CONVERSATIONS ON JUSTICE FROM NATIONAL, INTERNATIONAL, AND GLOBAL PERSPECTIVES

The question of what constitutes norms for global justice is of considerable concern for all those interested in world peace and cooperation. In order to explore these global norms Jean-Marc Coicaud, while working at the United Nations University, initiated a project centered around conversations with leading theorists and policy practitioners in global affairs. *Conversations on Justice from National, International, and Global Perspectives* features world-class authors and activists from around the world, and from a variety of disciplines, discussing the central questions of justice at the national, international, and global levels. Made up of a compilation of dialogues, this volume's unique format makes it highly accessible and even fun to read. The insights and observations of these leading intellectuals and scholars provide a rich contribution to theories on how global justice might become a reality.

Jean-Marc Coicaud is Professor of Law and Global Affairs at Rutgers School of Law, Rutgers University. He is also an elected member of Academia Europaea (European Academy of Sciences), and a Fudan Distinguished Chair Professor at Fudan Institute for Advanced Study in Social Sciences, Fudan University, Shanghai. He has published 15 books and over 100 scholarly articles and chapters in the fields of political and legal theory, international law, international organizations, international relations and comparative politics. Before joining Rutgers University, Jean-Marc Coicaud worked for the United Nations Secretariat and the United Nations University in New York and Tokyo, including as a member of the speech-writing team of the United Nations Secretary-General and a research director.

Lynette E. Sieger is a Ph.D. candidate at the Division of Global Affairs at Rutgers University. She specializes in global, legal, and political theory.

Conversations on Justice from National, International, and Global Perspectives

DIALOGUES WITH LEADING THINKERS

Edited by

JEAN-MARC COICAUD

Rutgers University

LYNETTE E. SIEGER

Rutgers University

CAMBRIDGE
UNIVERSITY PRESS

CAMBRIDGE
UNIVERSITY PRESS

University Printing House, Cambridge CB2 8BS, United Kingdom

One Liberty Plaza, 20th Floor, New York, NY 10006, USA

477 Williamstown Road, Port Melbourne, VIC 3207, Australia

314–321, 3rd Floor, Plot 3, Splendor Forum, Jasola District Centre, New Delhi – 110025, India

79 Anson Road, #06–04/06, Singapore 079906

Cambridge University Press is part of the University of Cambridge.

It furthers the University's mission by disseminating knowledge in the pursuit of education, learning, and research at the highest international levels of excellence.

www.cambridge.org
Information on this title: www.cambridge.org/9781316510094
DOI: 10.1017/9781108186759

First published 2019

Printed and bound in Great Britain by Clays Ltd, Elcograf S.p.A.

A catalogue record for this publication is available from the British Library

Library of Congress Cataloging-in-Publication Data
NAMES: Coicaud, Jean-Marc, interviewer. | Sieger, Lynette E.
TITLE: Conversations on justice from national, international, and global perspectives : dialogues with leading thinkers / edited by Jean-Marc Coicaud, Rutgers University, New Jersey; Lynette E. Sieger, Rutgers University, New Jersey.
DESCRIPTION: Cambridge, United Kingdom ; New York, NY, USA : Cambridge University Press, 2018. | Includes bibliographical references and index.
IDENTIFIERS: LCCN 2018020101 | ISBN 9781316510094 (alk. paper)
SUBJECTS: LCSH: Justice. | International law. | Law and globalization. | LCGFT: Interviews.
CLASSIFICATION: LCC K246 .C65 2018 | DDC 340/.114–dc23
LC record available at https://lccn.loc.gov/2018020101

ISBN 978-1-316-51009-4 Hardback

Contents

Acknowledgments

First and foremost I want to thank John Berger, Senior Editor with Cambridge University, for having believed in this book project and for publishing it in one of Cambridge University Press's collections. In addition, I want to thank a number of people who over the years have been instrumental in having the book become a reality. To begin with, I want to thank the contributors to the book. They are leaders in their fields, so I am truly grateful for their participation. I am very thankful for their commitment and fortitude in remaining part of the project till the end, especially since it took much more time than initially anticipated to complete. Without their initial agreement, in the early 2010s, to take time for the interviews, without their patience and willingness to respond to my additional questions over time and make changes to the conversations in the final stages of the project, this book would have never seen the light of day. I also want to thank Francis Lowe. In the early days of the project, Francis took care of its logistic and technical aspects, such as contacting the contributors, arranging for the schedule of the interviews, videotaping them, and travelling with me on location whenever necessary to interview the contributors. He was a model of professionalism, resourcefulness, and reliability, without whom, undoubtedly, the project would not have been able to start. Later on in the project, the contribution of Lynette E. Sieger was also instrumental. Lynette, a Ph.D. student of mine at Rutgers University, transcribed the first, videotaped version of the conversations, which was a necessary step for moving forward toward the book. Transcribing each conversation – each of them lasting from sixty to ninety minutes – was a particularly time consuming endeavor since the original number of the conversations amounted to thirty, out of which we ended up choosing thirteen conversations for reasons of space limitations. As each conversation was taking its final shape, Lynette helped to ensure that each conversation was as clear as possible. I also want to thank Zhang Jin, whom I called upon for the conversation with Wang Hui. I relied on her expertise on China to help me to craft some of the questions for the conversation with Wang Hui, and translate its Chinese portions and Wang Hui's intellectual profile. On China again, and other matters, Jacques Delisle and Daniel A. Bell are friends whose views I always seek. Their support has been constant, for which I thank them. I also want to thank my friend and law colleague Daniel Schlein for having taken the time to review and edit the introduction and conclusion. His suggestions and corrections have contributed to improving the style and the content of the texts. The preparation of the manuscript and the book was finalized during the academic year 2017–2018, while I was on sabbatical from Rutgers School of Law and spending time as a Distinguished Fudan Scholar at the Fudan Institute for the Advanced Study in Social Sciences (IAS-Fudan), Fudan University, Shanghai. I am very grateful to Rutgers University for the sabbatical, and especially, at the Rutgers School of Law, to Dean Ronald Chen and Vice-Dean Reid Wesibord, who made it possible, as it would have been challenging to finalize the manuscript without time off. I am also very grateful to Fudan University, particularly to Sujian Guo, Director of IAS-Fudan, for hosting me and helping to make my stay in Shanghai a productive time, Catherine and Françoise and real pleasure.

In France, in my hometown of Les Herbiers, my sisters Catherine and Françoise, and brothers-in-law Serge and Roland, their children Xavier, François, Florence and Pierre, and the kindness of longtime childhood friends (Gabriel and Didier) and local neighbors and friends (Guy Bibard, Jacqueline Poupet and Patrice and Lucette Martineau) are always a source of warmth, reassurance, and anchoring. I am grateful to them.

I thank my wife Jin and children Joseph Tao and Haibo Louis-Henri, whose love and affection give meaning and purpose to my life. They make me a better person, and want to be a better person. The love and support of my parents-in-law is also a big part of our daily lives. Without them New York City would not be the same and I want to thank them for this.

Finally, I dedicate this book to my parents, Joseph and Juliette Coicaud. I have been blessed to have them as parents. I cannot say how deeply grateful I am for the continued love and support. Je dédie ce livre à mes parents, Joseph et Juliette Coicaud. Il faudrait plus que des mots pour dire combien je leur suis reconnaissant. Leur amour et leur soutien m'ont toujours accompagné depuis mes jeunes années en Vendée.

Jean-Marc Coicaud

My first thanks go to the contributors for all that I have learned from them through working on this project. Their willingness to go through several drafts of the chapters and biographies always in good spirits made this process easier. Second, I acknowledge my gratitude for the mentors who led me through the somewhat convoluted path of global studies. Academic programs and scholars who do interdisciplinary scholarship are not easy to find, so I especially appreciate Dr. Joel Rosenthal for introducing me to the work of Dr. Coicaud, and Dr. Deen Chatterjee for introducing me to Dr. Coicaud and the Global Affairs program. I thank the Carnegie Council for Ethics in International Affairs because it was through their programing – centered on interdisciplinary issues and practice – that these important ties were made and fostered. Dr. Coicaud proved to be an advisor comparable to none. The scope of his intellectual imagination and the range of projects he conceives of and brings to fruition are impressive. I am indebted to Dr. Coicaud for inviting me on this adventurous journey. A special thank you goes to Ann Martin, whose support was felt in many ways, personally and professionally, throughout this project. Finally, my work would be impossible without the constancy of the strong ties to my siblings (Rand, Astrid, Beatrix, Nicole, Shadna, and Sabrina). I especially thank my partner, Seis Kamimura, for his unending encouragement, love, friendship, and support.

I dedicate this volume to my nieces and nephews who are entering or about to enter college and who have demonstrated a passion and commitment for social justice. Emma, Reagan, Brigitte, and Asa. May you contribute to making our world more just.

Lynette E. Sieger

1

Introduction

Setting the Stage for Conversations on Justice

Jean-Marc Coicaud

Conversations on Justice from National, International, and Global Perspectives focuses on issues of justice, including political, economic, social, cultural, and legal justice, from the national, international, and global perspectives. At the outset, the title of this book requires three points of clarification. First, bringing together "national," "international," and "global" perspectives is meant to refer to the fact that, today, matters of justice are not by and large self-contained and as such they cannot be addressed only at the national level. Rather, they are to some extent part of interactions that are taking place between the three levels. Second, referring to justice from an "international" perspective alludes to the interstate relations at work in the international system. In this context, the nation-state more than the individual is the primary right-holder, and international justice amounts to first and foremost the moral assessment of interactions among states. Third, referring to justice from a "global" perspective alludes to the way in which in recent years scholars – particularly in philosophy and global political theory – have come to address questions of justice by making the individual the primary right-holder (cosmopolitanism).[1]

This book is the product of a multiyear project that began when I was still working for the United Nations and, more precisely, for the United Nations University. It continued after I became a Professor of Law and Global Affairs at Rutgers School of Law, Rutgers University. This brief introduction addresses five types of issues: the unusual format of the book; the rationale for the book; the methodology used to conceive and build the book; the biographical sketches of the contributors; and the main themes and the organization of the *Conversations*.

[1] For a case study analysis of the convergences and divergences as well as hierarchies that can exist among these three levels as applied to matters of justice, see for instance Jean-Marc Coicaud, *Beyond the National Interest: The Future of UN Peacekeeping and Multilateralism in an Era of U.S. Primacy* (Washington, DC: United States Institute of Peace Press, 2007).

I THE UNUSUAL FORMAT OF THE BOOK

The format of the book is rather unusual, especially from an academic standpoint, in at least three ways. To begin with, usually when a book brings together a group of contributors around a topic, it tends to do so within the framework of an academic discipline. This book instead assembles contributors from a variety of fields, from philosophy to political science, law, international relations, sociology, and economics. Second, most books mobilizing a group of academics do so in the context of scholarly chapters. Again, this book deviates from a standard approach as it is a collection of conversations or dialogues between myself and various other scholars. Third, from the start a key concept of this book was to ensure that the issues it covers would be accessible to a large audience. In that respect, the goal was to introduce important authors who are interested in various aspects of justice but are not necessarily specialists, as well as their thinking on issues of justice, to a broad readership within academia and beyond.

II THE RATIONALE FOR THE BOOK

A multifold rationale prompted the unusual format of the book. Six reasons in particular led me to believe that there was intellectual and practical value in investing time and effort in this enterprise. These reasons concern (a) the context in which the book project emerged and developed; (b) the importance of targeting an interested but not necessarily specialized audience, and the choice of the conversation format that followed in order to achieve this objective; (c) the need to bring in one venue the various national conversations taking place on the interface between the national, international, and global dimensions; (d) the value of fostering an interdisciplinary approach; (e) contributing to improvement of the academic curriculum on issues of global relevance; and (f) helping the next generation to focus on new research and intellectual perspectives.

II.a The Context for the Emergence and Development of the Project

The project started when I was still directing the United Nations University Office at United Nations Headquarters, in New York.[2] At that time, there were compelling reasons to reflect upon questions of justice and the connections

[2] The United Nations University (UNU), headquartered in Tokyo, Japan (where I also served for a few years in the late 1990s and early 2000s), with thematic research centers around the world, is a think tank for the United Nations. It focuses on issues of global security, development, and the environment. Interestingly, the United Nations University is one of the very few United

between the national, international, and global levels that shape them – reasons that since then have continued to be pressing and, at times, grown even more urgent. Five are worth brief mention.

First, there is the economic context. In the early 2010s, the 2008 financial crisis was still a major topic of public discourse. That was all the more the case considering that its devastating repercussions extended well beyond the financial sector and affected the daily lives of people in many countries, both developed and developing. Today millions are still suffering the aftermath of the crisis and it is far from certain that all of the problems that led to the crisis in the first place have been resolved. As a matter of fact, not only are major sources of the financial crisis still largely unaddressed (such as the relatively light regulation of derivatives trading) but we are witnessing efforts to roll back those protections that were instituted in the Obama era. Moreover, if a few years ago the gap between rich and poor had started to emerge as a serious concern, recently it has become a central issue among the public at large.[3] The rise of populism, in part a product of the growing disparity between rich and poor, and itself part of the side effect of globalization with its winners and losers, shows that the problem is not only economic and social, but also political, and as such undermines the fabric and sense of community.[4]

Second, the problems at work in the early 2010s in the field of security and their implications for justice have by no means receded. Arguably, they are as acute as they were a few years ago. To be sure, with the defeat of ISIL and the arrest and prosecution of their partisans, terrorism is somewhat on the defensive. That said, it certainly cannot be said that the threat has disappeared. This is especially the case considering that its root causes have not really been fully addressed, in particular in the Middle East and in Europe. Moreover, one of the regions where terrorism finds its most fertile ground, the Middle East, is all too often crippled by problems like authoritarian political regimes, failed

Nations organizations that are headquartered outside the West. As one of the few UN institutions not based in a Western country, it could contribute a valuable perspective on global affairs since the United Nations, despite being a global organization, remains by and large a Western-centric institution, a situation rather outdated in light of the international redistribution of power that has been taking place in recent decades. The United Nations University has an office at the United Nations Headquarters in New York whose mission at the time was to function as a bridge between the United Nations, academia, and think tanks around the world, with special emphases on the connections between global politics, global governance, and global policy questions as they are particularly addressed and dealt with in the context of the United Nations Headquarters.

3 Consult, for example, François Bourguignon, *The Globalization of Inequality* (Princeton, NJ: Princeton University Press, 2017).

4 In his conversation, Chapter 13, Michael Spence stresses that it is dangerous for a whole society and the international system to let inequalities get out of hand.

states, high youth unemployment, and rather destructive involvement of Western influence, all factors contributing to the perpetuation of regional instability and volatility.

Third, climate change and its implications, with their problems related to justice, already on the map a decade ago, can now less and less be altogether ignored and underestimated. The urgency of the situation is illustrated by the increasing changes in extreme weather and climate events (such as heat waves and droughts) and the strong evidence confirming that some of these phenomena are related to human activities. Consequently, environmental issues are more and more becoming a major focus of the work of international organizations and international law.[5]

Fourth, the unfolding changes in the international redistribution of power, with their possible consequences for the evolution of the international system and various aspects of justice, only emerging a few years ago, are now on full display. With the relative decline of the West (the United States and Europe)[6] and the rise of China, which aspires to become a comprehensive power that is influential worldwide, the transformations looming on the horizon are prone to have a deep impact, including on questions of justice from national, international, and global perspectives.

Fifth, and finally, because of the growing globalization and interdependence of countries around the world, international organizations, especially the United Nations, are now more indispensable than ever. And yet, it is as if nation-states regard international institutions, including the United Nations, progressively less seriously and with commensurately less respect. International institutions appear to be becoming less relevant and adaptable to the problems and demands of the present than ever before, let alone responsive to the demands of the future. Hence the imperative, in part addressed by this book, of exploring how the central role of international organizations in terms of norm production and officialization concerning matters of social, economic, cultural, and environmental justice, can be revitalized.[7]

II.b Audience and Choice of the Conversational Format

A second rationale for the project was the need to extend the discussion of the issues at hand beyond a specialized and limited audience and, in part for this

5 For instance, see in this volume the conversation with Mireille Delmas-Marty, Chapter 9.
6 Refer, for example, to the conversation with Charles A. Kupchan, Chapter 12.
7 David Held, among others, addresses this issue in his conversation, Chapter 14.

reason, to employ interactive conversations that, without being simplistic, are more accessible than scholarly articles or chapters. This rationale is also related to the paradoxical situation in which we find ourselves when it comes to information and knowledge.

On the one hand, contemporary societies, especially Western developed societies, are viewed and certainly present themselves as information and knowledge societies. In them, the production of and access to information and knowledge is very high compared to the past. Institutions of education and research, mass media and social media are among the resources at the public's disposal of people for information and education. On the other hand, despite the plethora of information and knowledge developed societies produce and disseminate, it is misleading to think that they are ideal or full-fledged information and knowledge societies. This is true for at least three reasons. First, information providers – whether mass media newspapers, magazines, radio, or TV – are all too often more interested in and driven by "infotainment" than by hard news. This state of affairs may not be the worst form of misinformation, spin, and manipulation but when it becomes part of a "fake news" culture, as seems to have been the case in the past few years,[8] this is certainly not helpful to the public.[9] Second, even information that is serious and credible cannot claim the mantle of true knowledge. If knowledge presupposes information, knowledge consists of more than information. It rests upon data constructing and offering a narrative that is meaningful and brings about meaning – that focuses, directly or indirectly, on public and civic interest. Third, access to knowledge is not as straightforward as we might think. Beyond the easy and perverse attractiveness of the brain-emptying mechanism that mass media at times amounts to, knowledge, already challenging to produce, can be ever harder to share and disseminate. If academic and research specialization can be viewed as a methodological tool and an expression of scholarly excellence, it also isolates itself from the layman.

And yet we can hardly afford to stay in the dark, both in terms of information and knowledge. As societies are becoming, all at the same time, more complex, more fluid, and more interdependent, the need for intellectual clarity on the issues that are likely to define our present and future, individually and collectively, becomes much more imperative and urgent. What is at stake is not simply the maximization of opportunities and minimization of the risks

8 Mike Wendling, "The (Almost) Complete History of 'Fake News'," retrieved on January 22, 2018, www.bbc.com/news/amp/blogs-trending-42724320.

9 See Oscar Wilde: "The public have an insatiable curiosity to know everything, except what is worth knowing." In *The Soul of Man under Socialism, and Selected Critical Prose* (New York: Penguin Classics, 2001), p. 148.

that these unfolding evolutions entail. Perhaps more basically but more fundamentally, what is at stake is keeping as much of our lives and our environment as possible under our control.

To some extent this requires a commitment on our part – a commitment to curiosity and learning. As human beings, as citizens, as professionals, equipped or not with a specialization, we are asked to extend ourselves beyond our comfort zone. But, of course, the burden does not or should not fall fully upon us. We require support and encouragement in this effort. This is one of the *raisons d'être* and one of the virtues of accessible knowledge – that it is straightforward enough to reach an interested but nonspecialized audience yet sophisticated enough to expand the mind, and the heart, of the audience.

With those thoughts in mind, adopting a conversational format seemed a productive option. A conversation is an informal way to introduce and be introduced to ideas, issues, and authors. Its interactive character, between the person who interviews and the person who is interviewed, is a dynamic way to address issues. A conversation, particularly when it features theoreticians, may also be an appropriate method to summarize and clarify some of the technical yet important points of an author's work and thinking. In addition, in the context of a conversation it is easy to show the relevance of these points by connecting them with concrete examples and situations. The contributors draw these linkages at times in the conversations that follow. Finally, the conversational format is an effective means of highlighting the human dimension of scholarship. Behind books, there is always an author, with his or her history, certainties, and hesitations. A conversational format may be more apt to display their existence and value than a traditional book, in which the author tends to recede behind the systematic exposition of the argument.[10]

II.c From National Conversation to a Global Conversation

A third rationale was to show how national conversations have been taking place and continue to take place on the interactions between the national, international, and global perspectives. I felt that the value of doing so was five-fold.

To begin with, conversations on the relations between the national, international, and global dimensions exist in each national context. But, within the limitations of our specific national frameworks and horizons, we either ignore the existence of those dialogues or we know very little about them. As we tend

[10] In his conversation, Chapter 7, Avishai Margalit stresses the importance of the personal dimension at work in philosophy, especially in moral and political philosophy.

to be oblivious to the "other" beyond our circles of familiarity, we often are by and large ignorant of how other societies and their members think about the increasing internationalization and globalization of the world and their impact on national communities and their citizens. This tendency is all the more unfortunate since, to some degree, the intertwining and even embedment of the national, international, and global dimensions are experiences we all share.

In addition, national conversations present similarities and differences, which are always enlightening to discover and highlight. To be sure, these similarities and differences have much to do with the specific conditions (history, level of development, place in the international distribution of power, etc.) of each country and even, within societies, of people's positions in their societies. But they also relate to whether or not and to what extent the relations between the national, international, and global levels are seen in a positive or negative light. Needless to say, at the heart of these similarities and differences are key issues of justice, and in more ways than one.

Moreover, academics play an important role in these conversations. Like any other actors in society, scholars are part and parcel of the conversations and the concerns associated with the evolving relations between the national, international, and global levels. While not necessarily limited and reducible to the national context in which they operate (for academics are frequently part of international networks of research that tend to contribute to their own internationalization and globalization, including the homogenization of intellectual concerns, ideas, and languages[11]), they certainly echo it. As such, and certainly within the social sciences, their scholarship has been so concerned by the relations between the national, international, and global levels that these relations are now one of the defining aspects of the identity of contemporary societies and of the people who live in them. Furthermore, academics must and indeed do play a particularly important role in the context of these conversations. Because it is their full-time job and responsibility, along with teaching, to think and write about formative issues, to clarify them, put them in perspective, and make sense of them in their positive and even more so in their negative and pathological aspects, their function and contributions are significant and valuable. Their impact is particularly strong when they combine analytical rigor with a commitment to improving the world.

[11] Incidentally, the intellectual community of the hard sciences is more prone to function on the basis of scientific, standardized, and by and large internationally cultural homogenous parameters than that of the social sciences and the humanities.

In addition, I felt that by highlighting, through the work of academics, the various conversations on national, international, and global relations and showing their value, it would be possible to facilitate the establishment of a global conversation per se on these relations. Such conversation is very much needed. As the countries and cultures of the world are becoming more connected, encouraging a meeting point, so to speak, a global conversation on how societies and their members handle the intertwining of the national, international, and global levels, is a must. In light of this interconnectedness, it is a must from the intellectual, ethical, and political points of view.[12] It is an intellectual must in the sense that knowing about the "other" (individual and collective) and how it positions itself in this new landscape is a minimum requirement to analyze and understand the nature and evolution of one's own society. A society that adopts a siloed and self-contained approach, if such an orientation was ever sufficient, is today simply not good enough. It is also a must from an ethical point of view in the sense that we have no choice but to negotiate our relations with others. Getting to know and taking into account the existence of others is both a starting point and a condition of possibility of a global ethics, of an ethics mindful of our rights and duties toward one another beyond our borders and, in fact, also within borders. Here the question of immigration and the various debates surrounding it is a case in point. Furthermore, relating to the "other" is a must from a political point of view as well in the sense that in order for the intellectual and ethical demands vis-à-vis the "other" to be translated into reality, into the DNA of societies and their members, and their relations, politics must play a central role. National, international, and global politics, for example in the context of international organizations, needs to put in place the supporting mechanisms for a global conversation to become an expression and a tool of a more pluralistic form of universalism, as alluded to by Delmas-Marty,[13] Wang,[14] and ONUMA[15] in their respective conversations.

Finally, what I hoped in having these conversations featuring scholars from around the world was to provide a means to contribute to the development of a denationalized approach to issues at play in societies and the relations of these societies, both in terms of research and teaching.[16] Indeed, as societies

[12] For more on this, see for instance Jean-Marc Coicaud, "Ethics and Politics of Global Knowledge" (Keynote Lecture, 3rd JoRISS Lecture Series, East China Normal University, Shanghai, December 6, 2017).

[13] Chapter 9 in this volume.

[14] See the conversation with Wang Hui in this volume, Chapter 3.

[15] Refer to the conversation with ONUMA Yasuaki in this volume, Chapter 10.

[16] The national and nationalized bent has traditionally been at work in most social sciences as they have developed, in the eighteenth and nineteenth century at the national level for the national level. In this regard, it is also very much at work in international relations and

and their fates are now increasingly connected, part of the intellectual agenda is to move beyond "knowledge nationalism"[17] and foster approaches that at the same time are mindful of, first, the local characteristics of social objects (societies) and the national, international, and global relations at work within and among them, and, second, of the growing and global levels that are not reducible to the local/national level. From this perspective, the "de-nationalization" approach points in two directions, once again both in research and teaching. It points toward not limiting the production and dissemination of knowledge to that of one society or country, as if this country was the only one to exist and could exist on its own (as such it is about internationalizing knowledge in its research and teaching dimensions, so that students and readers know more about the world beyond their own societies). And it points toward identifying and analyzing the level of social activities taking place and having relevance at the international/global levels (globalization of knowledge).[18]

II.d Interdisciplinarity

A fourth rationale for bringing to life the book in its present form was an attempt to practice and encourage interdisciplinarity.[19] After all, if specialization and working within the frame of one discipline are a focused way to develop sound expertise and achieve results in research and thinking – a reality

international law. This is not surprising considering that both modern international relations and international law are built around and to serve the nation-state. There are additional noteworthy features to the national and nationalized bent of international relations and international law. For example, in the United States, where it is the most developed and often provides paradigms of knowledge, the field of international relations is anything but international in the sense that it by and large amounts to a US-centric vision and analysis of international relations – hence more often than not its character of "intellectual ideology" rather than knowledge per se. As for international law, echoing Yasuaki Onuma's thinking, international law cannot be seen as very international if by "international" we refer to diversity of cultures, including legal traditions. Modern international law is essentially a Western construct that only makes room for others on its own terms and in the margins. As such, when, as part of its progressive dimension, it recognizes rights to other cultures or legal traditions, it is still somewhat alienating. On this latter question, Jean-Marc Coicaud, "Le droit international et la question de la justice," in *Annuaire Français des Relations Internationales* (Paris: Université Panthéon-Assas, Centre Thucydide, volume XVIII, 2017).

17 See Ulrich Beck and his call for "methodological cosmopolitanism" in *Cosmopolitan Vision*, translated by Ciaran Cronin (Cambridge: Polity Press, 2006), pp. 17–18.

18 We go back to this issue and others alluded to here later in this introduction when we discuss the research and curriculum agenda.

19 Interdisciplinarity involves the combining of two or more academic disciplines into research and teaching.

that to some extent accounts for the organization of research and teaching institutions along divisions of labor and disciplines – it is a theory and practice of knowledge that is more a methodological, if not an epistemological, commodity (even if it is an essential one) than a reflection of the reality of reality. Indeed, the reality of reality is not to be segmented, as the categories of knowledge are, but integrated and all-encompassing (in a way all aspects of [social] reality are in one piece of [social] reality, really or potentially). Hence the virtue of adding, on top of monodisciplinarity, interdisciplinarity in order to have a more comprehensive picture of reality, of the different layers of which reality is composed and of the different aspects through which we can view it.[20] To be sure, *Conversations on Justice from National, International, and Global Perspectives* is a rather modest exercise of interdisciplinarity, and this in two ways.

A first aspect of this modest interdisciplinarity is the fact that only a few disciplines are featured and represented, essentially in the social sciences. This is the case for three reasons. Very prosaically, there is, first, a matter of space limitation. A book can only cover so much. Second, there are my own intellectual limitations. Beyond the social sciences and the humanities I am not intellectually equipped to engage in conversations with scientists in the fields of physics, mathematics, biology, etc.[21] A third and more positive rationale, given the book's focus on justice, was the need to highlight disciplines engaged, at least in part, and each in their way, with questions of justice and societies, such as economic justice, social justice, political justice, cultural justice, etc. Moreover, the social sciences are on the front line when it

[20] When studying at Harvard University, I attended a seminar on justice co-taught by John Rawls and Amartya Sen, Rawls being a philosopher interested in economics, and Sen an economist interested in philosophy. It was enlightening to see how the combination of philosophy and economics can help develop an analytical understanding of questions of justice that philosophy and economics alone would perhaps have difficulty delivering. The combination of law and philosophy or of philosophy and history is probably likely to generate similarly fruitful insights on justice.

[21] As a matter of fact, if there is a domain of interdisciplinarity that is absolutely essential and destined to become even more so in the future, it is the one bringing together the hard sciences and the social sciences. Relatively few people are trained in these two areas and are able to function and speak at the intersection of the two. Yet the relations and the interface between hard sciences (fundamental and applied sciences, be it in the areas of natural or medical sciences) and social sciences are decisive. Without some sort of expertise in them and their relationships and impacts, it is difficult to tackle some of the defining issues of our time, including in terms of ethics, politics, and justice, such as the environment, artificial intelligence, biotechnology, etc. This type of interface is one of the areas in which much progress has to be made in training the next generation of professionals, scholars, and civil servants.

comes to the interactions between the national, international, and global levels, as a significant part of their work has now come to focus on these issues.

A second aspect of this interdisciplinary modesty is the fact that the conversations contain few methodological and epistemological considerations per se. There is no systematic development of the conditions under which such interdisciplinarity is possible or not, and to what extent, and the advantages and disadvantages that interdisciplinarity entails. On the other hand, it is also true, as mentioned before, that the book gives voice to a variety of disciplines. More to the point, and perhaps more importantly, there is the fact as well that most authors featured in the book are themselves ardent supporters of an intellectually eclectic approach, of a form of interdisciplinarity. While all of them are strongly anchored in their individual disciplines (that is, they are strongly grounded in the disciplines in which they were trained, and in which they acquired their reputations for excellence), at times they ventured beyond their initial areas of expertise and embraced a more comprehensive and holistic, a more interdisciplinary, intellectual trajectory and enterprise.

Boaventura de Sousa Santos, for example, became a master at combining law and sociology and then expanded his intellectual interests in the direction of the sociology and the politics of knowledge. Wang Hui also aptly mixes history, philosophy, sociology, history of ideas, and literature to support his keen examination of China and its modernity. Eclecticism also characterizes Mireille Delmas-Marty, whose legal scholarship is deeply influenced by philosophy and even poetry. Similarly, one of the trademarks of ONUMA Yasuaki's work has been the use of the history of ideas and legal history to develop a critical analysis of international law and how it should evolve in the future. Finally, Charles A. Kupchan stresses in his conversation that as an international relations specialist he has come to value and mobilize history as a key aspect of his study of international politics and the identification of some of the main tendencies that shape it.[22]

II.e *For a Better Academic Research Agenda and Curriculum*

By featuring a plurality of disciplines in the context of the *Conversations* and, modestly, showcasing interdisciplinarity, my rationale has also been to encourage its development in the framework of universities' studies and programs, when it comes to both research and teaching. For it is true that in recent years interdisciplinarity has been embraced as a valuable approach by many in the

[22] Conversation with Charles A. Kupchan, Chapter 12.

social sciences (in the field of global affairs, in particular). But often interdisciplinarity is more an appearance than a reality. The intellectual difficulty of the exercise, let alone the existing institutionalization of knowledge, organized along disciplinary lines, largely explains this state of affairs. This is not surprising. After all, it is challenging enough to master the key elements of a discipline or subdiscipline. It can only be even more challenging to develop intellectual literacy in several of them, let alone bring them together in a productive way. There are many methodological and knowledge hurdles that must be tackled and overcome in order to generate meaning and compelling interdisciplinary research and teaching.

In my own experience I have encountered this reality as director of a graduate program in global affairs at Rutgers University. Most of the research produced in the program belonged first and foremost to one academic field rather than several. As for the curriculum, the best we could achieve was to organize what I call "juxtaposed interdisciplinarity," that is to say we mobilized a variety of disciplines on global issues but without "integrated interdisciplinarity," i.e. tackling one or a series of issues through the lens of several relevant disciplines in one course.[23]

That said, it is not because a path is challenging that one has to give up and return to old habits, or consider that old habits are the only good habits. In the end, intellectual creativity in academia is often the mark of scholarship transcending disciplinary frontiers. It is therefore worth it to persist and seek a new balance between the practice and theorizing of one discipline and the practice and theorizing of several.

II.f The Next Generation

Finally, this project is also meant to contribute to the education of the next generation. Each generation faces, in its experience of the present and trying to build a life for itself, a world that is in part old, in part new. For those in charge of training the new generation – adults, parents, and scholars as educators – this includes having the responsibility to help the young, including younger scholars, as much as possible to negotiate the right balance between the old and the new. This is not an easy task. For the scholar-teacher one of the challenges that this responsibility entails is, while investing years of effort in acquiring knowledge, accepting the fact that the value of this

[23] On the issue of interdisciplinarity in the context of global affairs, Jean-Marc Coicaud, "Reflections on Some of the Challenges of Global Affairs as an Academic Field," in *Journal of Globalistic and Globalization Studies* (Volgograd: Uchitel Publishing House, June 2013).

knowledge rests in part in remaining open to questioning and challenge, and in accepting and embracing knowledge as only one step, one stepping stone to go further on the never-ending road of learning.

Precisely by sharing with the readers, including younger readers, what has been their journey, their certainties and uncertainties in the midst of the difficult questions they have spent years attempting to clarify, the contributors to these *Conversations* illustrate how even for the best academics, knowledge is the constant experience of growing by learning and trying to move forward regardless of the challenges. If only for this, they offer a valuable knowledge lesson.

III THE METHODOLOGY OF THE BOOK

As for the methodology in developing this book, the first step was identifying the scholars most likely to shed light on issues of justice from a plurality of perspectives. Here, the objective was not only to find leading authors in their respective academic fields from various regions of the world but also authors who in their work and their ways of thinking have an interest in other disciplines and a curiosity about the world beyond the cultural context in which they mainly operate. Indeed, not all major scholars are curious about other disciplines, are eager to integrate as much as possible other fields in their way of thinking and writing, or are keen to factor into their academic world other cultural and intellectual perspectives. I sought out authors who had a rather open and syncretic understanding of their discipline and their work.

Over time I interviewed more than thirty authors. Most of them certainly would have been valuable additions to the *Conversations*, especially since all the interviews were interesting and insightful. But in order to make the length of the book manageable, it was necessary to limit the conversations to thirteen authors. The selection was not without ethical dilemmas, with which we continue to struggle. In the end, we focused on the relevance of the scholarship itself.

Overall, in order to prepare for the conversations, I read most of the work of these authors, or at least their most important work. I also made sure to read their latest publications, so that the conversations reflect as much as possible their most recent intellectual development and work. On the basis of reading the works of the contributors, I built a script for each conversation. The script was meant to serve as a guide for the conversation, but not an overly rigid one. Over time, the conversations evolved as they were transcribed, edited, improved, and updated, all the way to January 2018.

The script of each conversation and the conversations were meant to elicit some of the main aspects of the author's thoughts and how he or she addressed the theoretical, practical, and policy issues of their time. Some of the conversations were translated into English from other languages (French and Mandarin) because not all the authors were native English speakers.

IV BIOGRAPHICAL SKETCHES

My colleague Lynette E. Sieger and I felt that a biographical sketch would be a useful way to introduce each of the contributors. Since each is a leader in his or her respective field of academic expertise, we concluded that it would be interesting for the reader to find out how they came to focus on and develop an intellectual agenda. As such, we asked them the following six questions: (1) What are your key achievements (educational, professional, social) that you would most like to highlight? (2) How did you come to identify/become interested in the key intellectual questions of your work? (3) Who have been the most influential thinkers for your intellectual development? (4) What are the central issues and questions around which your intellectual/social project is organized? (5) What are the issues on which you intend to focus in the future and why? (6) What is your advice for emerging scholars in the field of global justice?

The answers that we received from the contributors varied in length and in substance, and it is on this basis, as well as on their curriculum vitae, that Lynette Sieger prepared the bibliographical sketches at the end of the volume. Each contributor reviewed and approved the biographical sketch.

One more point on the biographical profiles of the contributors featured in the book. They all hold or have held prestigious academic positions and have had and are having very successful careers. Most of them are in their 50s, 60s, and 70s. Given their accomplishments, they could be expected to relax a bit and take it easy. This is especially so for those contributors who are now in their 70s and are already emeritus professor. And yet remarkably none of these scholars are eager to rest on their laurels. They all remain extremely active and deeply engaged in advancing the frontiers of their professions and fields. In fact, some of them are now busier than they have ever been. This sustained activity is really a testimony to their commitment and passion for ideas and learning.

V JUSTICE AND ORGANIZATION OF THE BOOK

As the title of the book indicates, its thread is justice. As such the conversations, from the specific perspective of each contributor, address various aspects of the question of justice and how it unfolds in the context of the relations and interactions between the national, international, and global levels. In the process, the ambiguous relationship between power and justice of course emerges as central (the discourse and practice of justice, and the values, norms, and institutions that come with them tend to be based on and express a situation of power; at the same time, in order to be credible, justice has to somewhat transcend its dependency vis-à-vis power). What emerges as well is the fact that justice in its relations and interactions with power appears to function both like a foundation (from which all the criteria of validity of social reality flow) and a horizon (toward which social reality aspires). The nature and dynamics of this state of affairs are explored via a variety of aspects, in its relations with economic, political, social, cultural, and knowledge issues.

That said, although the conversations with David Miller,[24] Thomas W. Pogge,[25] and David Held[26] touch upon the definitional elements of justice, most of the conversations do not unpack systematically the core meaning of justice. They refer more to issues of justice in action rather than seek conceptual clarity of it. This is the case both for justice in general (which in fact concerns also justice at the national level, since it is at this level that traditionally it has been most developed) and for justice at the international and global levels. However, there are a number of key assumptions and considerations about the issue of justice that are at work and built into the conversations. Some of these key assumptions (and in no way do I mean to suggest that they are all there is to think and know about justice) are outlined in the next section in connection with justice in general and justice from the international and global perspectives.

VI JUSTICE IN GENERAL, AND FROM THE INTERNATIONAL AND GLOBAL STANDPOINTS[27]

One of the ways to define justice consists in saying that it is about what is owed to actors based on their rights. But, obviously, this definition, far from ending

24 Conversation with David Miller, Chapter 5.

25 Conversation with Thomas Pogge, Chapter 8.

26 Conversation with David Held, Chapter 14.

27 This section of the introduction builds on Coicaud's "Le droit international et la question de la justice" and "Deconstructing International Legitimacy," in Jean-Marc Coicaud and

the discussion on justice, rather opens it in the sense that it introduces a series of complex questions that are at the heart of the understanding of justice and the debates it brings about. That is the case for justice in general and even more so for justice at the international and global levels.

Justice in General – When it comes to justice in general, the definition mentioned in the preceding paragraph introduces fundamental questions in at least eight domains of determination (and judgment) applying to the identification and the projection of what is just.

- Right(s) holders and community of justice: To begin with, there is the question of the determination of who has rights, of who is a right(s) holder. Indeed, it is upon the condition of being recognized as having the right to have rights that a sense of justice can apply to and benefit an actor. It is this recognition of an actor having rights vis-à-vis other actors (with the duties that are associated with them) that is constitutive of a sense of community in which justice is taken seriously.
- Substance of rights: There is then the question of the determination of the substance or of the content of rights that enter into the composition of justice. In a given society or community, this determination happens in relation to the main normative cultural, economic, social, political, etc. structures that give shape and meaning to the identity of society and its members, and their relations.
- Distribution of rights: The determination of the distribution of the rights owed to actors concerns what we could call the differentiated nature of these rights, i.e. the fact that the rights allocated to those who have rights are not always the same. They change based on the identity of a community and the place actors, individual and collective, occupy in it. In this regard, within a community the allocation of rights is not necessarily the same for all since societal life is characterized by hierarchies, *de facto* and *de jure*. This is so even in communities/societies that are committed to equality (such as democratic societies). In this perspective, it is the responsibility of the system of organization of society and its culture of justice to justify, i.e. give good reasons[28] in order to account for the *de facto and de jure* inequalities and their implications for the life of actors. Needless to say, this is especially important in a community/society shaped by values and norms of

Hilary Charlesworth (eds.), *Fault Lines of International Legitimacy* (New York: Cambridge University Press, 2009), pp. 29–86.

28 On the question of justification, Rainer Forst, *The Right to Justification*, translated by Jeffrey Flynn (New York: Columbia University Press, 2012).

equality. When a community or society is unable to provide good reasons to justify the existing inequalities, the differentiated and somewhat unequal distribution of rights (and duties), the legitimacy of these values and norms and the public institutions and political leadership that underwrite them, as well as the overall sense of justice, run the risk of being weakened, if not contested and even rejected altogether.

- Threshold of realization or actualization of justice: The degree of realization or actualization of the rights that enter into the composition of justice is central to the sense and nature of justice. For, in order to be credible, it is imperative for a culture of justice (values, practices, institutions, etc.) to be perceived as sufficiently in the service of rights, i.e. sufficiently real, realized, or actualized. If this is not the case, the culture of justice risks denigration. Worse, the public may reject the fundamental values of justice themselves. Such rejection certainly occurs where corruption is systemic. People can become so disenchanted that they stop believing that justice is even at all possible. In these circumstances, it is not only the social organization of right and wrong that is disavowed. The very idea of right and wrong is susceptible to disappearance. In order to avoid this situation, the role of a system of justice (its values, laws, institutions, actors, practices, results) is to ensure as much as possible the respect of the rights of the actors recognized as having rights. This requires achieving a reasonable threshold of realization or actualization of justice. This state of affairs presupposes ensuring the respect of the rights as they are defined, but also helping them to evolve if the perception of realization of the rights, including who has and should have rights, requires for them to evolve.
- Instance of determination of what is just: The instance of determination of what is just, related to the identification of right(s) holders (who has rights and is a legitimate actor), the substance of their rights, and their distribution, concerns first the question of knowing who has the right, that is to say also the power and the authority to indicate what is just. This amounts to the question of knowing who is in position to have this role, it being understood that in a community (at least in a stable, well established, and functioning one) whoever (people and institutions) is in this position exercises power in ways that echo the normative, cultural, economic, social, political, etc. constitutive structures of society (identity, modalities of operation, relations among actors, etc.). As such, these structures contribute to form and validate what is perceived as just/legitimate, as well as the processes and mechanisms that project and protect what is perceived as just/legitimate.

- Evolution of what is just: The evolution of the determination of what is just – that is the evolution of what is right, of who has rights, of what these rights are, what their distribution is and how this is decided – constitutes another essential aspect of justice. The determination of these aspects of justice is not, in theory as in practice, fixed, or fixed forever. The nature of justice is, to some extent, to evolve, to be dynamic. It evolves over time, in ways that are more or less extended and deep, in ways that are also more or less slow or rapid, if not more or less peaceful or violent (the quest for justice via revolution is prone to be violent). These changes take place in relation to the transformations that affect the context of justice. They can include the identity of a community/society, the form of a political regime, if not a political system, the level and the modalities of development of a community/society, the relations of power, the expectations of actors, etc. From this perspective, it is not surprising that the dynamic nature of justice is one of the elements that make it a complex enterprise. This enterprise has to amount to a system and culture that satisfy the claim of validity of justice in the midst of the possibility of change and plasticity. There is here a balance between stability and change that is not easy to find, let alone maintain.
- Debates and struggles around the determination of what is just: In these conditions, the debates and struggles around each of the domains of determination mentioned previously are essential to the conceptualization, negotiation, realization, and evolution of justice and its demands. Indeed, because justice is one of the values and objectives most sought after in a social universe that tries to reach a type of stability based not mainly on force but on the qualitative consent of actors, because as such it is meant to seek, rest on, and express qualitative consent, it tends never to be definitively established. While it is something to which we aspire and that in turn inspires us, justice is prone to constant debate and challenge. Justice and how it is determined are all the more debated and possibly a source of struggles and conflicts that, as indicated before, they are closely associated with a situation of power (material and immaterial).[29] In order to make this power dependency of justice acceptable it is necessary for those in

[29] The fact that the values, norms, vocabulary, and institutions of the ethics of contemporary international criminal justice, such as the International Criminal Court (ICC), have been created under the impulsion of the West and are largely inspired by its vison of the world is a case in point.

powerful positions to respect those who are not power holders and recognize that they have rights. Experience shows, however, that this requirement is a tall order since for those in power, even in a democratic context, thinking and acting first and foremost on behalf of the rights of others all too often appear to be more the exception than the rule:[30] hence the never ending debates, struggles, and conflicts concerning justice and its demands.

- Justice and reflexivity: Ultimately, if justice amounts to a quest for qualitative consent (as distinct from manipulated and inauthentic consent) among actors aware of the rights of others as much as their own rights, this presupposes that at the heart of the nature and dynamics of justice is a form of (critical) reflexivity, or of (critical) return on oneself. As such, and this is true to some extent even in a hierarchical community, justice is about an actor recognizing rights for itself only to the extent that it also recognizes rights of others. This is to say that, as for all fundamental positive human social values, for instance friendship and love, justice is at the same time the good that is exchanged among actors living peacefully and what allows the pacific exchange to take place. It is this reflexive sharing of the human condition that is at the same time the foundation and the horizon of the possibility of thinking about and realizing justice.

Justice, International and Global – Since *Conversations* addresses issues of justice at the intersections of the national, international, and global levels, it makes sense to go beyond justice in general and add a few considerations about justice as it is perceived and unfolds at the international and global levels.

In this regard, when it comes to justice at the international and global levels compared to justice at the national level we have a lower level of development and commitment, as well as a higher level of complexity. This is the case because the world continues to be structured by and around a national bent (nation-state).[31] The tensions that competition among national interests can create undermine justice both at the international and global levels.

[30] Yet this is a key condition for the legitimate exercise of political power. Refer to Jean-Marc Coicaud, *Legitimacy and Politics: Contribution to the Study of Political Law and Responsibility* (Cambridge: Cambridge University Press, 2002).

[31] An illustration of this state of affairs is the fact that disciplines classically concerned with justice (including the social sciences and humanities, philosophy, and law) have mainly focused on justice within an established community. It is only in a secondary fashion that they have dealt with interstate justice (international justice) and more recently global justice (making the individual the primary right holder).

- Low development of and commitment to international and global justice:

  The low development and support of justice at the international level is the result of three factors. Despite the increasing recognition of the importance of human rights since the end of World War II (even more so since the end of the Cold War), the fact that international justice rests principally on the power of states and their good will tends to make it a secondary consideration. At the same time, such power makes international justice possible (for example, without states the International Criminal Court would not have been established) but limits it as well. In addition, the persistence of the eminently interstate character of international relations and international law goes hand in hand with the preeminence of national interest. This is to say that by and large the international system and international law make room for and care about international justice (human rights) only to the extent that it does not affect negatively, or not too negatively, the national interest of countries, particularly the most powerful countries, be they democratic or not. As a result, it is not surprising that international law and international institutions, which have the responsibility of ensuring cooperation between states, are limited in their support of the development or content of international justice.[32]

  In view of these constraints, it is not surprising that justice is even less developed and supported at the global level. The rights of states trump the rights of individuals. For example, the most progressive aspects of international law recognize the importance of human rights, and therefore of the individual as a right(s) holder from the international standpoint. But it does not follow that they make upholding human rights an absolute imperative. In fact, respect for human rights is a secondary, if not marginal, objective of the foreign policy of states, including those of democratic countries. For the most powerful of states, when forced to choose between their national interest and human rights, tend to opt for the former rather than for the latter.[33]
- Complexity of international and global justice: The complexity of the question of justice at the international level (focus on relations between states) and even more so at the global level (focus on the individual) has

[32] See the remarks of José Alvarez in his conversation, Chapter 11, on the need to reform international organizations, including the United Nations, in particular when it comes to the defense of human rights.

[33] On these issues, consult Coicaud, *Beyond the National Interest*.

> largely to do with the fact that it is not very developed. From this perspective, the continued national bent of the international system and the tensions it creates between the rights of states and the rights of individuals not only limit but also introduce a high level of complexity to the possibility of justice at the international and global levels. This complexity, having much to do with the dilemmas that the tensions between the rights of states and the rights of individuals produce, is at work both theoretically and practically.

At the international level, the theoretical complexity of justice exists at all the levels of determination mentioned previously (see pages 16–19). Concerning right(s) holders, a key problem is the ambiguity of and tensions in international law between the state and individual as right(s) holders. Their relations, although they put the state on top, are somewhat in flux and therefore not always clear -cut concerning what is owed to states and what is owed to individuals. The debates surrounding international humanitarian interventions and the Responsibility to Protect (R2P) are part of this story.[34] In these conditions, the determination of the substance of the rights of states and individuals, as well as of their distribution, does not benefit from a real consensus. Consequently, finding a satisfactory compromise between the right of states and the rights of individuals constitutes a huge challenge, almost as big as ensuring that the rights of all states are respected in the midst of the logic of power that continues to prevail in international relations and international law. From this perspective, it is difficult to have a precise idea of the degree of realization required of the rights of the rights holders in order to have the sense that the demands of justice are satisfied. It is all the more the case considering that the instances of determination of what is just internationally are far from unified. They rarely speak more or less with one voice or enjoy a high level of credibility and legitimacy. This is particularly the case in times of international crisis.[35] Rights and their evolution are therefore a constant source of debates and struggles that can turn into open conflict. Arguably, this situation has much to do with the fact that states are often blind and deaf to the approach of reflexivity that is at the core of justice. Each state is prone to focus entirely on what is owed to it and neglect as much as possible (to the extent that

[34] Refer, for example, to Jean-Marc Coicaud's "International Law, the Responsibility to Protect and International Crises," in Ramesh Thakur and William Maley (eds.), *Theorizing the Responsibility to Protect* (Cambridge: Cambridge University Press, 2015).

[35] The criticisms addressed to international organizations, the United Nations to begin with, for paralysis in exigent circumstances (Syria in the 2010s, for example) are a case in point.

it can get away with it) what it owes to others. In the end, these theoretical complexities go hand in hand with the practical and policy difficulties one encounters in attempting to take individual and human rights seriously in the international realm regardless of the short-term interests of states.

These challenges are destined to be even more at play when it comes to cosmopolitan justice, to justice at the global level. Here, one of the fundamental difficulties, which already exists in the context of international justice but is more serious in the context of global justice, concerns the levels of determination of justice touched upon previously. This difficulty leads to the following question: How is it possible to reconcile a cosmopolitan and universalist agenda (primacy of the rights of individuals) with the particularistic logic of nation-states from both the theoretical and practical standpoints? In order to answer this question, it is necessary to consider that nation-states are unlikely to cease being the main realm of socialization and belonging of individuals. Moreover, cosmopolitan engagement in the service of global justice should not necessarily lead to a homogenization of ways of life and thinking, or even of modalities of development.[36] All these considerations render conceptualization, negotiation, and implementation of acceptable lines of demarcation between universalistic (cosmopolitan) and particularistic approaches real challenges.[37]

VII ORGANIZATION OF THE BOOK

Having offered these remarks on justice in general and justice in the international and global contexts, I turn next to the organization of the book. It contains four main parts: "Global Knowledge/Global Thought"; "From Thinking Globally to Global Ethics"; "International Law and Global Justice"; and "World Order and Global Policy." This organization is a bit artificial, and there is also some overlap between these themes and the conversations they

36 ONUMA Yasuaki, in Chapter 10, and Abdullahi Ahmed An-Na'im, in Chapter 4, each in their own way make this point. This is also an issue at work in the question of secularism addressed by Neera Chandhoke in his conversation, Chapter 6.

37 The following authors, among others, touch upon these issues: Mathias Risse, *On Global Justice* (Princeton, NJ: Princeton University Press, 2012); Amartya Sen, *The Idea of Justice* (Cambridge, MA: The Belknap Press of Harvard University Press, 2009); Thomas Pogge and Darrel Moellendorf (eds.), *Global Justice: Seminal Essays* (St Paul, MN: Paragon House, 2008); Thomas Pogge and Keith Norton (eds.), *Global Ethics: Seminal Essays* (St Paul, MN: Paragon House, 2008); Simon Caney, *Justice Beyond Borders: A Global Political Theory* (Oxford: Oxford University Press, 2005); and Inge Kaul, Isabelle Grunberg, and Marc A. Stern (eds.), *Global Public Goods: International Cooperation in the 21st Century* (Oxford: Oxford University Press, 1999).

entail, if only because each conversation tends to cover a rather wide range of issues. But the sections and their succession have their logic as well. Part I (Chapters 2, 3, and 4) is in part dedicated to the interactions between power and knowledge. Part II (Chapters 5, 6, 7, and 8) pays much attention to values, norms, and institutions in relation to issues of international and global justice. Part III (Chapters 9, 10, and 11) focuses in particular on the place and role of international law and international organizations. Part IV (Chapters 12, 13, and 14) examines the trends at work in the international system, including how it is shaped by economic and geopolitical forces and how demands for justice could be better institutionalized at the global level. Part V (Chapter 15) offers brief concluding remarks.

The summaries below are not full accounts of the conversations but rather simply brief introductions to some of their key points.

Global Knowledge/Global Thought – Part I explores the relations between power and knowledge and what this means for the pursuit of justice. Boaventura de Sousa Santos's conversation, "Global Order and Global Knowledge" (Chapter 2), addresses the need to examine the power and knowledge relationships between the West and the non-West and, consequently, find a better balance between the two. A significant part of the conversation explores this issue and related questions of democracy at the local, national, and global levels by referring to the research project "Reinventing Social Emancipation" that has occupied Professor de Sousa Santos for several years. Part I continues with a conversation with Wang Hui, "China and Thinking Globally at the Turn of the Century" (Chapter 3). One of the issues that Wang Hui touches upon is the conditions under which it could be possible to establish better terms of intellectual dialogues and understanding between East (in particular China) and West. Such dialogue is both especially challenging and needed in light of the legacy of the somewhat tense relations since the nineteenth century between China and Western powers. The conversation with Abdullahi Ahmed An-Na 'im, "Oh, [Muslim] Believers: Be Just, That Is Always Closer to True Piety" (Chapter 4), ends Part I. It focuses on the challenge it can be to reconcile being a Muslim committed to peaceful international relations with the sense of universalism promoted by the West.

From Thinking Globally to Global Ethics – Part II concentrates mainly on the values of justice and on the various ways to identify and pursue them at the national, international, and global levels. It begins with the conversation with David Miller, "Extent and Limits of Global Justice" (Chapter 5). In this conversation Miller indicates that he is committed to cosmopolitanism, but within limits. He favors what he calls weak cosmopolitanism (the view that "all human beings have to be considered as objects of ethical concern") and rejects the strong version of cosmopolitanism (the view that "we actually owe all human beings equal treatment, regardless of any special relationship we have with them"). In particular, immigration is one of the highly contentious issues with which a theory of justice has to contend. In the conversation with Neera Chandhoke, "Minority Rights, Secularism, and Justice" (Chapter 6), the focus is on the interplay that takes place between the values and norms of justice at the global and local levels. Secularism serves as an entry point for this discussion. As such, Neera Chandhoke argues that secularism, a concept that historically emerged in the West, is a notion that was borrowed in India in the early 1950s and adapted to local conditions in order to regulate debilitating religious strife and assure the minorities of their safety. The conversation also addresses the need to factor in the specific conditions of developing countries, including the sense of agency of people in these countries, to put forward sound arguments on justice, especially when it comes to global justice. In "Decent Society, Memory, and Compromise" (Chapter 7), Avishai Margalit stresses that he has always been more attracted to what he calls "negative politics" (the idea "that what draws us into moral politics is injustice rather than justice") than "positive politics" (including "positive ideals"). He argues that this is the case because "negative aspects are more readily recognizable than recognizing and dealing with positive ideals." As such, Margalit believes that the "urgent question for today is how to prevent injustice, rather than how to promote justice." It would be interesting to ask Thomas W. Pogge if he agrees with this way of thinking. In his own conversation, "Global Ethics and Global Justice" (Chapter 8), Pogge, a fierce critic of the international order and how it not simply tolerates global poverty but to some extent organizes and facilitates it, draws in particular a distinction between international justice, which concerns first and foremost the moral assessment of interactions among states and has been around for centuries, and global justice, a much more recent concern that makes the individual human being the main rights holder and is therefore far more demanding in terms of justice. Pogge believes that global poverty could easily be addressed and solved and that it is essentially the self-serving interests of the powerful and their insistence on always having more that is largely responsible for the deplorable situation in which the world finds itself today.

International Law and Justice – Part III deals mainly with international law and international organizations, including the United Nations, and their relations with matters of justice. Mireille Delmas-Marty's conversation, "International Law as the Articulation of Universalism and Pluralism"

(Chapter 9), refers to the conditions under which law would be able to express a form of pluralistic universalism. She suggests a model of legal pluralist universalism that is at the same time descriptive and prescriptive. It is descriptive in the sense that the legal features Delmas-Marty highlights are already at work in the evolving nature of law. And it is prescriptive in the sense that as the world of law is shaped by contradictory forces, it is essential to encourage the forces oriented toward justice to prevail. As such, Delmas-Marty insists that at the international level cooperation should prevail over competition. This calls for a new conception of sovereignty, more geared toward solidarity. In his conversation, "International Law and the Question of Its Transcivilizational Possibility" (Chapter 10), ONUMA Yasuaki emphasizes some of the key aspects of his thinking about international law and the history of international law. In this regard, one of ONUMA's important theses is the somewhat unbalanced and non-international character of international law, essentially based on and officializing Western views. This is what leads ONUMA to advocate a trans-civilizational approach to international law, which allows international law to be more mindful of other non-Western legal traditions. Finally, José E. Alvarez, in "International Organizations and Global Justice" (Chapter 11), explores the role of international organizations as major actors of international law. Despite all their limitations and even pathologies, international organizations have a key role to play in the networks of norms and institutions of global governance. Alvarez identifies the challenges and opportunities that are now facing international organizations. In addition, he shares his views on the need to internationalize international law and what this means for research, teaching, and practice.

World Order and Global Policy – In Part IV Charles A. Kupchan, in "Global Justice and Global Peace" (Chapter 12), examines the conditions of justice as a source of global peace. In particular he identifies the various phases through which, to use the title of one of his books, "enemies become friends." In addition, Kupchan reflects on the changes at work in the international distribution of power, including the rise of China, and their likely implications for the evolution of the international system. In "International Economics and Development" (Chapter 13), the Nobel Prize winner A. Michael Spence highlights the importance of growth in order to achieve economic progress and justice. In this regard, he insists on the need to analyze and understand what has happened in the post-World War II period, i.e. a change of growth pattern. Since World War II, developed countries have continued to grow, but, more importantly, developing countries have grown at a relatively high rate and have to some extent caught up, at least some of them, with the developed world. He adds that growth, especially sustainable growth, is not just about economics but about good governance as well. The last conversation of Part IV, "Principles and Institutions of Global Justice" (Chapter 14), features David Held. In this conversation, Held puts forward his view of the central principles and the best institutions for a world order that would take the demands of global justice more seriously. The conversation centers around the extent and limits of a democratic agenda at the global level and how it could be expanded. This includes giving more importance to global policy.

*

Part V is the concluding section of the book. Jean-Marc Coicaud and Lynette E. Sieger, in Chapter 15, titled "Tomorrow and the Quest for Justice," summarize some of the lessons of the conversations, identify pending issues, and outline potential lines of research for global political theory in the years ahead.

PART I

GLOBAL KNOWLEDGE/GLOBAL THOUGHT

2

Global Order and Global Knowledge

Boaventura de Sousa Santos

I. REINVENTING SOCIAL EMANCIPATION

JEAN-MARC COICAUD (JMC): *Professor Boaventura de Sousa Santos, you have been teaching and conducting research in the field of law for many years but your approach to law is not very conventional, compared to mainstream legal scholarship. You have a strong interest in the sociology of law. In addition, over the years you have done a lot of work on non-hegemonic knowledge, including in the area of legal knowledge. This has led you to publish at a high speed. And to this day you continue to be incredibly productive.*

For this conversation I would like to focus on your multiyear, international, and collective research project, which has led to the publication of several volumes bringing together scholars from various parts of the world. The project has been called "Reinventing Social Emancipation: Towards New Manifestos."[1] *Indeed, for me this project encapsulates what has been your intellectual and political fight for decades. Producing better knowledge on the world and, altogether, contributing to producing a better world. Can you tell us about this project that has kept you busy for the last years?*

BOAVENTURA DE SOUSA SANTOS (BSS): The primary reason for launching and undertaking this project has really been the need to reinvent social emancipation. Social emancipation is a very important idea of the Enlightenment. It is the idea that we aspire to create a better society, a more just society, one that frees us from the bondages of current injustices, discriminations, suppressions, and marginalizations.

[1] Boaventura de Sousa Santos, *Democratizing Democracy: Beyond the Liberal Democratic Canon* (New York: Verso, 2005), *Another Production Is Possible: Beyond the Capitalist Canon* (New York: Verso, 2006), *Another Knowledge Is Possible: Beyond Northern Epistemologies* (New York: Verso, 2007), *Voices of the World* (New York: Verso, 2010), and *Epistomologies of the South: Justice against Epistemicide* (Abingdon, UK: Routledge, 2014).

The paradigm of social emancipation developed by Western modernity is undergoing a deep and final crisis. Social emancipation must, therefore, be reinvented. It must be understood as a form of counterhegemonic globalization relying on local–global linkages and alliances among social groups around the world which go on resisting social exclusion, exploitation, and oppression caused by hegemonic neoliberal globalization. Such struggles result in the development of alternatives to the exclusionary and monolithic logic of global capitalism, that is to say, spaces of democratic participation, non-capitalistic production of goods and services, creation of emancipatory knowledges, postcolonial cultural exchanges, and new international solidarities. The social sciences produced in the core countries from the nineteenth century onward have exhausted their capacity for renovation and innovation (as we know the social sciences were originally developed in the Western countries, in probably no more than five countries – England, France, Italy, and Germany, later on the United States). As a result, they have ceased to be the conscience of progressive social transformation to come and have rather become devices of legitimation, if not consecration, of the status quo and the social injustices it reproduces. By creating a network among a considerable number of social scientists working in countries which have been peripheral to the production of hegemonic social scientific knowledge, the project favored the emergence of a scientific community determined to develop new paradigms of social knowledge, relations among different types of knowledges, and engagement between knowledges and social action.

At the same time, the world has changed a lot since the time social sciences were developed. In particular, countries that are now becoming more important in economic and political terms – such as India, South Africa, Brazil, and China – have their own ideas and yet they are not very well known. In this perspective, one of the goals of the research project has been to get a better understanding and knowledge of the diversity of the world and of the young scientists who, in India, South Africa, or Brazil, are part of this diverse world. In the process, my goal is also to bring more knowledge, more ideas, more concepts, and more styles of writing into the social sciences of the world, and by doing so I am trying to improve social sciences as well.

JMC: So, one of your intellectual and political concerns is to go beyond the Western paradigm, the Western canons, and also to embrace a bit of an activist approach in tackling the issues at hand?

BSS: Well, my point is that if we stand a little bit outside of the West, we can see there are in fact a lot of social scientists in the non-Western world who are committed to trying to address and overcome the social problems of their countries. The social problems are so acute and so present that they knock on the doors of the universities and research centers. These are people who are not really isolated in ivory towers and are trying to bring their work to the foreground of politics. We therefore cannot make this very clear distinction between knowledge on one side and politics on the other side.

This is all the more true considering that social scientists more and more around the world feel that they are socially responsible for their countries and for the fate of the people who are oppressed and discriminated against, impoverished, silenced, and they would like to give voice to these people. There is a sense of social and political responsibility that is growing among social scientists and this, I think, brings together new kinds of knowledge with new kinds of politics. These two things go together.

Of course, I am not conflating knowledge and politics. They are two very different areas, but they communicate and feed on each other. There is a real opportunity for mutual enrichment. In my international research I have been guided by two main ideas. On the one hand, the idea of providing new knowledge about experiences of local innovation from democracy to cooperatives around the world, about which we tend to know little. On the other hand, empowering people to conduct politics based on this knowledge. Indeed, once people know that in different parts of the world there are more people who share the same ideas or similar ideas on fighting against social injustices and struggling for the end of discrimination, be it gender, racial, or caste discrimination, it has a triggering effect. It empowers people. People realize that they have struggles in common, which they tend not to know. In the end, the type of engaged scholarship I am interested in and which I have been practicing is about fostering encounters and providing meeting points for younger generations both in terms of knowledge production and reinventing politics.

JMC: You mentioned that in your view scholars and academics in the non-Western world – in Africa, Latin America, and Asia – are more aware of the demands of social responsibility than in the West, partly because in the West academics are captives of their wealth and stuck in the ivory tower. Can you tell us more about this idea?

BSS: The intellectual is someone who was trained to learn, not to teach. And knowing how to learn can help movements, citizens, and organizations to see the difficulties, contradictions, and tensions within their everyday lives, their transforming activity, or their political action. Intellectuals are facilitators; they facilitate communication because of their profession, they contribute and find out about other spaces and experiences that can help to contextualize a struggle, to find a better-informed conversation. That is why intellectuals must work in their offices, but also with movements and organizations. They have to explain and speak in, and understand other languages. And they also have to be able to explain themselves without footnotes, without words that people do not understand. We know that our specializations, especially in the social sciences and humanities, are specializations of words, but I cannot go to discuss with citizens and groups based on the *différence* of Derrida or Deleuze, because people do not understand it – and I say this while I have a very high regard for Deleuze as a great intellectual and philosopher of our time. That is something that we can do and that I am also doing this in my work. I know that when I am working I have to translate for myself. Intercultural translation begins with me.

JMC: What you are telling us is that, in a way, the professionalization of ideas can lead to two things: one which is good, and one which can be bad. On the one hand, the professionalization of ideas can lead to the deepening of knowledge and of science. On the other hand, it can separate this knowledge from social concerns and in the process it undermines the ability of knowledge to be good and socially useful, correct?

BSS: This is precisely the dilemma, the sense of the paradox that we are facing as social scientists. In fact the great social scientist Max Weber already mentioned this state of affairs. At the beginning of the twentieth century he indicated that the development of sciences and bureaucracies, together with professionalization of society, would produce the disenchantment of the world and the disenchantment of the people. Therefore, now, in order to re-enchant the world, to change it for the better, we need utopia, we need new ideas. This calls for a new meeting point between science, politics, and culture.

JMC: In fact your thinking about progressive knowledge and a progressive political agenda is also about finding ways to better organize and produce knowledge.

BSS: Yes, I think that new ways of production of knowledge are needed. More and more we need collective forms of knowledge and also a plurality of knowledge, what I call an ecology of knowledges. For instance, in the West, we have given absolute priority to science and to scientific knowledge. At the same time, we know that science is very limited. Science is very important for certain purposes but not for all purposes. If I want to go to the moon I need science and scientific technology. But, if I want to protect biodiversity in the Amazonian region I need indigenous knowledge.

So, scientific knowledge alone is not enough. We need other kinds of knowledge. Yet, around the world, particularly in the West, we have been destroying and neglecting other forms of knowledge. This is rather unfortunate considering that if one looks at the world as a whole as a unit of analysis, one can see that four-fifths of the population of the world in its everyday life does not rely on scientific knowledge. It relies on common knowledge, on popular knowledge, on traditional knowledge. But, in fact, we have silenced this type of knowledge that structures the daily life of people. We have not given value to it. Well, in my view, it is very much time to rediscover it and to reconnect it with scientific knowledge. I think about these issues in the context of my research on the epistemologies of the South. Scientific knowledge should not be pursued and celebrated at the exclusion of common and traditional knowledge. They have to work together. We have to respect both, each for their different purposes, if we want to be able to address and solve the crises the world is facing today.

II. DEMOCRATIZING DEMOCRACY

JMC: Your research project "Reinventing Social Emancipation: Towards New Manifestos" led to the publication of five volumes. Bringing these volumes to life has occupied you for many years. Let us review briefly each of the volumes to give the reader a flavor of your thinking and that of your colleagues. The first volume was entitled Democratizing Democracy: Beyond the Liberal Canon *(Verso, 2005); and, of course, since you gave this title to the first volume I assume that you think that there is a need to democratize democracy. Tell us a bit about this.*

BSS: There is, even in the West, a very rich tradition of different models of democracy, of different conceptions of democracy. But in the last thirty years we have given exclusive priority to representative democracy, that is to say a model of democracy through which the citizens do not decide issues. They simply elect the decision-makers of our society. Representative democracy is of course a great advancement of our world and it should be praised for that. But it is not the only model and in fact sometimes it is a very weak model of democracy. It is what I call a model of low-intensity democracy because people sometimes vote for different parties; but, first, there is not much of an alternative among the parties and, second, the parties violate their promises very often. The crisis of political representation that we have been witnessing in a number of Western democracies in the last decade or so, with more recently, the rise of populism such as in the United Kingdom, the United States, and France, is part of this story.

For instance, I will just mention Europe. Fifteen years ago, in 2003, the citizens of Europe by far voted against the invasion of Iraq but, in fact, a number of their governments, which had been elected by them, were in favor of the invasion and went ahead regardless of public opinion. And the examples of this kind of situation have only multiplied in recent years. Hence there is a crisis of political representation. The citizens do not see themselves represented by their representatives. This is not to say that democracy as a representative democracy is not valid but, rather, that we really have to enrich it with other forms of democracy.

For instance, in the "Reinventing Social Emancipation" project, we refer to forms of participatory democracy, particularly at the local level. In this regard, there are immense innovations, particularly in Latin America but also in Africa, where we see emerging forms of local democracy that are sometimes called participatory democracy, or even sometimes communitarian democracy. The constitution of Bolivia, for instance, tells us that there are three models of democracy that are equally valid in the Republic of Bolivia: representative democracy, participatory democracy, and communitarian democracy, the latter being the form of democracy that is prevalent among indigenous people. In Africa, in rural areas and sometimes in urban areas, we also see forms of communitarian democracy taking place.

With this plurality of forms of democracy, the idea is to broaden the canon as to what counts as democracy. It is not just representative democracy that exists and has legitimacy. There are other forms of democracy and they can complement each other. They do not necessarily conflict. And this dimension of complementarity is what I mean by "democratizing democracy." This is one aspect of what I have in mind when it comes to reinventing our ideas and practices on democracy. Another aspect concerns the fact that for some reason we have reduced our democratic discussions to the public sphere. Yet I think there is no need to restrict ourselves to the public sphere. We should have democracy within families. We should have democracy within communities. We should have democracy in our enterprises, and in our offices. Democracy is something that should be cultivated everywhere and in every place, in different terms of course, but there is no need to restrict democracy to the public sphere.

JMC: To go back to the crisis of political representation, your expression of low-intensity democracy is a nice way to coin this crisis. The crisis is at work in your view both in developing and developed countries. Is it something that is recent or has it been at work for many years?

BSS: It is getting worse. In my research I can see that low-intensity democracy is becoming even lower intensity, and this is for two reasons. One has to do with the fact that neoliberalism has become the main form of capitalism, and it has globalized itself. In this regard, global capitalism tries to avoid democratic deliberation. Very often we see that structural adjustment and conditionality violate the local constitutions of different countries. We have seen it in Greece in the past years, in the context of the adoption of austerity policies, but also in Ireland or in Portugal. So we can see that democratic culture, that is essentially nationally based, is besieged by international constraints.

Another reason accounting for the fact that low-intensity democracy is deepening is that corruption is growing; and it is growing because, in the field of political theory, there has always been a distinction between two very important markets, namely the political market of ideas and the economic market of services and goods. While the first market is dominated by values that have no price, the second market is the market of values that have a price tag. That is to say they can be sold and they can be bought. In this context, what we see today is that the economic market has contaminated the political market. Politicians, therefore, sell their votes and are being bought by powerful economic interests. In other words, there is a fusion and a contamination between economic power and political power. At times this state of affairs is illegal; at times it is not illegal. It is as if corruption has become the new normal. For instance, lobbying may be legal but it is certainly a form of contamination of the political realm through economic power. Of course, if all economic interests were equally well organized that would be fine, as Rousseau used to say. The problem is that some interests are much better organized than others and this distorts the political game and, ultimately, undermines political democracy. Unfortunately, I only see this tendency growing. Hence the fact that in the past years we have often been going from low-intensity democracy to an even lower intensity. If only for this we need to renovate and refurbish our democratic ideals and practices.

JMC: *You are telling us that the economic market with values that have a price is dominating and polluting the political market, which at heart is about, in principle at least, values which have no price. Is it not a fundamental problem since values which have no price are the most precious, as they are about organizing and negotiating freedom and equality and justice, and so on?*

BSS: That's right. Our opinions, our political ideals, the life options and choice they entail, even our ideologies are not for sale, or they should not be for sale.

JMC: The paradox and the interesting thing is that priceless things are the most valuable things. Going back to the issue you raised earlier of alternative forms of democracy, how do you dovetail formal forms of democracy and local forms of democracy? Can they complement one another? Can they work together?

BSS: Yes, they can work together. It is a complex issue because here we have a scale problem. There are forms of democratic interaction that take place at the national level or at the international level – let's take the United Nations General Assembly, for example – and then there are other forms that need a more local context, a more local scale, for assemblies that deliberate on complex issues. But in some countries you can already see that complementarity exists and is at work between these different scales. This was, for instance, the case in Brazil, which is a federal republic, between 2003 and 2016 where there have been attempts to solve the problem of scale.

JMC: You mentioned earlier that democracy should go beyond politics and take place, for example, in the context of the family and so on. Why do you think it is important to not view democracy as simply to be pursued in the political context but also to be pursued, conceived of, and exercised in the family and other contexts?

BSS: Democracy has to be part of the daily culture and life of people because for most people in the world, the democratic exercise as it is unfolding in the political realm is just a distraction in their lives. They vote every four years or every two years. They read the newspaper. They might also pay attention to political discussions and debates. But, most of the time, most of their lives are spent in their families, with their employers, in their communities. Moreover, in these areas we see lots of discriminations, lots of silences, lots of despotism, of conflicts. And bringing democracy to these aspects of people's life is getting a chance to address and solve these problems. For instance, in employment today we see the erosion of the rights of workers. What we used to call labor law was a magnificent body of legislation, which was meant to protect the weaker party of labor contracts, the employee, that is to say the worker. But we are witnessing today, in Europe and beyond, a tendency toward the erosion of these rights.

In the end, people are running the risk of having no real experience of democracy even though they live in democratic countries. This is why I think it is important to expand the experience of democracy and make it part of a wider culture of sociability.

JMC: What about global democracy? We now live in a world in which societies are more and more intertwined, interdependent, and so on. So, do we need to democratize global levels of governance?

BSS: Absolutely, and that is probably the most difficult challenge, or at least one of the most difficult. Looking at the world, one aspires that we should be heading toward a global civil society and a global political community. But sometimes it looks like we are more heading toward a global civil war. Against this background, we are living in a time in which we have to make very important decisions on how countries and people interact with one another, on whether or not countries and people are going to be able to respect each other. This is why, in my view, we truly need a profound reform of the United Nations. The United Nations, now led by a fellow countryman from Portugal, Antonio Guterres, could and should be a beacon for a more democratic world not just among the states but among the peoples and among organizations of the world. After all, although "imperialism" is an old word, which most people do not identify any more with, we still have today many powerful states that are imposing their will on the world.

The worldwide reality of today is certainly one in which democracy seems to prevail. But in reality it is more what we call "the market" that dominates the world. Take rating agencies, which are certainly not elected entities. And yet, as happened in the context of the financial and economic crisis of a few years ago, it suffices for them to downgrade the credit of a country to, in the process, alter the daily life of people. This is not democracy. In fact, it is despotism because no one has elected these agencies to tell us how to live. So, at the international level, we need more democratic accountability, especially when it comes to financial actors and capital markets, in particular the financial markets. How to make them democratically accountable? If you ask me today about increasing democracy at the global level, one the first things that comes to mind is that we need to regulate financial markets. Without regulation of financial markets most countries are at the mercy of speculation that may destroy the lives of peoples.

JMC: Do you think that we could see an improvement in this area?

BSS: The problems our economies are facing will not be solved if we continue to let financial speculation go unchecked. What is needed is a culture of political deliberation, and a culture of deliberation that is not limited to the official political sphere but that is permeating all levels of society. A culture of deliberation throughout society has to become part of our social DNA, so to speak.

In any case, I think we cannot move toward a stronger form of democratic rule without imagining and putting in place alternative economies. This is what the second volume of "Reinventing Social Emancipation", titled *Another Production is Possible: Beyond the Capitalist Canon* (Verso, 2006), tried to explore. It focused on all the other forms of economic activities that are taking place in the world and are not identifying with a capitalist logic (cooperatives, mutualities, credit systems, farming of occupied land by landless peasants, water systems, fishing communities, ecological logging, etc.). These initiatives are those in which local/global linkages are most difficult to establish, if for no other reason than they confront more directly the logic of global capitalism behind hegemonic globalization, not only at the level of production but also at the level of distribution. They often survive by finding ways of accommodating at least some hegemonic impositions. Another important facet of alternative production systems is that they are never exclusively economic in nature. They mobilize social and cultural resources that make inter-thematic linkages a necessary condition of their success. A market economy is of course possible and, within limits, even desirable. On the other hand, a market society is impossible and, if possible, would be morally repugnant, and indeed ungovernable. Nothing short of market fascism. Alternative production systems are one possible response to market fascism.

III. ON PRODUCTION BEYOND CAPITALISM

JMC: This second volume is clearly a systematic criticism of capitalism and its economic and social modalities. In this book, you call for encouraging a "solidarity economy" and "social economy," based on reciprocity and mutuality. Can you tell us more about this?

BSS: These are things that have been taking place for a long time at the grassroots levels in different countries, like in peasant economies and so on. But, today, you also find them, increasingly, even mentioned in constitutions at the country level. For instance, in Latin American, in Ecuador and in Bolivia, the model of economic development endorsed by these countries is a Quechua concept, called Sumak Kawsay. This concept means "good life," "living well." Living well is not living by accumulating wealth. It is living by respecting nature, by respecting the possibilities of collective growth of the communities, by taking seriously reciprocity and mutuality. These ideas and principles are already established in the constitutions of these countries. Translated into reality, these ideas and principles are prone to have a policy impact on the extraction of minerals and natural resources. They call for respecting the territories of indigenous people because these are sacred territories, not just natural resources. It is altogether a different conception of equality, and of nature itself. We all know, however, that noble constitutional principles are undone by realpolitik.

Needless to say, this type of approach contrasts with capitalist agriculture, which in fact has developed and "prospered," so to speak, on the elimination of traditional peasant economics, with the destruction of ecological equilibrium in the process. Today, many hundreds of thousands of peasants throughout Africa and Latin America continue to be displaced because of the acquisition of land as part of capitalist agriculture.

In contrast to capitalist agriculture, I favor peasant and solidarity agriculture and other forms of economy. Capitalist economy, including capitalist agriculture, as it stands now not only produces huge injustices in the world but also ecological degradation and destruction of the planet. This is a very serious problem and we should start addressing it. One way of addressing it is to think about alternatives to development, new forms of dealing with nature, with our communities that are great for creating a global equilibrium that will keep our planet intact for future generations. The fact of the matter is that we are currently destroying the possibilities that future generations will have to enjoy the planet as we are enjoying it at this point, even already with the problems of global warming.

JMC: These models of social economy and solidarity economy are, I think, rather influential in Latin America. But what is their impact in the US, which is so committed to capitalism? What is their impact in Asia, which is all about rapid growth and development, such as in China, with all the environmental problems that this has brought? And what is their impact in Africa? Is there a chance that these alternative models of economy could become one day part of a worldwide reality?

BSS: Well, clearly there are struggles taking place between the capitalist economy and alternative models of economy. This is certainly the case in the context of agriculture. At this point, for instance, in India we see a very nasty struggle going on, and sometimes it can be very violent, between peasants and the mega projects organizers particularly in agriculture but also at times in industrial development. We see the same happening in China, with all the displacements of peasants that are really destroying their ways of life. At this point, China continues to enjoy high economic growth rate and its cities appear to be able to absorb all the people displaced from the countryside. But suppose that at one point economic growth slows down in China, what will happen? All the countries that have gone through rapid development and high growth rate have encountered a slowdown, like in Europe and the United States. So what will happen when a similar situation takes place in China?

Africa also has its own problems and could go through a situation of crisis, even deeper than the one it is already in.

In fact, when it comes to agriculture, we have to invent new rights, such as rights to land, rights to water. These are things that cannot be privatized and, yet, more often than not, such privatization is happening. For example, the constitutions of Argentina or Uruguay or the constitutions of Ecuador and Bolivia indicate that people have a right to water, and therefore that water cannot be privatized. But such privatization has already taken place. Needless to say, this presents a danger for the populations that cannot afford to buy water.

A new social and economic common sense seems to be emerging pointing to postcapitalistic and postdevelopmentalist future paradigms in non-utopian terms, that is, by translating these visions into concrete political agendas. Grassroots organizations and citizens' initiatives have been launching social experiments that aim to build alternatives to capitalist infinite accumulation and environmental degradation. They cover such diverse fields as co-operatives, fair trade, barter economy, time-sharing and exchange, solidaristic economy, degrowth economy, social currencies, reciprocal investment and lend networks, social markets, care economies. These initiatives are giving rise to new fields of scientific research and gradually enter the public opinion debates. The trend need a broader scope and international outlook, multiple opportunities for social experimentation in order to become a central factor to overcome the present absence of equity, human dignity, and social justice.

JMC: *How then do we deal with the tension where, on the one hand, we see that emerging countries, such as China, Brazil, India are really adopting capitalist practices and ideology, and, on the other hand, the UN agenda, which is in part about trying to preserve and create spaces for priceless common goods. How do we conceptualize and negotiate the tensions and how do we find a middle ground?*

BSS: This is a very important question. I think that in order to answer that question, we need different kinds of knowledge that would be able to intersect with each other in a more intercultural way.

In a way your question already leads to another issue, which is essential, that of interculturality and rival knowledges. That is to say, if we do not respect other ways of being, other ways of understanding of the world, we will never be able to address and solve the challenges we are currently facing. The understanding of the world by far exceeds the Western understanding of the world. There are many non-Western ways of looking at the world, of looking at nature. So, in order to develop a common understanding, we have to know more about the diversity of the world.

In other words, we need a more intercultural type of knowledge, combining, as I said before, scientific knowledge and other kinds of knowledge by which most of the population still lives today.

We need a more intercultural understanding of the world because the alternative to intercultural understanding is war. It is the clash of civilizations, and I do not want that. I want a dialogue but a dialogue in intercultural terms. The goal is not to impose my single vision and priority of universalism, which we do very often in the West. We talk about universals like human rights in an absolutist way. But these are very Western and at times they do not respect other conceptions of human rights or human dignity. And the same applies to knowledge. We should respect others' knowledges not because everything goes or everything has the same value, but because we have to understand our differences and respect our differences. There is no other way than this in order to avoid global war among different paradigms resulting in much needless destruction of human lives.

IV. THE POSSIBILITIES OF KNOWLEDGE BEYOND WESTERN EPISTEMOLOGY

JMC: *This is the core of the third volume, which is entitled* Another Knowledge is Possible: Beyond Northern Epistemologies *(Verso, 2008). It seems that what is key for you is to understand the other as a way to better see and understand ourselves. In this regard, I think that the underlying intellectual and political agenda of this way of thinking amounts to exploring the conditions under which it is possible to know what is right and pursue what is right without being self-righteous?*

BSS: That is right, we have to have a sense of humility. In a sense we have to learn ignorance, in that I have to consider that my knowledge is very relative. Social sciences do not allow me to know everything, so it is important to be aware of our own ignorance of other knowledges. Knowledge is always incomplete and all cultures are always incomplete and problematic. This is why we need a dialogue among cultures and knowledges, and a dialogue that does not impose my terms to the other. I have to respect the other side. For example, I just cannot say "well, you have to defend human rights." Human rights have to be part of a culture that comes from within, and not be imposed from the outside.

We need not think that we are the depository of truth or of rightness or the only valued ethics. I am really prepared to risk that what I consider right may be considered wrong by someone else and that I may have to argue with this someone else to ensure that my reasons are understood, and that myself I understand the reasons put forward by the other side. Mutual understanding requires an intercultural conception of human dignity.[2] In a way self-respect calls for taking the other side seriously. For instance, some cultures will think that the individual is the most important thing while others will consider that the community is the most important thing. Well, in my view, self-respect and respect for the other requires us to not disregard the other's view but to discuss it. And it is all the more the case considering that we are prone to having a problem if we emphasize individualities but we also have problems if we only emphasize the community. So it is key to have a culture of discussion about differences of views. This in my view is the only alternative to war.

JMC: So it is the ability to listen but also, as you say, the ability to reinvent the way we understand and practice learning and teaching?

BSS: Precisely, and I think that much of the important production of knowledge that goes on in the world today takes place outside of our universities, our research centers. As we were discussing in the beginning of our conversation with the idea of the ivory tower, our universities have really kept themselves isolated from the other forms of knowledge that exist outside and around us. Sometimes, universities are at the center of the city and they have no idea what the people think just across the street. I think we have to open our universities. We have to change our education system. And yet, I see the dominant trend going in the opposite direction. The tendency is now to make universities more professional, more elitist, more global. There is also the tendency of franchising knowledge, and this is a disaster. If this tendency prevails, in the long run this will be the end of the university as we have traditionally known it. Rather than franchised and worldwide standardized knowledge, we need cognitive diversity. As I said before, we need more intercultural knowledge, we need to open ourselves to different forms of understanding and knowledge of reality, that is at least my idea.

JMC: You mentioned the expression "franchising of knowledge." How do we go about avoiding this tendency? What is the main problem with this tendency and how do we create alternative models of production and dissemination of knowledge?

BSS: Well, the first thing we can do, in my view, is to fight against the liberalization of services, of which education is a part. What is the most

[2] More on this in Boaventura de Sousa Santos, *If God Were a Human Rights Activist* (Palo Alto, CA: Stanford University Press, 2015).

profitable area in services of education is what the World Bank calls the tertiary education, which is basically university education. If these services are to be liberalized, then a few global universities, Oxford, Harvard, or Yale – which, by the way, is my alma mater – are going to be able to sell courses around the world that will reflect the views of the Anglo-American world. These universities are excellent but they reflect the realities of the Western developed world not the ones of Bangladesh, not the ones of China, not the ones of other countries, particularly those peripheral countries struggling to keep or restore their universities devastated by the World Bank diktats on education.

We need to fight this idea of franchising global knowledge and selling it throughout the world. We need more bottom up knowledge, reflecting and generated by the needs of common people. Modern universities, when they were created, were at the core of a national project. Look at the University of Sao Paolo in Brazil for instance, or UNAM in Mexico, Jawaharlal Nehru University in New Delhi. But if we are going to franchise knowledge, these national projects, that is to say the diversity of the world, disappears. It becomes invisible, and to me this is a major concern.

JMC: This is indeed a very important issue. So what kind of institutions of knowledge regarding research and teaching should we develop for the future? On the one hand we have global universities which are selling a particular form of knowledge at the global level, and then we have national universities that often tend not to adapt to the current evolution of the world. So what is the way to invent new forms of institutionalization for research and teaching for tomorrow? Should it be a combination of innovation at the local level and at the global level?

BSS: Well, think about the United Nations University, headquartered in Tokyo. I think the idea of the United Nations University is a good one. It could be a good starting point for cooperation, non-commercial cooperation, among universities around the world. In fact, what we need is non-commercial cooperation at the international level, especially in the area of knowledge production and dissemination. You know that in the middle ages universities were very transnational. The professors that taught in Bologna would also teach in Paris. We need more non-commercial interaction and more non-commercial cooperation among universities and global knowledges. In this regard, if the United Nations University were to be reformed in a way designed to give voice to a diversity of university projects around the world, it would be tremendous. It would be a great alternative to the commodification of knowledge that is now under way.

JMC: You are thinking about using it as a forum geared toward bringing together global policy and global thinking integrating a variety of intellectual cultural and traditions, so that it would be possible to think about global issues while combining local, national, and global dimensions?

BSS: I am in absolute agreement. That would be the way.

V. GLOBAL VOICES

JMC: The fourth volume of the project "Reinventing Social Emancipation" is about Voices of the World *(Verso, 2010). It is about personal stories and the idea is that behind ideas you have human beings, you have personal trajectories. Why did you think it was important to feature personal voices?*

BSS: Well, no matter how diverse social scientists are, they are still expressing and focusing on scientific knowledge. So I also wanted to feature people who are directly engaged in social struggles. This is why I felt it was important to hear from the leaders of social movements – traditional leaders, leaders of landless movement, leaders of national liberation in South Africa, Gandhian leaders in India, trade union leaders, etc.

The idea was simply to let these leaders of social movements tell their experience as they feel it, as they live it. So, you have the voices of these people through very long interviews. Some of them talked hours and hours, which means that there is an oral history dimension to the book. These leaders explain how they came about to be who and what they are, what kinds of knowledge they resorted to, what kind of experiences they encountered, etc. So this is a different book compared to the other volumes of the project. These voices are really different voices of the world and it is marvelous to put together voices from two indigenous leaders in Colombia with two traditional leaders in Mozambique or two women leaders of social movements in South Africa. It shows a fabulous diversity of experiences. This is the diversity that we need to know more and on which unfortunately we still continue to know very little. Sadly it is quite rare to bring such diversity of experiences and voices together. It is quite rare to find a forum where this diversity can be talked about, made visible and valuable. The irony is that with all the media technology we have, we do not have more diversity. We have less diversity.

JMC: Concerning this diversity that you feature in the book, do you find common traits? Do you find commonalities?

BSS: I see commonality. People use different languages to speak about social emancipation. The title of the project was social emancipations, not social emancipation. I wanted to refer to emancipation in the plural because there is not a single conception of emancipation. In fact, what I am seeing is that people have a sense of dignity, a sense of individual and collective dignity, and they struggle for a society that allows for their dignity to flourish. And for many of them often the idea of a better society, of a more just society refers to a collective well-being, not an individual well-being. This is why for them it is absolutely evil for a hedge funder to make millions of dollars while another family would take thousands of years to make that kind of money.

That said, through these voices we also see that there are different conceptions of what it is to fight for a better society. For instance, for these leaders justice is not only about justice in economic terms. Justice is also about cultural justice and environmental justice. As indigenous people have a different conception of nature, for them nature is not a natural resource. It is Mother Earth and its well-being is the source that generates all other well-being. This is an important lesson not just for the word of indigenous people but for the world in general. Particularly in light of the ecological catastrophe we are heading for.

JMC: When you have societies and people exclusively dedicated to making a lot of money, would you not say that in the end they are suffering from what we could call spiritual poverty?

BSS: Absolutely.

VI. LEARNING FROM THE GLOBAL EXPERIENCE

JMC: Finally, the fifth volume is about the overall and theoretical findings of the project. What are the key intellectual and perhaps even human findings of the project in your view?

BSS: Well, I have come to think that the Western world is becoming smaller and smaller. In a way, and for centuries, the Western world has been teaching the rest of the world and, at the same time, by and large, it has been unable to learn from the outside world. So by the end of the project, and this is also true for the current research I am now involved in, I came to think that it is important to explore what are the lessons that the US and Europe can learn from non-Western countries, for progressive politics and progressive knowledge.

This of course does not mean that I am romanticizing the non-Western world. There is much suffering, much despotism, and much corruption on the other side. But there is also much innovation. So while up to now the West has been in the modern era in a teaching position, it is now crucial for us in the West to sort out where are the areas and the conditions under which we can learn. Under colonialism and neocolonialism, we in the West lived as if the rest of the world was underdeveloped and therefore had nothing to say. We cannot think that way any longer. We have to learn from other experiences. We have to start learning how to learn from the global experiences of the world.

JMC: So, it is about reversing the order to try to create a better order at the global level.

BSS: That is the goal. And this is really what I try to explore and outline in my book, *Epistemologies of the South: Justice against Epistemicide*[3] and in my new book *The End of a Cognitive Empire: The Coming of Age Epistemologies of the South Coming of Age.*[4] In these new books, I take the logic of my thinking one step further.

JMC: The whole "Reinventing Social Emancipation" project was very much a critic of the current intellectual and political order, at the national and international levels. You seem to be pursuing further this critical approach in Epistemologies of the South. *Is it the case?*

BSS: The "Reinventing Social Emancipation" project began from the growing awareness that the social sciences had exhausted their ability to renew and innovate. Pursuing an approach that involved reinventing social emancipation, it began to explore what is now termed the "Epistemologies of the South," fostering an understanding of knowledges and practices that have been made invisible by mainstream social sciences. I further developed the idea of global learning through the epistemologies of the South in a very large project funded by the European Research Council (ERC) titled: "ALICE – Strange Mirrors, Unsuspected Lessons: Leading Europe to a New Way of Sharing the World Experiences" hosted by the Center for Social Studies of the University of Coimbra (www.alice.ces.uc.pt). I say more on this project below.

3 De Sousa Santos, *Epistemologies of the South. Justice Against Epistemicide*, Routledge 2016.

4 De Sousa Santos, *The End of Cognitive Empire: The Coming of Age of Epistemologies of the South*, Duke University Press, 2018.

JMC: Also, you refer to the notion of cognitive justice, which is a very intriguing notion. What do you mean by this term?

BSS: The long, historical duration of capitalism, colonialism, and patriarchy elucidate a past of unequal relations among knowledges. In many cases, those relations led to epistemicide.[5] Since scientific knowledge is not distributed in a socially equitable way, its interventions in the real world tend to serve the social groups having more access to such knowledge. Ultimately, social injustice is based on cognitive injustice. However, the struggle for cognitive justice will never succeed if it is based only on the idea of a more equitable distribution of scientific knowledge. Beyond the fact that such a distribution is impossible under the conditions of global capitalism, scientific knowledge has intrinsic limits concerning the kind of interventions it furthers in the real world.

JMC: It is very useful that you bring together a critique of political (and economic) order and one of intellectual order. For knowledge is often also an expression of power. The French philosopher Foucault has explored this line of thinking. Do you think that we are making progress on this front? Is knowledge, that is scientific and academic knowledge getting less ideological, less power-aligned, or are things getting worse?

BSS: At the beginning of the twenty-first century the most disturbing thing is that we have accumulated so much knowledge about social transformation and yet it is increasingly difficult to imagine a better society than the current one, even if the current one seems so fatally flawed, promoting unprecedented violence and repugnant social inequality. At the beginning of the twentieth century, there was a real lack of scientific knowledge about society. One hundred years later, we know much more, and yet the results are not brilliant. We have so much knowledge about our societies, but this knowledge is apparently useless. The knowledge we developed at universities is not preventing our societies from living under massive forms of false consciousness. Think of the process by which victims turn against victims and oppressed people elect their very oppressors into government. Look at South Africa, where poor South Africans have been turning against immigrants from Nigeria, Mozambique, and Zimbabwe. These immigrants, although they have less than 1 percent of the wealth in South Africa, are victims of racism and xenophobia. The white population makes up 8.4

[5] Dominant epistemologies have resulted in a massive waste of social experience and, particularly, in the massive destruction of ways of knowing that did not fit the dominant epistemological canon. It is this destruction that Professor de Sousa Santos calls "epistemicide."

percent of the population and they have 86 percent of the wealth in South Africa. Victims turning against victims. In the 2016 presidential elections in the United States of America poor white workers turned against the poor Latino workers. In Europe, impoverished middle classes are led to believe that their enemies are the migrant workers and the refugees. Has the knowledge about society that we have accumulated over the last century contributed to making us more insensitive to social injustice or more cynical or skeptical about the possibilities of struggling for a better society? Should we develop other types of knowledge that allow us to produce radical diagnoses of our societies, becoming more aware of social experience in the world that is an experience of suffering, but also an experience of creativity and innovation that we are often not aware of?

JMC: *For many years you were an active participant of the World Social Forum,*[6] *which played an important role at the global level. Where does the Forum stand today? Does it still play an active role in terms of shaping the global political, economic, and political agenda? It seems that it is not as visible and as active as it was in the 1990s? Does it mean that the international political, economic and climate has changed, and not for the better?*

BSS: The World Social Forum (WSF) met for the first time in Porto Alegre, Brazil in 2001. This was an event of extraordinary importance.[7] It signaled an alternative form of globalization to the globalization being promoted by global capitalism, at a time when capitalism was increasingly assuming its most exclusive and antisocial version: neoliberalism. This was not the first expression of an alternative form of globalization, but it was unquestionably its most consistent one. It put on the international agenda the struggles of the movements and social organizations fighting all over the world against the many faces of social exclusion: economic, racial, ethno-cultural, sexist, religious, etc. The WSF was, at the same time, both a symptom and a potentiality of the hope harbored by the oppressed social groups. It emerged in Latin America because the subcontinent was then the world region where the popular classes were more consistently translating hope into forms of progressive government. The great novelty of the WSF and its most precious

[6] The World Social Forum is an annual meeting of civil society organizations, first held in Brazil 2001. It is an effort to develop an alternative future through the championing of counter-hegemonic globalization. The World Social Forum can be considered a visible manifestation of global civil society, bringing together non governmental organizations, advocacy campaigns, and formal and informal social movements seeking international solidarity.

[7] More on this in Boaventura de Sousa Santos, *The Rise of the Global Left. The World Social Forum and Beyond* (London: Zed Books, 2006).

asset was that it facilitated relations of mutual knowledge among the social movements and organizations involved in all kinds of struggles in different countries and according to historically very distinct political cultures. At the beginning, such an objective was well served by a culture of free and consensual discussion, as well as by the refusal of the WSF, as such, to make any political decisions. This does not mean that, from the very beginning, there was no political debate among the more committed activists, a debate that became increasingly intense in the course of time. However, by the end of the first decade of 2000 the international conjuncture had changed in ways that were dramatically opposed to the objectives of the WSF. Undermined by their own internal contradictions, the progressive governments of Latin America were in crisis. US imperialism, which had been focusing on the Middle East for a decade, came back in force to the continent. The first signal was the forced resignation, in 2009, of President Manuel Zelaya, a democratically elected president in Honduras. It became the first test of a new kind of institutional coup under democratic guise. It would repeat itself in Paraguay in 2012 and in Brazil in 2016. Neoliberalism, fully backed now by global financial capitalism, invested strongly against every policy of social inclusion. The financial crisis provoked the social crisis and, as a result, the movements had to focus on national and local struggles. Actually, these struggles were increasingly more difficult because of repression and persecution. Under the excuse of the "war on terror," the paranoia of surveillance and security rendered extremely difficult even the international mobility of activists, as illustrated in the context of the World Social Forum meeting in Montreal in 2016, when more than 200 visas were refused to activists of the Global South.

Under such circumstances, what would the viability and usefulness of the WSF be? At a time when not only social policies but also democracy itself are at risk, would the continuity of the WSF be sustainable, a WSF reduced to a mere forum of debate and self-prevented from making decisions at the exact moment when neofascist forces are taking power? Such questions indicate an existential crisis of the WSF. Lately, however, as I watched the dynamism of the preparation of the WSF of Salvador (March 13–17, 2018), I came to conclude that the WSF may yet adjust to the dramatic conditions and challenges of the present time.

JMC: As you mentioned earlier, you are now involved in a new international and collective projective, funded by an Advanced Grant of the European Research Council Union, titled Leading Europe to a New Way of Sharing the World Experiences. This research builds on all the work you have done over the years and tries to push further the ideas we have explored in this conversation. Do you have already preliminary findings? And if so, what are they?

BSS: Has the knowledge about society that we have accumulated over the last century contributed to making us more insensitive to social injustice or more cynical or skeptical about the possibilities of struggling for a better society? Should we develop other types of knowledge that allow us to produce radical diagnoses of our societies, becoming more aware of social experience in the world that is an experience of suffering, but also an experience of creativity and innovation that we are often not aware of? The ALICE project is precisely about these questions. We conducted our research in some countries outside Europe, namely Ecuador, Bolivia, Brazil, South Africa, India, and Mozambique. Then we compared results with issues at work in Portugal, Spain, the UK, France, and Italy. We tried to understand how we could see realities arising from different continents. Here are some of our reflections and findings.

An epistemological shift is necessary in order to recover the idea that there are alternatives and indeed to recognize, as the bearers of potential alternatives, the struggles against oppression that go on being fought in the world. Such a shift lies in what I call the epistemologies of the South. We must change the world while constantly reinterpreting it; as much as change itself, the reinterpretation of the world is a collective endeavor. Six corollaries derive from this thesis.

First, we do not need alternatives; we need rather an alternative thinking of alternatives. Second, the constant reinterpretation of the world can only be possible in the context of struggle and, therefore, cannot be conducted as a separate task disengaged from the struggle. Third, as much as struggles mobilize multiple kinds of knowledge, reinterpretation cannot be provided by any single body of knowledge. Fourth, given the centrality of social struggles against domination, if, by an absurd hypothesis, the oppressed social groups ceased to struggle against oppression, either because they did not feel the need or considered themselves utterly deprived of the conditions necessary for struggle, there would be no room, and indeed no need, for the epistemologies of the South. George Orwell's *1984* is the metaphor of the social condition where there is no room for the epistemologies of the South. Fifth, we do not need another theory of revolution; we need rather to revolutionize theory. Sixth, since the work involved in constantly reinterpreting the world while changing it is a collective work, there is no room for philosophers conceived of as vanguard intellectuals. Instead, the epistemologies of the South call for rear-guard intellectuals, intellectuals that contribute with their knowledge to strengthening the social struggles against domination and oppression to which they are committed.

JMC: In the past two or three years, populism has become a major force, in Europe and in the United States. In 2016 in particular we have had Brexit in the United Kingdom, the election of Donald Trump as President of the United States. And in 2017, both in France and in Germany, the extreme right has progressed very significantly in the general elections. Of course this has been a long time coming but how do you analyze this state of affairs? And how do you interpret it in light of your own research? Should we be optimistic or pessimistic for the future?

BSS: Starting from the last question. There is not much ground to be optimistic. We live in societies that, for the past thirty years, have been in permanent crisis. When the crisis becomes permanent an insidious and for the most part invisible twist occurs: rather than calling for an explanation, the crisis is used to explain everything. In social sciences, we say that the crisis ceases to be a dependent variable and becomes an independent variable. The government cuts salaries and pensions because of the crisis. It privatizes the system of pensions because of the crisis. It privatizes health, again because of the crisis. So, instead of being explained, the crisis explains everything. The only thing that is not in crisis in our society is the crisis itself. All the rest seems to be in crisis. This leads to the politics of resentment, when people turn against each other; victims against victims and the oppressed against the oppressed. Populism is the politics of resentment.

Western modernity has repeatedly been under the illusion that it should try to save humanity by destroying part of it. This is a salvific and sacrificial destruction, committed in the name of the need to fulfill radically all the possibilities opened up by a given social and political reality over which it is supposed to have total power. As a result the global image (and self-image) of the West has been characterized by the discrepancy between high expectations and dismally broken promises: the promise of social justice and human rights; the promise of anti-colonialism; the promise of democracy and the end of authoritarian political regimes; the promise of cultural diversity and peaceful conviviality. The expectations were as high as the frustrations were deep in light of a resilient dissonance in realpolitik. This is how colonialism operated, bringing about the genocide of indigenous peoples, i.e. eliminating them under the pretext of guaranteeing their salvation. This is how it was in the period of imperialist struggles, which caused millions of deaths in two world wars and many other colonial wars. This is how it was during Stalinism, with the Gulag, and during Nazism, with the holocaust. And now today, this is how it is in neoliberalism, with the collective sacrifice of the periphery of the world system and of the popular classes everywhere. The contradictions of sacrificial destruction are coming home to roost.

JMC: Finally, as way to end our conversation, what is your advice for emerging scholars in the field of global justice?

BSS: Proceed by questioning all the time and in action (outside your office) your concept of global justice by dedicating 50 percent of your time to working with social movements and organizations that struggle at the grassroots level against capitalism, colonialism, and patriarchy.

3

China and Thinking Globally at the Turn of the Century

Wang Hui

I TEACHING AT TSINGHUA

JEAN-MARC COICAUD (JMC): *You have been teaching at Tsinghua University in Beijing for many years. What are the issues on which you focus in your classroom?*

WANG HUI (WH): Before I began teaching at Tsinghua in 2002, I was with the Chinese Academy of Social Sciences. At Tsinghua, I teach in two departments: Chinese literature and history. Usually, I teach both Chinese intellectual history and modern Chinese literature. Recently, I am focusing more on twentieth-century China. I also teach a course on theoretical issues. The title of the course is "Texts and Ideology."

JMC: *Given that Tsinghua is an elite university, most of your students are destined to have a successful career once they graduate. As such, your students are an interesting sample of how the new generation is evolving and seeing China and its role in the world. Since you started teaching at Tsinghua, have you seen an evolution in how students envision their careers, see China, and the role of China in the world?*

WH: Students at Tsinghua are very diverse, and what they do after graduating from Tsinghua varies also quite a bit. For the students specializing in the humanities, the best option is to continue to do research and find a position in a university or a research institute. This has been the case of the students who have worked under my supervision, especially my Ph.D. students. In this regard, a number of my students go abroad for about a year to do research in the context of their Ph.D. studies. They often go to the United States, in particular Harvard, UC Berkeley, NYU, Stanford, and Duke. Some of them also go to other universities and research institutes in the Asia region, in Japan and India. This is to say that, compared to the students of my generation, current students have certainly a better sense of the international academic landscape.

At Tsinghua, I also have many international students, coming from the United States, Europe, Japan, South Korea, Africa, etc. In addition, a number of my students are Chinese ethnic minority students.

Such student diversity was rare during the time I was a student. This is to say that things have changed a lot in the past decades. And, of course, such diversity has an impact on how students think about the pursuit of their future professional career, as well as on how they see China and its role in the world.

At Tsinghua, in addition to teaching in the Department of Chinese Literature and Department of History, I also lead the Tsinghua Institute for Advanced Study in Humanities and Social Sciences. The Institute serves as an academic and intellectual platform to invite distinguished Chinese and international scholars to spend time at Tsinghua in order to do research, give lectures, and organize workshops.

JMC: A few years ago I spent a research summer at Tsinghua and I was surprised by how many Tsinghua students are eager to study abroad, especially in the United States. How do you explain this attraction of the young Chinese generation to the United States?

WH: At the end of the nineteenth century, studying abroad, in the West or in Japan, became a trend. This trend stopped during the war period and in the early years of the communist regime. But after the Cultural Revolution, as part of an "Open Policy" approach, the Chinese government encouraged Chinese students to study abroad. Initially, the people travelling abroad to study were mainly graduate students and visiting scholars. But now things are quite different. Many families who are relatively wealthy send their children to study abroad. There are a variety of reasons for this situation. Some of the most important factors are the following: first, it is very competitive to get into a Chinese university, especially the best ones. In general, it is more difficult to enter Tsinghua and Beida (Peking University) through the examination process (Gao Kao) than to study abroad, even in the top universities. Second, most people who decide to study in the United States and other developed countries tend to think that the quality of higher education in these countries is higher. Third, studying abroad is also a way for a student to strengthen their ability to speak a foreign language. Fourth, in China the demand for people who have an international and first-class higher education is high, and the professional opportunities offered to them are quite good. All this encourages people to study abroad. That said, there are also downsides to this state of affairs. For instance, nowadays, for Chinese students having studied abroad and interested in coming back to China after their studies, it is more and more difficult to find a very good job, particularly in Beijing.

JMC: In the United States, we always present Tsinghua as the MIT of China (while Peking University is often presented as the Harvard of China). Is the comparison a good one? How would you describe what has been the role of Tsinghua in contributing to the development of China in the past decades?

WH: Presenting Tsinghua as the MIT of China is to a certain extent accurate because both universities have strong science and technology credentials, as well as humanity and social science studies with their own characteristics and strengths. At the same time, Tsinghua is now eager to restore the status and reputation it had as a comprehensive university before the 1952 reform of Chinese universities.[1] In fact, nowadays, most of the Ph.Ds produced by Tsinghua are coming from the social sciences. Do not forget that before 1952, Tsinghua had the best faculty in the fields of humanities and social sciences. But with the reorganization brought about by the reform of 1952, these subjects were transferred to Beida (Peking University) and the Division of Philosophy-Social Sciences at the Chinese Academy of Sciences.

It is difficult to summarize Tsinghua's contributions to China in a few sentences. But some of its most important contributions include: firstly, compared with other Chinese universities, Tsinghua has certainly the highest number of first-class scientists of any Chinese University. As a matter of fact, many Chinese achievements in the past decades, in terms of industry, national defense, advancing the frontiers of sciences, etc., were accomplished by Tsinghua University scholars or graduates. Second, Tsinghua is also engaged and active in politics. For instance, Joel Andreas wrote a very interesting book, *Rise of the Red Engineers: The Cultural Revolution and the Origins of China's New Class*,[2] which studies the Cultural Revolution and the origins of China's red engineer class. In this perspective, in addition to many scientists, there are a number of important political figures coming from Tsinghua, including two General Secretaries of the Communist Party.

JMC: Tsinghua is a top university in China and of course it now ambitions to become a top university in the world. How is Tsinghua working to achieve this goal? More specifically, in the humanities and in the social sciences, since this is your area of specialization, how does Tsinghua intend to become a university of

[1] Following the 1952 reform of higher education, such disciplines as engineering, agriculture, and medicine were separated from comprehensive universities to established specialized colleges. While there were a total number of forty-nine comprehensive universities in 1949, only fourteen were left in 1953.

[2] Joel Andreas, *Rise of the Red Engineers: The Cultural Revolution and the Origins of China's New Class* (Stanford, CA: Stanford University Press, 2009).

global intellectual reputation and influence? Does the university have major plans in this area?

WH: Both Tsinghua and Beida are making plans to become world-class universities, or even among the top world-class universities. But of course it is difficult for me to say if we are going to succeed and the extent to which we are going to succeed. When it comes to the humanities and the social sciences, I believe Tsinghua has still a long way to go. But it is certainly making progress. In the past years Tsinghua has made major efforts to attract talented scholars. It has also started a Ph.D. program focusing on developing countries, with a concentration on history, culture, and politics in non-Western regions. In any case, we also have to think about the following questions: What is a world-class university? Which criteria should be used to measure world-class universities? The question of criteria is not an easy one.

II BRIDGING ACADEMIA AND PUBLIC DISCOURSE

JMC: *Before teaching at Tsinghua, you served as one of the executive editors for the journal* Dushu, *for more than ten years, from 1996 to 2007. At the time* Dushu *was arguably the most influential literary journal in China.* Dushu *was also important in terms of the development of intellectual and academic relationships between China and the West. So tell us a bit about how the journal started and what was the initial idea at the time of the creation of* Dushu?

WH: *Dushu* magazine started in 1979, soon after the end of the Cultural Revolution. In the 1980s this journal played an important role for public and political discussions. It was the beginning of the opening of China.

JMC : *By training you are a specialist in literature and you started your career working on Lu Xun. You are also someone who is very much interested in the field of philosophy and, as you mentioned,* Dushu *initially focused more on social sciences. What led you to decide to become an editor of* Dushu?

WH: In the 1980s most of the essays in *Dushu* magazine were coming from the humanities. As such, it was viewed as a literary journal. But when I took the post of editor, since China was undergoing a process of great transformation, I thought it was necessary to involve more intellectuals from the social sciences and arranging for them to work with scholars from the humanities in order to foster high-level public academic debates. The goal was to reflect upon the urgent issues that China was facing.

JMC: *When you started as the editor, what were the issues on which you wanted the journal to focus?*

WH: *Dushu* was very much favoring a pluri-disciplinary approach. The objective was to bring clarity on political and social contemporary issues but also on Chinese history from a pluri-disciplinary perspective. For instance, we touched upon the crisis of agriculture and rural society. Also, in the early 2000s, we addressed questions dealing with the war against terror, nationalism, and globalization as well as many other issues.

III FOSTERING DIALOGUE BETWEEN CHINA AND THE WEST

JMC: A big role played by Dushu *was to foster exchanges between Chinese and Western intellectuals and academics, was it not?*

WH: Yes, in the 1980s, at the time *Dushu* was starting, a lot of reviews were starting to be written by Chinese intellectuals on Western scholarly works. And, later on, in the 1990s, the interaction between Chinese intellectuals and Western intellectuals intensified. This was in part due to the fact that a huge amount of translation of Western books into Chinese took place at this time. In this context, *Dushu* tried to create an intellectual public space for intercultural intellectual dialogue. We also invited intellectuals from America, Europe, and Asia (Japan, Korea, and India, as well as from Taiwan and Hong Kong), to contribute to the journal and become part of the intellectual debates in China.

I should add here that part of this intellectual strategy was also motivated by the idea that the problems that China was facing at the time – like the Asian financial crisis, nationalism, etc. – were not exclusively Chinese. They were global. This is why we worked very hard at putting forward different voices, not only from China but also from around the world.

Interestingly, this global dimension of problems and challenges that at the time we felt existed has only increased since the 1990s and the 2000s. Interdependence among nations has deepened in the past ten years and, in fact, the kind of global conversations and debates *Dushu* was trying to encourage is probably all the more relevant and needed today.

JMC: As Dushu *editor, you felt it was important for Chinese intellectual and public debates in China to be exposed to international scholarship and international ideas. Why did you think it was so important?*

WH: First of all, intellectually speaking, we should be open to any intellectual tradition that we can learn from, to every kind of intellectual tradition. I think this is part of what it means to think and to do scholarship: to be open and curious about what others have to say. Second, as I just alluded to earlier, nowadays most issues cannot be understood only from a national perspective, including from a national Chinese perspective. We need to have a global perspective. For example, it is important to understand the questions that arise in China from a global perspective. As such, a major concern I had when I was editor was regional integration in Asia. So we invited scholars from Korea, Japan, as well as from Hong Kong, Taiwan, and other places to reflect on this question. In the process, we became more aware of the processes of regionalization that have taken place in the age of globalization. This led us to encourage comparative studies of regional integration in Europe and Asia, in Europe and China.

JMC: You said that through Dushu *you wanted to feature Western scholarship and to have Chinese scholars learning about the West. Over the years if you had two or three key ideas coming from Western scholarship that were featured in* Dushu *and which you think were important to bring to Chinese public debates, what would you say they were?*

WH: Different kinds of issues. For sure, globalization and related issues of international law concerning war and problems with the nation-state and sovereignty is one of them. But the most important thing was introducing and reviewing a variety of topics coming from Western academia, as a way to encourage the negotiation between Chinese knowledge and Western knowledge.

JMC: As an editor you also envisioned this international intellectual dialogue as having to be guided by and built around interdisciplinary studies. Why did you feel it was important to bring historians, philosophers, economists, literary critics, anthropologists together, talking to one another and being together in one place?

WH: To begin with, a lot of Chinese intellectuals were curious about what was happening in the West. In addition, in the modern Chinese intellectual tradition, most of the journals and magazines that have expressed and shaped this tradition have had an interdisciplinary and comprehensive approach. Even with the Chinese literati, in early Chinese history, such a comprehensive approach existed. And so in the context of this tradition, one can find all kinds of topics, disciplines, all kinds of scholars from different disciplines involved in the discussion. This is part of the modern Chinese intellectual tradition, and *Dushu* wanted to position itself as part of this tradition. It was part of our strategy.

IV CRITICAL APPROACH AND IMPACT

JMC: It seems that what was also important for Dushu *was to put forward a combination of social and political critique and social sciences?*

WH: Going beyond the division between specialists and public intellectuals is important, in fact essential. Today a lot of the so-called public intellectuals are not really public intellectuals. They are more like media intellectuals. They just play the role of intellectuals in the media. But they have no real knowledge and they do not do the substantial research on the issues they are talking about. Obviously, this is a problem, and at *Dushu* we wanted to address this problem and rectify it.

At the same time, a lot of the scholars who focus on their own research limit it to their professional work. Needless to say, this is necessary in order to build a sense of expertise. But at the same time, it is important to have specialists engaged in public debates together with other scholars, so that the public can benefit from their knowledge and their discussions. In this perspective, most of the contributors to *Dushu* had a field of specialization. However, when they contributed to *Dushu*, we asked them to write in a readable style, not as it tends to be the case in an academic journal. The strategy and the objective were to have high-quality academic work but presented to the readers in an accessible fashion. I think that this is one of the key ways an intellectual and editorial enterprise can contribute to good public debates.

JMC: You wanted to have the best of academia, the best of academic knowledge, scholarship, and thinking, made available as widely as possible, so that you would be able to shape intellectual debates, public debates, beyond the university?

WH: Yes, because we wanted to address a broad audience.

JMC: How was Dushu *received in academic circles? Was it viewed as a useful contributor or as a critique of the system?*

WH: *Dushu* was broadly received as an intellectual journal as well as a political journal. *Dushu* magazine had a great impact on academic thinking and research because it put the spotlight on a lot of issues that became important in the social sciences and the humanities but also from a social and political standpoint, at times generating debates in the media.

JMC: Did Dushu *have an impact beyond academic and intellectual circles?*

WH: Yes, I think so. For example, it is through *Dushu* magazine that the crisis of agriculture and rural society, including the widening gap between urban and rural areas, between urban and rural populations, unfolding at the time, became a matter of public debates. Later on, the government responded to the debates and changed its policies. We also tried to address the fact that from the late 1990s to the early years of the 2000s China was facing a serious challenge with the collapse of its social welfare system, especially its medical system. Against this background, we highlighted the injustice or the inequalities that existed in these areas. We invited contributions from scholars who were working on the social welfare system. I really believed that *Dushu*'s work in these areas had a great impact on academic research and that at the same time it raised public awareness.

As a whole, *Dushu* did not have the direct intention on advising policy circles but, through media attention and real public debates and public discussions, a number of policy and political implications followed.

V YESTERDAY, TODAY, AND TOMORROW

JMC: How do you reflect on the intellectual life of the 2000s and do you think that intellectual life in China has changed since then?

WH: I think the general situation is quite different. Because of what is now the huge influence of mass media, people seem to be less interested than in the past in theoretical thinking and reading about difficult issues. This is a problem because without valuing academic research and theoretical thinking, it is difficult to maintain a meaningful and reflective way of thinking about complex issues. The culture of public debates that I tried to emulate when I was editor of *Dushu* is to some extent really in crisis. Moreover, compared to a few years ago, a significant amount of intellectual public discussions happen now on the internet. But, of course, the modalities of discussions on the internet are quite different. It is not so easy to have substantial and lengthy debates on the internet.

JMC: How do you see the situation evolving for public and critical discussions in China in the coming years? For instance, nowadays it is not easy in China to access international websites. How does this affect the ability of Chinese intellectuals and academics to have open debates?

WH: There is a serious problem of censorship in China. Different from the past, the current censorship system utilizes a lot of electronic technology, such as key words. I describe this trend of censorship as de-politicized censorship, as distinct from censorship in the past that was politically motivated and oriented in a much more direct fashion. That said, while the technologies used by the censorship system become more and more advanced, the anti-censorship methods are themselves also more and more sophisticated. For instance, everybody knows about the Great Firewall of China[3] but everybody knows as well about the means to circumvent censorship via the internet.

[3] The Great Firewall of China is the combination of legislative actions and technologies enforced by the People's Republic of China to regulate the internet domestically.

Also, personally I think that censorship is not necessarily an absolute obstacle for lively debates and the emergence of different ways of thinking. As a matter of fact, we always have had censorship since the 1980s. Sometimes it was stricter. Sometimes it was looser. But it has always existed. To be sure, today we have now the Great Firewall, but there are still many opportunities and venues for academic and intellectual debates. The key is for intellectuals to engage in high-level discussions and be able to create a sense of public space with a cultural logic that is different from government-controlled public media.

VI FROM NATIONAL TO GLOBAL DEBATES

JMC: You mentioned that compared to a few years ago, the modalities of public debates have profoundly changed with the arrival of the internet and social media. In this regard, do you think that the internet could become a support for organizing discussions among Chinese intellectuals but also between Chinese intellectuals and Western intellectuals? Relatedly, do you think it would be useful to have some sort of World Intellectual Forum, the way that there is World Business Forum (Davos), etc.?

WH: Yes, this could be very useful. But of course one of the difficulties is the language issue. Here, there is an immediate challenge of translation. As a matter of fact, when I was editor of *Dushu*, we worked with intellectuals from other countries to publish in a trans-lingual fashion, so to speak. We published in Chinese, Korean, Japanese, as well as in English. But this proved difficult because of translation issues. In addition, it is not easy to establish a proper editorial policy designed to attract an audience from different countries. Yet it is necessary to try this type of experience, and now perhaps more than ever.

Another challenge to the possibility of global intellectual dialogue, particularly on global issues, is the fact that there are significant differences between intellectual traditions across cultures. For example, from the late nineteenth century down to the twentieth century, Chinese intellectuals have had the tradition of studying the West and its major intellectual productions – classical, modern, and contemporary. We have had a broad interest in what happens in the Western world, especially, in terms of theoretical developments in the fields of economics, sociology, anthropology, humanities, and so forth. In the process, we have come to know quite a bit about the West and its intellectual traditions. Even if one is not a specialist of the West, the general interest that Chinese intellectuals have had for the West has led them to be quite knowledgeable about Western views and knowledge. I do not think that this is the case in the West. In the West one has to be a specialist of Asia to be interested in Asia and know about Asia, of course including China. This is a major challenge for the possibility of a balanced intellectual dialogue. This may have somewhat changed in recent years. There is more interest in the West for Chinese intellectual production. This is in a large part the result of the newly gained prominence of China on the world stage. But there is still a lot of progress to be made.

JMC: Would launching an online network bringing together scholars from around the world and publishing in a variety of languages help to promote global dialogue and knowledge?

WH: As I just alluded to above, here one of the main problems is one of translation. For instance, it is not easy to translate and make readable for a Western audience interesting and inspiring ideas coming from Chinese intellectual history. Through the process of translation nuances are often lost. To have a dialogue on specialized ideas, concepts, and words in their own context is an essential task but also a very challenging one. As the world is now more globalized, it is critical to go in this direction of what we could call "trans-lingual practice" but it is not easy.

JMC: We always talk about the globalization of the world, we talk about the fact that societies are more interdependent and intertwined. Yet political discourse and intellectual discourse and knowledge tend to remain very national and nationalized in the humanities and social sciences. Against this background, would you not say that we have neither a global space for debates nor truly the intellectual tools to think about the world as globalized, or globalizing?

WH: Yes, I agree. And yet such a global space and global tools are absolutely necessary. There are a number of global organizations, like the World Social Forum (WSF), that touch upon issues related to developing countries, the South, dealing with regions such as Africa, Latin America, and Asia. In this perspective, it is of course very important to think about the most urgent economic and social problems of developing countries. But what is also needed are new intellectual perspectives to understand the framework and the worldviews in the context of which these issues are interpreted and analyzed. This is essential in order to have a real dialogue between intellectuals from different backgrounds. To be sure, we are facing common problems and as such we have common interests. But we also have to learn how to communicate and negotiate better our intellectual and cultural differences, so that we can improve our mutual understanding. This is not an easy task.

JMC: Historically, in the field of philosophy, Western philosophers have conceived of and explored the notion of justice mainly at the national level. But today we cannot think about economic justice, social justice, cultural justice, simply at the national level. Often, our intellectual tools, our philosophical tools are not really adapted to think about global issues. They are not really based on dialogue among intellectual traditions, among cultural traditions, so there is a need for all these traditions to know about and learn from one another.

WH: Yes, that is true. To touch upon the issue of global justice, or social justice, from different intellectual backgrounds should not be simply arguing about the particularity of each intellectual tradition. It should also be about trying to address universal issues from the particular perspectives engaged in the discussion in order to broaden and deepen our understanding of universal issues.

For example, in relation to the issue of global justice, a few years ago I wrote a paper on Amartya Sen's famous article *Equality of What?*[4] The paper is now part of my book *China's Twentieth Century: Revolution, Retreat and the Road to Equality*.[5] In this paper I tried to think about the question of equality from the point of view of Chinese intellectual history and put forward a number of ideas in order to give a more comprehensive meaning to the notion of equality. Indeed, in Chinese intellectual history, there is a rich tradition in terms of thinking on issues of equality. And in this tradition, the focus is somewhat different. Take for instance the famous intellectual and philosopher from the early republican period, Zhang Taiyan.[6] In his work he combined Taoist thinking together with Buddhist thinking and, more specifically, referred to the notion of "equality of all things."[7] In this regard, one of his key questions was: *How can equality be understood not only formally but with respect to differences within society and also within the cosmos?* In other words, his analysis of equality focused on the relationship between equality and

4 Amartya Sen, "Equality of What?," *Tanner Lecture on Human Values*, delivered at Stanford University, May 22, 1979, available at tannerlecures.utah.edu.

5 Wang Hui, *China's Twentieth Century: Revolution, Retreat and the Road to Equality* (London: Verso, 2016), chapter 6.

6 Zhang Taiyan (1868–1936) was a Chinese philologist, literary critic, philosopher, and revolutionary. His philological works include *Wen Shi* (文始 "The Origin of Writing"), the first systematic work of Chinese etymology.

7 Wang Hui, *China's Twentieth Century*, chapter 7.

difference. Well, from my point of view, this is an interesting approach, which is very relevant for today. For example in China, take the question of minorities. They often are facing problems of discrimination, of inequality. They suffer from the divide between urban and rural areas, between coastal and inland areas, as well as from the gap between the poor and the rich. But they suffer as well from the difficulties and challenges associated with their specific lifestyle. So the question is: How can we combine the recognition and respect for their lifestyle, which is quite different from others, and at the same time offer them real equality? How can we combine these two issues? Addressing this question is all the more important considering that it is not specific to the Chinese context. It is also at work in other parts of the world. And this question is also related to matters of global justice. It is a challenging issue but I think that Chinese thinking can also contribute to the global discussion on this aspect of justice.

JMC: The humanities and social sciences bodies of knowledge are highly nationalized. For instance, in France when we study history and literature we first and foremost study French literature and French history. In the US it is American literature and American history. How do we globalize our mind? How do we globalize our knowledge while maintaining a national identity and a national body of knowledge?

WH: There are different approaches, of course. But, first people need to learn from others. In China when one visits a bookstore one can find a massive number of translated books. In comparison, when one visits bookstores in European countries or in the United States, it is difficult to find the same phenomenon of massive translation from China or other non-Western countries. This contributes to create a somewhat unequal intellectual relationship. It is not so easy in the West to learn about the non-West. Second, we need to find a way to create a new paradigm for an understanding of our history that goes beyond national literature and national intellectual history. Most historical narratives in the nineteenth and twentieth centuries are national histories. To this day, despite the intellectual efforts made for instance by the world history approach and its various schools, it remains the dominating paradigm. We need to find a way to go beyond that.

VII ON CONTEMPORARY ISSUES AND CHINESE INTELLECTUAL HISTORY

JMC: Over the course of your intellectual and academic career you have written on the contemporary social problems of China and its place in the world, like in your books China's New Order: Society, Politics and Economy in Transition,[8] The End of Revolution: China and The Limits of Modernity.[9] *But you have also written a massive opus on the intellectual history of Chinese thought,* The Rise of Modern Chinese Thought.[10] *Why did you feel it was important to spend ten years of your life writing on Chinese intellectual thought and what are the key ideas and questions that you were trying to address in this Chinese history of intellectual thought?*

WH: Well, concerning your first question, the fact of the matter is that when we talk about contemporary issues like neoliberalism, social inequalities, and social differentiation, all these issues are now at the same time both a Chinese phenomenon and a global phenomenon. As such, I have been interested in addressing them in the Chinese context. But in order to do so, one also needs to have a real understanding of the global context in which China operates. Otherwise it is difficult to make sense of the Chinese situation. The old ways of understanding a country by simply focusing on this country is limited and limiting. This is why my focus on China integrates a variety of perspectives, such as taking into consideration local perspectives as they are connected with the national, regional, and global dimensions. I also try to analyze contemporary issues from a historical perspective. This is to say that there is a real intellectual interaction, so to speak, between my historical studies and my engagement in contemporary issues.

As for my intellectual history of Chinese thought, it is difficult to summarize the four volumes of my book in a few sentences. But, generally speaking, I tried to introduce a new paradigm for the study of intellectual history and, more specifically, of Chinese intellectual history.

When I talk about the rise of modern Chinese thought, I do not only refer to the interactions between Chinese thinking, Western thinking, Indian thinking, or any other intellectual tradition. It is more how those different elements became integrated into the pattern of Chinese thinking. In that way Chinese thinking is not only Chinese but also made up of different components. As such, in the book, I try to get rid of the national framework when thinking about Chinese intellectual history. For instance, at one point I venture into some sort of comparative study of imperial experiences earlier in history in

8 Wang Hui, *China's New Order: Society, Politics and Economy in Transition* (Cambridge, MA: Harvard University Press, 2003).

9 Wang Hui, *The End of Revolution: China and the Limits of Modernity* (London: Verso, 2009).

10 This four-volume book, *Rise of Chinese Modern Thought*, published in Chinese in 2004, is not available in English. A translation of the introduction to the book was published in English under the title *China from Empire to Nation-State* (Cambridge, MA: Harvard University Press, translated by Michael Gibbs Hill, 2014).

Asia (Mongolian empire, Manchurian empire, Qing Dynasty), the Middle East (the Ottoman empire), and Europe. In this perspective, I try to do comparative history but by avoiding the framework of traditional comparative literature, which is still based on national literature and national history. This is what I mean when I say that in this work I tried to change the paradigm usually associated with intellectual history.

Part of renewing the paradigm of study of Chinese intellectual history calls for thinking about the dichotomy between empire and the nation-state. The nature and history of political entities in Asia are quite different from what they have been in Europe. And yet most of the time Europe, European history, European state-formation is taken as the main entry point and framework of analysis and understanding, with the Western teleological narrative of modernity that this approach is associated with. This is not correct as it tends to overlook the specificities of Asia, including of China, with their modalities, rhythms of development, temporalities, etc. I think it is important when thinking about history not to be the captive of the nation-state as it has emerged and developed in Europe. So, as an intellectual historian, I try to keep in mind, first, the need to be reflective or critical when it comes to the intellectual tools, the concepts and frameworks of analysis at disposal, and, second, the need to look into history from a comparative perspective.[11]

JMC: When you do intellectual history, you seem to be very much interested in the relations and interactions of ideas and the kind of political and economic contexts in which these ideas emerged, how they are shaped by these contexts and how they shape this context.

WH: Yes, that is true. And this is an attitude that goes back to my own reflections on the condition of knowledge. We are now trained in universities within certain disciplines and we take the division of disciplines for granted. However, history, for instance in Confucian thinking, is not only historical record or historiography. It also serves political purposes and values. As a result the term "history" cannot be reduced to the positivist approach of historical studies. We must also find the significance of the category "history" in our historical and intellectual discourse. In this perspective, we simply cannot universalize ideas. We need to approach and try to understand them in their historical context. On the other hand, we also have to try to draw some universal implications from the study of history in the contextual setting. This is how I attempt to understand ideas in their historical context, by accounting

[11] On this question, refer to Wang Hui, *The Politics of Imagining Asia* (Cambridge, MA: Harvard University Press, 2011).

for the constructive factors of ideas, by factoring in the historical, political, and intellectual forces that play a role in the creation of social reality. The interaction between the interpretation of ideas and the interpretation of political, social, economic, cultural practices is important.

JMC: In other words, you view intellectual history through understanding how intellectual history is produced and organized in concrete terms? In this perspective, you seem to think that doing so helps to translate ideas from one culture to another because understanding the context in which they are produced and organized helps to borrow them in another context?

WH: Yes, because, in the end, we need to avoid reductionism either way.

VIII ECONOMIC DEVELOPMENT AND CHINESE MODERNITY

JMC: To go back to contemporary issues, in your work on contemporary China you are quite critical of how development has taken place in China. Most people in the West are constantly focusing on the fact that since the opening up of China in the 1980s many millions of people have been lifted from poverty because of China's development policies. But in your work you also stress the negative dimensions of development policies, particularly in connection with your analysis of globalization.

WH: Yes, that is true. Let me summarize a bit my views on this matter. First of all, my critique of development policies in China does not necessarily mean that I am entirely negative toward the development policies. Development and economic growth represent a real achievement in China. I certainly do not deny that. On the other hand, I am critical of development policies, especially as it has been the case since the late 1990s, when moving far in the direction of neoliberalism. Basically I am critical of this approach. I see it as a crisis that has contributed to widen the gap between rich and poor, between urban and rural, and between coastal and inland areas. It also brought about very serious problems when it comes to the environment. This is to say that my critique is more than anything else a critique of the neoliberal model of development.

JMC: In this regard, what are your thoughts on the rise of populism in recent years, in Europe and the United States? One could say that populism in the West is in part a rejection of neoliberal policies and the negative impact they have had for millions of people. What do you think should be done in order to address this problem?

WH: The consequences of neoliberalism, such as the polarization between rich and poor, the ecological crisis, the concentration of capital in a few hands, all these are the basic reasons and the background for the rise of populism in recent years. Economic crisis is a periodical phenomenon of capitalism, so one of the questions that we have to ask ourselves in the current context is the following: Why is it that neoliberalism as it works today has led to a political crisis that took the form of populism? I think that part of the answer to this question has to do with the crisis of contemporary politics and, more specifically, the crisis of democracy.

At the core of this crisis of democracy is the fact that party politics, traditionally one of the key aspects of representative democracy, has moved further and further from the population and its daily problems and preoccupations. As a result, the democratic system as it exists today can no longer respond to the needs and demands of people. For example, in the United States, the rise of the Tea Party[12] has to some extent echoed the decline of the Republican Party's ability to represent a constituency. As for the Occupy Wall Street[13] movement, it illustrated the radical political appeals beyond the so-called "left-liberal" wing of the Democratic Party. Here the bottom line is that left or right populist movements cannot obtain political expression through the traditional political parties of the democratic system. In this perspective, the crisis of contemporary democratic politics cannot be disconnected from the economic and social crises caused by neoliberalism.

JMC: Another intellectual concern of yours is the question of modernity. Why is the notion of modernity and different aspects of modernity in China so central to your intellectual thinking and your political critique?

WH: Modernity is a very broad issue and to this day a lot of scholars argue that it is difficult to give a clear definition of this concept, so maybe we should just forget about it. However, in the context of China, for example in the 1990s, partly because development was based on the ideology or teleology of modernity, this notion of modernity is quite important. That said, my use of this category of modernity is based on a reflective perspective. I do not simply treat modernity as telos but I try to argue that it is necessary to reflect, and to reflect critically on modernity itself. Basically, in the context of modernity, development and

[12] The Tea Party movement is an American conservative movement, loosely allied with the conservative wing of the Republican Party.

[13] Occupy Wall Street was a protest movement that began in September, 2011 in New York City's Wall Street financial district, receiving global attention and spawning a surge in the movement against economic inequality worldwide.

economic growth provide us with many positive things. But, at the same time, sometimes it produces very serious problems, as I mentioned earlier.

So this is one of the ways in which I think about modernity – by reflecting critically. But my thinking on modernity is also related to the history of China in the twentieth century. In China, after the Cultural Revolution, the dominant ideology has been the negation of the Cultural Revolution. But this negation of the Cultural Revolution is not only the negation of the Cultural Revolution. It is also the negation of twentieth-century Revolutionary and Socialist history. This is a problem because in China the Republican and Socialist Revolutions of the twentieth century are part of the modernist project. Against this background, it is important for me to highlight the continuity between the different modernist episodes in Chinese history of the twentieth century down to now. What has preceded the 1980s in China should not be viewed in the context of a dichotomy, with pre-1980s twentieth-century China not being really modern, and post-1980 China being really modern.

This is to say that, as a whole, I believe that, on the one hand, it is necessary to conduct a critical reflection on modernity. As such, I do not envision modernity as part of a teleology. But, on the other hand, it is necessary as well to understand the whole history of twentieth-century China in the context of the modernity project.

IX CHINA'S GLOBAL ROLE

JMC: With its worldwide economic influence China is now a power of global importance. Do you think that at one point China will also become a comprehensive global political actor, able to shape world politics the way the United States has been able to do so since the end of World War II? In your view, what kind of global political actor will China be and do you feel that there are Chinese values or principles coming from Chinese philosophy that will become part of the international intellectual discourse of global justice, international law, and so on?

WH: I think that China is already a global political force. But this is not really a new phenomenon. For quite a long time China has been a global political force, but in different ways. For example, during the Cold War period, China was already an important actor, playing a role in the Cold War structure. After the establishment of the People's Republic of China (PRC), China was at war in the Korean Peninsula with the United States. In the late 1950s, China also had disagreements with the Soviet Union, which later led to military conflicts. In the course of these events the bipolar structure of the Cold War gradually changed. The Chinese engagement with Third World politics played a significant role as well. And I also believe that China did play some role in the deconstruction of the bipolar structure of the Cold War. In addition, the Cultural Revolution was a catastrophe in China but at the same time played a central role in 1968 movements in the West and other places. So in this sense, prior to now, at other moments of the post–World War II period, China was already a global political force.

But of course, in recent times China has changed a lot, and so has its role in the world. For example, in Africa, besides Europe and America, China with India and other emerging economies are playing larger and larger roles. Incidentally, this entails both positive and negative aspects. Positively, the new presence of emerging countries gives African countries more options and possibilities. They can put traditional powers in competition with new powers and get the best deals possible. But on the other hand, China, India, Brazil, or other new economies have to really avoid the old American and European colonial patterns in African countries. This is a crucial issue, especially in the new global context. A few years ago I was in Senegal for the World Social Forum. I could see that the Asian–African relationship had been tremendously transformed, and not always in a positive way. In this regard, there are surely issues of global justice that are overlooked. These issues of global justice need to be addressed in the context of Africa's interests. Moreover, Chinese intellectuals following these developments need to think about China's own internationalist legacy. In this regard, one of the questions that Chinese intellectuals have to think about is: How to connect this Chinese legacy and tradition of internationalism with policies mindful of global justice issues? For example, to refer to something that I allude to earlier: How can we develop equality while maintaining respect for differences? These are big challenges. Needless to say, the solutions to these challenges are not easy but Chinese intellectual traditions can contribute a lot. To go back to the theme of dialogue we talked about earlier in our conversation, their contribution should be part of a dialogue with intellectuals from all over the world – that is to say not only with intellectuals in the West but also, and this is especially important, with intellectuals from African as well as from Latin American and Asian countries. This is urgently needed if we want to address the problems mounting around the world.

JMC: In your recent book in English, China's Twentieth Century,[14] *you talk about the fact that the crisis of political representation and legitimacy affecting a number of Western democratic regimes is not specific to these regimes. You*

[14] Wang Hui, *China's Twentieth Century*.

argue that there is also a problem of political representation and legitimacy in China. In this book you also stress the paradox that while China has become the factory of the world, its working class as an organized force is not in good shape. Could you share your thoughts on these issues and tell us what kind of impact these issues could have on the role of a rising China at the global level?

WH: After World War II the Chinese political system, especially the relationship between party and state, has been shaped by the people's war of liberation. Mao Zedong called this system "People's democratic dictatorship." For a long time, there has been no doubt about the legitimacy of this system. But in the past thirty years, this system has changed tremendously. In my own work I call the political aspect of this transition the transition from a "party-state" system to "state-party" system.[15] In the "party-state" system, the party's leadership rests on political leadership and ideological leadership, so to speak. But in the "state-party" system, the party (that is the Chinese Communist Party, CPC) functions as well as an administrative power. In other words, there is an expansion of the CPC's scope and power in the sense that the party has been transformed from being a political organization to being a core part of the state apparatus. This creates a sense of disconnect between the political dimension and the social dimension, with the sense of broken representation that follows.

This type of analysis leads me to argue that the question of crisis of representation should not simply be framed as a problem for democracies. It is also a problem for the socialist political system. And in order to address this problem it is important to focus on how to overcome the sense of broken representation at play and how to bridge the gap between the political dimension and the social dimension. In the context of China, this would call for at the same time invoking China's political heritage and learning from the strengths of other political systems.

In any case, as I just said, it is important to think about the crisis of contemporary political representation and how it could evolve in the future by going beyond the binary framework (democracy-socialist regimes) shaped by Cold War ideology. In this regard, in a way, Western societies have not been very self-reflective because not many people, including the intellectual elite, in the West are willing to seriously study other non-Western experiences and political traditions, including the ones of modern China, and think they could possibly learn from them. For them, there is not much to learn from other traditions. In my view, this attitude amounts to a missed opportunity.

15 *Ibid.*, pp. 39–40.

JMC: Toward the end of your book in English, China from Empire to Nation-State,[16] *you say that "the forms of sovereignty, models of identity, and global relations created by modern revolutions are currently facing a deep and wide-ranging crisis. Therefore, efforts to reinterpret forms of sovereignty and the crises of legitimacy produced by the revolutions and the historical changes of the nineteenth and twentieth centuries play an important function for understanding changes in the contemporary world and what lies ahead." What are your current thoughts on these issues?*

WH: In fact, I have been thinking about these questions for a long time. My book *The Rise of Modern Chinese Thought* is relevant in this regard. The first volume discusses the relationship of "Principle and Things" (Li and Wu), mainly focusing on Chinese premodern political thought and ethical practice. The second volume "Empire and Nation-State" is an attempt to reinterpret sovereignty, models of identity, and global relations in the context of the seventeenth to nineteenth centuries. The following two volumes discuss the work of Chinese modern thinkers concerning the tremendous changes that took place in the nineteenth and twentieth centuries. The book you mentioned, *China from Empire to Nation-State,* is the introduction of this four-volume work.

After the publication of *The Rise of Modern Chinese Thought*, I shifted my main research focus to the twentieth century, and *China's Twentieth Century* includes some of the findings of my research in this area.

Currently I am working on editing in Chinese a two-volume collection and just finished the last essay, which discusses the Russian Revolution and the Chinese Revolution. In this text, I discuss the theoretical debates surrounding these two revolutions in the twentieth century. This entails analyzing the evolution of concepts such as sovereignty, models of identity, and global relations, etc. in the twentieth century, especially in the context of the changes faced by China and the world.[17]

X THE FUTURE OF CHINA AND WORLD ORDER

JMC: In November 2017 I attended a conference on globalization organized by the Fudan Institute for Advanced Study in Social Sciences. At the conference, most Chinese academics seemed to be quite confident that China was about to replace the United States as the leading power in the world. As someone who has

16 Wang Hui, *China from Empire to Nation-State,* p. 143.

17 On this issue, Wang Hui, *China's Twentieth Century,* chapters 1, 2, and 3 in particular.

written a lot on Contemporary China, its evolution, and its characteristics, do you think that it is the case?

WH: China is already the second world economy. Soon it will surpass the United States and will become the first. But the per capita income is still much lower in China than in the United States. So there is an obvious internal disparity. Polarization between rich and poor, differences between urban and rural areas, regional differences, the ecological crisis, etc., are also generating a number of major problems in Chinese society. There is therefore still a long way to go in terms of looking for a suitable or right development path. But no matter what, China, India, Brazil, and South Africa, plus Japan and Korea (which have already become developed countries), these countries are profoundly changing the geopolitics and geo-economy of the world. The world order, which was European-centered in the eighteenth and nineteenth centuries and American-centered in the twentieth century, is now radically different.

But it is an exaggeration to say that China is going to replace the United States. American hegemony was formed in the period of colonialism, imperialism, and the Cold War. If only because of this, for a long time it is going to be impossible to replace its military power. The replacement of one hegemon by another is what people's imagination focuses on in times of transition. But what I think is more important is which new values and principles will be generated in the context of the changes we are currently witnessing and whether or not these new values and principles will be able to transcend the hegemonic logic of the nineteenth and twentieth centuries.

JMC: Assuming that China indeed takes over the role of leading power in the world, what could be the implications of this on Chinese foreign policy?

WH: It is difficult for me to make an accurate judgment. But what I can predict is that China will not become a hegemon like America. In this regard, it is useful to focus on three aspects and periods in order to make sense of Chinese foreign policy and how it could be oriented in the future. First, following the Korean War in the 1950s,[18] especially after the Bandung Conference,[19] there are the Five Principles of Peaceful

[18] The Korean War (June 1950–July 1953) was a war between North Korea (with the support of China and the Soviet Union) and South Korea (with the principal support of the United States).

[19] The Bandung Conference was a meeting of Asian and African states, most of which were newly independent, which took place on April 1955 in Bandung, Indonesia. The twenty-nine countries that participated at the Bandung Conference represented nearly one-quarter of the Earth's land surface and a total population of 1.5 billion people, roughly 54 percent of the Earth's population at the time. The conference's stated aims were to promote Afro-Asian economic and cultural cooperation and to oppose colonialism and neocolonialism by any nation. The conference was an important step toward the Non-Aligned Movement.

Coexistence[20] and Third World Internationalism. Second, there is the period following the “open door policy,”[21] with a diplomacy and foreign policy more engaged with other countries as well as in international organizations. Third, there is the moment of multilateralism that has emerged in the early twenty-first century, including the Shanghai Cooperation Organization, ASEAN+3 (China, Japan, and Korea), one (China) plus sixteen (middle and east European countries), the BRIC Development Bank, the Asian Infrastructure Investment Bank, etc. And, of course, more recently, there is the “Belt and Road Initiative.” It is important to know about these aspects and reflect on them because Chinese foreign policy is not going to change suddenly. For example, China–Africa relations experienced changes through the Mao Zedong and Deng Xiaoping era, and it is also changing significantly today. However, there is still certain stability. Therefore, rather than imagining what policy China, if it ever becomes a world leader, could have, it is more fruitful to analyze the history and evolution of its foreign policy.

JMC: Do you think that Chinese leadership has a clear idea of what it wants to do, of what kinds of policy it would like to pursue in the hypothesis China becomes the leading power in the world?

WH: I am not sure. Learning from the trends of Chinese foreign policy, and from the demands from Chinese society, can be useful.

JMC: At this Fudan conference, again, one of the major issues that emerged from the discussion among Chinese academics was the one of Chinese soft power. In essence, the debates addressed the fact that it is not enough to have massive material power to achieve great power status. It is also necessary to have the support of soft power, of values. Do you think that China has the kind of values that could become the source of an effective soft power?

[20] The Five Principles of Peaceful Coexistence are a set of principles meant to govern relations between states. Their first formal codification in treaty form was in an agreement between China and India in 1954. They were enunciated in the preamble to the “Agreement (with exchange of notes) on trade and intercourse between Tibet Region of China and India,” which was signed in Peking on April 29, 1954. This agreement stated the five principles as: Mutual respect for each other’s territorial integrity and sovereignty; Mutual non-aggression; Mutual non-interference in each other’s internal affairs; Equality and cooperation for mutual benefit; and Peaceful Coexistence.

[21] Open Door policy describes the economic policy initiated by Deng Xiaoping in 1978 to open up China to foreign businesses that wanted to invest in the country. This policy set in motion the economic transformation of modern China.

WH: In the context of international relations, soft power is principally focused on the nation-state as a subject. As such, it has mainly been understood in the context of international competition. This is certainly how Joseph Nye, who has coined the expression of "soft power," refers to soft power. But when discussing values or culture, soft power cannot only be a tool of competition for hegemony. It should also be a resource for improvement.

For example, after the Bandung Conference, China initiated the Five Principles of Peaceful Coexistence, and later Third World Internationalism. These principles include important values and define the relationship between China and other Asian, African, and Latin American countries. This was an important contribution. As such, although at the time China was very poor and its military power not strong, this approach, along with the idea of socialism, brought China many sincere friends in Africa and Latin America. In this perspective, if China, based on its own historical tradition and social conditions, can really develop a socialism which is different from twentieth-century socialism and fits the new historical condition of the twenty-first century, Chinese experience could provide something useful to other regions, countries, and people of the world. That would be a constructive form of soft power.

JMC: In China, we often hear the expression of "socialism with Chinese characteristics" or of "democracy with Chinese characteristics." Do you think that one day we will have "world order with Chinese characteristics"? In this regard, in your book The Politics of Imagining Asia, *toward the end of it you argue that "... the core of Eurocentrism lies in its having established rules according to the demands of Western interests and then having universalized them. Any critique of Eurocentrism must thus involve the reformulation of those rules themselves."*[22] *As the international order is changing, especially under the influence of the rise of China, do you think that it is possible for China to play a role in transforming the international rules, particularly in the context of international law?*

WH: Without any doubts, China will participate in the shaping of the new world order, but its involvement will only be one of participation. In this regard, China's "Belt and Road Initiative" (BRI)[23] has generated debates in the past years, including in terms of skepticism and criticisms in the West. And

[22] Wang Hui, *The Politics of Imagining Asia*, p. 260.

[23] The Silk Road Economic Belt and the twenty-first-century Maritime Silk Road, also known as the One Belt and One Road Initiative (OBOR), The Belt and Road (B&R), and The Belt and Road Initiative (BRI), is a development strategy proposed by the Chinese Government that focuses on connectivity and cooperation between Eurasian countries, primarily the People's

here what is important is to make sure that this initiative does not lead to the types of mistakes of expansion and power politics made by European countries and the United States in the past.

So far the "Belt and Road Initiative" has been discussed mostly by economists and international relations scholars. They care about finance, investment, resolving overproduction, looking for new opportunities of market extension, as well as game theories between countries. These are not new things from the modern history perspective. My approach is different. For me, if the "Belt and Road Initiative" is only a material initiative but not a spiritual one, then it cannot contribute to re-shaping civilization. If this initiative cannot bring a new direction when it comes to values, then even if it brings about short-term economic benefits, its contribution to world history will be minimal. "Belt," "road" constitute concepts that are very meaningful. Unlike how previously in history the expansion of empires took place by continuous occupation of land, these concepts refer to interaction methods, to connections between different cultures, societies, languages, civilizations, religions, and customs. They mean or should mean that economic processes must be embedded in forms of culture, society, customs, beliefs, and daily life and not let economics be the dimension that controls everything. Therefore, the "Belt and Road Initiative" should not be a plan of expansion, a plan of territory expansion, but a plan of connection, communication, and interaction. It should not aim at super-national integration but, through networks of connection, at allowing different actors to participate in the process of interaction according to their own condition, status, and willingness. This should not be a plan belonging to historical capitalism but a plan of rebuilding civilization that goes beyond historical capitalism.

If the world is changing along these lines, does it mean that it is adopting Chinese characteristics? I do not think so. This should be a process allowing different groups, regions, and cultures to participate. It should be an exploration toward commonality and not singularity, combining diversity and equality. I know what I say here is idealistic. But if we do not participate in the related discussion using our own way, capital and its logic will lead everything. And then we will give up on the future.

Republic of China (PRC), the land-based Silk Road Economic Belt (SREB), and the ocean-going Maritime Silk Road (MSR). The strategy underlines China's push to take a larger role in global affairs with a China-centered trading network. It was unveiled by Xi Jinping in September and October 2013 for SREB and MSR, respectively.

The change of world order should not amount to a hegemony replacing another. It should be an evolutionary process that admits diversity, encourages participation, and favors more democracy and openness.

XI GLOBAL INTERCULTURALITY

JMC: *In this same book,* The Politics of Imagining Asia, *in the chapter dealing with "Weber and Chinese Modernity," you conclude by stressing the need to expand Habermas's concept of "intersubjectivity" to the study of other cultural and linguistic communities. Being able to communicate with other cultural and linguistic communities and understanding their point of view is indeed key for the building of a sense of intercultural and global community? What do you think could be some of the ways to nurture and foster such intercultural and global community?*

WH: In order to answer your question, let me refer to the concept of "society of intra-systems," which I have been using to describe the Chinese civilization and the dialogue of cultures within it. And it certainly can be used beyond this, to foster an intercultural and global community.

What does this concept mean? It means that within a society there are many systems, mutually intertwined, and that society is composed of these intertwined systems. Now, what does the concept or notion of "system" itself mean? It means that it can be language, religion, ethnicity group, and even civilization, such as Muslim civilization, Tibetan civilization, etc. Against this background, the uniqueness of Chinese civilization is that it can incorporate internally different cultures and civilizations. What do I mean by "incorporate internally"? I mean that it has an existence that is holistic and does not cancel the characteristics of different cultures/civilizations it entails and are gradually formed over time through long-term contacts and mutual interpretations. It is a kind of social relationship that uses both integration and diversity as its internal factors.

Extrapolating, the notion of "society of intra-systems" can be useful to think about the fostering of an intercultural and global community. It is very much related to the need to understand our own internal diversity based in how we relate and interact with others. It is also related to the need to understand the internal civilization that each of us is and then create a new subjectivity, individual and collective, on this basis – a new subjectivity, individual and collective, that makes room for others and recognizes the place that others play in its constitution.

For example, our history, individual and collective, is not the history of a single region, a single ethnicity, a single religion, and a single language. Our history is one that is intertwined, including with conflicts and identification. What shapes us is not only our ancestors but it is also our friends, chance encounters, such as love and marriage, friendship, conflicts, etc. All these can change the path of life. As such, it is dangerous if identification only develops toward singularity.

In essence, the concept of "society of intra-systems" can help us make sense of the notion of civilization and of the relations among civilizations. This is especially the case today at the global level, when there are many connections and interactions among the various cultural blocks around the world.

XII THE WAY FORWARD

JMC: What are the projects which you are now working on?

WH: Connected with my ongoing thinking on equality, I am doing research on the social form of democracy and its crisis. It is important to think about this because in China we often talk about democracy and the form it could take. Yet, in democratic countries in the West, as I mentioned earlier, democratic regimes are going through a crisis. The traditional pattern of the democratic political system is in crisis. There is a crisis of political representation with mainstream political parties having lost a significant part of their credibility. The public sphere, especially the media, which is crucial for democracy, appears problematic for a lot of people. Against this background, one of the questions that I am thinking about is: What could be the conditions for the rule of law in China? What kind of political culture can make the rule of law really effective in China?[24]

JMC: Finally, to conclude our conversation, what would be your advice to young scholars beginning to work on issues of global justice today?

WH: My hope is that the new generation will call upon interdisciplinarity, as well as theoretical and empirical approaches, to address the key issues of diversity, equality, big-scale mobilization and migration, the return of religion and different traditions, as well as the crisis of political-social models or patterns shaped in the nineteenth to twentieth century.

24 Refer to Wang Hui's latest book in English, *China's Twentieth Century*.

4

Oh, [Muslim] Believers: Be Just, That is Always Closer to True Piety

Abdullahi Ahmed An-Na'im

I ON MUSLIMS AND GLOBAL JUSTICE

JEAN-MARC COICAUD (JMC): *One of your most well-known books is titled Muslims and Global Justice.*[1] *Why did you focus on the theme of Muslims and global justice?*

ABDULLAHI AHMED AN-NA'IM (AN): The mandate of the Quran to all Muslims is to always be truthful and do justice. For instance, verse 8 of chapter 5 of the Quran can in part be translated as follows: "Oh, [Muslim] Believers ... be faithful to God, witness to the Truth. Do not be dissuaded from doing Justice because of the injustice perpetrated by others. Be Just, that is always closer to true piety." Drawing on this dominant theme in the Quran, I take this focus on Muslims and global justice in the book you mention here for two main reasons.

First, as a matter of principle for me, the theme of justice required putting the human person at the core of the inquiry. As a Muslim myself, I am exercising my agency, my responsibility, to contribute to defining and to realizing global justice. Of course, the fact that Christians and people affiliated with any other religion or belief do or do not identify as believers is not something that I am addressing. For me, as a Muslim, and I believe for all Muslims who wish to identify as such, being Muslim is integral to our world-view and core identity. That is why I approach global justice in this instance from my perspective of being a Muslim.

Second, and from a pragmatic strategic perspective, my focus on Muslims as people should enable all concerned to locate the issues for Muslims and their communities in their particular historical context. This focus on

[1] Abdullahi Ahmed An-Na'im, *Muslims and Global Justice* (Philadelphia: University of Pennsylvania Press, 2010).

Muslims and their communities in context is crucial for facilitating possibilities of change or reform in their beliefs and policies regarding issues of global justice. A focus on "Islam and Global Justice," for instance, is disempowering to Muslims and other concerned actors because it frames issues in terms of "this is Islam, take or leave it!" Faced with that stark choice, I know that as a Muslim I will choose Islam over whatever else is presented as an alternative. In contrast, when the issues are seen as about the attitudes and practices of Muslims as people in their respective historical context, then the way is open to exploring ideas and strategies for better understanding and transforming negative aspects of the beliefs and policies of Muslims regarding global justice.

Two further points should be noted here. The first point is that this approach is not limited to Muslims, but should equally apply to all people of every religious, cultural, or ideological persuasion, in their respective contexts. The second point is that the possibility of and responsibility for change and transformation is primarily for the people concerned, Muslims in my case, but other peoples also have an important role to play in facilitating and reinforcing what the people do in their context and for their religion or belief in their communities. For global justice in particular, the more all societies around the world collaborate in establishing and promoting fair and effective norms, institutions, and mechanisms for mediating disputes, keeping the peace, and promoting economic and social development, the more will Muslims (and others) be encouraged to reflect critically on their own values and behavior in support of such shared commitment to global justice.

JMC: The starting point of the book is a very personal starting point and also a starting point which has to do with the specific condition of Islam and how people in Islam identify with the religion.

AN: Yes, it is, because of what I said in the preceding answer about the reasons for my focus on Muslims and their human agency for change. I am therefore raising the challenge to myself to begin with, then to my communities of Muslims and non-Muslims who share the values and vision I am presenting in this book, and to humanity at large. In my view, none of the identities human beings have is exclusive or unique. Since Muslims everywhere, like other human beings near and far, share fundamental concerns with other human communities, their identities overlap, interact, and adjust to other identities.

Moreover, there is such diversity among Muslims and their communities that it is grossly misleading to assume that they are all the same even regarding what it means to be Muslim. It is particularly misleading to identify Islam as Arab or Middle Eastern, because Arabs make up only about 12 percent of the total world Muslim population. There are more Muslims, or as many Muslims, in Sub-Saharan Africa (I am from Sudan) as there are Muslims in the Middle East. India and Pakistan have the second and third largest Muslim populations in the world (estimates vary about which is second to Indonesia). So, what it means to be Muslim depends on self-understanding and contextual experience of highly diverse populations across vast regions of the world. Islam began in Arabia in the seventh century, but has spread and adapted to preexisting belief systems and cultures around the world, from Senegal, to Indonesia, to Uzbekistan, Central Asia, to West China.

JMC: *You started the conversation with the idea that in the Islamic world there is a stronger sense of identification between believers and the religion than is the case in Christianity. How would you explain this phenomenon?*

AN: I would not presume to evaluate how strongly Christians, or any other religious community, identify with their religion. I should also avoid thinking of Christianity as European or so-called Western, or, to distinguish European Christianity from African or Asian Christianity. Historical and cultural factors in each region influence perceptions and experience. For instance, to what extent has what we now call Western Christianity been shaped or influenced by European Enlightenment or modernity, and how far has that in turn influenced African and Asian Christianity? What I can and wish to affirm from my perspective as a Muslim, having grown up and lived most of my life in Sudan, is that my identity as a Muslim is central to my commitments and obligations to global justice.

JMC: *This is why it is important for you to think about global justice on the basis of this strong sense of identification with the religion?*

AN: Yes, most certainly for myself, but by the same token, I should not presume to speak for anyone else without their permission and delegation. As a matter of self-determination, I should neither speak for others nor concede their claim to speak for me without my person and delegation. From this perspective, it must be the human agent, the human subject, who defines global justice and participates in realizing it. Whatever that person is, however she or he chooses to identify, her or his understanding of global justice and how to realize it is integral to that purpose.

Integral to this approach is also exploring possibilities of interreligious and cross-cultural solidarity and alliance-building. While each human being is entitled to participate in defining and realizing global justice, none of us is capable of achieving and sustaining that conception alone. We must all therefore engage in strategic and inclusive collaboration with others in realizing shared visions and commitments to global justice. In view of emphasis on human agency and self-determination, persuasion and consensus-building are the only necessary means for collaboration in achieving and sustaining global justice.

JMC: In your work you say that one of the basic purposes and meanings of your research in general as well as in the context of global justice has been to try to reconcile the fact that you are a Muslim with your commitment to peaceful international relations and the protection of universal human rights. You seem to say that somehow this reconciliation is a bit challenging. Why is this the case and what are the main difficulties with trying to reconcile the two?

AN: Yes, the reconciliation I seek is challenging, but should be familiar to Muslims because Islam itself succeeded in spreading and laying roots across the world since the seventh century because Muslims struggled to reconcile the precepts of their religion with the norms and institutions of preexisting local religion and culture. Peaceful international relations and the protection of universal human rights happen to be the features of our present value systems as Muslims, which we must strive to reconcile with the precepts of our Islam. In doing so, we would be on the true path of Islamic traditions through fourteen centuries of intellectual, theological, and ethnical history. That history is reaffirmed by the remarkable diversity of Muslim societies and communities, from West Africa to West China to Southeast Asia. Muslims of today must adapt better to global interdependence by reexamining the relevance and authority of Sharia in their lives if they are to reclaim that glorious historical influence.

Part of the challenge is to heal the profound trauma of European colonialism and neocolonial hegemony on the consciousness of Muslims, locally, regionally, and globally. One of the challenges I am responding to in my *Muslims and Global Justice* book is why and how to strive for peaceful relations with former colonial powers and current neocolonial powers. We sometimes strike at our neighbors out of frustration for not being able to strike at a more powerful and distant nemesis. The response I propose in the first chapter of *Muslims and Global Justice* (pp. 60–64) is that Muslims must abide by their own principled commitment to peaceful international relations, and not out of nativity or weakness.

I should also add here that all human societies should feel the challenge of the requirements of achieving peaceful relations and protection of human rights because those humane objectives are counter to deep socialization into perceptions of the need for violence against other societies and domination and exploitation of other human beings. All human societies have to struggle with their challenges in this regard in their own ways because that is the only way that can achieve sustainable positive outcomes. For Muslims, one part of that challenge is what Sharia means today, and how it affects Muslims' lives socially, politically, legally, and otherwise. In other words, because there is a highly developed jurisprudential and theological tradition that Muslims strongly identify with, they have to understand what that means in the post-colonial globalized world that we live in today. That is how I define one distinctive aspect of the challenge for Muslims, namely, Sharia, peaceful relations, and human rights, without suggesting that this is the only challenge to Muslims everywhere in the exact same way. The reality of some challenge is true of every society on its own terms. My responsibility as a Muslim is to seek reconciling interpretations of Sharia with principles of peaceful international relations and protection of human rights as a critical part of the challenge facing Muslims in general.

JMC: *Based on what you are saying, it seems that there is a double challenge. On the one hand, there is the legacy of colonization, and on the other hand, there is also the need to somehow find bridges and commonalities between Sharia and the field of international law, which is essentially a Western field.*

AN: Yes, that is true. But, for international law to be truly international, it has to cease to be Western and to become global. For human rights to be truly universal, they have to be reconceived as global not only as Western, and I think that that is part of the challenge. The discourse of human rights in Western societies tends to assume that these are rights which we – we being people of the West that is – or international law define, is something that we have invented and everybody else has to conform to.

My question is: Given the historical experience that yes there was colonialism, that yes international law has been developed by European nations, what do the rest of us, everyone else in the world, have to say about this? Sharia, by the way, does have a dimension of international relations to it, but it is a premodern notion of international relations and it was not founded on the state or the so-called nation-states and intergovernmental relations as we have them under international law. So, how do we retain a sense of authenticity and authority of Sharia in relation to what international law must be today? So, there is no question of going back, there is no question of sort of unwinding the historic experience. The question is: Here we are in the twenty-first century; we are Muslims, but we are also many other things. Being Muslims does not exhaust who we are, although it is critical to our self-understanding.

II DE-COLONIZING THE MIND

JMC: I want us to discuss the legacy of colonization. Why do you think that, to this day, it is such a defining element of the Muslim identity?

AN: Not only of Muslims but also of other Africans and Asians; all former colonies are struggling with their colonial legacies, though the colonial experiences of Muslims and other colonized communities were different. French colonization of Muslim West Africa was very different from British colonization of Muslim East Africa, and the same was true of the Dutch in Indonesia and the British in the Indian sub-continent. For Muslims throughout Africa and Asia the struggle is coping with their postcolonial condition, which persisted everywhere, despite the physical departure of colonial administrators and armies. The struggle then is with what colonial powers left behind, in the hearts and minds of the colonized, which could not be expunged overnight on the eve of political independence. I think this is one of the challenges that we face, that we have not really achieved decolonization until we cease to think in postcolonial terms and engage in deliberate and systematic decolonization of our hearts and minds, beyond mere political independence.

This is the phase we can see in the so-called Arab Spring, and we see it in many other parts of the world, in Eastern Europe, when people come to exercise responsibility for their lives and stop blaming other actors and assume their obligations as the primary actors in their own lives. Part of the challenge of the colonial is that it has created a global reality integrating so-called nation-states, a European concept and institution, imposed through colonialism, though this concept and institution has not evolved from organic experience of the colonized people as it has evolved out of the experiences of European societies. The decolonization of our hearts and minds does not mean that we have to negate and erase this internationalization of European concepts and institutions. Instead, the challenge is to really take the initiative in asserting our own voice and experience in the political stability and economic development of our societies. As I see it, the primary challenge is to accept the ways colonization has shaped the global economy, politics, security, and otherwise, but that does not mean conceding our own interests and concerns for the benefit of former colonial powers.

JMC: In relation to the idea of postcolonialism as still being part of a colonized mind and of a colonized heart, it is interesting that you say that in your view the Arab Spring was part of this decolonization process. Also, based on what you are saying, it seems that the idea of having a decolonized mind is about stopping to feel and to act as a victim and really becoming a full-fledged agent, right?

AN: Precisely, that is exactly my point. In doing so, fortunately, we do not have to do it alone. I do not accept the notion of clash of civilizations, which is a simplistic and negative self-fulfilling prophecy. I like to think of various human experiences around the world as part of the same human civilization and in that regard I do not see any problem in benefiting from the experience of any society, whether they are Western or Eastern, whatever they are. I benefit from the experiences of other societies, and build on their achievements while still asserting my own sense of who I am.

Therefore, in our struggles, whether in the Arab Spring or in Eastern Europe or anywhere else, we are not alone but we have to accept the primary responsibility. That is why I was heartened by the Arab Spring because here are populations who are saying "enough is enough, we refuse to submit to authoritarian dictatorial rule and we are willing to take the risk and accept responsibility." Still the international community can help in that process but it should not attempt to take over, or seek to negate the human agency of the local actors. The fact that liberation movements in the Arab world and elsewhere tend to stagnate, sometimes regress, is only to be expected. As I see it, "regression is always part of progression"; no society anywhere at any phase in human history has achieved constant, irreversible development forward. We should therefore integrate setbacks and delays in the grand design of our social movements and political mobilization.

JMC: In relation to the importance of decolonizing heart and mind, you seem to think that a decolonized mind and heart would be an open one – one secure enough about itself to embrace others and plurality and diversity. Then the question is: If a decolonized mind – both for the former colonized and the colonizer – is an open mind and an open heart, what are the conditions to make this happen and how does one nurture these conditions?

AN: Yes, I very much like your reading. That is exactly what I mean, that it is a question of being self-confident, without being defensive or apologetic, or claiming some sort of exceptionalism. Since in every human society people tend to think of themselves and their community as exceptional, it is not really helpful to rely on such claims. Instead, we should focus on being who we are and being confident about who we are, and to think of how do we engage the other globally? It is true that when people feel under attack, they tend to entrench and become conservative and defensive, but we can counter that primordial impulse by identifying as part of a global community, under rule of law, international law, and human rights, in order to feel secure enough to come out of the shell.

Now, what are the conditions for this to happen, you are rightly asking. To me, indispensable requirements include strong and accessible global normative and institutional resources. The UN Charter, the experiences of the various specialized agencies of the United Nations, in health, development, human rights, the global presence of the United Nations, all these are tremendous resources that can be truly global and not just Western, and for that reason I take tremendous pride and confidence in the weight of the United Nations. Establishing and sustaining such resources require consistent commitment and investment of effort and material support, but the need for that will be on high intensive scale in the initial stages, and decline over time.

This is not to say that we should not expect any problems, because everything human will have problems. In any case we cannot succeed without something like the United Nations, and since we do have the United Nations now, we should work with it instead of trying to do without it. For me, it is a global community coming together in development, in technology, in the environment, in human rights; there are all these possibilities of collaboration. The normative and institutional resources we already have in these and other fields make it possible for a Muslim to come out and say, "when I engage, I am not engaging my former colonial masters, I am engaging my fellow human beings, and our collective international community at large." And that is why I think it is now possible, more than ever before, to truly decolonize because we have the resources, the international experience, and institutional presence that makes it possible.

JMC: You are suggesting from a philosophical and human point of view that unless one is at peace with oneself, it is very difficult to be at peace with others?

AN: Yes, and I think that it is dialectical. The extent to which I am at peace with myself will facilitate my being at peace with others, which will come back to help me to be more at peace with myself. If I may come back to the point about Islam, for me as a Muslim, Islam is the resource for my coming to peace within myself and through that I can engage, but it is not going to be the same understanding of Islam that prevailed a thousand years ago. For me, that is why the challenge for Muslims, myself and others, is to understand Islam in today's context, not to be dreaming about something romantic and hypothetical of what it might have been otherwise. We live in the world. Islam is part of who we are; it does not exhaust who we are, but it can be a positive resource or it can be a negative force and that is how I deal with the issues.

III SHARIA AND NATIONAL AND INTERNATIONAL LAW

JMC: *Earlier, you talked about the normative and institutional resources that we should call upon as a way to bring about a decolonized mind and a decolonized world. So, how do you see the role that Sharia can play in this perspective?*

AN: The first point I start with is to affirm and emphasize that Sharia is a human understanding of Islam, and does not exhaust Islam itself. Sharia is never the totality of Islam and it is never Islam as such. Since it is a human interpretation of Islam, it can change through being reinterpreted. Sharia is not an end in itself; in fact Islam is not an end in itself. Islam is a means to the end of liberating and fulfilling our humanity. It is the means of liberation for the human person who believes in this religion to be at peace and to exercise and to pursue justice.

As a human understanding of Islam, Sharia must be interpreted and practiced in an historical context, and not in the abstract. So the crisis in this connection is that Muslims of today tend to think of precolonial, premodern interpretations of Sharia as immutable. I think that is a mistake because, being the outcome of human interpretation, Sharia cannot be immutable, and must instead respond to the challenges that face Muslims at any time and at any place. The value of Sharia is not in its immutability but in its adaptability, in its ability to interact with and to be transformed by the experience of Muslims. Insisting on the immutability of Sharia is the source of the tension we see between that rigid, premodern conception of some aspects of Sharia and modern international law and human rights norms. There is no problem with that so long as we understand that Sharia was then responding to the needs of its communities, and Sharia today has to respond to our very different needs in a globally integrated world. So, the problem is not with Sharia; it is with Muslims' refusal to recognize the contextual understanding of Sharia.

JMC: *What you said about Islam and Sharia, that it is a tool to achieve inner peace and peace with others, tends to be common to all religion. Would not you say so? Also, for those in the West who do not know what Sharia is, what would be a good translation of the term "Sharia"?*

AN: Actually, the term Islamic law is misleading because it represents Sharia as a code of law, but I think of Sharia more as a normative system. So, Sharia is the normative system of Islam, which is different from state law; it is different from positive law. As I have explained in my book, *Islam and the Secular*

State,[2] enacting Sharia as the positive law of the state changes its nature from being the normative system of Islam to being the political will of the elites controlling the state. Enactment as positive law also deprives Muslims of the freedom to choose among competing views of Muslim scholars, and forces Muslims who live in a so-called nation-state to follow views they may not accept as valid from a religious point of view. A Sunni Muslim may be forced to live by Shi'i norms in Iran, and a Shi'i Muslim may be forced by Sunni norms in Saudi Arabia, although both may regard the doctrine followed by the state where they live as invalid.

So, for me the value of Sharia is in its community-based practice, not in the coercive enforcement by the state. The state is a political institution that is designed to serve particular functions like keeping law and order, providing essential services to citizens, and regulating external trade and other relations. State institutions and officials are neither qualified nor competent to regulate the religious life of believers in their communities. The mistaken belief of Muslims that Sharia can be enforced by the European model of a centralized, bureaucratic, nation-state, imposed by colonial administrations derives from our defensiveness and contradictory feelings about colonial administration. We seek political independence from colonial powers, but when the colonial administrators leave, we continue to follow their models of administration of justice and rule of law. Perceptions of being under siege also cause us to cling to a false hope that we can somehow resurrect Sharia out of the past to "save" us from our present political strife and economic collapse. Instead of chasing the mirage of an Islamic state to enforce Sharia, Muslims should be seeking promoting national consensus and genuine economic development.

JMC: How do you explain that conservatism and an understanding of Sharia on the basis of the past is so prevalent today and that your progressive view, your focus on adaptability rather than on immutability, is not really very often part of the contemporary culture of the Muslim world?

AN: I have two responses to propose here. First, if we consider what the vast majority of Muslims around the world *actually do*, as opposed to what a tiny minority of "Islamists" say, I believe that I am part of that vast majority more than Islamists claim to be. It is commonly accepted that the global population of Muslims is estimated at 1.6 billion, who constitute the dominant majority of the population in some forty-three countries (www.pewforum.org/2009/10/07/mapping-the-global-muslim-population/). All Muslim-majority countries are

[2] Abdullahi Ahmed An-Na'im, *Islam and the Secular State: Negotiating the Future of Shari'a* (Cambridge, MA: Harvard University Press, 2010).

members of the United Nations and contribute to all the activities of the UN and other international organizations in the promotion and protection of human rights, etc. These countries have been fully active partners in combating international terrorism, and maintaining international peace and security. In my view, there is no rational or scientific way of distinguishing Muslim majority countries from any other group of countries regarding peaceful relations and protection of human rights. They determine and implement their domestic and international relations by the same factors and practices used by all other postcolonial countries. Only four or five out of the total of forty-three Muslim majority countries may be regarded as exception to the general rule I am describing here because they may also engage in sponsoring terrorism, and that is likely to be due to legacies of European colonialism, like the Kashmir conflict between India and Pakistan, rather than being inspired by traditional notions of Jihad. Of course, much more can be said in clarifying all these claims, but I believe they are largely true. My point here is simply that what I am saying in my writings, public lectures, and briefly discussed in this conversation, is in fact consistent with what the vast majority of Muslims around the world are actually doing domestically and in their regional and international relations.

Second, it is also true, however, that the majority of Muslims I am referring to above are "the silent majority," who do not engage in public discourse to explain or defend their policies and practice regarding peaceful relations and human rights from an Islamic perspective. It seems to me that this has to do with the siege mentality and diminished self-confidence I mentioned earlier. If I am confident in my own beliefs and comfortable with who I am, I would not feel the need to prove to others my religious piety or fidelity to Islam. Conversely, diminished self-confidence may lead me to seek the approval of my peers and fear of the stigma of infidelity to immutable Sharia.

JMC: I agree with you, and this is not something specific to Islam. Very often a sense of psychological insecurity creates all kinds of problems and leads to war. So the question is: In the context of Islam, how do we engineer a sense of self-confidence, a sense of inner security in people, in political culture, so that a sense of openness prevails?

AN: When you ask: "how do we engineer?" I wonder who is the "we" in this question. To me, the "we" must be Muslims in internal discourse about Islam and Sharia from a theological perspective because intervention by non-Muslims will probably lead to rejection of whatever strategy is proposed as neocolonial. This is particularly true in the postcolonial context and how the insecurities Muslims feel about continued neocolonial hegemony.

What external actors can and should do is to enhance normative and institutional resources for the rule of law in international relations and protection of human rights. These are the resources we need to invest in. The more we show that these are global resources and inclusive of all of humanity and not just Western, the more Muslims will have confidence in these institutions and resources and will work with them. In my work I emphasize the need for absolute fidelity and compliance with international law, especially from the more powerful states. Greater damage is done to the credibility of international law when it is violated by powerful states than when it is violated by weaker states. The more developed parts of the world, the so-called Global North, comply with international law, the more Muslims will have confidence in this system and be inclined to abide by it. But when they see international law being opportunistically manipulated, ignored with impunity, or used by developed countries as a tool of power rather than an administrator of justice, then Muslims will have no interest in compliance and may even resort to open rejection. A globally inclusive "we" should try to create conditions for Muslims and other peoples to trust international institutions, invest in the rule of law, and engage in relationships in good faith, openness, and self-confidence.

IV INNER-DISCOURSE AND CROSS-CULTURAL DIALOGUE

JMC: It seems that one of the underlying arguments that you make throughout your work is that what is key is to pursue what is right without being self-righteous, to pursue what is right while being open and not self-righteous in one way or another. In your work you call for reimagining global justice in the context of revisiting and renewing the sense of dialogue not only between the West and the Muslim world, for instance, but also within each of these poles, within the West and within the Muslim world. I understand you to believe that the need of dialogue is much greater within each of the poles, within the West, within Islam, than in fact between Islam and the West.

AN: Absolutely, yes. To me the key question is about two processes: internal discourse and cross-cultural dialogue. I think that we have to engage our own tradition for a critical understanding of what it should be today as opposed to what it may have meant in the past; and through that internal transformation and internal discourse, we create common ground with other cultures. Then we can engage in cross-cultural dialogue to build consensus around the central values of justice, peace, and human rights.

It is a dialectical process. The more we transform internally, the more we have common ground to engage in dialogue, gaining confidence from that dialogue, giving back to internal transformation, and I see the two processes as reinforcing each other. Therefore, other societies, such as Western countries or states, should support the right of Muslims to engage in internal discourse and cross-cultural dialogue, without attempting to dictate the outcomes of discourse and dialogue. In other words, we support each other in engaging our respective internal transformations but not our patronizing attitudes, like the so-called civilizing mission of European colonialism. Instead of the Western attempts to require non-Western states to earn admission with Western criteria, the process should be about persuasion for consensus-building around values of global justice and human rights.

JMC: In essence, you are telling us that perhaps more important than cross-cultural dialogue is the dialogue within ourselves. Unless we see ourselves honestly, unless we come to terms with ourselves, we are not going to be able to come to terms with others. So, in a fundamental way, reconciliation with the other begins with reconciliation with oneself.

AN: Absolutely, because where else will acceptance of the other come from? One of my heroes is Mahatma Gandhi and the way that he really brought the sense of responsibility for our lives by living our values, when he said "be the change you wish to make in the word." Whether or not this is an accurate record of what Gandhi said, the meaning is clear and consistent with Gandhi's philosophy and approach to life. So, if I want to have justice I must be just myself; if I want to have peace I must be at peace with myself. I believe this to be the message of Islam and other religions, too; namely, that dialogue is the way to anchor change within the human person and then from there into the community through collaboration and trust. Otherwise we have claims of absolute values on the one side contesting claims of absolute values of the other side, with no way for mediating such conflict of values. But when you have willingness to engage in self-criticism on both sides, the possibility of dialogue becomes more realistic.

JMC: Your argument about global justice is, to a certain extent, a spiritual argument: let us work on inner peace to find external peace. But, the world in which we live is anything but spiritual. It is a world of consumption and so on. So how do we go about this spiritual dimension, which is key, I agree with you, in order to achieve global peace in a world which is less and less spiritual?

AN: The world is what we make it and what we see in it. The outcome is not a given, and therefore the question of perception and understanding is critical. It is all in the eyes of the beholder. To me as a Muslim spirituality is everywhere, and I may fail to see it but it never ceases to be there. If I may go back to something you said about religion and spirituality, I think that the object of all religions is spirituality, but all religions get hijacked by power. So institutionalized religion is a distortion of what the essence of the religion is about. Ironically, whether it is Jesus Christ or Mohammad, they were spiritual revolutionaries in their communities and led exemplary personal lives. As soon as their communities became viable entities, the politics of the day hijacked the religious values into a power game.

Therefore, the challenge for each believer is to recapture and recover the essence of the spirituality of his or her religion, in my case Islam. It is only then that Islam can have the difference it intended to have in my mind and in my life. If you think of the first generations of Muslims who transformed themselves and their primitive, violent communities of Arabia into a global community of justice, knowledge, and spirituality, that was a narrative of self-transformation before it became transformation of the social and political environment and of the world around them. That is what we need to replicate. To me the tradition is not about imitation of the past. Instead it is about reenacting the original conviction and transformative vision of the founding communities.

V ACTIVIST SCHOLARSHIP AND GLOBAL PUBLIC POLICY

JMC: In your work you seem to be interested in applying philosophy to concrete situations, as a way to improve the world. If this is the case, what kind of institutions should we have in order to ensure that spirituality, the quest for inner peace as a way to achieve peace in general that it entails, is nurtured and taken seriously?

AN: I do not believe in scholarship for scholarship's sake, or in the possibility of neutrality on public policy and social justice concerns. Failing to take a position is a position in favor of the *status quo*. I believe that scholarship is such a gift and a privilege that we must render it in the service of justice and peace and a good life for everybody. Therefore, it is always about my responsibility out of my conviction on human rights and global justice. The agency of the person to me is critical. We keep complaining about international institutions like the United Nations as being ineffective or being paralyzed by the power dynamics, as if to say: given the world as it is, what can we do about it? With such a stance nothing will change.

To me scholarship is not just an endless prognosis of the problem but it is a setting up of an agenda for action. If, for example, we have deadlock in the Security Council, which paralyzes it from being able to act in protection of international peace and security and protection of human rights, this is to be expected. This is the nature of power politics. Then, what is the responsibility of us as citizens of our states? At this point I am a citizen of the United States. I think the most effective power in changing the policy of the United States are the citizens of the United States. Therefore, if the citizens of the United States fail to keep their state on the path of justice and human rights, then foreign policy will fail. Conversely, every failure of US foreign policy, at the Security Council or elsewhere, is a failure of the citizens of the United States to exercise their democratic responsibility of holding their government accountable not only for its domestic policy but also for its foreign policy. The institutions we have are valuable. They are not perfect and we should constantly engage in them in understanding what they are and what is wrong with them, but the question is to what end? Is the object to discredit the United Nations or to make it more effective and more sustainable as a global actor? That role is for every single human person. It is not only for governments to promote global justice. That is for the people of the world, acting through their states.

JMC: The UN was based on ideals, values, and dreams, and the challenge is to make sure that the way the UN is being institutionalized does not betray these ideals, values, and dreams. This is also true for democracy. What you are telling us is that, ultimately, those responsible for the fate of institutions – whether they rise or fail – are individuals. But very often individuals are busy with their lives, with trying to survive and so on, so that they do not really invest much in the quality of their institution. Against this background, how can we address this situation?

AN: I think that we should recognize that yes, we are busy with our lives, but what should we be busy about? Take for example democracy. Sometimes we hear that we need to develop before we can be democratic. My position is that we need democracy in order to develop, but that requires a proactive, dynamic view of democracy. When I say democracy, I mean the rule of law as critical for development, for peace, for protection of the environment. I am concerned with such issues because they are about the very survival of human beings and human society. We should engage in self-governance with accountability and transparency because it is our livelihood, because it is our security, not simply fashionable ideals that are at stake.

So the problem is not that people are busy, the question is what are they busy about. Do we have a sense of ends and means? Do we have a sense of priorities? Yes, I do need to do this, that, and the other but, ultimately, I need to be well informed, engaged, and proactive. In the so-called now-established democracies – France, Britain, the United States, Germany, any of these countries – it took a long time to build democratic institutions. Fortunately, we in the developing world today do not have to take as long because we can build on their experiences.

This reflects what I said earlier on borrowing and being open, so we can build faster, but still there are no short-cuts. We have to build our institutions, we have to stand up for our rights, and we have to exercise our responsibilities in order to realize these values. It is true that, ultimately, governments vote at the United Nations for our states, but how are those governments authorized to vote for the people? I think in democratic states, the voting at the UN is more representative of the will of the people, while in despotic states it is not. This is why we need to take our freedom into our own hands, so that our government acts for us and when it acts at the United Nations it acts in our interests and not in the interests of ruling elites who manipulate the process.

JMC: Yes, but eventually the ultimate product of a more democratic world, for instance in the Muslim world, would not mean that the regimes would look like Western democracies. I guess it would be a hybrid in cultural and political terms.

AN: Precisely. I think that the questions of constitutionalism, democracy, human rights, all of these values and institutions have to be rooted in local culture. You cannot transplant democracy or the rule of law, because both must be homegrown. But, in being homegrown, these norms and institutions can benefit from the experience of other societies. In my book *African Constitutionalism and the Role of Islam*[3] my argument is that constitutionalism for African societies must be African. What that means is not that it has nothing to do with constitutionalism anywhere else in the world, but that it is legitimized, justified, and motivating for the peoples of Africa when they see it as their own and not something that is imposed on them from the outside.

[3] Abdullahi Ahmed An-Na'im, *African Constitutionalism and the Role of Islam* (Philadelphia: University of Pennsylvania Press, 2006).

VI SHARIA AND DEMOCRATIC PRINCIPLES

JMC: In the context of this democratization and development that you call for, what kind of a resource is Sharia? In specific ways, how can it be helpful?

AN: I think that the notions of accountability and transparency which are critical to democratization can clearly be rooted in Sharia. The fact that Muslims can never abdicate responsibility, that we are always responsible for our actions, that God knows all that we do and all that we fail to do, and will always hold us accountable, these beliefs and values can be cited to ground democratic principles in Islamic cultures. The ideals of fairness, of earning an honest living, of moderation in lifestyle, not to be consumption oriented, the requirements of simplicity of lifestyle, of sharing wealth and resources, all of these are Sharia values that are supportive of democratization and development among Muslims today.

The point I am emphasizing here is that there are in fact tremendous resources for accountability, responsibility, transparency, and honesty within the corpus of Sharia, and have been since the seventh century. So, for example, corruption – when officials are accepting bribes and giving favors or kickbacks –, that is a fundamental breach of Sharia and yet those aspects of Sharia are never highlighted by ruling elites because that is against their selfish interests. They talk about punishments, they talk about limiting the rights of women, in order to distract from their own failures to comply with Sharia. The ruling elites of Muslim-majority countries are therefore facing the following challenge: Are they conforming with Sharia when they oppress their citizens, kill peaceful demonstrators, or engage in corruption? All of this is clearly against Sharia, so why is Sharia invoked when it is convenient and disregarded when it is not?

JMC: What is their answer?

AN: The question has not been put to ruling elites effectively. What the leaders do is to distract their populations from the real issues. Let me put forward a very controversial point. I think that in the Middle East region Israel is not the problem. The problem is the corruption, the incompetence, the lack of responsibility and democracy of Arab rulers throughout the region. Israel has become a convenient excuse and distraction. So for decades, since Abdel Nasir in 1950s' Egypt, Baath regimes in Iraq and Syria, monarchies of Saudi Arabia and the Gulf States, and other rulers throughout the region keep invoking the Israel–Palestine conflict as a distraction from their failure to deliver on their promise of independence and development and self-determination. Other distractions include the conflict over Kashmir for Pakistan, and the Western Sahara for Morocco, and the conflict with South Sudan for Sudanese regimes.

The answer, as I see it, is for the peoples of the region to refuse to be distracted, and challenge the deceit and hypocrisy of their ruling elites, to turn the Palestinian cause as a challenge for development and democratization, instead of a convenient distraction and a way to escape responsibility by blaming others. It is first and foremost the peoples of the region who have to take matters into their hands because their ruling elites will never relinquish power voluntarily or permit genuine democratization and development. To be clear on this point, I am not contesting the seriousness of the struggle of Palestinians for justice and self-determination, but I am condemning Arab regimes for using Israel as a distraction from their own failures and corruption.

JMC: In this context, the importance you give to the notion of responsibility is, I think, very much connected to the equally important notion, for you, of shared vulnerability. The way you envision responsibility as connected with shared vulnerability is a way for you to move people away from victim identity and victim mentality, is this correct?

AN: Yes, the idea of shared vulnerability is that as human beings we are vulnerable to the same kinds of dangers and risks of disease, poverty, and violence. These are shared vulnerabilities which should give us a common ground to act toward securing ourselves as a global humanity against these vulnerabilities. One of these vulnerabilities could be psychological, a vulnerability toward abdication of responsibility. If you think of public health, for example, of contagious disease, there are many things that we can do for ourselves without calling on the international community to do this, that, or the other. We know that there are many things which are harmful to health and yet we continue to do them, which is what I call a psychological vulnerability toward escaping responsibility. The response should be to confront ourselves with our responsibility by doing what we ourselves can do before asking others to do it for us.

JMC: Your understanding of the connection between responsibility and vulnerability is interesting. In English there is a difference between being tough and being strong. I myself believe that strength is based on recognizing and embracing vulnerabilities and then growing from them and allowing a sense of responsibility to flourish; while being tough is denying vulnerabilities, which is a false sense of strength, and in fact, very often, rejecting a sense of responsibility. It is telling that at the very core of responsibility and empowerment is the recognition, even the embracing of vulnerabilities not only as an individual but also as humanity.

AN: Exactly. I see that as being local as well as global. There is a phrase I use in *Muslims and Global Justice* about acting locally and thinking globally, but also thinking globally and acting locally. It works both ways. We have to have a global view of things while acting locally, and we also have to have a local understanding and act globally. I see vulnerability as an immediate situation that I can do something about, whether through local action or global action in coordination and solidarity with others. In agreement with your sense of vulnerability as something between tough and strong, I see violence as weakness and peaceful resistance as strength.

JMC: Absolutely. I often say that in every terrorist there is a terrorized person, so the key is to move beyond being terrorized so that one does not feel the need to exercise terror and violence.

AN: If the violent person thinks that his violence demonstrates strength, it is the obligation of the rest of us to confront with evidence to the contrary, to help see how violence is in fact weakness. That is why the question of responsibility is so critical. It is our responsibility to prevent violent actors from achieving their objectives, or attracting favorable attention of young people or the media. It is also our responsibility to show that being just and humane takes more courage than being violent and aggressive. It takes more courage and more strength to be peaceful than to be violent. If on the scale of human values one wants to be strong, one should be peaceful and just, not violent and oppressive.

I think these are some of the challenges that we have to confront each other with within our own communities. For me as a Muslim from Sudan, the fact that we in Northern Sudan have not confronted our own racism, our own violence, our own oppression of other people of the same country are the reasons why we are ending up with a divided country. I take full responsibility as a Muslim from Northern Sudan for my failure in making unity attractive for people of the South. It is not that they made the mistake of choosing secession as their road to self-determination; it is my mistake of failing to make unity with justice and equal citizenship realistic enough for them to want to remain in a united Sudan. If they had no reason to break away they would not have elected to break away. So that is the way I put it: What is my responsibility, what is my failure, and what can I do to fulfill my obligation and recover from my failure? It is never too late to recover, though not in different ways. Both North and South Sudan are facing the same challenges of peaceful relations, development, democratization, and protection of human rights, and both countries must respond to those challenges in their own context.

JMC: So what you are saying is that political bullies are bullies out of fear. This leads to the next question: How do we find ways to manage fear so that political bullies cease to be structured by fear and to project violence out of fear?

AN: I would not make it easy for them by saying that "we understand you are a bully because you are afraid, and you are not really responsible." I may understand that to be true, but I would not allow them to escape their share of responsibility. I must put an end to aggression and violations of human rights, and I must stand firm in rejecting violence and injustice. My understanding of the psychology of violence is that it is out of weakness and fear, that violence can be unleashed but my action will be to resist violence immediately. So anything I can do to help the violent person to come to terms with his own fear is in the manner of my response, but not at the expense of acting decisively. For me, human rights are to be respected here and now. Understanding what are the root causes of their violation is part of the process of protecting those rights, but it is not a reason for postponing their immediate realization.

JMC: We should not excuse the behavior of political bullies. While understanding them we should also make it a point to stop them?

AN: Yes, and part of stopping them is understanding where they are coming from, as we take decisive action to stop and prevent them from bullying others. The relevance of understanding is a factor in my strategies of resistance, but I do not concede violence or postpone resisting it out of understanding of the fear of the violent person. It is simply an understanding of the strategy of effective and sustainable response.

JMC: Finally, you recently published What Is an American Muslim? Embracing Faith and Citizenship.[4] *How do the key ideas in the book help us to think better in the context of the recent debates and controversies in the United States over immigration policies and terrorism?*

AN: In this book I call on my fellow American Muslims to join all citizens of the United States in contributing to defining our national identity, to draw on its benefits and participate in the obligations of our equally shared citizenship of the country. Instead of passively waiting to be assimilated in the dominant

4 Abdullahi Ahmed An-Na'im, *What Is an American Muslim? Embracing Faith and Citizenship* (New York: Oxford University Press, 2014).

preexisting so-called national identity, or expecting others to save us from the loss of our religious and other identities, American Muslims should proactively engage in the formation and transformation of the national identity of the country. Since key aspects of what is commonly called the national identity of the country have significantly changed and continue to change and evolve, American Muslims have the right and obligation to contribute to these processes. As I illustrate in chapter 2 of this book, by briefly discussing the experiences of Catholic, Jewish, and Mormon communities, American Muslims are not the first or only religious community to face prejudice and exclusion in the United States. In the rest of the book I also highlight ways in which American Muslims can draw upon the experiences of those and other communities in affirming equal citizenship without surrendering their distinctive identities. I am also calling on my fellow American Muslims not to think of themselves as a "minority" in the country because that is not true even if we define ourselves in exclusively religious terms, in view of the significant diversity of religious belief and practice among American Muslims. In contrast, it is both factually true and strategically useful for American Muslims to appreciate and cultivate the many ways in which we share with the rest of the population of the United States our political, cultural, educational, employment, and other formations of identity. Yet, if we think of ourselves as a minority, we will be treated by others as if that is true. Even if we are perceived and treated by others as a minority, we can still exercise our human agency to break away from such negative characterization and stereotyping.

In my view, the dialectic ideas and strategies for negotiating the relationship between religious (racial, ethnic, cultural, etc.) identity and citizenship I applied to the case of American Muslims in this book can be useful for other American communities, and be adapted to other similar situations around the world. The key factor in such deliberations and responses to marginalization and exclusion is the assertion of the agency of the human subject to participate in the process of self-liberation. Just to be clear on this point, there is no role for violence in the proposed strategies, simply because it tends to serve the interests of dominant privileged elites at the expense of marginalized communities. At the same time, the proposed strategies should empower marginalized communities to advance their peaceful demands for social justice and individual freedom.

Finally, it may be relevant to note here that I am currently writing a book manuscript under the working title: "Decolonizing Human Rights: From State-Centric Legality to People-Centered Practice." The core thesis of this manuscript is that the human rights paradigm has been colonialized by liberal values and institutions, to the exclusion of serious consideration of the cultural values and institutions of the rest of humanity, thereby repudiating the universality of human rights. As a consequence of this liberal perspective, sovereign states are supposed to be the sole bearers of human rights obligations and exclusive protectors of those rights within their own territories. Paradoxically, this means that national courts and institutions can only protect the civil rights of citizens and resident aliens, and not the rights of human beings as such. To break out of this deadlock, I am calling for local cultural transformation to uphold human rights values through political mobilization. In other words, there is a positive role for the state to play, but that role should be founded on local cultural values and monitored through grassroots political mobilization.

More specifically, the proposed people-centered practice does not delay or prevent the protection of human rights by states simply because there is no protection of human rights (as the rights of the human as such) by any state anywhere in the world. Whatever rights are protected by any state are the rights of citizens and lawful residents, not the rights of the human being regardless of such conditions of membership or qualification. In other words, the book manuscript I am writing proposes a possibility of protection of the rights of the human being as such, instead of waiting in vain for protection of the rights of the human by the state. Whatever the perceived limitations of the rights of the human as such in local practice, they are to be redressed through cultural transformation and political mobilization, instead of expectations of the illusionary promise of legal remedies.

JMC: As a way to end our conversation, a last question: What is your advice to young scholars starting to work in the field of justice?

AN: My primary suggestion to the young generation of Muslims everywhere is to assume immediate responsibility for change in their own communities, while benefiting from the incremental nature of social evolution. On the first count, I would recall the point I made earlier about human agency and responsibility. Nothing happens without the agency of human beings, and whatever is negative about what is happening, it is people who can change it for the better. On the second count, young people should not despair because of the apparent magnitude of the problems facing their societies and immediate communities. Positive change begins with where we are, what we already do, by planning and acting to enhance what is good and redress what is negative. In the final analysis, only we can honor or shame ourselves by our action or failure to act, regardless of what others think of us.

PART II

FROM THINKING GLOBALLY TO GLOBAL ETHICS

5

Extent and Limits of Global Justice

David Miller

I ON FRAMING GLOBAL JUSTICE

Jean-Marc Coicaud (JMC): *Let us begin our conversation with addressing the question, why is it important to think about global justice today?*

David Miller (DM): We cannot avoid thinking about global justice once we begin to look at the world in two connected ways. We have to recognize that states are interdependent, and acknowledge the impact that rich states in particular have on the life prospects of people living in poor societies. And then we have to see that these relationships are open to change. Rich states could begin behaving differently, or international institutions could be reformed to the benefit of the global poor. Once we recognize these things, then unavoidably we are bound to ask what can justify the global inequalities that we see around us. What makes them legitimate? Once we get to that point, we start thinking and talking about global justice.

JMC: You write in one of your books, National Responsibility and Global Justice,[1] *that it is a very new field and a very new area of inquiry, which started twenty or thirty years ago more or less?*

DM: Yes, the concept itself only emerged over that time period. Now it is widely used. Of course, people for many years before that were talking about issues of development ethics, and about international law and the limits it placed on state sovereignty, but the idea of global justice itself is new and reflects a different way of thinking about the world order on the part both of the global rich and of the global poor.

[1] David Miller, *National Responsibility and Global Justice* (Oxford: Oxford University Press, 2012).

JMC: As a matter of clarification, what is your definition of justice and how do you define global justice compared to international justice and national justice? Clearly there are similarities but probably also significant differences.

DM: Yes, well it is hard to give a simple definition of justice that captures all of its dimensions. Obviously, it has to do with what people can claim from each other as a matter of right and we can ask what that means in different contexts. One way of addressing the question is to remind ourselves that the idea of social justice itself only appeared a little over a century ago. Social justice is about justice between citizens – citizens of the same state – about what they owe to each other, and about how their institutions should be framed so that they can deliver the various entitlements that each member has qua citizen. Later on, around the middle years of the twentieth century, more attention was given to the idea of international justice, which has mainly to do with regulating relations between states. So it applies to issues that arise in international law and more generally what states can and cannot do to each other – respecting one another's sovereignty, keeping treaties, refraining from aggressive war, and so forth.

The shift up to the level of global justice occurs when we begin to ask the question: What do human beings merely as such, and regardless of any special relationships between them, owe to each other as a matter of justice? Here we are thinking about human beings simply as individuals and asking what claims they can make on each other, and how we can respond to those claims, individually or collectively. So that is a fresh perspective that goes beyond the first two and potentially gives rise to new and quite demanding obligations of justice.

II MORAL AND POLITICAL, AND STRONG AND WEAK COSMOPOLITANISM

JMC: In your work you argue that most philosophers writing on global justice today describe themselves as cosmopolitan, and it makes sense as a strategy to think about oneself as a cosmopolitan if you are going to think about global justice; but it does not seem to be the case for you.

DM: Well, I find the cosmopolitan label confusing and rather vague. I am not sure that it signals very much other than a general concern for global questions. So I would prefer not to be defined either as a cosmopolitan or as an anti-cosmopolitan – though I know that some people would want to describe my position as anti-cosmopolitan. I think that the real issues arise as you begin to define these terms more carefully and then some differences do begin to emerge, but the labels themselves I do not think are so important. There is a growing consensus about this by the way – that it is unilluminating to categorize people writing on global justice as either cosmopolitan or anti-cosmopolitan.

JMC: As a way to bring clarity into this confused and confusing notion, you distinguish between what you call strong and weak cosmopolitanism and then moral and political cosmopolitanism. Can you tell us a bit more about these distinctions?

DM: Yes, let us take those distinctions in reverse order, starting with "moral" and "political." That is a relatively straightforward distinction to draw. A moral cosmopolitan holds a certain view about our ethical relations to other human beings and, connected to that, about the nature and extent of our obligations to them just by virtue of their humanity – so it is an ethical perspective. Political cosmopolitans are those who think that we need to have political institutions at the global level, for reasons of legitimacy and justice. They believe that a world made up of independent states is no longer justifiable. The most radical version of political cosmopolitanism argues in favor of the creation of a single World State. But in practice political cosmopolitans tend to draw back from that extreme, recognizing the dangers it would pose, and argue for something less. They want to have international institutions of various kinds exercising significant but limited authority over states – a beefed up version of the United Nations, for example.

Now, what about the distinction between weak and strong cosmopolitanism? This is a distinction internal to the moral cosmopolitan perspective and it is a bit harder to pin down, but it goes something like this. The weak view is that all human beings have to be considered as objects of ethical concern. In other words, when we make decisions, whether as individuals or collectively via our states, we must always consider the potential impact of what we are doing on every human being. We cannot just leave a whole section of humanity out and say that they do not matter morally speaking. Further, we have to give them equal consideration in the absence of good reasons for discriminating. We cannot say that a white-skinned person should count for more than a black-skinned person or a Christian more than a Jew. That is the weak cosmopolitan view – it is a view about how we must think about our fellow human beings when we are deciding how to act. The strong view goes beyond this: It says that we actually owe all human beings equal treatment, regardless of any special relationships we have with them. In other words, it says that there can never be good reasons for favoring those who are close to us, or related to us in some other way. In particular, there are no fundamental reasons for recognizing special responsibilities or obligations to our fellow nationals – I say "no fundamental reasons" because strong cosmopolitans will often want to argue that there can sometimes be derivative reasons for attending to the claims of compatriots first. The best way to discharge a universal duty might be to begin with those close at hand. I do not want to caricature their position. But fundamentally, strong cosmopolitans believe that national boundaries, or any other boundaries for that matter, are morally irrelevant. There are just human beings who can make claims on us and we must respond to them all in the same way.

JMC: Keeping in mind these distinctions, what is the position that you embrace? Your position is on the weak cosmopolitan side, right?

DM: Yes, exactly. I support weak cosmopolitanism and reject the strong version.

JMC: And so what precisely would be the normative principles at the core of your weak notion of cosmopolitanism?

DM: Well, the central idea is one of showing moral concern for all human beings, and in my view one important way of capturing that idea is in terms of human rights. It should be of concern to us whenever we see that there are people whose human rights are not adequately protected. But this does not mean that, as citizens of a particular state, we have undifferentiated responsibilities to protect the human rights of everybody. Our first responsibility is to act to ensure that the human rights of those around us are secure. Nonetheless human rights failures in other societies should be of concern for us, and we are likely to have secondary responsibilities to protect them, whether this means providing food aid, granting asylum to victims of persecution, or in the extreme case intervening physically to prevent mass violations being perpetrated. We cannot just be indifferent, as weak cosmopolitans, but nor on the other hand do we have to abandon our special responsibilities to those close to us.

JMC: In this context, much of your thinking on global justice is about examining the tensions between the national demands of justice and the global demands of justice, and drawing the line. One of the key points that you mention in your work is that clearly we have special obligations to our fellow citizens. So how do you draw the line between national and global demands? And why is it that we owe something special to our fellow citizens? What is the normative foundation for your claim in terms of special duties toward fellow citizens?

DM: There is a qualitative difference between what we owe as a matter of justice to our fellow citizens and what we owe to human beings worldwide. As applied to fellow citizens, justice very often takes a comparative form, and in particular an egalitarian form. It matters whether one co-national is treated better or worse than another – gets fewer rights or resources, for example. We could think of equal voting rights, or equal access to the legal system, or equality of opportunity in education and in the labor market. These comparative aspects of social justice are made very evident in the writings of philosophers such as John Rawls, for example. But there is nothing equivalent to this when we think about our global duties of justice. As I suggested a moment ago, the most important of these concerns the global minimum that everyone is entitled to, which is best spelt out in terms of human rights. There may be reasons to worry about global inequalities – not least the impact these can have on the human rights of the global poor – but they are not problematic simply as inequalities in the way that domestic inequalities often are. I do not believe that principles like equality of opportunity apply at global level, for example.

Now, you asked what the basis for this contrast between social and global justice was and that is an interesting question, not an easy one to answer. We need to look for special features of the relationships that hold between citizens but not between all humans worldwide. Some, like Rawls, argue that the key feature is that citizens cooperate together to create large gains that they could not achieve by acting alone. Others, like Thomas Nagel, claim that obligations of social justice arise because citizens are together responsible for the coercion they exercise on one another via the state and its machinery of law. I believe that both of these explanations provide part of the answer, but we need to add a third element: The sharing of a national identity which motivates citizens to feel special concern for one another and be willing to provide one another with various forms of assistance even when those being aided are unlikely to be able to reciprocate. If you juxtapose these three elements, as happens to a large extent when nation-states are formed, then you have an explanation for why we have special obligations of justice to compatriots that we do not owe to people globally.

JMC: In your view it does not have to do with issues of scarcity of resources, allocation of resources, or taxation? The key is sharing an identity and engaging in reciprocal practices?

DM: Yes, of course the resource question is important when it comes to implementing ideas of justice, but I think that at the foundational level scarcity of resources is not the key. We could feasibly engage in a lot more global redistribution if we thought that was what justice demanded – and for strong cosmopolitans, of course, that is what justice requires – but the underlying issue is really one of working out what we owe to people toward whom we stand in qualitatively different relationships.

JMC: *What happens to these two notions is at the core of your thinking about special duties being owed to our fellow citizens, i.e. sharing an identity and engaging in reciprocal practices, as the world is becoming more and more globalized? With globalization the sense of identity and engagement in reciprocal practices is evolving. It is widening and deepening at the global level. Does that mean that somehow your position on these issues will have to change?*

DM: Yes, I am perfectly willing to accept that. My general view about justice is that it evolves in line with our practices and our relationships. So when these things change, then we begin to think about new forms of justice, and maybe abandon some old ones. If it were the case that the world as a whole began to function in the same way as the nation-state now does – which would be a massive change from where we are now – then of course everything I have said would apply at the global level. What is much more complicated are the various halfway houses we might pass through on the way to that destination. Take the case of the European Union. Where it has begun to take on some of the features of a nation-state – but not all – we have to think about what demands of justice emerge in that context. Should we begin talking about pan-European social justice, for instance? If so, what should the content of that idea be?

III DUTIES OF GLOBAL JUSTICE

JMC: *Do you feel that the trends toward globalization are somehow changing the landscape in the context of which we think about what is owed to the national and what is owed to the global? Do you think we are witnessing a trend that will force us to somehow revisit this idea of special duty to the national and duties to the global?*

DM: I do not believe that the forms of globalization that exist at the moment should force us to have that rethink. In a sense, the fact that we talk about global justice at all involves a significant rethink, which was my opening point. Economic globalization, the fact that economies are becoming more interdependent, is one of the main factors along with the globalization of the mass media that have inspired us to think about global justice in the first place. Some people believe that national identities are fast disappearing, to be replaced by global ones, but I am much less convinced that that is happening, partly because of the big cultural cleavages that still exist in the world today. These create very strong barriers against the emergence of a single global identity.

JMC: So, clearly you think that this distinction will continue to remain relevant and significant. Against this background, in terms of the respective duties at the national and the global level, in your view, what are the specific things that we owe to our fellow citizens in this kind of a globalized and yet still nationally anchored world?

DM: As I suggested, what we owe our fellow citizens is best spelt out in terms of duties of social justice. What this requires is fairly familiar: equality before the law, equality of opportunity, providing people with a generous minimum of education and health care, and so on. I think the more difficult and in some ways more interesting issue now is how to conceptualize global justice. We have already talked a bit about the idea of protecting human rights for everyone. That is the most urgent demand but it does not exhaust the idea of global justice and I would want to add two other ideas to that.

One is what I would call fair terms of interaction. In other words, when societies interact, when states interact, much more is required of them than simply that they should adhere to current international law. So, for example, there arise questions about the fairness of trade, the rules that govern trade and investment, and also of course questions about resource use, resource depletion, and last but by no means least global warming. In all of these areas what we need are principles to allocate fairly the costs and benefits of interaction. In each case in which societies are interacting, they are producing benefits or else they are avoiding creating global harms of various sorts, as in the case of steps to prevent global warming, and then there is a question of how these costs and benefits should be shared between them: this is what I am calling the problem of establishing fair terms of interaction.

The second principle I would add to the theory of global justice concerns national self-determination. I take it is as given that this is something of considerable value to those who already enjoy it. We want to be in a position where we can decide many things for ourselves and our national societies, but of course some of these decisions may have effects that work to the detriment of people outside. So in terms of equity it is important that people elsewhere have real and not merely formal opportunities to do the same; in other words, the right of self-determination is one that every society should enjoy. It then becomes a matter of justice that both the international order we create and the way that individual states behave should not undermine the possibility of self-determination elsewhere – for example, by creating a neocolonial relationship of dependence between one state and another. This will also have consequences for how access to material resources is governed, since a nation that wants to be self-determining needs to keep control of the essential resources that fuel its economy. So that would be my third demand of global justice.

JMC: These three principles – fair terms of interaction, self-determination, and access to material resources – would be at the core of what you envision in terms of what we owe to strangers at the global level. Let us examine a bit their implications for key aspects of global justice. For example, there is the protection of human rights. Here, of course, the question is how far should we go about this? Is it enough to engineer norms at the global level? How do we make sure that we implement and enforce them? How do we go about this, for instance, in the context of humanitarian interventions? In the 1990s it was in the name of human rights that the West favored interventions in the Balkans and so on. So how far should we go in protecting human rights at the global level? Is it enough to simply generate norms or should we go beyond this?

DM: Well, it has to involve more than that. There are some situations, extreme situations, in which people's human rights are directly threatened, such as natural disasters, which are likely to call for an equally direct response from foreign states as well as NGOs. But there are also some situations for which humanitarian intervention is the only possible response. I start from the position that the protection of human rights is in the first place the business of the state of which any person is a citizen. It is clear, however, that in the world today for various reasons some states are going to fall down on the job, and in that case external intervention, which may include humanitarian intervention, is going to be called for. We are then confronted with a problem, which is to decide how extensive the ensuing responsibility is. And that is a very difficult question to answer. People are easily misled into thinking that protecting the human rights of outsiders is just a matter of everybody making a small sacrifice, each paying a small amount into a large pot, which is then used for that purpose. But in real cases of forcible intervention, what you actually find, very often, is the opposite: a small number of people making quite a large sacrifice to carry out the human rights mission. These will be soldiers, medics, aid workers, and so on, who may be exposed to high levels of personal risk. We need to ask what can justify us asking them to make this sacrifice. So, I think there is a big question about how to understand the responsibilities that correspond to human rights.

JMC: How do you dovetail in a satisfactory fashion the active protection of human rights in the context of humanitarian intervention and the principle of national self-determination? How do you assess that a given situation is bad enough to justify intervention in a way that it does not go against your principle of national self-determination?

DM: Of course, it will vary. In natural disaster cases I think that we can assume that the state that is being helped will be happy to receive the help so there's no real issue of self-determination there. In some of the other cases, we may be facing a situation in which there is no real opportunity for collective self-determination. If political authority breaks down, or a society falls into civil war or a conflict of that kind then what national self-determination means, concretely, becomes very unclear. We may be unable to say who belongs to the nation that could exercise self-determination and who does not – think of the situation in Syria as an example of that. In these cases, part of what you may be doing in intervening is actually recreating a situation in which self-determination becomes possible again. The dilemma for the intervening powers is that they have to decide, from the outside, what the relevant units are going to be. Should the integrity of the previous state be upheld, or should borders be redrawn so as to allow new peoples, such as the Kurds, to become self-determining? It should be obvious that this is not a question that can be answered by democratic means – we cannot know in advance who the relevant "people" includes.

The case is different if an intervention is undertaken to protect human rights against the express wishes of a national government. That is philosophically a more difficult case, because we would have to weigh the competing values at stake: the human rights of the oppressed group against the majority's right of self-determination – assuming that the government does indeed reflect the wishes of most of its subjects.

JMC: Concerning the principle of fair terms of interaction, in particular when it comes to trade, what would make the situation better? For instance, how would you proceed in order to create institutions matching as much as possible this principle?

DM: I think that a good theory of fair trade is something we badly need but unfortunately it is going to be a complicated theory because it has to include at least the three following components. First of all, there must be some kind of formal procedural equality in the sense that societies are treated equally when the rules of trade are being negotiated; that is already acknowledged formally at least when these negotiations occur under the auspices of the WTO. But this formal requirement by itself is not enough. We need to add two more substantive conditions for trade to be fair. To begin with, when societies are in general interacting with one another for their mutual benefit, which must surely include economic trade, there should be a fair distribution of the surplus that is generated, and I would argue that should mean an equal distribution. In other words, both parties should gain equally relative to the baseline when they are not interacting, which in this case means not trading with each other. How these gains are to be measured is rather complicated, but it would be hard not to agree that current trade patterns fall badly afoul of that principle: Trade is very one sided, with a large part of the benefit accruing to rich countries and very little to poor countries, so we can say there is a substantive fairness issue to be addressed.

Then there is another requirement, which is that trade should be conducted in a way that is respectful of human rights. What this means more concretely is that trade practices should not be established that involve some of the participants having to sacrifice basic rights in order to engage in them. This would include such things as trading in the products of sweatshop labor, and trading commodities at prices that leave the primary producers of those commodities below the subsistence threshold. Trade on those terms might still be mutually advantageous compared to the no-trade baseline, but it would not be fair. So I believe that the human rights agenda should be built into the trade agenda as well, and this would count as a third way in which we could make the terms of interaction between societies fair.

JMC: You feel that at the moment we are very far away from such a situation?

DM: Yes, I think that we are. I am not an expert on this (it is not my main field) but reading the literature it seems all too clear that, for reasons that will be familiar, when trade rules are set they are set very much in the interests of richer societies.

JMC: Assuming that you have made the case for better-terms trade, how do you go about convincing people who are in charge of policy-making or who are in political leadership positions to improve the situation?

DM: Part of the argument has to be ethical. Given that the notion of human rights has gained widespread legitimacy, an argument about trade that links it to human rights should not be a hard argument to make. Alongside that it needs pointing out that it is in the longer-term interests of even the rich countries not to have a world in which there are millions of desperate people, because a world like that is going to be unstable, it will create huge pressures for migration, and it will also create the circumstances under which terrorism flourishes. So the two argument for improving trade practices go hand in hand: ethical argument that appeals to equality and human rights, and the prudential argument about why a fairer world is beneficial even to people living in rich countries.

JMC: I agree with you that the ethical argument has to be completed by a prudential argument. But how do you explain then that decision-makers seem not to want to listen and not to want to take into account these arguments?

DM: Well, I think there is a lot of persuading to do. We have to be willing to make these arguments to national electorates. People have to understand that they are subject to global duties and that they may have to make small changes in their daily lives (such as paying a fair price for imported clothes) in order to fulfill them. It should not be a difficult argument to make. People readily understand that a person in a Third World country growing cocoa or coffee or making textiles ought to earn sufficient wages to live a decent life. We often take a very negative view of politicians, but since they respond to what they think are the demands of their constituents, these ordinary citizens are the people we need to persuade that there are global duties that they must respect.

JMC: But in times of crisis, for instance in time of economic crisis as is the case today in the US and in Europe, it becomes even more difficult for this argument to be heard. In times of crisis people are focusing on their own fate and they are not necessarily eager to be open to ethical arguments beyond their own fate.

DM: In these circumstances, one good rhetorical strategy is to try to link together people's sense of national pride with issues of global justice. So, if a politician can argue that actually it is an honorable thing to do for a nation to commit to a certain level of foreign aid, or to commit to lobbying for fair trade practices, it can become a matter of national pride that we should do this. Even now politicians do sometimes talk in this way, which is heartening to see. The same kind of argument can be made for policies to reduce greenhouse gas emissions: We can take pride in being in the forefront of efforts to combat global warming.

JMC: So you feel that not all hope is lost.

DM: I am optimistic about this. I think that once people understand the issues they will respond positively. The fair trade movement has been quite effective in getting people to look more closely at what they are buying. And you may not have to convince everyone. Once the demand for fairly traded products reaches a certain level, it may be in the interests of shops and supermarkets just to announce that all of their stock is fair trade certified.

JMC: Concerning the principle of national self-determination, as one of the guidelines for global justice in a world that is not a cosmopolitan world, how do you decide when it is time for a country to split up or not?

DM: This is difficult. Of course, there will be simple cases such as some of those that occurred when colonialism came to an end, where you clearly have a national society that is ready for self-determination, though even at that time there were harder cases too – think of the still-unresolved question as to whether it is was justifiable to partition India, for instance. The more difficult cases are typically those in which state borders and national borders do not coincide perfectly, and so there are two political communities living side-by-side but with partially overlapping claims to territory, so that they cannot be cleanly disentangled. Under these circumstances one cannot assume that the classic nation-state solution is going to be the best for either side. The way forward is likely to involve a more complicated arrangement with partial self-determination for different regions, perhaps involving a federal constitution. The general point is that there are different ways of achieving self-determination for national communities. They may each hanker after having their own state, but sometimes geographical factors mean that that is just not possible without denying another community's self-determination claims.

IV EGALITARIANISM

JMC: The principles at the core of your vision of global justice do not amount to egalitarianism. In fact, in your work you argue that what you call global egalitarianism is not the answer for global justice. So what is your argument about egalitarianism and the fact that it is not the answer?

DM: I have two main arguments about this. One argument asks the question "equality of what?" If we are going to make people equal, in what respects is it going to be done? My claim is that in a culturally plural world it will be difficult to find a single currency that it would make sense to use as a currency of global policy. So we often use crude monetary criteria like per capita GDP as a way to measure the extent of global inequality, but income measures can hardly capture everything of significance in people's lives. If you think of all the components that go into making someone's life better or worse, you would need to include such things as public services, health, education, amenities, cultural resources, and so on. My central point is that people living in different places will attach different values to each of these things. We cannot just amalgamate them all together in a single index. In one place, for example, religious opportunities, opportunities to engage in religious practices, may be very important, in another place it may be sport or it may be music and one cannot presume that one should count for more than another in compiling an overall index of well-being or success in life. So then we confront a real question about how to conceptualize equality at the global level, if we are going to aim for it, we first of all need to know what it would mean to achieve it.

But the other argument is different and it takes us back to the significance of national self-determination. What I claim here is that people want, and have a right, to make collective choices about how their society is going to develop. In broad terms it is then fair that they should bear responsibility for the consequences of the choices that they make. If they decide, for example, to opt for economic growth and they succeed in achieving high economic growth rates, it is quite reasonable that they should become richer over time. If on the other hand they decide that economic wealth is not so important, but that they want to concentrate on preserving a very rich cultural heritage or to protect features of their natural environment, which means choosing a slower rate of growth, then that choice too must be respected. An obvious corollary, however, is that even if societies were to begin from a position of equality on one particular dimension (such as per capita GDP), the effect of self-determination will be to break that equality as time passes. To preserve it, you would need to nullify the effects (on that dimension) of the collective choices different nations have made.

V ON JUSTICE AND AGENCY

JMC: How do you argue about taking and exercising responsibility for who you are and what you do, and failing to succeed in a world that, as you said earlier, is not a fair world? Take for example the case of a committed political leader in a developing country, really eager to improve the overall fate of the country but encountering unfair terms of trade.

DM: I believe it is rarely the case, though it may happen occasionally, that a country is so beset by intractable problems that there is no scope for the exercise of political responsibility at all. Normally, the fate of any particular country will be determined by a mixture of collective responsibility and its circumstances, including the position from which it starts in any time period, which as you rightly say may be unfair. So it is not my claim that whatever happens in today's world is fine because it is all a matter of individual and collective responsibility. My argument is only that where it is clear that responsibility does apply, global justice cannot demand that we should try to correct for its effects in the name of equality.

JMC: What about situations in which there is a limited sense of responsibility. For instance, when a country is suffering from inequalities for which it is not entirely responsible? How do we address this in philosophical terms and how do we redress the situation in economic and political terms?

DM: It can be helpful to think of responsibility as involving two dimensions, which we might call constraint and control. Let us take control first. The first condition for national responsibility is that the people in the country are actually in control of what their government does, in other words that the government behaves in a way that is responsive to the beliefs and the interests of the people. That is obviously most easily achieved where the form of government is democratic but I would not want to say that responsibility only obtains in democracies. I think there can be cases where the government is sufficiently responsive because it shares very widely held cultural beliefs, for example, and there are various systems of accountability operating within the society. That is the control condition: People must have access to mechanisms, democratic or otherwise, that put them in charge of their own collective destiny.

The second condition is the constraint condition, where the question is: What room for maneuver have they got? If they are a very poor country, if they are heavily indebted, if the International Monetary Fund (IMF) is issuing very restrictive injunctions to them, there may be very little scope for choice, and in that case, of course, responsibility is not going to apply. But provided that both the control and constraint conditions are met, then it does. Take as a clear example at one end of the spectrum–Iceland. I have great admiration for the Icelanders, but it is obvious that the huge economic collapse they experienced following the 2008 financial and economic crisis was in large part the result of embarking on ventures which in hindsight Icelanders themselves would say were very foolish – so afterwards it has been up to them to reposition themselves and sort their economy and their financial institutions out. I do not believe that anybody would think that we owe Icelanders special forms of aid because they decided to invest very heavily in certain kinds of banking services. That was their decision: They are very much a democratic society and nobody was forcing them to pursue those policies, so here is a case where collective responsibility must apply; it is a very easy case. At the other end of the spectrum, if you take societies like Somalia or Sudan, desperately poor and with failed states, it is very hard to see how the responsibility conditions could apply there.

JMC: So at the center of your theory of justice at the national and global level is, in fact, the notion of responsibility and the notion of agency. The last thing that you would want is a theory of justice being associated with victimhood. You want to really have at the very core of a theory of justice a full-fledged individual agent.

DM: Exactly, yes. That is very important to emphasize. It is a serious fault with much current thinking about global justice that it tends to work with a picture of people who live in poor societies as passive victims: They have claims and we have obligations toward them. Sometimes that picture does apply, but not always or in general. One should always try to adopt a dual perspective, seeing very poor people as on the one hand in need of immediate help, but on the other as potential agents with choices to make. The imperative is to put them in a position where they can act on that potential and thereby become fully responsible agents.

JMC: You seem to say that the notion of responsibility is so important that short of having it there is no human dignity.

DM: Yes, I think that is both true and very important.

JMC: Regarding this notion of responsibility, as a way to structure your thinking on global justice, you distinguish two forms of responsibility: outcome responsibility and remedial responsibility. What do you mean by these two types of responsibilities and what is their respective impact on a theory of justice at the global level?

DM: Well, outcome responsibility, whether it is applied at the level of individuals or of groups, collectives, nations, is the responsibility you have as an agent for the results of your actions. Suppose you act in a certain way, and your action has an outcome that is not just accidental but it is one that you either intended or at least should have foreseen would occur, then being outcome responsible means that you should bear that outcome. If it is beneficial to you, then you should reap the reward; if it is harmful to you, then you should bear that too; and if it is harmful to somebody else, then of course you have to respond appropriately to that person – in some cases by making good the damage you have caused.

Remedial responsibility is a very different idea. It arises in cases in which people are in situations of need, or are being harmed in some way, or are victims of injustice. Typically, they will have little chance to remedy these circumstances themselves, and so we look to find some other agent to whom we can attribute responsibility for putting their situation right. And that is what I mean by remedial responsibility: being picked out as bearing a special responsibility to attend to somebody whose position calls for remedy. Now sometimes the two forms of responsibility converge, because if you act in a way that harms somebody else, then very often you subsequently bear the remedial responsibility to help them. So if I carelessly knock you over, then I should pick you up again: Outcome responsibility entails remedial responsibility. But there are other cases where they come apart – for example, natural disasters where there are likely to be remedial responsibilities but no outcome responsibilities because the disaster was unforeseen.

JMC: In line with the notion of responsibility and the sense of agency you develop in your philosophy, you feel that nations have a sense of responsibility not only to the present but to the past as well. So tell us a bit about the practical implications of this philosophical approach, especially in terms of the question of reparations because of colonization?

DM: Practical implications are more difficult to draw but the principle is relatively clear. We start from the premise that nations are historical entities, formed over many generations, so to identify with a nation is to see yourself as belonging to a community that stretches back in time. Indeed the origins of nations are often lost in a mythical past, but in any case they are thought to reach back for several centuries at least. So when we belong to a nation, we also identify ourselves with those who came before. Furthermore we are the beneficiaries of the national past: In many material and cultural ways, we benefit from the inheritance that our ancestors left us – the physical and human capital, the improved land, the built environment, and so forth.

Given that this is so – that we are linked to our predecessors by ties both of identity and of tangible benefit – if it turns out to be the case that in the past the nation we belong to acted in harmful ways toward others and if that harm persists so that it continues to have repercussions for people today, then in principle we do owe compensatory responsibilities to those who suffer from it. In practice things are not so simple. For one thing the past is disputed territory. There will be argument about whether what a nation did to outsiders was harmful on balance, or whether the harms it perpetrated came accompanied by offsetting benefits. Debates about colonialism often take that form. A further question is whether past harms can be shown to persist into the present. Answering that is going to be complicated by the fact that the communities on whom the harm was inflicted are likely to have made better or worse choices in the intervening years. If compensation is the issue, we need to be able to quantify the extent of the damage, and for the reasons I have given that will be difficult to do.

JMC: It is a very difficult question, debated both in Europe and in the US. So, from a theoretical standpoint, it is quite clear; but as a practical matter it is quite complicated?

DM: Yes, the clearest practical case is where resources have been wrongly seized and transferred and are still held by the party that took them, while they remain important to the society from which they were taken, either for practical or symbolic reasons. Here there is a strong case for restitution. Cases of past exploitation are more difficult to deal with. I have referred already to the case of colonialism, which often involved exploitation, but simultaneously contributed to the development of the societies that were colonized, as Marx in particular pointed out. Without knowing what would have happened in the absence of colonization, it is difficult to judge whether its impact was harmful or beneficial on balance. For that reason, acknowledging responsibility for the national past is often a matter of offering apologies for particular episodes of wrongdoing where the moral balance sheet is clearly negative.

VI IMMIGRATION AND ISSUES OF GLOBAL JUSTICE

JMC: In 2016, you published with Harvard University Press,[2] a new important book on the issue of immigration. In the past decade or so, immigration has become a major issue in the West, in Europe and in the United States. In the recent elections in the US and in Europe, it was a major campaign theme. The crises in the Middle East have only made the issue more timely. In this new book, you once again refer to the notion of "weak cosmopolitanism" in order to address this issue of immigration. In this regard, one of the key points you make in the book is that there is not a right to immigration. What do you mean by this?

DM: I had written briefly about immigration in my earlier work on global justice, but I felt the issue had become so important that it deserved a fuller treatment. Most philosophers who address it are drawn toward an open

[2] David Miller, *Strangers in Our Midst. The Political Philosophy of Immigration* (Cambridge, MA: Harvard University Press, 2016).

borders position. Although they acknowledge that some border controls are probably necessary given the world as it is, in general people should be as free as possible to move around the globe. In my view this freedom comes at the expense of other values we should care about. Nation-states have a legitimate interest in deciding who should join them as residents and future citizens.

Immigration, as such, is neither a legal nor a moral human right. There are certainly many people who can make a strong claim to enter a new society on the grounds that this is the only way in which their human rights – whether to bodily security, subsistence, freedom of conscience – can be safeguarded. But the vast majority of people currently being admitted to rich Western countries want to move for other reasons. They have interests such as entering higher education, finding a better job, or experiencing a new culture, that are served by immigrating. I am not arguing that states should shut their doors to all these people, but they are entitled to decide who to admit and who to turn away. Current citizens may have an interest in controlling population growth, protecting their language and culture, or maintaining a generous welfare state, all aims that immigration is likely to impact.

JMC: Also, could you explain to the reader the four main values on which your views on immigration are based, that is weak cosmopolitanism, self-determination, fairness, and integrated society. Why do you think these four values are related to one another and are central to a philosophy of immigration?

DM: Weak cosmopolitanism tells us how we must react to the claims of the stranger who asks to be admitted to our society. We cannot just ignore her or turn her away regardless: We must consider her interests. If she is a refugee, and therefore liable to be persecuted if she is sent back to her home country, we must take her in, or at least make sure that she is accommodated in a safe place. Since there are many millions of people who can make such a claim, we need to devise schemes to share the burden of processing and admitting asylum seekers between states. On the other hand, if the stranger cannot press a claim for refuge, we still owe him consideration, and an explanation for our decision whether or not to admit him. This should take the form of a consistent, publicly announced, policy for selecting immigrants that incorporates defensible grounds of selection, such as whether the immigrant has special skills that the society needs.

Self-determination is an important factor in this debate because large-scale immigration is likely to change the character of the host society over time, and today's citizens have a legitimate interest in controlling the direction of change. Think of the case – an unlikely one, I admit – where half a million Chinese, only a minute fraction of the total population of China, want to move to Iceland. I believe that Icelanders would have good reasons to resist this movement, to protect their culture and way of life. This involves no judgment that being Icelandic is better or worse than being Chinese. When states decide who to admit, they are in fact making a decision on the future of the country since those admitted on a permanent basis must be allowed in due course to qualify for citizenship and enjoy all the rights and opportunities that existing citizens have.

This is where fairness comes in: Immigrants who are accepted must be offered a fair deal. In the late nineteenth century there were large-scale migrations, especially across the Atlantic, but on arrival the immigrants were effectively told to sink or swim. They were heavily dependent on finding communities of people from the same background for material support. At the beginning of the twenty-first century, we have governments supporting large, inclusive, welfare states that immigrants are entitled to benefit from as a matter of social justice. So we have to consider what impact immigration will have on these systems.

I think the importance of integrating immigrants should be fairly clear by now in the light of recent terrorist events. We want to avoid the creation of what have been called "parallel societies," not least because such divisions can lead to intolerance and, in the last resort, sectarian violence. We should not be ashamed to encourage immigrants to identify strongly with the nations they are enjoying, and becoming a citizen should be a time of celebration, as it is in countries like Canada that have gone furthest in making large-scale immigration a success.

JMC: Toward the end of the book you also reflect a bit on the European migration crisis of 2015. Can you tell us how your philosophy of immigration helps to think about this crisis and, possibly, would have helped to handle the crisis better?

DM: From my perspective, what happened in Europe in 2015 was something of a disaster, and is likely to poison debate over immigration for years to come. For the best of humanitarian reasons, but with little regard for long-term consequences, EU states decided initially to allow migrants to enter Europe uninvited and move across the continent to their preferred destinations. Although many of those who arrived would indeed have qualified for refugee status, or at least for temporary protection, the chaotic nature of the events prevented those status determinations being made. Equally, it proved impossible, as the EU had hoped, to distribute refugees between member-states on the basis of agreed quotas.

In my view, it would have been far better for the EU to have taken a tough line to prevent migrants from crossing the Mediterranean or the land borders from Turkey, meanwhile increasing the level of on-site support they offered to refugees from Syria encamped in neighboring countries. This would have allowed the most vulnerable among them to have been identified and offered resettlement in European states in an orderly way.

JMC: In your view, what is the next big immigration crisis and what should be done to either prevent it or address it properly?

DM: I do not have any predictions to offer about specific future immigration crises. What is clear is that heavy immigration pressure on wealthy democratic states is going to continue, and may actually get worse as developing societies get richer, since it is rarely the poorest in the world who have the means to cross borders. To address it we will need to be more proactive in identifying those with valid claims to asylum, and more willing to contribute to international schemes for placing refugees in host societies according to their capacity to receive them. We should also experiment more with properly policed temporary migration schemes that allow people to work for short periods before returning home, taking with them skills and capital that will contribute to development. What we should avoid at all costs is the emergence of an underclass of illegal migrants living on the fringes of society and shorn of all the entitlements and protections that citizens can rightly claim.

JMC: Finally, what would be your advice to young scholars starting to work in the field of justice?

DM: I think it is important to recognize the complexity of the question. When people began to think about global justice, the question they asked was whether the principles they were familiar with in domestic contexts, such as equality of opportunity, applied at global level as well. Battle lines were drawn up: You were either a cosmopolitan or a statist. We need now to get beyond that simple opposition. "Global justice" covers a multiplicity of more concrete questions – trade, aid, migration, climate change, humanitarian intervention, etc. – and it is unlikely that any single principle is going to help us think about all of them. So I would recommend focusing on one of these more specific topics, and then working out a theory that is relevant to that topic in particular.

6

Minority Rights, Secularism, and Justice

Neera Chandhoke

I CONTEMPORARY DEVELOPMENT OF MINORITY RIGHTS IN INDIA

JEAN-MARC COICAUD (JMC): *Let us begin with speaking about minority rights. In the context of debates on justice, both at the national and the international levels, it is a topic that has been on the map for a long time. But it has acquired increased importance in the recent decades, for instance in the 1990s in the Balkans and in Africa. And of course, it is also an issue of premier importance in India. Since you have written extensively on the topic can you tell us about your understanding of minority rights in the Indian context?*

NEERA CHANDHOKE (NC): The focus on minority rights in India originated in a distinct political context in the 1980s. The context was marked by the rise of the religious right, attempts to transform a plural society into a unified and homogenous nation-state, and targeting of the Muslim minority. The strategy of targeting Muslims foregrounded historical injustices perpetrated by Mughal rulers on Hindus in the past. The alleged destruction of a Hindu temple in the town of Ayodhaya in 1538 by a Mughal general of Emperor Babar and the construction of a mosque on that exact site formed a central plank in this saga of injustice. According to historians, there is no evidence that a temple stood at precisely the site of the mosque, which was subsequently demolished by the cadres of the right-wing party the Bharatiya Janata Party, in 1992. But history can be twisted in any direction, and the leadership of the (BJP), through the deployment of incendiary rhetoric and mythological allegories, propelled serious and sustained political passions in the public domain. Even as resentment and the desire for vengeance overtook Indian society, the leaders of the right-wing party emphasized the need to demolish the Babri mosque. Before the demolition, hate speech catapulted violence against the Muslim community. The demolition was followed by a series of violent riots resulting in mayhem, death, and destruction. The charged political context motivated scholars to launch a discussion on the adequacy or the inadequacy of secularism. As a result, I decided to defend the minority rights that have been granted by the Indian Constitution.[1]

JMC: In the Indian context it is as late as in the 1980s that the notion came to the fore, and it was in the context of religious minority rights.

NC: We need to bring a historical perspective on the issue of minority rights. In the 1920s India witnessed ferocious communal riots between Hindus and Muslims. The leaders of the mainstream party, the Indian National Congress, tried to allay tensions and insecurities of the Muslim minority by incorporating minority rights in the Motilal Nehru Constitutional Draft. The draft authored by the leaders of the nationalist movement in 1928 committed that the right of minorities to their religious practices, educational institutions, and scripts would be protected in independent India. The Constitution of India reiterated the commitment to minority rights in Article 29 and particularly Article 30 of the Fundamental Rights Chapter. These two rights add to the generic right to religion codified in Article 25 of the Chapter.

In the same decade, Gandhi tried to bring warring religious communities into a wide-ranging freedom struggle, under the banner of the phrase *sarva dharma sambhava*. The phrase, which is inscribed in the sacred text of the Hindus, the *Advaita Vedanta*, holds that all paths to the truth are equal. This was interpreted politically to indicate both toleration and equality of all religious beliefs. The concept is Hindu, but for Gandhi it meant nothing less than equality of all religions. The implication was that in independent India, no group would be given special preference, or discriminated against, on grounds of religious affiliation. From the beginning, therefore, minority rights or collective rights were about the rights of religious communities.

The leadership continued to hold fast to this normative principle after independence, even though the country had been partitioned in the name of religion. Given the deep polarization of Indian society, and given the brutality that erupted in the wake of the partition, India could easily have swung in the direction of majoritarianism. In the Constituent Assembly, one representative suggested that any consideration of minority rights should be postponed until Pakistan's stand on minorities became clear. In response, Dr. Ambedkar, the Chairman of the Drafting

[1] See Neera Chandhoke, *The Rights of Religious Minorities* (Delhi: Oxford University Press, 2003).

Committee, stated resolutely that the rights of minorities are absolute rights. Whereas minority rights were made an integral part of fundamental rights, secularism remained the unstated principle of the democratic constitution till 1976 when it was incorporated in the Preamble of the Constitution.

The concept of secularism was first spelled out in 1951 by the first Prime Minister of India, Jawaharlal Nehru. The word "secular," he said, is not a very happy one because it cannot be translated into an Indian language. And yet, for want of a better, we have used it. It "does not obviously mean a state where religion as such is discouraged. It means freedom of religion and conscience, including freedom for those who may have no religion."[2]

Strictly speaking we do not need to proclaim secularism to grant freedom of religious belief. This right is part of the fundamental rights that are assured to every citizen. The right to equality is also a part of a generic fundamental right. The principle of secularism goes further and secures that the state will not be aligned to any religion, and that it will not discriminate against religion. *It is this specific commitment that establishes the credentials of a secular state.* Or that secularism outstrips the right to freedom and equality, and stipulates that the state will maintain an impartial attitude toward all religious groups.

Given the partition of the country on religious grounds, the commitment that the state would not align itself with any religious group was essential to set the fears of minorities at rest. It was equally necessary to send a clear message to the majority community, that it would have no privileged position because of its demographic strength. The principle needs to be constantly reiterated to ward off majoritarianism.

JMC: Why specifically the 1980s? What was the political and cultural context of the time which put this notion on the map in the Indian context?

NC: The 1980s were characterized by what is called the collapse of the "Congress System." After independence in 1947, the Indian National Congress ruled the country for about twenty-five years. At the turn of the 1970s, the socialist leader J. P. Narayan launched a massive political movement against the authoritarian policies of the central government under the leadership of Prime Minister Indira Gandhi. Leading a major movement for "total revolution" in the country, he called for "party-less democracy." Many Indians concurred with his view, for not only had the political party failed to discharge its responsibility toward the people but it had also rapidly degenerated into a corrupt, unrepresentative, and power-hungry

[2] Jawaharal Nehru, *Jawaharal Nehru: An Anthology*, S. Gopal (ed.) (Delhi: Oxford University Press, 1980), p. 327.

machine. It could no longer assure citizens that it represented the interests of the people.

This is cause for some regret, for it was precisely the ability of the Congress to represent and accommodate all class, caste, and group interests *within* the organization, that had been acclaimed by scholars. In fact, the respected sociologist Rajni Kothari conceptualized the Indian model of democracy as the "one party dominant system" or the "Congress System." Factions representing different interests carried on the rather complex activity of negotiating and bargaining with the leadership *within* the party organization.[3]

The decline of the Congress and the crisis of representative politics took place in a context of rising expectations. An entirely new generation had grown to maturity in post-independence India, a generation that had no memory of the freedom struggle, and a generation that measured the achievements of a party in terms of its ability to meet the aspirations of the people. It was at this exact moment that the party of the religious right, the Bharatiya Janata Party, managed to fill in the political vacuum by foregrounding identity politics.

II SECULARISM AND THE PROTECTION OF MINORITY RIGHTS

JMC: *In the context of your work you have argued that secularism is one of the mechanisms that one can call upon to somehow ensure the protection of minority rights. Why is it the case in general and, more specifically, in the Indian context?*

NC: In India secularism was designed to regulate debilitating religious strife, to assure the minorities of their safety, to set at rest any apprehension that the state would align itself with the dominant religion, and to protect diversity. The concept of secularism had historically emerged in the West as a formula to put an end to the religious wars that had devastated Europe in the sixteenth century. It was on the principle of secularism that communities that had gone to war over religion, and societies that tolerated torture of non-believers throughout the period of the Inquisition, could learn to live together.

India faced similar problems. The anti-colonial struggle provoked separate and potentially divisive identities to define themselves not only in opposition to colonialism, but also in opposition to each other. This posed a distinct threat to the coherence of the new nation. The articulation of the principle of secularism as equality was designed to allow people to live together in civility. Of equal importance was the need to protect pluralism. Notably, the empirical

3 Rajni Kothari, *Politics in India* (New Delhi: Orient Longmans, 1970).

proposition that India is plural does not easily transit to the normative proposition that plurality is of value. The gap between the two propositions has to be bridged. What other normative concept can bridge the gap except secularism as equality of all religions?

The distinctive feature of secularism in India has been defined by the Supreme Court as equality of religions. But as every egalitarian is aware, the application of formal equality in a constituency that is unequal, or in a society composed of majorities and vulnerable minorities, lands up reproducing inequality and vulnerability. I see substantive equality and minority rights as integral to the root concept of secularism.

JMC: You just mentioned that this understanding of secularism is quite specific to the Indian context. So, if you had to compare the notion of secularism in the Indian context with how it unfolded in the European or US context, what would you say are the points of difference and the similarities?

NC: Political secularism or simply secularism is not a stand-alone concept. In modern Europe it rose to prominence on the shoulders of a social process, the secularization of society that took place in the wake of the Enlightenment. Now that secularization has been seen as one of the vanities of modernity, and now that religion has made a comeback in the public domain, political secularism has been abandoned by those who once enthusiastically embraced the concept. It needs a new theoretical home. And what other home can our society provide except democracy? The argument in my work suggested that secularism should be viewed as a companion concept of democracy, as an extension of the principle of substantive equality.

III SECULARISM AND THE MEANING OF WORDS

JMC: How to make secularism a companion concept of democracy and an extension of the principle of substantive equality?

NC: In order to accomplish this transition, we have to distinguish between the various meanings of the term "secular." Words are tricky things and we can never be sure/certain/confident/assured that we have used the right word to express/convey what we wanted to say. An interesting exchange between Alice and Humpty Dumpty in Lewis Carrol's *Through The Looking Glass* might illustrate what I am trying to say: "I don't know what you mean by 'glory'?" said Alice to Humpty Dumpty. The latter smiled contemptuously, "of course you don't-till I tell you. I meant there's a nice knock-down argument for you!" "But 'glory' doesn't mean 'a nice down argument,' " Alice objected. "When I use a word" Humpty Dumpty said scornfully, "it means just what I choose it to mean-neither more nor less." "The question is" said Alice, "whether you can make words mean so many different things." "The question is," said Humpty Dumpty, "which is to be master-that's all."

Lewis Carroll, mathematician and logician, excelled in the subtle art of satire and word play. Coded in this exchange between Alice and Humpty Dumpty, which appears a piece of delightful literary nonsense at first sight, is a message. The search for unequivocal meaning, Carroll seems to tell us, is doomed.

Consider the term "secular"; it can be used descriptively to, say, distinguish education based on modern rational and "scientific" pedagogies from religious education. Or it can be used to depict processes of critical engagement with ideas, systems of thought, and beliefs. Modernity brings with it an interrogative stance toward all beliefs, especially religion. Secularization is a social process that entails the privatization of religion.

Political secularism is a normative concept. It is an attribute of a democratic state. The democratic state does not distinguish between people and groups on the basis of religion. The belief is that no one should be privileged or disprivileged for reasons that are outside their control, particularly birth into "this" or "that" religious community. To distinguish between people on basis of ascriptive characteristics is morally arbitrary. The attendant presumption is that people have good reasons for subscribing in belief system X or Y, and this should be tolerated. The proviso is that their beliefs and the actions that follow therein do not cause harm. In history, secularism emerges as a companion concept of secularization.

IV SECULARIZATION AND RELIGION

JMC: But you tell us that in recent years we have seen an evolution?

NC: The wheel has turned full circle, and since the end of the twentieth century, Western political philosophers, theologians, anthropologists, and postmodern thinkers have declared the onset of a post-secular age. Religion has made a spectacular comeback to the public domain in at least two ways. One, political philosophers have come to subscribe to a not-so-new belief that secularization has led to spiritual impoverishment. Human beings no longer have access to resources that can help them negotiate deep philosophical problems. Two, religion has entered the public sphere as a powerful and evocative form of politics: Making demands upon the state, and legitimizing state-breaking and state-making projects. Western political philosophers have tried hard to come to terms with the resurgence of religion. But in the ultimate analysis they subordinate religious vocabularies, strategies, and beliefs to some form of "reasonable restrictions" or "reasonable consensus."

For instance, in a speech titled "Faith and Knowledge" in October 2001, Jürgen Habermas piloted the concept of post-secularism to the center-stage of political theory. "We," he said in the aftermath of the attack on the Trade Towers in New York, "are in a post-secular age." The speech recognized that out of the destruction wrought on the symbols of America's economic and political hegemony, religion had gained a new lease of life.[4]

Since the 1990s, Habermas had been moving in the direction of recognizing religion as a resource for resolving some of the most troublesome ethical problems confronted by human beings, for example genetic engineering. There is need, he argued, to institute a dialogue between religious and nonreligious citizens. Religious citizens must develop a self-reflexive and pluralistic view of modernity, so that secular beliefs can be viewed as disagreements that can be worked through rationally. And secular citizens must develop a non-reductionist, reflexive, and accommodative attitude toward religion.

The burden Habermas places on secular citizens insofar as they are urged to understand and appreciate religious vocabularies is much less than the burden placed on religious citizens. Religious vocabularies have to be translated into secular ones the moment arguments in the public sphere enter domains of law-making. That is why Habermas sets institutional thresholds between the "wild life" of the political public sphere, and formal proceedings within political bodies, and allows only secular contributions to pass through. In parliament, for example, the standing rules of procedure of the house must empower the house leader to have religious statements or justifications expunged from the minutes.[5]

Considering that one of the tasks he sets before himself is to work out rules of coexistence between religion and nonreligious politics, Habermas could have considered that India has had a long experience of negotiating a problem that Western philosophers have come to recognize as serious only at the turn of the twenty-first century. How do a democratic public sphere and a democratic state negotiate and manage the inclusion of religious voices in the public sphere?

4 Jürgen Habermas, "Faith and Knowledge," 2001, www.freidenspreis-des-deutschen-buchhandels.de, accessed on February 12, 2017, p 2.

5 Jürgen Habermas, "Religion in the Public Sphere," *European Journal of Philosophy* (Vol. 14, no 1, 2006), pp. 1–25.

India had no choice in this matter. In the early nineteenth century, the colonial state embarked on a project of understanding, translating, codifying, and freezing a plural and decentered religion like Hinduism into the mold of Judeo-Christian notions of what religion is, and what it should be. These attempts fetched sometimes anxious, and sometimes assertive, responses by Indian intellectuals and political leaders.

Investigations of Hinduism and later Islam in the nineteenth century, rationalist reformulations and orthodox defenses of practices shaped an emerging public sphere in which religion was debated, discussed, and ultimately made the anchor of a nationalist project. Reeling under a barrage of criticism by Christian missionaries, influential Western philosophers, and colonial officialdom, nationalist leaders and social reformers set out to refashion Hinduism along the lines of foundational texts. From the early nineteenth century onward Indians were surrounded by, swept up in, and swamped by discussions on religion, new interpretations, new modes of measuring and critiquing received wisdom, and anxious defenses by orthodoxy, in a newly constructed public sphere. In India, modernity arrives through processes of intense reflection on, critique of, and politicization of religious identities, not through the privatization of religion as in Europe.

Public debates on religion inevitably led to the politicization of religious identities. Indians who had lived with each other in neighborhoods and workplaces became aware of their identity as members of not only a religious, but also a demographic majority, or minority group. Colonial policies gave an added fillip to this politicization through practices of group representation *vied* separate electorates, offers of public goods to members of a community, politics of enumeration, and in general policies of what has been termed "divide and rule."

Unlike Europe, in India political secularism was not the companion concept of secularization. Political secularism as a policy that regulated the relationship of the state to different religious groups was institutionalized amidst the politicization of religion and the polarization of religious identities.

V SECULARISM, RELIGION, AND GENDER RIGHTS

JMC: Your remarks introduce the issue of translation in political philosophy, which is an important one. Often when we use concepts in different contexts we run the risk of thinking that the concepts have the same meaning but very often it is not the case. Also, in the context of your work, you use the notion of secularism not simply as a way to handle the issue of religious minority rights but also as a way to think about what you call substantive inequalities in economic terms and in gender terms. From your point of view, what is the link between secularism, minority rights, and tackling substantive inequalities in economic and gender terms?

NC: The granting of collective rights to religious minorities was accompanied by a special concession: Christians and Muslims could retain their own personal laws. Personal laws relate to marriage, dowry, dissolution of marriage, parentage and legitimacy, guardianship, adoption, gifts, wills, inheritance, and succession. They are, therefore, crucial for gender justice. The acceptance that the Muslim and Christian minority could be governed by their personal laws was a response to minority insecurities in troubled times. Whether this was a wise move or not has been a matter for some debate, because it brought into question both the role of the Indian state in providing a secular public sphere and its self-arrogated role as a social reformer. Though article 44 of the Directive Principles of State Policy stated that the government should enact a Uniform Civil Code in due course, the time has still not come for the realization of this particular commitment.

The problem is that immediately after independence the government set out to reform the personal laws of the Hindu community through a series of legislations known collectively as the Hindu Code Bill. But it stayed away from reforming Muslim or Christian personal laws. That is, government intervention in the affairs of religious groups proved to be *selective*.

The Hindu right, capitalizing upon the selectiveness with which Congress governments have intervened in religious affairs, accused the government of practicing pseudo-secularism. It is not that the Hindu right dismisses secularism. The argument goes deeper. If secularism means equality of all religions then minority rights and retention of personal laws violate the basic precepts of secularism. It may appear ironic that the religious right, devoted as it is to the establishment of a majoritarian state, has no problem with secularism as the doctrine of strict equality relating to religious groups, until we recollect that the doctrine of formal equality is profoundly indifferent to background inequalities.

Matters came to a head in the mid-1980s with the Shah Bano case. The case was not the first of its kind in independent India. Nor was the Supreme Court judgment the first time the judiciary had ruled on the issue of maintenance of divorced Muslim women. But in 1985 the decision of the Court to grant to Muslim women the same rights as other women aroused a storm of protest from patriarchal sections of the Muslim community. The scale of the protest can only be understood as a response to the massive mobilization of the Hindu right in the mid-1980s. Whatever the reason, the unprecedented protest of the Muslim community had important political implications.

The controversy snowballed into a major political problem as thousands of Muslims took to the street to demonstrate against the judgment. Ultimately, Prime Minister Rajeev Gandhi's government, then in power at the center, bowed before the uproar. In February 1986, the Government introduced a Bill in Parliament which sought to exempt Muslim women from the protection provided to other women. The Muslim Women (Protection of Rights on Divorce) Bill in essence abrogated the limited right to maintenance.

The passage of the Bill aroused angry demonstrations as liberal, left, and feminist sections who considered the Bill as regressive and as a violation of gender justice mobilized against it. Oddly enough, protestors shared a common ground with the Hindu right, which attacked the Bill on the same grounds. In the process, defenders of secularism were laden with two more theoretical tasks: One, to justify selective state intervention in religion and square this with secularism; two to try to locate minority rights into the secular project.

JMC: How was your argument on Secularism received in the context of intellectual and public debates in India? And, beyond the debates themselves, what has been the evolution of the situation on these issues?

NC: Secularism seems to have vanished from contemporary political discourse in India, and whatever remains of the concept is subjected to contemptuous remarks, mockery, and dismissal by the religious right. The near disappearance of secularism from political imaginations and visions of how a plural and complex society can be held together, is short-sighted, for the binary opposite of secularism is majoritarianism at best and theocracy at worst.

At the same time we have to recognize that the concept is in crisis. It has been subjected to overuse, and invested with too many expectations. Secularism is not a robust concept like democracy or even justice; it is fragile. Yet the concept has had to shoulder the onerous task of nation building and national integration, take on the politically explosive construction of a uniform civil code, bear responsibility for the rearrangement of hierarchical and exclusionary relationships within communities, and even stand in for democracy. Secularism has been subjected to an overload. Unable to bear the weight of too many diverse political projects and ambitions, it might even implode.

Yet moments of crisis need not lead to unmitigated gloom, or abandonment of the concept. Reversals in the biography of concepts, and the practices associated with them, provide an opportunity to reexamine, rethink, and clarify what the concept means, what it stands for, and what the political context of the concept is. Such moments can be productive because they compel us to reconsider the foundational presumptions of secularism. They allow us to rescue a beleaguered concept not only from angry and abusive opponents, but also ardent supporters and fervent advocates. As part of this rethinking we might need to cut away theoretical flab and dispense with extravagant expectations and hopes that the concept of secularism has come to be embedded in India. The argument in my current work tries to put secularism in its place, by locating it in democratic theory, and by interpreting it as a procedural principle.

VI KNOWLEDGE PRODUCTION AND GLOBAL SOCIAL JUSTICE

JMC: As a political philosopher, as a political theorist, you are calling upon the Western tradition. And you are using this Western tradition and adapting it to the Indian context. As an intellectual how do you go back and forth between these two worlds? Also, what is your strategy to optimally use analytical and normative terms belonging to the two traditions in order to understand and put forward a progressive agenda in the Indian context?

NC: This is an anxiety that besets most of us who try to avoid the trap set by "universalism" on the one hand, and "indigeneity" on the other. The problem is exacerbated by the realization that liberal theorists in the West simply do not pay attention to political predicaments in countries in the Global South, which are complex, contradictory, and resistant to neat resolutions. When in the course of a work on "Contested Secessions"[6] I started looking at the literature on secession authored by Western liberals, I found that they were just not looking at troublesome cases, such as Sudan or Kashmir, which involve violence, third-party intervention, and the rights of minority groups which do not wish to secede. Liberal theory, despite its universalistic pretensions, does not really take into consideration troublesome cases. That is perhaps why liberals have been able to create neat theories and neater principles of justification. Research on my current work on "Rethinking Pluralism, Secularism, and Tolerance"[7] has intensified disenchantment

6 Neera Chandhoke, *Contested Secessions* (New Delhi: Oxford University Press, 2012).

7 Neera Chandhoke. *Rethinking Pluralism, Secularism, and Tolerance*, Sage Publishers, in press.

with Western philosophy. Western philosophers barely pay attention to the Indian experience with plural society, the Indian variant of secularism, affirmative action policies, and theories of toleration. Western theories appear too neat, too sterile.

For instance, the coexistence of secularism and religion in India has neither been completely harmonious nor wholly discordant. In some cases, social practices associated with religion have been subordinated to secular and democratic politics. In other cases, the judiciary has acted as a holding mechanism, and warded off attempts by majority groups to take over the state, and serious communal riots. In some cases, practices that are deeply anachronistic exist side by side. And in other cases, subordinated sections within religious communities have been inspired by democracy to challenge patriarchy and caste oppression. The Indian case teaches us that though we have little choice but to accommodate religion in the public sphere, the outcome of the coexistence of secular and religious principles is extremely untidy and unwieldy, generating as they do different sorts of political dilemmas and scenarios.

JMC: So, you are trying to find a kind of middle ground?

NC: I started with that ambition, but I have changed my mind since then. The argument in my current work on secularism suggests that all of us live in frighteningly blinkered worlds simply because time-tested projects of living together have broken down. We have to rethink this project together, simply because we confront common dilemmas. We need to reach out to other sites of theory production and see whether we can together reflect on issues that bedevil accepted notions of recognition, redistribution, and voice. If conventional notions of secularism have broken down it may be time to rethink the project in the light of other historical experiences, say that of India. We may need to go "beyond secularism," not to dismiss it but to recast it in new mold and strengthen it. In the process, we may well succeed in realizing the universal and inclusive presumptions of global democracy or cosmopolitanism.

In short, global theory needs to expand beyond Eurocentrism to engage with other philosophies and histories, and to mediate its own Eurocentric preoccupations. Conversely, we who live and work in the Global South have to sift out what is valuable in Enlightenment philosophies of equality, freedom, and justice. We have to, to put it bluntly, listen to each other. The right to equal political voice can perhaps be then realized.

JMC: That would be a way to bridge theoretical concerns with specific realities?

NC: I do not want to rush into the debate holding aloft a "me too" pennant and suggest that the canon of Western thought should be expanded to include writings from the Global South on the complexities of the human condition. What I wish to point out is that cultural particularity and universal norms are fated to live together and constitute an unresolvable dilemma. We have to negotiate this dilemma, not seek to resolve it. This recognition shifts the problem of living together, somewhat. For now we have to address the question of how we see ourselves as part of a shared history and shared knowledge systems. We need to develop a social ethic of seeing the other as part of oneself. For this we might have to go beyond the vexed issue of universalism versus cultural particularism that has been criticized strongly by postcolonial theorists. The task is to bring to the fore theories forged in other contexts and times that may well prove relevant to the needs of European societies that have undergone a process of social transformation. Finally, the idea that the universal and particular are closed off categories is a mistaken one. Every site of production of knowledge is a condensate of multiple streams of thought. Gandhi himself was what he was; a great moral leader and a giver of remedies for the maladies of the human condition, because he drew inspiration from a variety of sources. His philosophy is indebted to three great spiritual and moral traditions: Hinduism, Jainism, and Christianity. Gandhian philosophy is constituted as much by the *Bhagvad Gita* as it is by the Sermon of the Mount. And he drew inspiration as much from Tolstoy and John Ruskin[8] as much as he drew inspiration from Vivekananda and other spiritual leaders in India. This should be the model deployed for comparative political theory.

JMC: One of the goals of political theory is to bring clarity on difficult issues but, of course, reality tends to be complicated. As a philosopher, how do you balance the need to clarify and the need to acknowledge the complexity of reality?

NC: Dilemmas, wrote the late philosopher Bimal Matilal, are like paradoxes, and genuine paradoxes are seldom solved. "They are generally speaking, resolved or dissolved. Those philosophers and logicians, who have tried over the centuries to solve the well-known logical and semantical paradoxes, have more often than not created new problems elsewhere in the conceptual apparatus, which exposes

[8] John Ruskin (1819–1900) was a leading English art critic and social thinker.

the non-existence of a universally accepted solution. Can moral dilemmas be put into the same category as unsolvable paradoxes?" Theologians, ethicists, and "strong-minded moral philosophers," he goes on to argue, have often been reluctant to admit the reality of moral dilemmas.[9] But we are, suggests the philosopher, fated to inhabit a world of irresolvable dilemmas. If there can be genuine unresolvable moral dilemmas in a moral system, then it would be as good as courting defeat in any attempt to formulate rational moral theories.

Matilal illustrates his argument with a story found in the great Indian epic the Mahabharata.[10] The Mahabharata, he suggests, is shot through with the meta-concept of *dharma*, which can be interpreted as moral and righteous conduct and the making of a normative order. But the concept of dharma is ambiguous and elusive, and within the structure of dharma-ethics we discover dilemmas. These are not culturally specific, Matilal hastens to add; they are universal, and can be effectively used to illustrate arguments in moral philosophy.[11] Witness for instance that moral dilemmas arise when the agent is committed to two or more moral obligations, but circumstances are such that an obligation to do x cannot be fulfilled without violating an obligation to do y. Dilemmas present irreconcilable options, and the actual choice among them becomes either irrational or is based upon grounds other than moral, even if we possess the relevant information to negotiate them.

This is contrary to the system of Kantian ethics. For Kant, objective practical rules should form a harmonious whole, and a system characterized by consistency, much like a system of true beliefs. The system presumes that two mutually opposing rules cannot be necessary at the same time. Therefore, if it is a duty to act according to one of them, it can prove contrary to the duty to act according to the other.

9 Bimal K. Matilal, "Moral Dilemmas: Insights from Indian Epics," in Bimal K. Matilal (ed.) *Moral Dilemmas in the Mahabharata* (Delhi: Simla Indian Institute of Advanced Studies and Motilal Banarsidass Publishers, 2014), pp. 1–19. Professor Matilal was the Spalding Professor of Eastern Religions and Ethics, University of Oxford, 1977–1991.

10 A hermit, Kausika, had vowed always to tell the truth because he desired above all to go to heaven and presumably break the endless cycle of rebirth. One day as he was sitting near a cross road, he saw a group of travelers rush by in an attempt to escape bandits who were chasing them. While passing the hermit they pleaded that he should not tell their pursuers the direction they had taken. But when the pursuers, who seemed to know that Kausika never lied, asked him what direction their quarry had fled, Kausika acted according to his commitment to always tell the truth. Paradoxically, he did not ascend to heaven even though he had spoken the truth. His commitment to the truth had violated his duty to save innocent lives.

11 Matilal accepts that morality is not an Indian term and its Sanskrit equivalent is not easy to find, except the ubiquitous dharma, but it would be wrong to argue that just because a particular term is not used in a tradition, then the social and political reality denoted by that term does not exist. In that case, one might argue that since the term religion did not have a Sanskrit equivalent in ancient India, the social reality we call religion does not exist (ibid., p. 6).

In Kantian ethics, truth telling gets the highest priority, as is promise keeping. This is equally true in the Indian systems of ethics that extols truth telling as *satya-rakhsa* (protection of the truth). No cultural relativism can be found here. But when two equally strong obligations – that of truth telling and that of saving lives – conflict,[12] keeping of a promise cannot be an unconditional obligation. In such situations we have to make a choice between different sorts of options that might minimize harm.

This implies that we bear moral responsibility for the choice we make. For instance, suggests Matilal, Kausika could have told the bandits that though he knew which way the travelers had gone he would not share this information, or simply kept quiet. But he interpreted his commitment to tell the truth unthinkingly and unimaginatively, and innocent lives were lost. We learn from Matilal that the dilemmas we find ourselves in might well prove intractable, but there is no reason why we cannot negotiate them with some degree of resourcefulness and ingenuity.

VII AGENCY OF THE GLOBAL POOR AND JUSTICE

JMC: What would be a less Eurocentric understanding of global justice coming from the non-Western world? What in your view are the issues which are forgotten and not addressed in the Western-centric approach of global justice?

NC: What is missing in the global justice debate, especially the one that addresses the important issue of poverty? One, the current debate, unlike earlier ones on the unjust global order viz dependency theory, is largely confined to Western intellectuals. Since these theories mainly concentrate on the duties of justice that the richer West has toward the global poor who live in the developing world, scholars from the latter part of the world are excluded from the debate by definitional fiat. These theories speak of obligations to the distant needy, but theorists just do not conceive of a universal humanity in which all of us have duties of justice to each other. Are we, who live and work in the developing world, fated to remain consumers of acts, whether those of harm or of duty, performed by the West?

Two, what is the moral status of the global poor in theories of global justice? Citizens of the affluent world can be persuaded to transfer some part of their resources to the global poor. However, the transfer does not proscribe asking

[12] *Ibid.*, pp. 8–9.

the question: Do not the poor who live in the regions of Sub-Saharan Africa, South America, and South Asia somehow remain faceless in these theories, as if they do not possess status, as if they are mere recipients of obligations that emanate from elsewhere, and as if they do not struggle for justice, sometimes realize justice, and thereby acquire agency?

The serving up of compassion to the laboring poor in countries of the South does little to enhance their status as people who count in their own right. People should be participants in the multiple transactions of society, they should be able to listen to world music, read the same books shortlisted for the Booker award as people who live in Rio or in Rome, engage in debates with other like-minded people, or agitate against the manifestly unjust policies of global institutions. They cannot do so because their energies, their capacities, their zest for life have been crippled by poverty.

JMC: So you argue that the debates on global justice portray the non-Western world in passive terms and do not put forward the sense of agency and the sense of responsibility that should be also at the core of the non-Western world? Implicitly, there is the idea that the Global South is the victim and that agency has to come from the developed countries but this should not be the only term of the debates?

NC: There is nothing wrong with the proposition that affluent citizens of the Western world should be obliged to transfer some portion of their resources to the global poor. The relevant question is: What about the global poor? What is the status that they are allotted in these schemes of transfer of resources from the rich to the poor world? Can poverty-stricken peasants in India, laboring under the iniquitous policies of the WTO, even *afford* to wait for the realization to dawn on Western governments and citizens that their actions have wronged people living in this part of the world, and that the wrong has to be compensated? The more significant point is: should the global poor be even doing so?

Monique Deveaux has argued that Thomas Pogge rightly emphasizes that coordinated efforts of governments and global economic institutions are needed to effect major structural changes in global poverty, which is the outcome of unfair practices of global institutions. But in recent years a more complex view of poverty as "multi-faceted powerlessness has emerged in development circles and among civil society organizations grappling with the effects of globalization."[13] The antidote to such powerlessness is participation

13 Monique Deveaux, "The Global Poor as Agents of Justice," *Journal of Moral Philosophy* (2013) DOI 10.1163/17455243-4681029, p. 8.

and input of poor communities in civil society campaigns, so that they acquire voice and impact national legislation. "In some Latin American countries, grassroots poor organisations have successfully fought for the implementation of poor-empowering 'social protection' schemes, such as minimum-basic income programs and cash transfers to the poor."[14] The poor have standing as moral agents because of their capacity for morally motivated action, to respond as best as they can to the poverty in which they find themselves and to undertake acts of solidarity with fellow persons living in poverty.[15] From the successful efforts of the rural poor to seize land in Mozambique to gain control of local government institutions using the Bolivian law of Popular Participation, pro-poor civil society groups and movements aim not only to change policy but also to lay claim to democratic power.

If political philosophers focus on the political context that shapes moral choices, they must also take cognizance of how political struggles that try to reshape those contexts that inhibit the making of choices allow human beings to make their own history, even if the histories they make are not the histories they wanted to make in the first place. Otherwise there is real danger that the status of persons whose condition is sought to be remedied, will be reduced to that of beneficiaries of transfer of resources from the West.

JMC: The way debates are being framed in global justice – even though it may be well intentioned – is a form of paternalism?

NC: Theorists of justice tend to overlook that ultimately justice has to be wrested from imperfectly just states, howsoever democratic they may be. If one of the main objectives of political practices is to realize justice, which is embedded in the democratic state, but which is often unrealized or partially realized, then these practices have to reshape the political context in which we live and work. As a World Bank study on moving out of poverty reports, there is little evidence that people remain trapped in a "culture of poverty," as Hegel or Oscar Lewis the American anthropologist had theorized. Poor people seldom are apathetic. They take initiatives, pursue small ventures, and often get ahead. Some do manage to move out of poverty, some obviously do not, but on the whole the picture is far removed from a "culture of laziness, passivity, and criminality."[16]

14 *Ibid.*

15 *Ibid.*, p. 9.

16 Deepa Narayan, Lant Pritchard, and Soumya Kapoor, *Moving out of Poverty Success from the Bottom Up*, volume 2, 2009.

JMC: In the end it is another way of not seeing the other and of not recognizing the other as a full-fledged agent and responsible actor?

NC: Western citizens cannot be held responsible for all sorts of deprivation that afflicts the poor in the developing world, but in the ultimate analysis this does not matter, or ought not to matter. What should matter is that a large number of the global poor are condemned to leading lives that are insecure at best and fraught at worst. Should not groups in the Western countries that are concerned about these issues join hands against the denial of human rights, ensure that the poor are not condemned to poverty, or that their rights are not left unfulfilled, particularly if national governments do not do anything about this? Do we always have to be institutionally connected to the causes of someone's ill-being to do something about it, as Thomas Pogge suggests? Arguably, the insecurity which stalks the rights of the poor in the developing world should be evoking positive duties on relevant agents irrespective of anything else. "So-called 'positive' duties to aid others are often regarded as weak, broad, imperfect, and meritorious," writes Larry Temkin, while "negative duties are regarded as strict, narrow, perfect, and unexceptionable. But these divisions are deeply misleading. Positive duties are still *duties*, and one acts wrongly if one *fails* to fulfil them … Failing to fulfil a positive duty can be significantly more open to moral criticism than failing to fulfil a negative duty, even if the latter involves a rights violation, and hence an injustice, while the former does not."[17]

JMC: Do you think that there is the tendency when we talk about justice to view the beneficiaries of discourses of justice as victims – within nations and among nations – while in the end the goal is to allow for the possibility of a full sense of agency for the people whom we want to benefit from justice?

NC: Arguably, the insecurity which stalks the rights of the poor in the developing world should be evoking positive duties on relevant agents irrespective of anything else. We can safely assume many of the activists and NGOs are motivated to act and to confront powerful global institutions and powerful states because they feel that universal human rights impose universal obligations on relevant agents. These agents can secure the realization of a right through a transfer of resources to the poor but they can also secure this transfer through advocacy, and what international human rights NGOs call strategies of "naming and shaming." In other words, a link between rights

[17] Larry S. Temkin, "Thinking about the Needy, Justice, and International Organizations," *The Journal of Ethics* (vol. 8, no. 4, 2004), pp. 349–395, p. 356.

bearers and relevant agents can be wrought by the language of human rights, and by the sentiment that if a right is recognized as human this is cause enough to evoke duties on the part of relevant agents.

Such an approach accomplishes two things, both of which are compatible with the basic proposition of human rights. Firstly, the global poor are not seen as victims who have to be given cash transfers because the West is guilty, but instead are treated as rights bearers and thus as people who possess moral irreducible status. Secondly, the one factor in politics that engenders awareness of injustice, of rights and of duties to those whose rights have been violated, is political mobilization. This makes people conscious of what is due to them, and what they have been denied. And this is what these networks of solidarity accomplish. There *is* perhaps much more to global justice than the negative duties of global justice theories. I do not by any means wish to dismiss the concept of negative rights. All I want to do is to argue that violations of human rights place obligations even upon those persons who have not participated, albeit indirectly, in these violations. This might still not be enough, but if we can compel recognition that universal rights command universal duties, it might suffice.

JMC: What strikes me is that often there is a lack of reflexivity in how we conceptualize these issues. On the one hand, philosophers in the West are, I think, well intentioned; on the other hand, at times they approach these topics in a way that may be critical but is not necessarily reflective.

NC: Yes, I do not think they even take into account the sensibilities of the worlds they are obliged to save from themselves. But the poor are not potato sack or potato mash. They have ambitions, desires, and above all a deep desire to be seen as agents in their own right.

VIII GLOBALIZING THEORIES OF JUSTICE

JMC: Western debates on global justice call upon a very narrow body of knowledge, essentially Western philosophy. In intellectual terms, which have political and policy consequences, would it be better to also call upon intellectual traditions beyond the West to think about justice at the global level?

NC: Consider the ways in which postcolonial critics have engaged with the project of global democracy. For one, global democracy theorists replay the same problem that was identified with formal democratic theories, that is the tendency to ignore background inequalities of wealth and various forms of power between the North and the South. Two, defenders of global democracy disregard the fact that the source of current inequalities between the West and the rest can be found in Europe's dark history of colonialism, and neocolonialism. Three, critics allege that cosmopolitanism seeks to push a quintessentially Western liberal agenda on the Global South, that the Anglo-American world has not hesitated to use armed force to do so, and that these efforts easily slide into new forms of empire.[18] Four, the philosophy that underpins the project, cosmopolitanism, is, it is argued, excessively Eurocentric. Even as John Hobson accepts that David Held's theory of cosmopolitan democracy stands outside liberal triumphalism, and even as he applauds Held's defense against charges of Eurocentrism, he suggests that Held's framework universalizes a particular Western conception of liberty and equality, a conception that is derived purely from the Western historical experience. "That Held believes passionately that his theory of the good is inherently universal and will genuinely benefit *all* peoples is *not* at stake. Rather, I want to point out that his theory exhibits that most seductive property which Eurocentrism offers its believers: that Western provincialism does not simply '*masquerade* as the universal' because it truly is the universal."[19]

JMC: The intellectuals supporting the modern canon of knowledge tend to view traditions as opposed to a progressive agenda. Against this background, how do you reconcile traditions and a progressive agenda, so that in the end we do not have a progressive agenda that is mainly an elite and Western agenda?

NC: There is much excitement over the project of comparative theory in Western universities. Comparison demands equal political worth and presumably equal voice. Yet, in the literature on comparative theory, representation from the South amounts to tokenism, a Gandhi here and a Tagore there, even as methodologies of comparison remain Western-centric. Epistemic systems from this part of the world remain unexplored. This is a great pity, for knowledge systems forged in the context of plural and divided societies might help in resolving dilemmas that stalk the projects of liberal societies, negotiating cultural plurality for instance. These systems might help Europe out of its current predicaments. But they do not find place in formulations of comparative democracy.

18 Costas Douzanis concentrates on the imperial dimensions of cosmopolitanism, *Human Rights and Empire: The Political Philosophy of Cosmopolitanism* (Abingdon: Routledge-Cavendish, 2007), pp. 153–176.

19 John M. Hobson, *The Eurocentric Conception of World Politics: Western International Theory* (Cambridge: Cambridge University Press, 2012), pp. 298–299, emphasis in the original.

JMC: Maybe we are focusing too much on the variety of intellectual traditions. After all, people from all walks of life, while being part of a specific tradition, also have a strong sense of what is right and what is wrong, and of their rights.

NC: I think that rights have become detached from any particular historical discourse and have become a part of everyday imagination, because they motivate projects that speak back to power. The focus on rights was very much a part of our freedom struggle in South Asia, as it was a part of the freedom struggle in Africa. The talk about rights in the context of liberation became part of popular consciousness, not because of the accomplishments of Western philosophy, but because political consciousness of what is due to human beings is integral to processes of political struggles. When people seek to make their own histories, howsoever badly they might make them, they become aware of their own status as people who matter, and who matter as much as anyone else. This is how the notion, the discourse, and the practice of rights become part of the way people think of themselves and of others.

X POVERTY, EQUALITY, AND THE ROLE OF GLOBAL CIVIL SOCIETY

JMC: You mentioned earlier the notion of global civil society. Are activists in India involved in the global civil society?

NC: To give one example, whereas 94 percent of India's work force is in the unorganized sector, the Indian Government has for at least four decades after independence failed to take the rights of this section of the work force into account. Policies were enacted for this sector only in the 1980s. Ratna Sudershan has argued that the decade of the 1980s witnessed two paradoxical developments. One, despite the large differences in the situation of the old and the new informal workers, and between workers in the developed and the developing countries, the forging of associative networks between them resulted in the formulation of a definite approach to social protection. Two, although globalization had expanded the informal sector, the process also provided the space for serious discussion on how to ensure the rights of informal workers to social protection. A number of such discussions in global forums led to the creation of international networks such as WIEGO or Women in Informal Employment. Over time, the network began to advocate the adoption of this right across the world.

Notably, members of WIEGO, who include representatives of several membership-based organizations from different countries, have been engaged in advocating the rights of informal workers not as an act of charity for the informal workers of the developing world, but as a technique for securing the rights of all workers who eke out a living in precarious work situations. International advocacy has played an important role in increasing the visibility of informal workers, and in generating commitment to providing universal social protection, at the very time globalization has created more workers in the informal sector.[20] This strategy seems to have been successful. For in December 2008 the government of India finally passed the Unorganized Sector Workers Social Security Bill.

JMC: Is the rising global status of India putting pressure on the government to tackle social issues?

NC: In India, trade unions are yoked to political parties and represent a very small percentage of the work force. For this reason India simply could not replicate the model institutionalized in the Scandinavian countries. In the twenty-first century, civil society organizations stepped into the field of social policy, and sharply foregrounded the responsibility of the state to its citizens. The enactment of several social rights as laws followed civil society campaigns, the filing of Public Interest Litigation in the Supreme Court, and a new phase of judicial activism.

In the run-up to the 2014 general elections, the Bharatiya Janata Party managed on a vote share of 31 percent to secure 282 seats in the popularly elected lower house of Parliament. Despite its stance as pro-corporate and pro-rich, once in power the central government moved toward establishing a social security regime. At the same time, it proceeded to slash expenditure on the social sector, in education, health, agriculture, livelihood security, food security, local self-government institutions, drinking water, and Scheduled Castes and Tribes sub-plan. The rights-based approach to well-being that had been emphasized by civil society interventions during the previous government has been replaced with the route to social policy from above. Significantly, these policies have been announced without any sort of civil society mobilization. The pattern adopted seems to be the one adopted by benevolent dictators in South East Asia: Social goods without political liberties.

JMC: Finally, what is your advice for young scholars focusing on issues of justice?

[20] Ratna Sudershan, "Social Protection, the Informal Economy, and Globalization," unpublished paper (2007).

NC: One, politics has to be recognized as chancy, unpredictable, and contingent. Scholars have to understand the ambiguities of the human condition, and that some of these dilemmas may well remain unresolvable. Neat and rigorous theory tends to stray far away from lived experience. Two, since many of the problems that confront the world are common, it is time that Western scholars explore the way scholars in the Global South have formulated, and tried to resolve these dilemmas. We have to reach out to each other and to other sites of theory production.

7

Decent Society, Memory, and Compromise

Avishai Margalit

I FROM IDOLATRY TO DECENT SOCIETY

JEAN-MARC COICAUD (JMC): *Your first major book dealt with the question of idolatry.*[1] *I remember discovering and reading the book while I was myself doing research in philosophy and law in Cambridge, near Boston. Afterwards, your books have dealt more directly with issues of justice. So, as a philosopher, why did you start your journey with the issue of idolatry? Is there a link between the book on idolatry and your subsequent books dealing with justice issues?*

AVISHAI MARGALIT (AM): *Idolatry* was my first book, but not the beginning of my philosophical life. I was trained in and practiced what is termed analytical philosophy. I dealt with topics congenial to this trend (trends) such as language, meaning, logical paradoxes, rational decisions, and more. I was particularly interested in cognitive illusions, caused by our use of metaphors not recognized as metaphors. My dealing with idolatry was very much the continuation of my interest in illusions. This is the case because I consider the religious criticism of idolatry as the forerunner of the modern unmasking of ideologies as cognitive illusions. So idolatry was not in my case the symptom of a mid-career crisis. It was an integral part of my former philosophical interests. Moreover, I was always interested in religion. So, this book dealing with the question of idolatry was an expression of this interest too. Yet my interest in religion was always a third-person perspective on religion. I was never engaged in a first-person quest for redemption. I never believed that one should be a believer. At the same time, I think that it is terribly important to understand why religion plays such a central role in the lives of so many people.

[1] Moshe Halbertal and Avishai Margalit, *Idolatry* (Cambridge, MA: Harvard University Press, 1994).

JMC: The book is also partly about trying to make sense of the fact that religion, and relations among religions can bring about violence.

AM: I do not think that there is an inherent relation between religion and violence. I also do not believe that there is strong empirical correlation between the two. The saliency of what seems to be sectarian religious wars recently may lead us to believe that religion has a dominant role in bringing about civil wars in the world, but this is simply factually wrong. On a retail level of small cells' acts of terror, religion today may play a significant role relative to other sources of violence. But even this limited claim should be confirmed and not be taken for granted.

JMC: After your work on idolatry you have chosen to work on social and political morality. Your approach to addressing justice has been through the notion of what you call the Decent Society.[2] *This notion is quite different from some of the most iconic approaches of justice in recent time. For example, it is quite different from the Rawlsian approach, which you mention at the beginning of the book. In fact, in the book, you argue that the urgent problem today is not related to the just society but rather to the decent society. So what do you mean by this? Why do you think that decency is more important than justice? Is your thinking on decency also about justice?*

AM: The book is really about what I believe is a decent society, namely a society that does not humiliate people. And humiliation, in the strong sense, is when you are treated not as a human being but as a number, as a machine, as an animal, as subhuman, as abnormal. I think that there is of course a strong link between a decent society and a just society. Still, the idea of a decent society is somewhat different from the one of a just society. A just society has to do with negotiating two basic values, equality and liberty, and there are various ways of striking the balance between the two. The decent society deals with something far more fundamental, to my mind, and that is to be treated as a human being, as a precondition to a just society.

II DECENCY, INJUSTICE, AND JUSTICE

JMC: You just mentioned that being treated as a human being is a precondition for a just society. How is this notion of precondition to be understood, especially when it comes to rights, and more specifically to human rights?

[2] Avishai Margalit, *The Decent Society* (Cambridge, MA: Harvard University Press, 1998).

AM: One way of viewing human rights is to view them as a protection of human dignity, which is the idea that all humans should be respected as human beings. So human rights give on this account positive content to human dignity. My strategy in treating humans as humans was different. It was a negative strategy: namely, avoiding humiliation rather than promoting dignity. Be it as it may, both strategies assume that a precondition for morality is the idea of shared humanity. And positive dignity and avoiding humiliation are both in the service of the idea that shared humanity is a precondition for morality and justice.

JMC: In the book The Decent Society *you mention that focusing on the notion of a decent society is a second best because it appears to be more manageable than identifying what a just society is. What do you mean by this notion of "second best"?*

AM: Well, let us take an example. In Catholicism, the ideal life for a woman can be viewed as a life devoted to Christ, i.e. becoming a nun. But this ideal is too much to ask from all ordinary women, so the second best for a woman is to be a mother with many children. It is indeed a mere second best, which is very different from the ideal life of chastity. Based on this example, we can see that the notion of a "second best" refers to the idea that in our list of priorities the second item on the list is a mere approximation to the first item, but it may look very different from what is at the top of the list. Moreover it calls for a different strategy to attain it compared to the one required to attain the top priority. Now, going back to the question of a decent society as a second best compared to a just society, we could say that while justice is at the top of our list of social moral life, a decent society is a mere second best. And, indeed, I believe that a decent society is a second-best society. Of course, the ideal is a just society. On the other hand, there are also just societies that can treat people very mechanically and indecently, and therefore not humanly.

JMC: How is it possible that a society that claims to be just and that, arguably, is just, does not treat people, members of the community humanly?

AM: For example, this happens when a society is distributing things justly yet in a manner that does not respect humans as human beings. A just society is a very valuable idea, but the question of humiliation is a different one. The two issues are connected but are different.

JMC: Can you tell us more on this idea that a society can be just and still humiliate its people, or at least some of its people. This appears to be a bit of a contradiction. Since this seems a fundamental idea in your understanding of justice and humiliation, could you expand on this?

AM: The notion of justice involved in a just society is a distributive notion of justice. It calls for distribution of resources among members of the society along principles of fairness. The market does not allocate resources according to the principles of fair and just distribution. So there is in a just society a need for bureaucracies to reallocate resources by taking what the market yields and reallocating according to what is just. In a just society, such bureaucracy must distribute resources according to a just principle. It may do it but, then, it can also do it in a mean-spirited way, for example by conveying a sense of disdain to those who are on the receiving end of the allocation, treating them as parasites and abject losers. This is not an unfamiliar scene, and in my book *The Decent Society* the chapter dealing with bureaucracy and the welfare state bears on this issue. This is what I mean by saying that a society can be just to the letter but indecent in spirit.

JMC: Going back to this notion of "decent society" in general, what are from your point of view the key elements that enter into your definition of a decent society?

AM: There are two types of decent societies. One is when the institutions treat you decently, be it the prison, educational institutions, the army, etc. It can be the whole institutions of the state when they treat you decently. Another type of decent society is when human beings, the other members of society, treat you decently. I still remember Czechoslovakia under communism. The state was not decent but the people were more or less decent to each other. But there are other places were the state can be decent and the people can be indecent. This is why I think it is important to conceptually distinguish these two types of decent societies.

JMC: You gave us the example of Czechoslovakia under communism, where the state was not decent but where people were decent toward one another. Can you give us an example of a place where people are not decent toward one another but where the state is decent toward people?

AM: Well the recent issue of immigration into Europe highlighted the possibility that governments may be more decent in their attitude toward the immigrants than the attitude of their general population. I believe that Angela Merkel, as an embodiment of the German state, was ahead of the general population in her decent attitude to the immigrants.

JMC: Also, don't you think that if a state and state officials do not treat people decently, if they are corrupt, for instance, it is then likely that this lack of decency from the state and state officials will serve as a bad example and will end up influencing and corrupting the attitude of people toward one another in society?

AM: My general point about a decent society and a civilized society is a conceptual one, namely the possibility of one society living without the other. But there is no question that in real life there is a close relation between the two. You just mentioned one possibility of corrupting a civilized society by state corruption. This is a good example.

JMC: Can you tell us about your distinction between a society where people treat one another decently, and a society where the state treats people decently?

AM: Yes, I call "civilized society" a society where people treat each other decently and I call a "decent society" a society where by and large the institutions treat individuals decently – and "decently" means here treating an individual as a human being. Of course, what is meant by treating an individual as a human being depends a great deal on the cultural interpretation of what it is to be a human being, as this can vary sometimes. There are a number of things that are culturally dependent in what it means to be treated decently and there are various interpretations of what it means to be human in different societies. That said, there is also a universal dimension to humiliation. Take for instance the gesture of spitting in the face of an individual. I think it is always an act of humiliation. I cannot think of instances where it is not a humiliation.

JMC: But of course, the ideal situation is when the state treats people decently, and when people treat one another decently. Do you know of any society being able to do this in a satisfactory fashion and what are the minimal conditions for this to be possible?

AM: Decency goes in degrees. So there is always room for improvement. Yet, I think that the Scandinavian countries, for example, are a good approximation of realizing the idea of a decent and civilized society.

JMC: Is it the case that in your thinking another word for "decency" is respect, respect for individuals?

AM: Yes, but respect has two meanings. One meaning refers to social respect, namely honoring your position, which is a vertical notion and understanding of respect, and I would call it honor. Whereas human dignity and human respect refer to a horizontal notion of respect; this horizontal meaning forces us to respect equally the most terrible human beings. It is this second meaning of respect in which I am interested.

III THE ROLE OF EXPERIENCE IN MORAL AND POLITICAL PHILOSOPHY

JMC: At the center of any theory of justice you have this idea of decency, but at the same time, somehow, it is left implicit. It is not unpacked or systematically explored the way you do it in your book The Decent Society. *So how did you come to think about this notion of "Decency" as a key requirement for a good society?*

AM: First of all, I have always been attracted to what I call negative politics rather than to positive politics. By negative politics I mean that what draws us into moral politics is injustice rather than justice. It is indecency and cruelty rather than positive ideals. As such, I think there is more urgency in addressing the negative aspects of politics. Moreover, these negative aspects are more readily recognizable than recognizing and dealing with positive ideals.

What has also played a significant role in my adoption of this approach has been my experience as an activist in the Israel–Palestine conflict. Interacting with people who came to Israel from the former Soviet Union and other countries has played a role as well.

Based on these practical experiences, I came to realize that humiliation is a major human concern, which is grossly underestimated. In many of the revolutions that we see now around the world, the craving for human respect and human dignity and lack of humiliationis, I think, a crucial motivation. Even before we start talking about equality of income or wealth, the issue of not being treated in humiliating ways is a crucial motivation for action. So, both in terms of ideas and in terms of personal experience, I came to realize that this type of approach is needed, and all the more needed that it has been largely overlooked or ignored.

JMC: So the personal dimension was quite significant?

AM: Yes, and this is especially the case since I think that in moral philosophy or political philosophy, if you do not come with your own experiences, you come empty handed.

JMC: In other words, it is not enough for philosophy to rely on book-knowledge. What is equally and perhaps even more important is the ability to see and listen, to experience life and the world and reflect on it, draw from it?

AM: Indeed. There is one type of philosophy that is about reacting to former books of philosophy, and usually this is the one that is practiced, that is done by academics. And there is another form of philosophy, which is basically "documentary philosophy." This latter form of philosophy entails reacting to what happens around you and trying to make sense of it.

JMC: *In this regard, the concrete situations you have been exposed to have been significant sources of ideas for your work?*

AM: Obviously, there are a lot of questions associated with the notion of "decency" but the one issue that struck me as central was the one of "humiliation," of how people are exposed to lack of decency. And in this context, the Israeli–Palestinian conflict and the way people had been treated in the Soviet Union made me think. And I felt that it was all the more urgent to address the topic since, as I alluded to earlier, it had not been addressed properly within political philosophy. To be sure, philosophers like Kant and others have dealt with human dignity. But they have not paid much attention to the negative aspect of humiliation, and how to avoid humiliation. And although this approach has been by and large ignored, I think it amounts to an agenda that completes the one offered by the positive notion of dignity.

JMC: *One would assume that when people focus on the positive or ideals aspects, they assume the negative dimension but it is not conceptualized as such; it is not addressed as such?*

AM: Yes, and this lack of conceptualization and the practical implications of this lack of conceptualization make us impoverished, less able to address and solve concrete problems. We do not have to wait for an ideal society to be realized to address problems of injustice and lack of decency. And this approach is not specific to moral and political philosophy. Take the example of medicine. I think that doctors understand illnesses better than health. In fact, in the field of medicine, doctors have a much clearer idea what disease is than what is health.

IV DECENCY AND RIGHTS

JMC: *As part of your focus on "negative politics," to use the expression you refer to earlier, you seem to approach the idea of rights differently?*

AM: We have two different bases for political or moral theory. One is a right-based theory, and the other is a duty-based theory. Obviously, rights are what we want for ourselves and duties are what we want others to have. I prefer to start with duties and not with rights. Let me give you an example.

At the end of World War II Stalin allegedly suggested that the Nazi leadership should be forced to travel naked in cages throughout Europe. I think that we have a duty to reject outright such a wretched suggestion. The reason is not the fear of violating, say, Himmler's human rights but rather our obligation not to humiliate him. Duty does not require a correlative right.

If I am sitting on a bus and a very old man or woman comes onto the bus, he or she does not have a right to my seat, but it is my duty to give him or her my seat. The main problem with rights is that it is very easy to advocate for human rights. But what people do not address enough is who has the duty to fulfill them. And this duty is the crucial element. Who is responsible for looking after rights? To ascribe to human beings rights of all kinds is easy. But what is hard is the duty to fulfill and to make the rights stick. So I tend to shift the main emphasis onto duties rather than on rights.

JMC: And you do so because at the center of your thinking and your concerns is the idea that what we owe to others is at the center of what decency is and of what a decent society is?

AM: Yes. We, for example, bury people. We do not treat people the way we treat cadavers of animals. We think that human beings need a proper burial. We think that it is crucial that we do not treat people as a waste that can be disposed of. This is part of what we understand as human dignity, of what we feel and think is needed to not humiliate human beings. And we expect that even when we lose our consciousness or die we will be treated with respect, even though we are not there any longer. In a fundamental sense, it is part of our notion of what it is to treat humans as humans.

JMC: Precisely, would not you say that one of the most horrific aspects of war, of killing in war and the lack of respect it displays, is not only that people are killed often in the most senseless fashion but that, in addition, as dead human beings, they are treated with no respect, buried, or not buried, with no sign of respect and human consideration?

AM: I think this is an important point. Mass killing numbed our sensitivity to the humane way of handling dead bodies in war: the bodies of our people but, no less, the bodies of our dead enemies. Such behavior gravely detracts us from our humanity.

V DECENCY, DUTIES, AND MEMORY

JMC: This is how we can see the connection between the notion of decency and your work on memory? Indeed, after having worked on decency, one of your next books was a book titled The Ethics of Memory.[3]

AM: I think so. Here the notion with which I start is the one of "community of memory." Against this background, I ask the following question: What, if at all, are the duties and obligations attached to belonging to a community of memory? My concern is not the politics of memory. I am not asking about the power relations that go with memory, for example in determining whose names are commemorated and whose names are omitted. Rather, what I am asking is about is the very duty to remember. Is there such a duty?

JMC: What are the duties when it comes to memory? What do we owe to the past? What do we owe to others who have suffered in the past? And how do we pay respect to the past?

AM: First of all, we do not want to die without a trace, as if we had never existed.

The prospect of dying without a trace is a problem. I would even say that it is an existential question, for all of us. To be remembered in some form by our family, by our friends is an expectation that we all have, and that we all hope will be fulfilled. To die and disappear, to die and be erased, like a deleted e-mail, is for us a terrible prospect, and a terrible feeling and thought. We want to leave a trace, at least most of us most of the time. I am not talking about a monumental trace. But, at least, we want to be remembered by the people with whom we have thick relations, be it family and friends, or our religious community or even our nation. We want to be remembered either individually or, sometimes, collectively. We simply do not want to vanish into thin air.

Now, I think that the ability to be remembered and, more generally, a community of memory are based on and constitute a community founded on thick relations.

JMC: Before going further concerning memory and the ethics of memory, can you clarify your use of the categories of thick and thin relations in your book The Ethics of Memory? *For instance your idea that treating another human being as a human being is the indication of a thin relation is quite striking. People could ask you: Can our shared humanity be seen as a form of thickness? Why describe this sharing, this community/relation of humanity as thin? Can you*

[3] Avishai Margalit, *The Ethics of Memory* (Cambridge, MA: Harvard University Press, 2002).

elaborate a bit on this idea of thinness regarding treating another human being as a human being?

AM: I do not use the terms "thick" and "thin" as honorific terms. We do distinguish the extension of a term, say, "daffodils," namely all the things referred to by the term "daffodil," and the intension of a term, that is the properties that all "daffodils" share in virtue of which they are called daffodils. Now if we compare the term "daffodils" to the term "flowers," the extension of flowers is much wider, and it includes, of course, all the daffodils, but its intension is smaller, for all daffodils share among their properties the property of being a flower. The scope of flowers is wider but the content of flowers is smaller: The content is conveyed by the properties the things have in common. In that sense we may say that daffodils are a thicker notion than flowers. Now, if we go back to being human and the terms of "thin" and "thick," we can say the following: Being human is much thinner than being a brother, for being a brother is being human and much more. The extension of humanity is wider. But the intension is narrower and thick and thin go by the intension, not by the extension. This is all pretty crude and a bit technical but I hope that it is of some help.

JMC: Now that you have clarified your thinking on this specific point, let us go back to the issue of community of memory.

AM: Well, as I alluded to, from my point of view, a thick relation is when we have history and memory, and an established relationship with others. Usually, the clear cases of thick relation are family and friends, and memory usually has to do with thick relations. That said, and this is one of the key points I focus in my book on *The Ethics of Memory*, the only case of thin relation which puts an obligation for us to remember is when humiliation occurred. In particular, in situations of genocide, of atrocities of momentous importance, then there is an obligation of the world to remember. Hiroshima should be remembered. Rwanda should be remembered. And, needless to say, the Holocaust should be remembered.

So the issue here is to be remembered by the humanity at large. In other words, the issue is memory as coextensive to humanity. But humanity does not amount to a political entity. We talk about cosmopolitanism but cosmopolitics is not a political unit. There is no established and institutional politics, political framework, for cosmopolitanism. Only nations or states benefit from a situation of political establishment and institutionalization. So the world is international, but it is not cosmopolitan. For example, the United Nations

(UN) is an international organization, but it is not a cosmopolitan organization. So, the question here is: Are there international obligations to remember tragedies that have happened in the world, at the world level? In order to answer this question, we have to focus on tragedies that function as I would call "signposts to humanity," signposts to humanity in the context of which humanity has been denied, as for example in the case of Nazism. Nazism's ideology and policies were geared toward denying the humanity of its victims. In such cases, the obligation of memory concerns the nation directly involved and more.

JMC: I lived in Japan for a few years and, not being a specialist of Asia, when I started living there I knew very little about the historical tragedies of the Asia region. Similarly, people in Asia tend to know little about the historical tragedies that have happened in Europe, the Holocaust and so on.

AM: I did not mention it, but of course the massacre of Nanking should be remembered too. Nanking is a glaring example.[4] My Lai is another event that should be remembered.[5] All these events are signposts to the world at large.

VI FOR A GLOBAL COMMUNITY OF MEMORY?

JMC: One of the challenges of thinking about justice at the global level, or of combatting injustice and injustices at the global level, is that memory is partial, that the community of memory you were referring to earlier is fragmented. There is no real community of memory at the global level. In the West we know about the Holocaust, but in other parts of the world, in Asia for instance, it constitutes a rather abstract and distant reality. Similarly, in the West, we tend to know little about the tragedies that have happened in Africa, in Asia, and other parts of the world. In these conditions, how to

[4] The Nanking Massacre, or Nanjing Massacre, was an episode of mass murder and mass rape committed by Japanese troops against the residents of Nanjing (then spelled Nanking), then the capital of the Republic of China, during the second Sino-Japanese War. The massacre took place over a period of six weeks, starting in mid-December 1937, the day the Japanese captured Nanjing. The International Military Tribunal for the Far East estimated in 1946 that over 200,000 Chinese were killed.

[5] The My Lai Massacre refers to the massacre of between 347 and 504 unarmed civilians in South Vietnam on March 16, 1968 by a company of American soldiers. Some of the women were gang-raped and their bodies mutilated. Subsequently, twenty-six soldiers were charged with criminal offenses but only a platoon leader was convicted. Found guilty of killing twenty-two villagers, he was originally given a life sentence but served only three and a half years under house arrest.

develop an intellectual and political agenda to tackle injustices around the world?

AM: I wish I had a useful answer to your question. But whatever the answer is, I believe that the way to go about expanding social justice, going globally as it were, is still through an international effort, namely by recruiting the commitment and the resources of existing states. We should avoid falling in the trap of believing that we are already in a global world, in which nation states are something of the past. It may come to that one day but the day has not come yet.

JMC: For a number of years, in the field of history, scholars have been trying to develop comparative and global history approaches, as a way to have a more balanced and comprehensive understanding and analysis of history, and of our shared humanity. Is there a similar movement in philosophy, in order to try to think better on issues of justice, and injustices, at the global level?

AM: Well, there is a "cosmopolitan" trend in current philosophy, with the assumption that the relevant community for dealing with moral and political issues, as well as with cultural issues, should be the community that comprises all human beings. Thus moral cosmopolitanism talks about distributive justice on a global scale and not just within the confines of a State.

JMC: In your work you refer to the notion of "shared humanity" as a fundamental element of the human condition that has to be respected and celebrated. But what might we make of this notion of "shared humanity" if there is no real sense of community bringing people together and being celebrated at the global level?

AM: I do not quite see why a shared trait should force one to view all that bear the trait as a community. I may cherish my trait of having red hair in me and as in others, but I do not see the urge to form a community of red-hair people. This may strike you as trivializing your question, since being human is a serious trait whereas red hair is a trivial one. But my point still sticks. The mere fact that the trait is serious does not fill the gap between a shared trait and a community.

JMC: Earlier, you mentioned there is no politics in cosmopolitan approaches, that there is no cosmopolitics, and of course you are right. But if you are talking about the culture of memory and if you want to somehow extend the sense of solidarity and of identification beyond the national, how do we encourage the making of politics at the cosmopolitan level?

AM: I am an internationalist, not a cosmopolitan. That said, the United Nations, as a world organization, should make the issue of humanity's memory, one of its major projects. I will give you an example for such a project. There is a need to find a place where historians from both sides, or from many sides, of a conflict can come and sit together, and work out their shared conflicting past. If they reach an agreement on what has led to the conflict, its modalities, etc., then their findings should be translated into the various languages of the countries that had been previously at war, so that the common findings can be integrated into schools' curricula. This may help prevent later irredentism[6] and I think that this is a very worthy project, which the United Nations should take on board. The project could be labeled as an "institute for contested shared history." For example, the conflict between Israel and the Palestinians is still a bleeding wound. Even if a political solution is going to be reached, it will not be enough. We will have to address issues of memory.

The UN could do something of great value by addressing issues of painful memories that may eventually be resurrected and erupt again. After all, irredentism is always lurking behind any political solution. To be sure, I do not make addressing painful memories a condition for finding a political solution, but it is very important.

JMC: In essence, you are advocating the creation and the cultivation of a world memory, as a way to address the issue of fragmented memory we discussed earlier. But, as we said, creating and cultivating a world memory is challenging considering that to this day most of the key academic disciplines in the humanities and the social sciences are nationally based. When one studies history, one first and foremost studies the history of the country to which one belongs and, in the process, one deepens the gap between this country and others, and so on. So how do we nurture world memory if our knowledge in the humanities and social sciences is nationalized or constitute a national type of knowledge?

AM: You are absolutely right, but I think the grip of the nation-states on history is loosening up. I really believe that you see more and more critical history occurring in many places. You are right that history is still in many places – especially in young states – perceived as a propaganda branch, with the aim of indoctrinating the young. But I think that this idea of using history

6 In the book *On Compromise and Rotten Compromises* (Princeton, NJ: Princeton University Press, 2010), Avishai Margalit defines irredentism as "a foreign policy aiming at regaining lost territories" (p. 69).

and memory for propaganda purpose is in retreat. The danger is still, as you said, that nation-states try to monopolize history. They are afraid of critical history. But there is more and more a tendency of historians to be independent, and this of course should be encouraged. And by being "encouraged," I mean making it possible for historians to work in institutions that make it easy for them to not be under the sway of the nation-states they are coming from.

VII SENTIMENTALITY, HUMAN DIGNITY, AND BEING A PHILOSOPHER

JMC: When we look at the totality of your work, one of the questions that seems at the center of your thinking is: How do we create for ourselves and others an open heart, so that we relate with one another with respect and dignity, both at the individual and collective levels? If this is the case, what could be the conditions of this kind of open heart or, if you will, of this open mind?

AM: I am as afraid of using the expression "open heart" as of using the expression "bleeding heart" because I want my political morality or ethics, or whatever it is, to be hardnosed, and not sentimental. There is always a fear of using the expressions of "human dignity" and of "honoring human beings" becoming sentimental and kitsch, of the sort that defies conceptual analysis. I think those terms like humiliation can be called upon in real hard politics, and not being just mushy and sentimental and an expression of muddled headedness. So, yes, I want open hearts and I want to be open to others, but I am afraid of the sentimental undertones of those expressions.

JMC: Because equally important for you is the need to draw the line between what is acceptable and what is not, and that is what you call hardnosed politics?

AM: Yes, that is right.

JMC: So how do you balance the two, this idea of a non-sentimental and not very effective politically open heart, and drawing the line as part of hardnosed politics?

AM: There is no algorithm on how to do it. In fact, it is a matter of tact, not of rules. It is like tactful behavior in society. You cannot say to someone how to behave tactfully. There are no rules per se. How to behave politely, tactfully, calls for a judgment, and balancing these two concerns that you are referring to is a matter of tact, and of a sense of proportion.

Myself, when it comes to my work on morality and politics, I am a late-comer. I came to deal with politics and moral philosophy very late in my career, actually only in the last twenty-five years or so. As I said before, initially, as a student, I was trained in a different discipline, in analytical philosophy, and for a long time I was afraid to touch topics of morality because I was afraid of kitsch morality, and I still am.

JMC: Your concern about not being sentimental in addressing issues of morality and politics explains perhaps your focus on how to address and avoid humiliation?

AM: I think so. That is part of it. There are two ways of viewing the world and working in the field of philosophy. One is being concerned with the rules and arguments, and another one is working by distinctions and examples. I am working mainly with distinctions and examples, and of course, here, the distinctions are very important.

JMC: In your work, you refer to two styles of philosophers.[7] *You say there are illustrators and explicators, and you see yourself as an illustrator. What do you mean by each of these two terms and their distinction?*

AM: I make the distinction between what I call "e.g. philosophers" and "i.e. philosophers." As I say in my book *The Ethics of Memory*,[8] e.g. philosophers (illustrators) trust, first and foremost, striking examples, in contrast with i.e. philosophers (explicators), who trust, first and foremost, definitions and general principles. As for me, my tendency is to be an e.g. philosopher rather than i.e. philosopher. I like to give examples and illustrate.

JMC: You just mentioned that you came to moral and political philosophy late in life. So the kind of philosophy which you practice now, is it the same compared to what you were practicing when focusing on logic and philosophy of language?

AM: As I said, I was always interested in politics. In fact, as I mention in the preface of my book *The Ethics of Memory*, I grew up in a political home.[9] But in terms of my own scholarly work, it is only later in life that I began to write on moral and political issues. My book *The Decent Society*[10] was published in 1998, and it was my first book in the area. It came after the publication of

7 Margalit, *The Ethics of Memory*, p. IX.
8 *Ibid.*, p. IX.
9 Avishai Margalit, *Views in Review. Politics and Culture in the State of the Jews* (New York: Farrar, Straus and Giroux, 1998), p. IX.
10 Avishai Margalit, *The Decent Society*.

Idolatry,[11] a book I wrote with a former student and now a friend of mine on idolatry and religious philosophy. As I alluded to earlier, the basic idea of the book dealt with worshiping the wrong god. It was a criticism of ideologies that attribute ultimate values to the things that do not deserve to be objects of ultimate values (this is what idolatry is), but it obviously had strong political underpinnings.

VIII RECONCILIATION

JMC: In your work of moral and political philosophy, you give much importance to the idea of reconciliation. In this regard, it seems to me that, of course, reconciliation among people or entities is important but in your thinking equally important is the idea of reconciling with oneself. Would you agree with this and is it something that has to be understood in connection with conceptions of memory and decency, because, in the end, it is difficult to be decent with others if one is not at peace with oneself?

AM: In fact, I have avoided this type of approach. In my work I have tried to start with human relations rather than with self-reference. From Socrates on, philosophers have addressed the question of how one should lead his or her life as a personal question. But this has not been my starting point.

I have started in an almost Marxist way. I have started with the questions: What kind of human relations should there be? What are relations and what should they be? Namely, the idea is to start with human relation as the basic unit, rather than with the self. So I did not start with how to work on myself and then how to approach the other. Rather, my starting point has been to think that in many cases we are what we are by the kind of relations we have. This has been a key point. Of course, I am not the only one or the first philosopher who has had the idea of starting with human relations as antecedent. As a matter of fact, in daily life we often start with the idea of relation rather than with a concept itself, and this how I go about my thinking. Take for instance height and weight. Basically, the way we go about weight or height is relational. We go about it by trying to understand what it means to be equal in height and weight, etc. This is the way we evaluate rather than by trying to find out, from a conceptual point of view, what is height and what is weight. So, in my thinking dealing with morality and politics, I do not start with myself. I start with the kind of human relation I want with others.

11 Moshe Halbertal and Avishai Margalit, *Idolatry*.

Reconciliation, from my standpoint, has to be understood as a symmetric relation. We both wronged each other and we have to reconcile. If there is no symmetric relation, then, in my view, the notion of reconciliation does not really apply. For example, there is no sense of reconciliation, let us say, between Germans and Jews because I do not think that the Jews did anything wrong to the Germans, so there is nothing symmetrical here. It is more of matter of a need for repentance and apology on the German side. Of course, I do not want young Germans to feel guilty for what their forefathers did. But I want them to feel responsible as long as they view themselves belonging to the German people. So, young Germans are not guilty because they have not done anything wrong but they bear a sense of responsibility the way children are responsible for their parents' debts. Children do not have to feel guilty for what their parents did but they should feel responsible.

In any case, reconciliation for me is only relevant in cases when two sides wronged each other. The interesting case is South Africa and its Truth and Reconciliation Commission because in the case of South Africa there is no symmetry (one side wronged the other side), and yet a Truth and Reconciliation was put in place.[12] This started with the idea that if you get the truth, this will bring reconciliation. But this is not necessarily true. Truth is a very good thing and reconciliation is a very good thing. But in the case of South Africa, there was an empirical assumption, the one that somehow truth would bring reconciliation, and I am not sure that this always happened. Truth can bring bitterness.

IX COMPROMISE, PEACE, AND JUSTICE

JMC: The decision to create the Truth and Reconciliation Commission in South Africa was part of a compromise approach, which in fact leads us to one of your last books, On Compromises and Rotten Compromises.[13] *In this book, you address the issue of compromise in the context of trying to address conflicts and achieve peace. How do you draw the line between compromise (and a good one) and a compromise that is rotten?*

AM: There are many types of compromises but the bottom line is that not all compromises are good compromises. Some are just bad deals. That said, what

[12] The Truth and Reconciliation Commission (TRC) was a court-like restorative justice body put in place in South Africa after the abolition of apartheid in 1994. Witnesses who were identified as victims of gross human rights violations were invited to give statements about their experiences, and some were selected for public hearings. Perpetrators of violence could also give testimony and request amnesty from both civil and criminal prosecution.

[13] Avishai Margalit, *On Compromise and Rotten Compromises.*

distinguishes a compromise from a rotten compromise is not just a bad deal. A rotten compromise amounts to making a deal with an inhuman regime – a regime which has installed a systematic practice of cruelty and humiliation. The Munich agreement was rotten, not just bad.

JMC: What is the importance of compromise in politics in general, and of compromise in politics today?

AM: Very important, but my concern is not with compromises in politics in general. My concern is compromise with inhuman regimes.

JMC: Can you give us examples of rotten compromises in politics?

AM: I mentioned various examples in the book. Munich, which I mentioned before, is one of them, because it is an agreement that was signed with Hitler, who was committed to destroy morality. Another case that I deal with is the one of the American Constitution. I asked whether the Constitution was based on a rotten compromise. More specifically, the question I ask in the book is whether agreeing with slavery in the American Constitution when it was drafted and adopted – although the word "slavery" was removed from the text – amounts to making the US Constitution a rotten compromise. And I come to the conclusion that "yes," the US Constitution was a rotten compromise. Now, there are of course lots of good things in the US Constitution and you may say that altogether it is a great constitution. But, to repeat the story I use in the book,[14] if one serves a soup with a cockroach, you do not say that the soup is great; you say that it is a shame that there is a cockroach in there. You say that the whole thing is bad. By contrast, if you find a fly in the ointment or in the honey you remove the fly and the soup gets fixed. I thought that slavery, the fact that the US Constitution went along at the time with the idea and practice of slavery, is a cockroach in the soup and that is a bad thing to have.

JMC: Why do you think that slavery spoiled the soup in the American context?

AM: Because slavery is the ultimate manifestation, apart from genocide, of an inhuman regime. That is really a combination of cruelty and humiliation. A slave is not treated as a human being but as a slave, as subhuman, and slavery, for me, is one the ultimate cases of cruelty and humiliation. Now you may say: "Do you accuse Aristotle of having slaves?" This looks ridiculously anachronistic. It is like accusing Julius Caesar for not treating his illness with antibiotics. So in order to assess the cruelty and inhumanity of slavery,

[14] *Ibid.*, pp. 54–61.

you have to keep in mind a question of context and horizon. And, precisely, the antislavery movement was within the horizon of the people who agreed to the American Constitution. So the American Constitution was a great thing in many ways. Also, many of the people who signed it expected that slavery would vanish soon. But it remains that they created a document that endorsed slavery to such an extent that I think it put a cockroach in the soup.

JMC: But in the end the American "soup" was able to go beyond this and somehow transcend this initial rotten compromise?

AM: Well, it took a terrible civil war for that.

X BETRAYAL AND JUSTICE

JMC: In 2017 you published a new and important book, On Betrayal.[15] *Why this interest in the notion of betrayal and what is the link between betrayal and what has been your interest in issues of justice, or decency?*

AM: There are two lines of research in my books which are roughly divided between thin and thick relations. My book *The Decent Society* as well as my book on *Compromise and Rotten Compromises* are in line with thin human relations, namely dealing with morality. My books *The Ethics of Memory* and *On Betrayal* are in line with thick human relations, namely dealing with ethics.

JMC: In the book you argue that betrayal is first and foremost related to thick relations, which you also see as ethical relations, such as relationships with friends, family, and core communities. So betrayal is less of a central notion when it comes to thin relations, relations of morality?

AM: Yes.

JMC: This leads you to argue that betrayal, while a central notion throughout history, is less central today because thin relations are getting more important than thick relations. What does this tell you about the state of the world today and about its core values?

AM: I still think that betrayal has a strong hold in our current world, on current traditional societies, but it has lost the tightness of its grip in less traditional society. This crude observation I believe holds true.

[15] Avishai Margalit, *On Betrayal* (Cambridge, MA: Harvard University Press, 2017).

JMC: Toward the end of the book, in the chapter titled "Class Betrayal," you argue that in advanced economies the social conditions for bringing about a just society do not exist. You connect this argument with the fate of the working class. Can you explain your views on the matter?

AM: The claim is that macro-justice, namely an overall just society, can be brought about by a collective agent, say a social class, which is both socially strong and would be well served by a just society.

It seemed that the working class suited this historic role, especially in the time of tool production industry. But information industry as well as other factors dismembered the scope and coherence of the working class as an historical agent and it is not clear which force in society is going to replace it as a candidate for the historical role of bringing a just society. There were remarkable moral political successes throughout history, which were not class based. A glaring example is the abolitionist movement in the US. But I am talking not just of moral advancement in one particular zone but an overall change. The women's movement is another glaring example of a moral success, but I wonder if it is a sustainable historical agent overall.

JMC: If this is the case, what are today the options for bringing about a just society, and a sense of global justice? Where to turn and how to proceed? Indeed, it is not as if people have given up on the idea and the need to try making societies and the world better. But if your analysis is right, how to proceed to nurture ideologies of peace (and justice) and combat ideologies of war (and death)? After all, one could argue that the crisis of democracy in a number of European countries and in the United States gives much relevance to this question.

AM: The urgent question for today is how to prevent injustice, rather than how to promote justice. There is asymmetry between good and evil. Refraining from evil takes precedence over pursuing the good.

I do believe that the rise of what is described as populism is a direct attack on the liberal-democratic society, which although it is not a just society is much better than the various versions of soft-fascism which are looming beyond the populist battle cry: "We the true people against you the phony elite."

The first priority for now, at least in terms of urgency, is to hold off the populist assault. Bringing about a just society is more important but less urgent.

JMC: Finally, what would be your advice to young scholars starting to work in the field of justice?

AM: The Scottish biologist and town planner Patrick Geddes, who among other things was the town planner of Tel-Aviv, coined the slogan "Think globally, act locally." I believe that this slogan holds true for the issue of global justice. I for one cannot improve on this succinct and illuminating advice.

8

Global Ethics and Global Justice

Thomas W. Pogge

I ON JUSTICE IN GENERAL

JEAN-MARC COICAUD (JMC): *Much of your work centers on the idea of justice. To begin our conversation, what should we understand justice to mean?*

THOMAS W. POGGE (TP): Justice is traditionally defined in terms of not harming anyone and of giving people what one owes them. So there is an association with negative duties: Justice is not about helping other people by being beneficent, benevolent, and so on, but rather it is about not harming them, not depriving them of their due. It is about not reducing others' standard of living, not taking anything away from them, not breaking promises made to them, and so on.

In recent years and decades an aspect of justice has become increasingly important that is often referred to as social justice. Social justice concerns the design of social institutions. One can of course harm people and deny them what they are owed not only directly face to face but also through the design of social institutions, of rules that govern the interactive life of a society or of the world at large – through rules that are unjust, that deprive people of what should rightfully be theirs. The design and imposition of social rules constitute one increasingly prominent way in which some people are harming others, treating them unjustly.

JMC: *That is a very general definition of justice, and is it a definition that applies throughout time or is it something that is simply for today?*

TP: Obviously, conceptions of justice have changed over time. We are now thinking, at least internationally, increasingly in terms of human rights. But human rights are not the construct that was prominent in the thinking, for example, of the old Greeks and Romans, or the ancient Chinese. So there are changes in how we conceive of justice. And yet, I think it is also important that, when we think about justice, we think about it as eternal or at least as quasi-eternal. In this spirit, we should ask ourselves whether our conception of justice is one that would have been applicable to, would have made reasonable demands upon, people in earlier ages. Not perhaps all the way back into the Stone Ages – that is why I am saying quasi-eternal – but certainly back to classical antiquity. If we are really convinced that slavery is wrong, that slavery is an injustice, a practice that unduly harms the people who are being enslaved, then we should be willing to project this judgment back in time and say that slavery was as unjust in ancient Greece and ancient Rome as it is, let us say, in the early nineteenth-century United States situation or indeed today, when the global number of *de facto* slaves is probably as high as it has ever been.[1]

JMC: Concerning the definition that you gave us of justice, would you say that it is really a definition that is built around these quasi-eternal principles of justice?

TP: One should distinguish between the concept of justice and various conceptions of justice. One feature of the concept of justice is that the demands of justice do not vary from day to day. Justice is not some sort of agreement that people make and then, when there are changes in the interests of the parties or in the distribution of bargaining power among them, renegotiate in order to adjust to the new realities. On the contrary, justice has a certain eternity or eternal validity, and you would not qualify as offering a conception of justice if you said "well now that I have become more powerful and you have become less powerful, now the just arrangement between us is a different arrangement." Justice is precisely not a mere accommodation of the interests of the various parties where each one demands and concedes what one finds it advantageous to demand or concede given the bargaining power of oneself and the other.

II ON GLOBAL JUSTICE

JMC: While historically thinking about justice has by and large taken place at the national level for the national level, in the past twenty years or so more and

[1] The International Labour Organization (ILO) puts the number of slaves today at 21 million (www.ilo.org/global/topics/forced-labour/policy-areas/statistics/lang–en/index.htm). But this estimate may be far too low. While the ILO reckons that there are 600,000 slaves in South Asia and the Middle East (ibid.), alternative estimates claim that there are 18 million slaves in India alone (*Wall Street Journal* at https://blogs.wsj.com/indiarealtime/2016/06/02/india-has-the-most-people-living-in-modern-slavery/).

more attention has been given to justice at the global level, and in this new context you have been one of the key voices. Why is it that now we have to think about justice at the global level and what are the differences and the similarities in terms of justice at the national level and justice at the global level?

TP: The main reason why we must increasingly pay attention to questions of global justice is because the rules that govern our day-to-day interactions are increasingly supranational rules or rules constrained and influenced by supranational rules. So, go back in time a few centuries and you would say that most of what went on in interactions among human beings – economic transactions, for example, employment relations, whatever – was governed by rules that were at most at the national level. But today supranational rules are much more consequential. There are many more of them and they increasingly preempt and constrain the rules at the nation-state level. These supranational rules are incredibly influential. We all know that the rules of the World Trade Organization (WTO) matter; and we need to think about these rules because they have so much influence in moral terms. We must ask ourselves "are these rules harming people?" and "are these rules giving people what they are owed?" These matters are becoming increasingly important.

Now, the difference between the national and global levels is one of subject matter. And there is also this important difference: That the kinds of moral intuitions one can appeal to within a national community are not necessarily available at the global level. So, it could be that, when you design a conception of justice for France, you can draw on a certain shared history, shared values, the French Revolution, let us say, and some of the great heroes of French intellectual history. But these heroes may not be even known, let alone respected and revered in other parts of the world, and we could not ask the rest of the world to accept a conception of global justice that is heavily focused upon French traditions and French thinking. So we must look for common elements; we have to find a perhaps thinner conception of justice, one that is widely shareable. This thinner conception will probably not be one that we can all agree is complete, but it can and should be one that we can all agree is at least the core of a reasonable conception of global justice. We must try to work with such a thin conception of global justice to shape our supranational institutions in such a way that at least the most severe, most obvious harms to people are avoided.

JMC: Essentially, you are telling us that at the national level there is a strong sense of moral community partly because there is a sense of shared history, which does not exist at the global level?

TP: Yes, this is true at least of many countries – though obviously not of all. There are some countries that are artificial constructs with great cultural diversity within them. But most countries and certainly most of the developed countries that have been around for centuries, like France, have a significant history, a significant body of traditions, of thinking about justice, and a certain commonality of experiencing morality, of thinking about morality, all of which you can draw upon and can design an ambitious conception of justice around. And that is alright. It is alright for countries to have ambitious conceptions of justice, maybe ones that are distinctive, that differ from those of other countries. There need not be one correct conception of justice that fits all countries. But the problem is that at the global level we do not have enough sharable material for a complete conception of justice that would be widely accepted; and so we have to work with something thinner.

III THE CHALLENGES OF THE GLOBAL MORAL COMMUNITY

JMC: One of the difficulties at the global level is that a sense of global moral community does not exist. So, how do we first identify the principles that would be usable at the global level and how do we go about implementing them?

TP: I think a good starting point is to look at the things that have been common themes in the moralities of many diverse cultures: common elements. The Golden Rule,[2] for example, is an element that has been developed independently in different cultures. I think that human rights are also a common theme, albeit not under this name. Here the idea is simply that human beings have certain basic needs and that these needs support high-priority claims on others for their fulfillment. Thus, everyone should enjoy access of adequate food, water, shelter, clothing, sanitation, health care, education, and participation in the social, economic, and political life of one's society, should enjoy freedom of movement, of expression, of worship, of association, should enjoy protection from arbitrary violence, punishment, expropriation. The endorsement of these freedoms is not partisan to any particular country or culture. Rather, it has emerged independently in pretty much all the different cultures of the world and therefore forms a sharable nucleus that has now been made explicit in the human rights documents that have emerged over the last seventy years since the Universal Declaration of Human Rights was adopted.

[2] The Golden Rule is the instruction not to treat others in ways in which one would not want to be treated oneself (negative variant) and to do for others what one would want to have done for oneself (positive variant).

This thin preexisting convergence makes it possible for countries around the world to agree on at least some minimal conception of justice – a conception that gives all human beings a certain standing, a certain dignity, a certain set of basic claims on the rest of humankind, and also a conception that is contained in any more-ambitious conception of global justice one might want to construct from within the standpoint of a more specific (e.g. national) culture.

In addition, we also need agreement that the basic claims of the minimal conception have great weight so that they normally outweigh any other moral contents that, from the standpoint of this or that culture, one might want to include in a conception of global justice. Such a twofold agreement would constitute the starting point you are asking about – the starting point that would enable us to say: We do not know exactly what a full conception of global justice would or could look like but we have enough to go on at least to have a critical vantage point to guide our assessment and reform of existing supranational institutional arrangements.

IV THE DISTINCTION BETWEEN INTERNATIONAL AND GLOBAL JUSTICE

JMC: We are talking about global justice as if global justice was more or less the same thing as international justice. But I would assume that in your mind international justice and global justice are quite different. And in fact, over time your focus has been very much on global justice rather than on international justice. What is the difference between international justice and global justice? And why do you think that it is much more important to focus on global justice than on international justice?

TP: International justice has been around for centuries. There is a very long tradition of international justice going back all the way to ancient times. International justice is concerned with the moral assessment of the interactions among states. States are interacting with one another, they sign treaties, they invade each other, perhaps fight wars and make competing claims over resources and territory; and international justice covers these interactions and the rules states do or should commit themselves to toward resolving their conflicts and competing claims. Here states are the players whose claims are in focus; they are the subjects of international law and international justice.

It is different with global justice. Here it is individual human beings who are the claimants, who are the ones who have the rights, and who are the subjects of the theory. So, we are trying to work out a theory of how international institutions ought to be designed, and specifically a theory that is responsive not to the claims and interests of states but rather to the claims and interests of individual human beings. This is an inheritance from the Enlightenment era that we are thinking that the ultimate units of moral concern are human beings. States matter only if and insofar as they are important to individual human beings. They do not have any importance in and of themselves but only insofar as individuals identify with them, individuals are protected by them, individual interests are enhanced by them. Now global justice is quite different from international justice in that, once you focus on the interests of individuals, you will want to impose very different rules on the world.

You will also assess the existing rules quite differently. Rules can be very convenient for states, that is, for governments: For example, states may work out a system under which it is considered always wrong to interfere in the internal affairs of other states. That is nice for all governments because they can do what they want within their own territory, but it is not a good arrangement for individuals because they can then easily be subject to oppressive and corrupt regimes that exploit them, oppress them, kill many of them, and so forth. So, if we make human beings the be-all and end-all of justice, then we get a very different perspective, a very different take on the assessment of supranational institutional arrangements.

JMC: So if we focus on global justice rather than on international justice, the principles of justice at the global level are going to be different because the beneficiaries and the actors for whom you are working are going to be different? And I guess the institutions expressing and implementing and protecting the sense of justice are going to be different, right?

TP: Absolutely, they are going to be quite different. If you follow what I said earlier about human rights being in the core of a conception of global justice, then our first question is always going to be how we can design and reform supranational institutional arrangements in such a way that we realize human rights insofar as reasonably possible. If you look at the same question from the standpoint of international justice you will say "how can we improve institutions at the supranational level in such a way that states enjoy greater independence and autonomy, are better protected against predators, stronger states in the neighborhood" and so forth. Of course, there is some overlap between these two concerns. But the supranational institutions that will optimally serve the former purpose may not be optimal for the latter, and vice versa. So, it really makes a significant difference which kind of justice you seek to implement.

JMC : Is it possible when we go from international justice to global justice, both concerning principles and institutions, to build on the legacy of international justice to somehow midwife global justice?

TP: Yes, I think this is possible to some extent. Some of the concerns that states have traditionally had and that one might plausibly attribute to states are concerns that can be justified by appeal to individuals. For example, states having a certain degree of autonomy, being left alone, not being interfered with by other stronger states; such self-determination (as it is often called) is an important value in international justice and would remain an important value in global justice. But even here there is a difference. On the international-justice paradigm, you would say that whoever is in power should enjoy this right to self-determination. Self-determination really means that a country's own rulers can determine how this country shall be governed, without interference from foreigners. But if you take the global justice paradigm you will regard not a country's rulers but its people as the true subject of self-determination. The country should be governed in the interest of the people, and if the people happened to rule, if the country happens to be governed in a broadly speaking democratic way, then indeed self-determination in the traditional sense is of great value. But the traditional international-justice type of self-determination has very little value if it is exercised by people like Sani Abacha,[3] or Mobutu Sese Seko,[4] or Suharto,[5] or Gaddafi,[6] or whoever your favorite dictator might be.

JMC: So, people are at the very core of the sense of global justice and of the demands associated with it?

TP: That's right.

V GLOBAL JUSTICE AND DIVERSE INTELLECTUAL TRADITIONS

JMC: Clearly, the global justice agenda is very much an outgrowth of what has been the culture of the Enlightenment?

TP: Yes.

JMC: So, how do we pursue global justice in a world that is somehow shifting toward Asia, toward countries that to some extent are themselves very much

3 President of Nigeria (1993–1998).

4 President of Zaire (Democratic Republic of Congo) (1965–1997).

5 President of Indonesia (1967–1998).

6 Leader of Libya (1969–2011).

attached to a more traditional version of national sovereignty, and therefore what could be the world order to come? How do we go about negotiating this evolution and bringing new versions of sovereignty of rights into the picture?

TP: This is a very good question, and I think there are two things to be said about it. One is that we have to look for these debates to happen in those countries themselves. It is not ultimately productive to come in from the outside and to say to a culture as ancient and as venerable as the Chinese culture, for example, "look guys, nice try for 5,000 years, but you have to start over because we have got some better ideas about how to run countries and how to run the world." This would obviously not be a winning approach. You have to look at the internal debates, really understand something, learn something about Chinese traditions, Chinese thinking, and find there the kinds of levers, memes, and thoughts that are continuous with our Western traditions and say it in a Chinese way if you can find commonalities. And you must also, of course, be prepared to learn from what the Chinese tradition can teach us about justice.

The second point is that one must focus on the essentials. Let me give you one example that seems important in the context of the Asian values debate you were alluding to. The example is that most people in the West, when they think about human rights, think about courtrooms. They say "well, having a human right means that there is some courtroom available somewhere: You go to the police, you make a complaint, you come before a judge, the judge decides, and you get your right." Now this is something that many people in Asian cultures find alien. They do not want a culture like the United States, where everybody, when anything goes wrong, is just looking for someone to sue. They say "we want to resolve our differences in a consensual way, we want to talk with one another, we do not want to run to some umpire or arbitrator whenever we feel hurt or we feel that something has gone wrong." And I think we should be sympathetic to this and think of human rights more generously.

We should ask: What does it really mean for a human right to be realized? Does it require that there be police stations and courts available everywhere for you to go to when you feel that your right has been infringed? Not really. What it means is that you have secure access to the object of the right. So, take as a concrete example, the right to adequate nutrition. China is managing to realize this right, to ensure that in the whole country everybody has enough to eat, without there being a legal system that polices this right. So, there may be no official place for Chinese citizens to go to claim their right in case they are hungry; but then there may be no need for such an official place because the economy and social support system work in such a way that everyone actually has access to adequate food: People have jobs, pensions, family members, or other support or institutions that collectively ensure that everyone has enough to eat. This is how I want to conceive of human rights. A human right requires that everyone has secure access to the object of this human right; it does not require that this access must be achieved in any specific way. How access is achieved is not important enough to be itself prescribed by the human right in question.

JMC: But in a way, it is the optimistic or happy scenario that you are telling us about. It is about achieving and recognizing the universality of human rights within the context of plurality or pluralism, right? But while human rights are the essentials on which we should focus in areas such as economic and social rights, cultural rights, civil and political rights, it is not always possible to find a balanced relationship between universality and plurality or pluralism. So when conflicts arise, how to proceed in order to find a balance between universality and plurality?

TP: When conflicts arise, then we may need to think about contraction. If some particular human right that we strongly believe in is contested in many countries, then perhaps we should not at this point insist on its inclusion on the list of human rights acceptance of which is required from all states as a precondition for their recognition as members in good standing of the international community of nations. For example, we should not say that any country that does not have a parliamentary democracy must be excluded from the community of nations, must not be allowed to be a full member in international organizations; this would be too demanding a standard, at least for now. Maybe in the long run we want to aspire to that, but for the moment, I think, we need to contract our notion of human rights in such a way that we focus on the goods that are widely accepted as essential.

It is widely accepted as essential that there be some form of democratic participation, but this may be weaker than parliamentary democracy. And again, it is widely accepted that there be some form of freedom of expression, but this may demand less than a completely free press on the Anglo-American model. In regard to social and economic rights we may actually be in better shape in that there is widespread agreement that each state's institutional arrangements, and also supranational institutional arrangements, must – insofar as is reasonably possible – be shaped in such a way that all human beings can meet their basic needs.

VI RELATIONSHIPS BETWEEN INTERNATIONAL AND GLOBAL JUSTICE AND INTERNATIONAL ORGANIZATIONS

JMC: Focusing on global justice, does it mean that we should abandon altogether what has been at the core of international justice or not? Can we bring the two approaches together?

TP: We should emphasize the continuities as much as we can and we should work for gradual changes toward a more global-justice-friendly institutional design. The example of self-determination, which I gave earlier, can help answer your question. Traditionally, it was conceived that whoever exercises effective power within a state should be recognized by outsiders as representing this state and should be allowed to determine its fate. Outsiders should defer to him or her or them, should not try to interfere or intervene in the internal affairs of the country. Now this is fine to a certain extent but, as I said, such deference should not be accorded to any old ruler or ruling elite.

Such deference is merited by a government insofar as it really represents the will and interests of the people. Insofar as this connection between the people and their rulers becomes tenuous – as in the cases I mentioned earlier – in those cases self-determination has little moral weight. Saying this goes against the traditional understanding of international justice according to which the equal standing of states required that outsiders should not invoke their own judgment about how legitimate or appropriate some government may be, according to which governments should all recognize one another as equals in a kind of gentlemen's agreement, regardless of whether they are dictatorial or democratic, fascist, liberal, socialist, or whatever. The new global-justice paradigm departs from this gentlemen's agreement by recognizing that it is *for the sake of a country's people* that outsiders should accord self-determination to it. In cases where the government is oppressive and unrepresentative, as for example in the case of Burma when it was ruled by a military dictatorship, self-determination has little moral weight or none at all.

JMC: But of course, for this agenda of global justice to go forward it needs advocates, and advocates beyond philosophy and philosophers. In the context of your work you interact a lot with the United Nations system, with practitioners, with member states. Do you feel that beyond the intellectual traction that the agenda of global justice has now, do you feel that member states and UN organizations are open to the idea of going beyond international justice in normative terms, in policy terms, and so on?

TP: Yes, I think that there is definitely a willingness to go beyond international justice. But, one has to be careful because this willingness may not always, or even often, be inspired by the same moral commitments that inspire me. It is often not about wanting to protect people better or something like that. It is often about gaining a better chance to implement one's own interests. Thus, strong states have exploited this idea of a people-focused conception of justice in order to advance their own interests. They say – in regard to certain oil-rich countries that are badly governed, for instance – "well look at this injustice! These brutal autocrats are oppressing the people, and we should help liberate the people through regime change."

Now, I am all in favor of liberating the people. But it is telling that this eagerness on the part of Great Powers to liberate oppressed peoples is so very strongly focused on countries that are resource-rich and unwilling to sell their natural resources on favorable terms. Oppression is ignored in countries that are resource-poor, like Egypt, and oppression is tolerated in countries that are willing to sell their resources cheaply, like Equatorial Guinea.

JMC: Also, one could argue that this global justice agenda is a liberal Western agenda. So, in your conversations, in your debates, in your interactions with colleagues, philosophers, policy-makers, from developing countries in Asia, in Africa, and so on, how do they view your plea for global justice and do they give you suggestions regarding how to go beyond the fact that it is partly a liberal Western agenda?

TP: Yes, what I find in the developing world is indeed the suspicion you are suggesting. I think the best way to deal with it is just to be very upfront about it. The global-justice concern that governments should be broadly representative of the needs and interests of the people they rule can be deployed in a one-sided way for partisan political ends. So can any moral principle or value. This is not a reason to abandon sound moral principles but rather a reason to criticize those who apply such principles one-sidedly. I can then say to critics from the developing world: "I share your suspicions and I reject one-sidedness at least as much as you do, if not more so, because I am a member of the Western culture and for me it is personally shameful to see the double standard with which countries that I have lived in and that I feel I culturally belong to are applying to their interactions with oppressive regimes."

We can avoid association with such politically motivated double standards by making our own theory clear and by criticizing forcefully some of the policies that Western states are pursuing. We can distance the theory of global justice from these dubious uses of it and we can also point to the great critical potential that this sort of theorizing about justice has for the domestic and foreign policies of developed countries. Developing countries – India and China are examples – could often profit greatly from some of the transparency, the concern for individual rights that are part and parcel of recent theorizing about global justice. The governments of these countries should provide to their people not merely security and opportunities for economic betterment, but also transparent institutions securing the rule of law and genuine democratic participation. Such calls for transparency and accountability of political power, for government by the people and for the people, have tremendous resonance in developing countries. And this resonance shows once more that these are valuable ideas that should not be dismissed just because certain Western powers are abusing them, are seeking to take advantage of them.

JMC: *Implicitly implicitly when we think, or when we try to think, about global justice, somehow we are calling for a greater sense of social and economic and political integration. Basically, this is what we have in mind. So the question is: Is it truly possible to achieve greater and better social, economic, and political integration while keeping in place structures having to do with the nation-state? How do we achieve greater social, economic, and better integration while having the nation-state still in place and motivated first and foremost by the national interest?*

TP: You are entirely right; we want more global integration and we want this because modern technologies, modern ways of life, the modern economy, simply make it necessary. If we all continue to puddle along in our respective nation-states according to our own principles and preferences, then we will ignore the ever-greater externalities that our conduct inflicts upon foreigners and we will then be caught in a massive collective action problem that will really seriously diminish our chances even to see the end of this millennium, let alone to survive and thrive beyond it. So, I think globalization in the sense of closer global integration is a necessity. And existing and newly emerging technologies are exerting strong pressures toward global integration.

So the interesting question is *how* it will happen. *Which* globalization will we have? Will we have a globalization that will serve the interests of all human beings or will it be one heavily dominated by a narrow "elite"? And then, secondly, as you were asking, will it be a globalization in which states will retain much of their current power and autonomy or will it be a globalization in which states will gradually fade away? Now, on that second question I think we should fight for a globalization that will gradually make states fade into the background. I do not want states to fade from the scene altogether. I think states as political units are important in enabling populations to maintain a common and distinctive culture. We do not want the whole world to be a US-style melting pot in which all cultures merge into one mono-cultural brew. It is a wonderful thing that we have alternative models of community, alternative models of social, economic, and political organization, underpinned perhaps by alternative philosophical, moral, or religious visions and ideas.

What I have in mind is something more like the European Union, where France, for instance, has a very distinctive culture and deliberately maintains this culture. The art, the novels, the movies in France continue to be distinctive and different from those in the rest of Europe. I mention France because it is the most distinctive country in the European Union, the one that has managed, I think, to the greatest extent to maintain its own personality and its own culture and is also most consciously pursuing this goal; and I think this is wonderful. Europe would be much poorer if everything ran on the Deutsche Bank model, from Northern Finland down to Sicily. So, it is good that we have this cultural diversity and good that we have political units like states. But why does it have to be only that one kind of unit? Why cannot we have nested units of several kinds, including provinces and autonomous cities and municipalities that allow their populations partially to shield themselves against the encroachment of the rest of the world, to maintain separate cultures, separate communities, distinctive ways of organizing themselves? Having such distinctive units on several levels would help ensure that none of them become so powerful or so invested with patriotic sentiment that collective violence can easily break out. So, a kind of globalized, law-governed European Union would be, I think, the best model for where I want the world to be.

VII THE EXAMPLE OF THE EUROPEAN UNION

JMC: But isn't it a paradox? You said earlier that for us to have a better, greater form of social, economic, and political integration, the state has to some extent fade away. Yet at the same time – and this is one of the lessons of the European Union – in order for integration beyond the state to happen we need effective, powerful states; and, of course, while it is a tool for this to happen, it also becomes an obstacle because a so-called post-national organization can be hampered by these states. So, how do we manage this kind of paradox?

TP: Well, we need powerful states in order to make the transition but we do not necessarily need powerful states at the end of this transition. Think once more about the future of the European Union. I am not trying to make any predictions, just laying out how it might go. At the moment, states within the European Union still dwarf the European Union itself in terms of their power, and you can see this easily not just in regard to military might but also in regard to economic strength, where the state budget of a single EU member state like Germany or France is some ten times larger than the entire budget of the twenty-eight-member EU.[7] Now this does not need to be this way, right? One possible future will see the European Union strengthen relative to its member states to the point where the EU might have a similar budget, on a *per capita* basis, as its member states. This trend might be accompanied also by a strengthening of subnational units so that, in the end, governance is more equally spread over the various levels rather than heavily concentrated at the level of the state.

And it is not just a matter of budget. The EU should seriously take on the functions that are better handled at the EU level than at the level of member states. This includes especially foreign and military policy. It would be very helpful in dealing with things like the crisis in the former Yugoslavia, or with our participation in the NATO operation in Libya, if, instead of having all these different countries each pursuing its own interests and policies, we had a common voice of Europe making decisions for all EU countries, if necessary by majority rule. So, I hope that Europe will get its act together in these ways. It would then be a model of what I also hope to see at the global level, namely a hierarchy of nested political units without one crushingly dominant level as we now have with the level of states absorbing the overwhelming majority of tax revenues. Governance functions and tax revenues should be more evenly distributed over all these levels, using the principle of subsidiarity as a guideline.

JMC: Clearly, you think that there are lessons that we can draw from the European Union. I tend to agree with you. One of the key lessons is that the exercise of public policy at the regional level is an interesting one and we should look into whether or not public policy at the global level is a serious scenario for the future in terms of a better form of integration. So if it is the case, in your view – and I know that you are very much interested in the practical aspects and implications of your theoretical thinking – if public policy at the global level is a scenario that we have to take seriously, what would be the intellectual and policy challenges? Perhaps, also, what would be the political challenges for global policy to become a reality?

TP: The great challenge is to make sure that the moral voice is heard and that the moral imperatives, the moral values that we want to inject in this globalization process, really play a role. Here one needs something a bit like judo. Moral motivations are, in the history of humankind and the foreseeable future, not going to be politically very powerful motivations; they are not going

7 The annual EU budget is currently about $150 billion, while the German and French annual government budgets are about $1500 and $1400 billion, respectively.

to play the dominant role in world affairs. We who are thinking about the question in moral terms and more specifically in terms of global justice must therefore try to collaborate with prudential forces in ways that redirect these forces somewhat, in a more moral direction.

The Great Powers are obviously in one sense pro-globalization and in one sense against, powers like the United States. On the one hand, they like globalization, not merely for the access it affords to markets and resources, but also because they worry about all these externalities, all these threats they need to control. The US puts it very openly and calls itself a nation with global interests. It has interests absolutely everywhere because it needs to control resources, it needs to control climate change, it needs to control military technologies, and it needs to control pathogens, bacteria, viruses, and so on. So, it needs to create a world in which all these matters are under some sort of common supervision, in which nations can no longer just do their own thing unmolested – North Korea style – within their own borders: build their own nuclear arsenals or other dangerous technologies, for example.

And this makes sense, of course. But the question is: Do we want this supervision to be run by the United States? We do not, I take it. Nor is there much chance of this coming to pass. The Chinese are not going to allow it to happen, the Russians are going to resist it, and the emerging powers of India, Indonesia, Brazil, South Africa, Nigeria are also not going to accept for long a world under US supervision. If the most serious threats posed by sovereign states are to be controlled – and we absolutely must learn to control them if we are to reach the fourth millennium – then we must persuade the United States to give up part of its own sovereignty, to accept the authority of supranational courts and legislative procedures. This would involve the US in a common quest to reduce international economic inequalities and to relieve the anxieties that other countries are feeling in the face of its enormous military superiority.

So, it is a kind of negotiation where different countries have a great deal to gain, I think, from a negotiated settlement that will restrict the sovereignty of states, what states can do unencumbered by other states. Each state has much more to gain from other states giving up some of this sovereignty than it has to lose from its own giving up some of this sovereignty. But, of course, progress in this direction can still be blocked if states cannot agree on precise terms. This is where morality can come in as an additional force that pushes things in the right direction. When one great power is blocking the way toward a rule-governed world order, we may be able to convince its population by showing that holding out for a better deal, for a continued hegemonic role, is not merely dangerous (because there might then be no deal at all), but also immoral by claiming special privileges that cannot be afforded to all. We could say to the US population, for example: "It would be wrong to use the superior military and economic strength you currently possess in an effort to lock in more favorable terms for oneself, to demand more supervision than you are willing to grant to others, to demand lighter burdens for yourselves in the fight against the common problems of undernourishment, disease, climate change, and so on. Any restructuring of our planet to make it safe for the future must take account of the interests of all human beings equally, with no extra weight given to the richest or most powerful nations or families."

JMC: You are describing a multi-polar world, with the European Union, Asia (China), and the US regions. One of the dangers is that these poles could be competing in a self-defeating fashion. After all, the European project is partly a project designed to have European countries, now too small to compete at the global level, working together and being able to compete globally. Another difficulty concerns the integration of newly emerging countries. How does one achieve better integration in the midst of such competition among powers and regions at the global level?

TP: I think you put your finger on exactly the problem because that is the other future ahead of us, the alternative to a rule-governed and just global order of equals. The other future is one where you have blocs of relatively powerful, relatively wealthy countries that coexist in an unstable and somewhat dangerous competition and organize the world so as to preserve their advantaged position against the other two-thirds of the human population, those who are either subordinates in one of the blocks or marginalized and impoverished at the periphery. This future is to be avoided, and it is a real danger because it may very well be the future that self-interested bargaining would produce.

Now, of course, I have hope that our actual future will not be determined by self-interested bargaining, that morality can make at least some difference. This hope is fueled in part by the positive experience of the European Union, which can serve as a prominent model. To be sure, the European Union is today imperfect in several ways, but with some luck it will be a much more appealing model in, let us say, ten or twenty years. And people everywhere will then aspire to the same kind of transition that Europe will have achieved: away from the power politics that dominated Europe for centuries and toward a law-governed cooperation under just and democratically legitimated rules.

The prospect of such rule-governed cooperation is strengthened by confidence that we can create a world of sufficiency, a world in which everyone can enjoy the essentials of a worthwhile life. This will not be a world in which populations around the world will all enjoy roughly the same standard of living; Africa will probably continue to have a lower standard of living for the foreseeable future. But it can and should be a world in which Africa – the African Union – will be accepted as an equal partner in working out the common institutions that govern the whole world.

The prospect of such a rule-governed, broadly democratic world is further strengthened by a culture of globalization. The creative leaders in science and technology, arts and humanities, music and movies, sports and entertainment, business and finance, politics and religion – these leaders increasingly come from all different demographic backgrounds. There is still great inequality, but this inequality is becoming increasingly "anonymized," that is, disconnected from its traditional markers such as gender, race, ethnicity, language, religion, nationality. And this makes it much harder to exclude entire regions or cultures from a meaningful role in global governance: harder to relegate them to the role of mere rule-takers (as was the fate of the "Third World" under colonialism and neocolonialism) and harder also to erect some literal or metaphorical "separation wall" between the privileged haves and the struggling have-nots.

JMC: On this issue of growing disparities between rich and poor, isn't it ironic that while the global justice agenda seems to be getting more and more attention, somehow we are having more and more trouble trying to achieve justice at the local level, partly because the gap is growing between rich and poor people?

But before addressing this issue of disparity between rich and poor, I want to go back to the question of Europe and the world. And on this I have two questions. First, concerning Europe, you are telling us there is something seductive about the European project. But one could also argue that the European project is a parochial one, at times giving the impression that it is essentially all about Europe, and one of the expressions of this fact is that we do not really have a European foreign policy. So how can the European model guide us when in fact it is quite parochial? Second, the nature and evolution of the relationships between Europe, China, and the US are somewhat puzzling. On the one hand, concerning the US and Europe, clearly they share the same values, they have more or less the same political culture, and yet it seems that they are less and less speaking the same language. On the other hand, China and America, although they do not have the same political values, they do not have the same political culture, seem to be more and more speaking the same language, which is the language of power and status. What do you make of this situation?

TP: I agree with you that Europe has not yet managed to forge a common foreign policy and a common vision of what it wants the world to be like in 2100. This is indeed a serious failing, which was painfully in evidence, for instance, during the Yugoslavia crisis. But this fact, that, as you put it, Europe has been all about Europe and the Europeans, does not disqualify Europe from being a model. If we think of Europe as a model for the world, then its lack of a common foreign-policy perspective does not matter – the world at large needs no foreign policy. In this global use of the model, what matters is not that Europe should *have* a vision of a future world but rather that it should *embody* such a vision.

And even if we think of Europe as a regional model, as a model for Africa, say, it would not be so bad for Africa to be, at least initially, all about Africa and Africans: about creating a continent-wide system of justice and democratically legitimated rules that would safeguard human rights and secure meaningful social, economic, and political participation for all inhabitants of that wonderful continent. But then it would indeed be even better, nonetheless, for such a unified Africa to develop also a common foreign policy, including common demands on the institutional organization of the world, all grounded in the shared interests, culture, and values of Africa. As with Europe, Africa will be more successful in making the world hospitable to its values and interests if it can speak with one voice in the international fora where global institutional arrangements are discussed, negotiated, and designed.

Coming now to your interesting remarks on Europe, China, and the US, I basically agree that, even though the US has close historical and cultural ties to Europe, its international politics now has more in common with China's. This is partly just a matter of the nature and geopolitical place of these three entities. China and the US are large, homogeneous states, each headed by an enormously powerful central government (with annual spending of $3 trillion and $4 trillion, respectively) – governments that both can plausibly harbor the ambition to dominate at least a substantial part of the world. The US seeks domination because it has enjoyed domination after World War II and also because it sees itself as possessing the best economic and political system as well as the best ideas for how the rest of the world should be organized. China seeks domination mainly because it wants to protect itself against the containment it was subjected to for much of its recent history and, even more urgently, against the horrendous destruction and humiliations it had suffered earlier, from the Opium Wars to the 1949 Revolution. The result is similar: Two powerful states with imperial ambitions and an "America First" kind of ideology.

Europe is different. It lacks the inner unity of the other two single-state power centers. Moreover, Europe's global importance is clearly in decline, as is most evident from its rapidly shrinking share of the global population, which contributes to its lacking the military power and economic strength to be a serious contender for world domination. Europe has then a natural interest in a world that is dominated not by some super-powerful state but by widely respected and morally plausible rules impartially interpreted by an independent judiciary. Europe could hope to do well in such a world, and Europe can also hope to derive soft power from promoting such a world in alliance with the rising powers of Asia, Africa, and Latin America and perhaps also Japan, Australia, Canada, and New Zealand. This is a somewhat hopeful prospect, actually: Europe as the least aggressive Great Power, preferred over the US and China by most of the smaller countries who share Europe's natural interest in the marginalization of military power and the ascendancy of effective legal mechanisms for the peaceful resolution of interstate conflicts.

VIII GLOBAL AND LOCAL INEQUALITIES AND JUSTICE

JMC: To go back to the tension between global justice and local justice, does it make sense to pursue global justice while justice at the local level is being undermined or under threat?

TP: First of all, it is not merely justice at the local level, but also justice at the global level. Inequalities are rising locally but they are also rising globally. So, in a sense, it is nice that we have this burgeoning concern with justice just at the moment when it is needed, right? In a sense that is a good thing. Yes, things are going in the wrong direction. The last thirty years have been a disaster for justice; I agree with that. Locally and globally things have gone very badly in the wrong direction in most countries and in the world at large, but that is exactly what we need justice for to try to reverse that trend, to try to raise consciousness, to make people aware of it.

Now the second thing is that the local injustice that is really on the rise, as you say, is on the rise for reasons that have deep global roots. I think globalization is a very important element of this increase in intra-national inequality. And there are two ways of looking at that. One way of looking at it is to say that as rules are shifting upward, as more and more of the rules that govern, let us say, economic transactions, financial markets, and so on are made at the global supranational level, the number of agents who can have meaningful influence on the shaping of this rule actually shrinks. You would think that if the rules are made at a higher level more people have influence: No, fewer people have influence. When there is a bill pending in the French Parliament we know what to do. We know ahead of time what the bill is, we can weigh in, we can organize petitions, we can have demonstrations and so on and so forth. If there is a treaty text pending at the supranational level you would be very lucky to find out what it is before it gets announced as adopted. And it would be very difficult for you to influence in any meaningful way, for you or for any citizen to influence in any meaningful way, what goes on in these supranational negotiations. But who has an influence?

Well it is a very, very small group of very powerful corporations and industry associations and banks and so on. They know these things beforehand and they can lobby through the most powerful governments like the US, China, and so on and really influence these negotiations, and their influence is almost unopposed because the rest of civil society is essentially excluded even from knowing what is being negotiated, let alone from being able to have any kind of influence. And that in turn of course means that when this very small group of powerful economic actors can design the global rules, the supranational rules, essentially as they please, then that enables them to design them in a way that strengthens their economic position at the expense of those excluded.

And those excluded include the rest of the people in their own country who are not at the table. So, for example, intellectual property rights are heavily regulated by the WTO agreement, through its Annex 1C, the agreement on Trade Related Aspects of Intellectual Property Rights (TRIPS), which prescribes what intellectual property rights protections countries must minimally adopt as a condition of membership in the WTO. Now look in the same WTO treaty and look for protections of workers, for labor rights. Nothing there. Labor rights are left to the discretion of the various member states, which are thus drawn into some race to the bottom, into a competition where they must attract foreign capital by offering ever more exploitable and mistreatable work forces.

JMC: But historically property rights in Western capitalism have always been more protected than labor rights or human rights.

TP: Yes, this is right. But there is still an important difference. In the domestic theater of decision-making, ordinary workers have much greater capabilities to fight for their rights, for instance by means of strikes and the ballot box. To be sure, money can exert an enormous political influence, especially in the US. But universal suffrage remains a powerful tool of resistance, enabling ordinary people to reshape political parties or to form new ones. If a large proportion of the population gets frustrated enough, then even large amounts of political money are not going to keep them down. And there are then limits to how unfair the rules can become to the poorer majority of a democratic country. These limits are absent at the supranational level, where governments have a much freer hand, where it is much harder even for a large majority of humankind to resist the imposition of rules that are blatantly unfair to them. In democracies, the voters can punish their incumbent politicians, to be sure. But these politicians will say – often truthfully – that the supranational rules they agreed to were, overall, the best deal they could get for their country, that accepting the TRIPS Agreement was better than declining to join the WTO.

JMC: *So, global justice requires a global polity in the context of which people would have a say and would be given the means to control the small elite?*

TP: Yes, this is what it requires! Not in any logical sense, but in a practical, political sense. We will not get just supranational rules without it. If we allow global rules to be made by a small elite of government representatives who basically do the bidding of the strongest lobbies in their own home countries, then we can expect highly unjust outcomes that completely disregard the interests of the vast majority of human beings. To avoid this, we need to move to a system where the interests of the large majority of humankind are at least clearly articulated in these negotiations, so that there is someone at the table who will point out the adverse effects of contemplated rules on poorer segments of the human population. It would be even much better, of course, if the interests of these poorer segments were represented by negotiators with a genuine voice and vote, competent people who could protect the interests of the global majority in the decision-making. What global justice requires here is that the interests of the poorer majority of humankind should be as well represented in international negotiations as the interests of the poorer majority of a national population are currently represented in the political process of the advanced democracies, of Norway, France, or Germany, say.

IX GLOBAL GOVERNANCE AND ACCOUNTABILITY

JMC: *How do we enhance the ways through which we can really increase participation and accountability at the global level? In the end, how do we do this?*

TP: I think the only way to do it is through the media and the people. Politicians are happy with the system as it is because it gives them cover for unpopular decisions. The large corporations and banks are happy with the system as it is because they have huge advantages in the game of supranational lobbying – in fact, they often lobby unopposed as only they have the inside information and expertise to meaningfully influence the agenda and outcomes at the WTO, G-20, UN, IMF, and so on. The shift from national to supranational rule-making in conjunction with the crushing advantage wealth confers in supranational lobbying goes a long way toward explaining that the poorest 80, even 90, percent of the US population have seen no meaningful improvement in their economic situation in the last thirty-four years.[8] They are no better off than their parents or grandparents were despite the fact that *per capita* productivity and the average income in the United States has risen quite nicely. But all these gains have gone to a small elite – to the big owners of capital and the top executives of the larger firms, to those who were able to bend the economic rules in their favor in national and especially supranational negotiations.

JMC: The issues that you are putting on the table as part of our conversation tend not to be at the center of the public political discourse, be it at the national level or at the global level. The politicians are not very eager to talk about this. Moreover, even when they are willing to talk about these problems, clearly they do not have the answers.

TP: Yes, the politicians, as I said, the politicians like the system as it is. They basically get large amounts of money and other support from the big banks, hedge funds, and corporations as well as from their top executives, and so long as the rest of the people do not really understand how the system works and more or less accept it, politicians are not going to rock the boat – with a few exceptions, of course, such as Bernie Sanders and Elizabeth Warren. But there is nonetheless a lot of popular discontent in the wake of the global financial crisis, and people do understand, of course, that their generation has not enjoyed the kind of economic gains that previous generations had enjoyed. People do understand that their prospects for a comfortable retirement were severely set back by the bail-outs and subsequent low-interest policies. And people do understand that tiny so-called elites – the leaders in business and finance as well as the top politicians, and especially those who manage to jump back and forth between political and commercial job (through the proverbial "revolving door") – are capturing the lion's share of economic growth. There is a lot of popular anger, especially in the US, and the next recession could turn quite ugly.

8 See the "hockey stick" chart in the *New York Times*, which also allows comparisons with earlier 34-year periods, at www.nytimes.com/interactive/2017/08/07/opinion/leonhardt-income-inequality.html.

X GLOBAL HEALTH

JMC: So this is the big picture on globalization. Perhaps as a way to finish our conversation, I want to link what has been your intellectual trajectory with all these issues. You started, many years ago, with a reading and a critique of Rawls's theory of justice, at least the international dimension of his theory. Then you worked on identifying the principles and responsibilities of justice at the global level, in particular in connection with world poverty; and now you are focusing on global justice in connection with issues of health. What led you to this journey and why is it that you are now focusing on health issues?

TP: I started with Rawls because I thought that he was a very important and widely revered theorist in the US context, who really had managed to appeal to and to resonate with much of the US intelligentsia. And I felt that some of the ideas he had introduced into the discussion were extremely useful, especially the focus on social institutions, on the way societies are structured and organized. I thought that Rawls's work could be very useful for getting people to think in the right structural way also about global institutional arrangements and their great influence on the evolution of economic inequalities.

I was then increasingly interested in issues of poverty because I appreciated the importance of the economy for the realization of all human rights, not merely economic ones. It is very difficult for people to be respected in the political sphere, in the social sphere, for their civil rights to be respected, if they are really poor and thus excessively dependent on others for employment and support as well as effectively unable to resist violation of their rights. It is also very difficult to shape rules in the political arena in a way that conforms to justice if economic power is so unevenly distributed that a few people can essentially dictate the terms under which everybody lives. So, I saw the economy as exceedingly important and I wanted to make progress toward a theory and also practice of global justice that understand why economic inequality is increasing, why poverty is persisting, why so many people are effectively excluded from political decision-making.

The health focus came in through a number of things. It was historically very contingent. I was invited to spend a year at the National Institutes of Health and just got interested in health issues. But health is an important part of that vicious cycle that keeps so many people from having a worthwhile human life. They are poor, and because they are poor they are vulnerable to disease; because they are poor they cannot then overcome their disease, they cannot go to the doctor, they cannot get the right medications, and then they become even poorer as a consequence of being sick and of not being able to work or as a consequence of being forced to stay home to look after a child that may be very ill. So disease is a very important part of the poverty nexus, and we who are relatively well-off and thus can maintain our good health well into old age, we just do not realize how important health issues are for the poorer half of the human population.

During my NIH year (2003–2004) I hit upon this wonderful idea of the Health Impact Fund (HIF) as something that could really make a difference to the health of the world's poor. The basic idea of the HIF is that we should reward the introduction of new medicines not by giving the innovators a monopoly patent so that they can sell the medicine at extremely high prices during its initial years, but that we should instead reward such innovators, from public funds contributed by many states, on the basis of the health gains they achieve with their new medicine during these early years. To receive these annual reward payments for one of their new products, innovators must forego patent-protected markups: They must sell the product at no more than the cost of production. So this is the basic idea, and I think it is a wonderful win-win where truly everyone would benefit from this new way of incentivizing pharmaceutical innovation. The pharmaceutical industry, for instance, would benefit through new profit opportunities in fighting diseases concentrated among the poor and also through a much-improved public image (selling life-saving medicines at prices that everyone can easily afford).

The HIF could also serve as a model in other areas of innovation such as green technologies, agriculture, and education. For example, in the area of seeds, or in the area of green and clean technologies, we could have similar win-win reforms that would allow the poor to use the innovation at cost. Green technologies could be used by anyone around the world without a licensing fee, and would thus diffuse much more quickly. And the inventors of such technologies would be amply rewarded in proportion to the environmental harms their innovation averts. In this way, the poorest, those who pay no taxes, would free-ride on the innovation efforts, but this would greatly benefit not merely them but also the rest of us: The poor would no longer be breeding grounds for diseases, would use clean technologies, would grow more food with less use of pesticides and fertilizers, and so on.

XI PHILOSOPHY AS RESPONSIBILITY

JMC: Professional philosophers do not necessarily think that it is proper for a philosopher to work on practical issues. So why do you feel that it is part of your mission, part of your responsibility, to really try to connect academic concerns, theoretical concerns, and very practical concerns?

TP: Well, there are two answers to that. One answer is related to your very first question in this interview, when you asked: What is justice? Philosophers tend to answer this question by giving you a string of other complex and abstract words. And then you have a nice colorful Christmas tree of high-level concepts, philosophical concepts, and they are explained one in terms of the others, but, in the end, you do not really know what the whole Christmas tree of concepts actually means in the real world. My point is that, if you really want to answer the question of what justice demands, then you must bring these concepts down to earth. You must define them not merely in terms of one another but must pin them down and say concretely what would count as a society that, say, satisfies Rawls's first principle of justice. How, for example, do we feed statistics about the frequency and distribution of various crimes into the question whether specific demographic groups in the US – young black urban males, say – do or do not in fact enjoy the physical integrity that Rawls's theory of justice entitles them to? These are not questions for economists or lawyers or other experts to answer. Philosophers have to bring their abstract theorizing down to earth as a condition of even saying something meaningful, of even explicating the very meaning of whatever principles they enunciate.

Now, the second point I want to make is that traditionally philosophy has been conceived as the love of wisdom; that is the root, the Greek root of the term. If you asked me what wisdom is, then I would say wisdom is understanding what really matters, what is really important. And one of the things that really matters is that in our world so many people are impoverished, deprived of secure access to the objects of their human rights. To be sure, severe poverty has always existed. But, in contrast to poverty throughout the ages, poverty today is easily avoidable without much cost to anyone. And it is really important that we eradicate such poverty, that we not continue enjoying the privileges of a good life at the expense of large numbers of people excluded from these privileges. So long as they are avoidably excluded, our own lives cannot be truly worthwhile, meaningful, or even decent.

Thus I think it is in the best tradition of philosophy when philosophers highlight issues they identify as important, as something that citizens ought to pay serious attention to. One such important issue, in my view, is the persistence of severe and avoidable poverty: The serious possibility that, through the institutional arrangements we maintain within the affluent states and especially on the supranational level, we are impoverishing and killing millions of people in the poorer regions. This is important, and citizens ought to pay attention to it. Pointing this out – with ample attention to the empirical evidence, of course, as well as to feasible avenues of reform – is very much continuous with the role philosophers have played since ancient times.

JMC: So, for you, focusing on bringing together theoretical concerns and practical concerns is an attempt to really make the life of all these people in need more meaningful but it is also a way for people who are more in a lucky position to make their own life more meaningful because if you are among the lucky ones and you do not care, the very meaning of your life is in question.

TP: Yes, absolutely, we more affluent people face a real danger of having lived at the expense of other people, whose severe impoverishment we are collectively responsible for. And even if we lived tolerably happily in a subjective sense, we would have lived a bad life. Citizens should be aware of this danger, at least, be confronted with it, and be helped to think about it constructively if they so choose.

JMC: As we are approaching the end of this conversation I want to ask you what are the questions you think that you will be working on ten years from now? What will be your agenda ten years down the road in the context of your concerns?

TP: I will probably remain for the rest if my life in this broad orbit of global justice questions. But I do want to get into some important issues other than the ones I have already worked on – though not at the expense of seeing through that Health Impact Fund project, if at all possible. So I see two possible futures ten years down the road. It is possible that I will still be involved in the effort to get the Health Impact Fund up and running and, hopefully, it will be much closer to realization then and perhaps I will even be involved in setting it up. To be sure, building and managing an organization like the Health Impact Fund requires many kinds of expert knowledge and experience, so I could only play a minor role. Still, if the HIF were to become a reality, affording poor people around the world easy access to the medicines they need, then I would regard this as quite a happy outcome.

It is also possible that I will cease work on the Health Impact Fund – either because the political will to institute it cannot be summoned or because it can move toward implementation equally well without my help. In this case, there would be two areas in which I would like to play a greater role.

One is offshore finance, or illicit financial flows, which I think is an extremely important topic.[9] Enormously large amounts of hidden wealth are

9 See Thomas Pogge and Krishen Mehta, eds., *Global Tax Fairness* (Oxford: Oxford University Press, 2016).

sloshing around a nontransparent netherworld of tax havens, populated with secrecy jurisdictions, letterbox companies, sham trusts, and anonymous accounts, along with an army of shady lawyers, accountants, lobbyists, and financial advisors. Such unaccountable money plays a pernicious corrupting role in politics, paying for unmerited privileges and undermining the equality of citizens. And often such money comes straight from the pockets of poor people, is siphoned off in poor countries through tax avoidance, embezzlement, and so on, and then parked in illicit locations, often with the connivance of Western banks or even *in* Western banks with the connivance of Western governments. I want to shine a bright spotlight on all this because doing so strikes me as another win-win proposition. Most people in the rich countries, most taxpayers, are hurt by these opportunities to hide wealth and, of course, the poor countries are losing massive amounts of money in this way. Again, here I think a grand coalition can be formed with prudential and moral interests to dry up this terrible morass, to stabilize the global financial system, and at the same time to ensure that the costs of government are also shared by many of the people who are now stashing their money away into secret accounts.

The second possible area of future work is climate change, pollution, and resource depletion, an area in which great progress can now be made because many people, especially young people, in both poor and rich countries are seeing that this is increasingly a problem that will affect their generation and the generations coming after them.[10] And, yet again, there is a lot of potential mobilization that I can maybe contribute to by articulating the concerns, by channeling them in a direction that makes them politically more effective and by unifying people behind a common platform. This is a global justice issue par excellence and one to which I hope in future years to contribute as well.

JMC: But it will mean retraining yourself, expanding your field of knowledge, learning about new areas. What gives you the energy, the drive to work so hard?

TP: The energy comes simply from the emergency, right? We are living in a world in which so much injustice happens, so much horrendous harm is suffered by people, and I feel that the costs of making the kind of effort I am making are miniscule, ridiculously small compared to the burdens so many poor people are bearing without choice. In view of this disparity, it would be absurd to prioritize a good vacation for myself over meaningful work toward

10 Thomas Pogge has already participated in drafting the Oslo Principles on Climate Change Obligations. See http://globaljustice.macmillan.yale.edu/sites/default/files/files/OsloPrinciples.pdf.

global justice: work that might, for example, bring the Health Impact Fund closer to realization. So long as I am healthy and have my wits about me, I will continue to do this work and, when I can do it no longer, I hope there will be others ready to go on.

JMC: Finally, what would be your advice to a young scholar working in the field of justice?

TP: For those emerging scholars interested in dedicating their life to research and teaching, the key is to stay in touch with the real causes of injustice and with the best people and organizations that combat or seek to reform these causes – whether these be NGOs, international organizations, government agencies, or individual writers or philanthropists. The point of this type of work is to bring positive change, and this we can only do through sizable collaboration/mobilization.

PART III

INTERNATIONAL LAW AND GLOBAL JUSTICE

9

International Law as the Articulation of Universalism and Pluralism

Mireille Delmas-Marty

I CRIMINAL LAW IN THE NATIONAL, EUROPEAN, AND GLOBAL SPHERES

JEAN-MARC COICAUD (JMC): *When in 2002 you started to teach at the Collège de France, the most prestigious academic institution in France,[1] you decided to have your Chair focusing on comparative and international law. But as a young scholar in the field of law, you started by focusing on criminal law. Your work in this area became an important aspect of your academic development and expertise, first, at the national level, then at the European level, and finally at the global level, notably with Professor Cassese. From your point of view, what are the big questions which brought you to the field of criminal law?*

MIREILLE DELMAS-MARTY (MDM): As you just indicated, I started my law studies in private law and criminal law. At the time, business criminal law was a field of study that was not much studied. My dual interest in private law and criminal law led me to work on the question of the responsibility of corporations and, more particularly, on transnational corporations. In this perspective, at the end of the 1970s, with a German colleague I set up a research team on their practices abroad. We analyzed the way transnational corporations used juridical differences from one country to another to avoid criminal justice and accountability – for example by selling in South America dangerous products or medicines forbidden in the North. As part of this research, we also did research on offences and offenders beyond the reach of the law, focusing, on the one hand, on political offenders and, on the other, on

[1] The Collège de France, founded in 1530, is the most prestigious academic institution in France. The Collège, which does not grant degrees, comprises over fifty professors in subjects including mathematics, chemistry, biology, history, philosophy, the social sciences, law, and other fields. The professors elected to the Chairs at the Collège de France are intellectual leaders in their fields.

economic offenders. Interestingly, these topics have now become a very significant area of research. With the establishment of the International Criminal Court (ICC), and the internationalization of war crimes and crimes against humanity, the idea of holding companies legally accountable for being complicit actors in criminal acts is becoming more of a possibility.[2]

JMC: Can you share some concrete examples that address these types of questions?

MDM: For instance, in Africa, in the Great Lakes Region,[3] a number of companies involved in mining and using militias to protect their interests on the ground have found themselves implicated in the crimes committed by these militias. And yet the Statute of the International Criminal Court does not allow prosecution of a corporate entity. The Statute allows prosecution of the heads of state even when holding office, but it does not allow going after corporations since they are not individuals but legal entities. Against this background, discussions have taken place and reform proposals have been circulated concerning the possibility of extending the statute of the Court, so that it can apply to corporate entities. This topic and the evolution of legal views on this question in the field of international criminal law are of great interest to me. Another, related, issue, although of a more philosophical nature, is the one of culpability or dangerousness.

JMC: What is the nature of the distinction that you establish between culpability and dangerousness?

MDM: The notion of culpability is, in principle, part of a classical framework in which it is presumed that the human being has free will. The idea is that a human being is not entirely free but also is not totally predetermined. And because of this significant dimension of free will as part of what it is to be a human being, a human being can be said to be responsible (in the sense of

[2] See the annual meeting organized by the Société française pour le droit international, "L'entreprise multinationale et le droit international" (University of Paris VIII Saint Denis, May 19–21, 2016). Also, in September 2016, the International Criminal Court announced in a policy document released by the ICC's prosecutor that "the Office will give particular consideration to prosecuting Rome Statute crimes that are committed by means of, or that result in, *inter alia*, the destruction of the environment, the illegal exploitation of natural resources or the illegal dispossession of land." This kind of extension could facilitate the persecution of chiefs of companies.

[3] The African Great Lakes are a series of lakes including Lake Victoria, one of the largest fresh water lakes in the world, and Lake Tanganyika. The African Great Lakes Region consists of countries that surround the African Great Lakes. These countries include Burundi, the Democratic Republic of Congo, Kenya, Rwanda, Tanzania, and Uganda.

accountable). It is on this basis that there is a possibility of imputation of responsibility, of criminal responsibility. This is the classical approach to the question of crime. But in recent years, we are seeing the reemergence of a type of thinking that was made popular at the end of the nineteenth century by the Italian School, with scholars like Cesare Lombroso[4] and others. This type of thinking amounts to saying that the real problem is not the effective crime itself but the ability to commit a crime. This is in essence the idea of dangerousness of an actor.

JMC: You mean the dangerousness of the individual?

MDM: I mean the dangerousness of the criminal, or more precisely of the potential criminal. Rather than focusing on the notions of crime and criminal, more attention is given to the notion of the potential criminal, or of the "born criminal," to quote the expression used by Cesare Lombroso. For Lombroso, the "born criminal" was an incomplete human being. He developed this idea on the basis of Darwin's theory of evolution and the reference that at the time he makes to the idea of "unfinished evolution," with some beings appearing as in between the animal and the human. Incidentally, this theory has been used by authoritarian regimes in Europe in the 1930s. In any case, my point here is that we are now witnessing some sort of a comeback of this notion of dangerousness, in Europe as well as in the United States. In Europe, in Germany and in France, for example, there is now the possibility of keeping people in prison who have served their sentence but who are viewed as continuing to be dangerous or a threat to society. This allows for the detention of people for an indefinite period.

JMC: This is the case for what type of crimes?

MDM: Initially, this trend was developed essentially for sexual criminals. But now the list of crimes entering into this configuration has expanded, with other crimes being added to the list. Interestingly, and this gives you an idea of the mind-set that this orientation is conveying, in Germany this tendency takes its roots in a law, the Enabling Act, enacted in 1933, and massively used at the time against political dissidents. This law had become obsolete but was revived by contemporary debates on the criminality of sex crimes and other serious kinds of crime.

[4] Cesare Lombroso (1835–1909) was an Italian criminologist and physician, founder of the Italian School of criminology. Rejecting the views held by the classical school, such as that crime was a characteristic trait of human nature, Lombroso argued that criminality was inherited, and that someone "born criminal" could be identified by physical/congenital defects.

II FEAR AND SURVEILLANCE SOCIETY

JMC: Do you think that this orientation that has taken place in Europe and in the United States is connected with the rise of terrorism in recent years?

MDM: Absolutely. In particular, we find this orientation at work in the notion of "unlawful enemy combatant,"[5] which has especially emerged out of the treatment of prisoners detained in Guantánamo.[6] In Guantánamo, some of the people labelled as criminals could not be brought to trial and judged because they are simply considered dangerous. Their detention has been open-ended, with no right to the presumption of innocence.

JMC: I would imagine that the latest events in terms of terrorist attacks, in particular in France, in 2015 and 2016,[7] are only encouraging a deepening of this approach?

MDM: After the terrorist attacks of January 2015, the Intelligence Act ("loi sur le renseignement") of July 24, 2015 added the component of anticipation to intelligence gathering. With the progress made by digital technology, especially in the context of big data, we are now able to aggregate so much information that the interpretation of it, by integrating techniques of profiling and prediction algorithms, is more a matter of the logic of anticipation than anything else. This amounts to a form of predictive justice that is particularly difficult to control.[8] It is all the more the case considering that anticipation

[5] After September 11, 2001, the notion of "Unlawful enemy combatant" has been referred to by the Bush administration as "a person who has engaged in hostilities or has purposefully and materially supported hostilities against the United States who is not a lawful combatant (including a person who is part of the Taliban, al Qaeda, or associated forces." On this notion, see for instance Nathaniel Berman, "Privileging Combat? Contemporary Conflict and the Legal Construction of War," *Columbia Journal of Transnational Law* (vol. 43, no. 1, 2004).

[6] The Guantánamo Bay detention camp is a United States prison located within Guantánamo Bay Naval Base, which fronts onto Guantánamo Bay in Cuba. At the time of its establishment in January 2002, Secretary of Defense Donald Rumsfeld argued that the prison was established to detain extraordinarily dangerous people, to interrogate detainees, and prosecute detainees for war crimes. In fact, Guantánamo has been used for indefinite detention without trial. Despite commitment of President Obama to close the prison, by the time he left office in early January 2017, although the total number of prisoners had been brought down dramatically, the prison had still not been closed.

[7] France has been the target of a series of terrorist attacks since 2015. In particular, in January 2015 over ten people were killed by terrorists in Paris. In November, still in Paris, terrorist gunmen and suicide bombers left 130 people dead in the streets of Paris and hundreds wounded. And in July 2016 over eighty people died, after a lorry slammed through a crowd celebrating Bastille Day in the southern city of Nice.

[8] M. Delmas-Marty, *Aux quatre vents du monde. Petit guide de navigation sur l'océan de la mondialisation* (Paris: Seuil, 2016), p. 30 sq.

takes place in a variety of ways. For instance, after the second wave of terrorist attacks in Paris, in November 2015, house arrest ("assignation à résidence") has become possible in the context of the state of emergency when it is felt that there are "serious reasons to believe" that the behavior of an individual constitutes a danger to public security and order. This is in contrast to the previous text, which referred to "an activity that is dangerous for public security and order."

JMC: From your point of view, what do this evolution and return of the notion of dangerousness tell you about the evolution of the legal and juridical culture of the moment, and of the political culture?

MDM: It shows that a culture of fear is more and more shaping the contemporary legal and political landscape. This is quite striking. In the past, I have been working with a colleague, Jean Delumeau, who used to hold the Chair of the History of Religious Mentalities at the Collège de France. He wrote on fear in the Western world, in particular from the Middle Ages to the seventeenth century. Jean Delumeau told me that when he started doing his research on fear, a few decades ago,[9] there were very few books on the history of fear, as if fear were taboo. After all, this makes sense since for a long time the focus of the official discourse was on reassurance. But, nowadays, this has changed drastically.[10] What has changed, I think, is the fact that now in the official discourse there is much attention given to fear, and even much use made of fear. Fear has become an instrument of government. This also means that the goal of the official discourse is firstly to alert society of a possible threat and risk; and we alert earlier and earlier. For example, in kindergarten classes, children are taught about all the risks they are running in the course of their daily lives.

JMC: Does this amount to a good prevention policy, or even a prevention culture?

MDM: Well, in any case, living is dangerous. So it is clear that pretending, or looking like you are pretending, that there is no risk is an illusion. The world is effectively dangerous, and perhaps increasingly so. But a culture of fear modifies the tolerance threshold. This means that there is an unstable equilibrium between the degree of protection necessary and the degree of

[9] One of the most famous books published by Jean Delumeau, *La peur en Occident* (not available in English), was published in French in 1978.

[10] See in particular Mireille Delmas-Marty, *Libertés et sûreté dans un monde dangereux* (Paris: Seuil, 2010), and *Terrorismes: histoire et droit*, with Henry Laurens (Paris: CNRS, 2010).

risk which we are willing to take for preserving liberty. This equilibrium and the proportion that comes with it have been changing in recent times. Relying first and foremost on the narrative of risk reduces the scope of liberties in the name of security. I should add that this is a rather endless, if not self-defeating, race since we will never achieve absolute security. There is not such a thing as a "zero-risk life."

JMC: Do you think this quest for absolute security, somehow paradoxically, encourages a culture of paranoia?

MDM: Exactly. This encourages paranoia or, simply put, it can generate a society that is not a politically totalitarian regime but amounts to a surveillance society. Needless to say, this is facilitated by technologies like the internet, which are both a tool of democracy and a tool of surveillance. This is therefore a situation that I find really worrisome for freedoms.

JMC: Liberties are being undermined in the name of security, which is leading to a surveillance society. How do you suggest that we tame or limit this evolution?

MDM: I think that we should work on what I call "ambivalences," or the dual dimension of a number of phenomena and processes. Take the example of the internet. On the one hand, the internet is an instrument of a surveillance society. It practically allows the surveillance of every human being. But the internet is also what has, to some extent, helped social and political movements, such as the Arab Spring, in countries like Tunisia and Egypt. So, the same technology can bring more liberty, or more surveillance, depending on how it is used. Incidentally, I would say the same thing about globalization. Globalization is often demonized, or, on the contrary, we see it as the source of the world's progress. I do not think that it is either positive or negative. Focusing on the negative aspects of globalization, think for instance about the fact that it has been demonstrated that globalization worsens inequalities instead of reducing them. The gaps between the poorest and richest have increased not only within countries but also worldwide. Also, international crimes persist, despite the creation of the International Criminal Court. Environmental damages, another serious type of issue, have also multiplied during the time of globalization. This is to say globalization has created new problems. But at the same time, and now referring to positive aspects of globalization, we have to recognize that globalization is offering means and opportunities which did not exist before, particularly by opening boundaries to goods, to people.

JMC: Globalization is both the problem and the solution?

MDM: Yes, globalization can be both the problem and the solution.

III THE ROLE OF CONCEPTS AND PROCESSES IN THE ANALYSIS OF LAW

JMC: Earlier you referred to the notion of "ambivalence." In relation with this notion, how can we use it so that we can encourage more positive developments?

MDM: As a lawyer and a legal scholar, I will argue that in order to achieve this we need to work more on processes than on concepts.

In my work, I am very attached to working on concepts. This is part of my methodology, if I may say so, in terms of reflecting and trying to make sense of the internationalization of law, particularly in the field of values on the issue of human rights or, indeed, on the other side of human rights, on international crimes such as crimes against humanity. That said, concepts do not necessarily tell the whole story of international law, and of the internationalization of national law. For example, and to continue using the example of human rights, if we take this great founding and iconic text, the Universal Declaration of Human Rights of 1948, and we read the articles one by one, as such focusing on concepts and principles, we might think that this text is an utter failure because none of these principles are well respected throughout the world. But if you examine what the Declaration has changed in the legal world since 1948, that is to say, if one takes this text, and other texts, not as the embodiment of fundamental concepts but as parts of the transforming processes of law, then chances are that we will see very different results and that we will have a positive view. The Declaration has had a tremendous impact. It was followed by and contributed to a number of landmark agreements and instruments dealing with human rights, including regional conventions in Europe, the Americas, and Africa. There were also more focused instruments such as the Convention on the Rights of the Child and the Convention on the Elimination of all forms of Discrimination against Women. The number of conventions that followed and in part build on the Universal Declaration is huge. It is such that we can say that these conventions introduced a form of legal revolution. This is to the point that now in a number of states, through the European Court of Human Rights, even countries like France and the United Kingdom, which consider themselves homes of human rights, may be prosecuted and sentenced at the request of a victim, of a single person who has been the victim of a violation of its rights. This is an extraordinary revolution, which to a large extent has derived from the Universal Declaration. By focusing on processes and not only on concepts or principles, we can see that revolution at work.

JMC: The negative side of an approach focusing on concepts is that the gap between concepts and reality may be wide, whereas if we focus on the process, we are able to see the triggering and interlocking effects?

MDM: Yes, I think it is a way to be aware of the dynamic of the internationalization of law and to try to understand how this dynamic takes place and unfolds. Working on movement, on the triggering, or blocking, or regressing factors, because processes are not necessarily linear, is a key aspect of law and of its evolution, in fact as much at the national level as at the international level.

Such evolution does not happen all at once. There are some offshoots. Take, for example, the International Criminal Court. We could say that Nuremberg is a first version or first draft of it. But Nuremberg was still a form of victor's justice. Afterwards, there have been projects that have led to nothing. It was not until the 1990s that the ad hoc tribunals for the former Yugoslavia and Rwanda were created (and I should say here, since you mentioned his name earlier, that my colleague and friend the legal scholar Antonio Cassese played an important role in the context of these ad hoc tribunals[11]). At the time, some criticized the ad hoc tribunals as possibly setting precedent for blocking the coming of a permanent international criminal court. But in fact that was not the case: on the contrary. Instead, these tribunals have served as a useful intermediate step, a kind of laboratory to test the feasibility of a permanent international criminal court. Subsequently, the Permanent Court was created by the Rome Statute. At the time, many commentators said that The Statute will never take effect because major powers, in particular the United States and China, were opposed to it. And it is true that during that period the United States concluded bilateral treaties in order to try to prevent a number of states from ratifying The Statute. Yet this did not prevent anything. The Court was created in 2002. Over time it began operating and, gradually, asserted its authority.

[11] Antonio Cassese (1937–2011) was an Italian jurist who specialized in public international law. He was the first president of the ad hoc international criminal Tribunal for the Former Yugoslavia (ICTY) and the first President of the Special Tribunal for Lebanon, which he presided over until his resignation in 2011 on health grounds. A prolific scholar, he published extensively on international human rights law and international criminal law.

In this regard, to the surprise of most commentators, the Security Council itself decided to seize the International Criminal Court (ICC)[12] on the issue of Libya. Regardless of what happened to Muammar Gaddafi afterwards,[13] it was a step forward that the Security Council Members, including those who had veto power like the United States and China, decided to join forces with the ICC on the matter. That said, we have also to keep in mind that in the fall of 2016 South Africa decided to withdraw from the ICC, while other African countries are also considering leaving the scope of ICC.

In any case, that is why the distinction between concept and process is useful as a way to see and understand international law both in a conceptual and dynamic fashion, so that we keep in mind the movements, the speeds, blocks, and hindrances, etc., through and by which national and international law evolve. Also, we have to keep in mind how the transformation rates may be different from one sphere of law to another.

IV LEGAL CHANGE AND THE GLOBALIZATION OF LAW

JMC: *This type of approach to law, and to international law in particular, is not very traditional. This is not the type of approach that is practiced by mainstream legal scholars?*

MDM: You are right. When I was lecturing at the Collège de France about what I have called "ordering pluralism," I was working on the issue of speed. As such, when I lectured for two hours on the issue of processing speed in normative spaces, it created some surprise among the audience attending the lecture. At the time, in fact, I was exploring two phenomena, what I have called "polychrony" and "asynchrony."[14]

[12] On February 26, 2011 the United Nations Security Council, by a unanimous resolution, referred Libya to the International Court of Justice. In May 2011, the chief International Criminal Court prosecutor, Luis Moreno-Ocampo, having grounds to believe that he had ordered attacks on civilians during Libya's uprising in the spring of 2011, issued an arrest warrant for Libyan leader Colonel Muammar Gaddafi, accusing him of crimes against humanity.

[13] Muammar Gaddafi died in October 2011. Captured by insurgents, he was killed shortly afterwards.

[14] Mireille Delmas-Marty, *Ordering Pluralism: A Conceptual Framework for Understanding the Transnational Legal World*, translated by Naomi Norberg, foreword by Stephen Breyer (Oxford: Hart Publishing, 2009), p. 119 sq and p.133 sq.

There is polychrony when a unique normative space can operate at different speeds. In Europe, for instance, we see this in the case of the Schengen Area.[15] In the context of the European Union it amounts to a group of states that is willing to go faster and deeper than others (in terms of integration) and that agreed on incorporating certain standards of freedom of movement before the others. As for other European Union members, they have the possibility to join when they want or when they can. Another example of polychrony, which I find more interesting because it concerns a global scale, is related to the Kyoto Protocol.[16] With the Kyoto Protocol, we have a text that includes an annex of different categories of countries that must comply with the Kyoto standards with a different schedule, which seems quite logical considering the differences of situation existing between countries. So, in essence, we have a reference to the idea of different schedules according to the situation of countries: a schedule for already industrialized countries, one for emerging countries, and another one for developing countries. This model, limited to two figures, was still too reductive. As a result, the Paris Agreement[17] (December 2015) enlarges the operationalization of the principle of "shared but differentiated responsibilities" that takes into account the national context in all its past (historical context) and present (economic, social, and cultural context) dimensions. This enlargement was necessary in order to evaluate the responsibility of each according to criteria allowing a more objective differentiation.

JMC: Is your research on the various rhythms of law linked to the overall reflection you have been conducting for the past ten years, at least, on the need to globalize law?

15 The Schengen Agreement was signed in 1985 by five of the ten-member Economic European Community (EEC). It led to the creation of the Schengen Area, established in 1995 in Europe, which includes twenty-six European countries that have abolished border control at their mutual borders. It mostly functions as a single country for international travel purposes, with a common visa policy.

16 The Kyoto Protocol, which was signed in 1997 and became effective in 2005, in an international agreement linked to the United Nations Framework Convention on Climate Change (UNFCC). It is meant to commit States Parties to reduce greenhouse gas emissions, based on the premise that global warming exists and that human-made CO_2 emissions have caused it.

17 The Paris Agreement entered into force on November 4, 2016, and aims to combat climate change, adapt to its effects, and provide enhanced assistance for developing countries to do so. In total, 197 countries are party to the Paris Agreement and as of April 2017, 144 countries have ratified the treaty.

MDM: In part. As I recall, my work in this field of law started with a book that I published in French in 1994, and which was then published in English in 2002.[18]

JMC: How did you come to think that it was imperative to address change and the mechanisms of change in law, including in terms of the European context, international law, and the globalization of law?

MDM: Actually, it is by observing what was happening in the field of law that I came to analyze these issues and to think that they were important. More specifically, by observing how the different legal spheres evolved over time I came to feel that the law no longer resembled what I had been taught as a student in the 1960s, and what I taught as a young professor in the 1970s, when the systems of law were identified to states. For example, at the time, there were few classes offered on the law of the European Community. This area was considered as somewhat marginal. But in recent years, the landscape has completely changed. The interactions among different levels and systems of law, from the national, regional, and international standpoints, on which I have been conducting much research in the past fifteen years or so, have become particularly visible in Europe.

Take for instance the European Court of Human Rights. At the beginning, when the states adopted the Convention for the Protection of Human Rights and Fundamental Freedoms in 1950, they thought that the most common solution to European problems would be a political solution. As a result, this Court was practically never called upon. But then, slowly, slowly but surely, it has acquired an authority and established itself as a to-go place, so to speak. In this context, in case of violation of human rights, any member of the Council of Europe – and I insist because it is the wider Europe, including, for example, Russia and Turkey – may be sentenced by the judges in Strasbourg for violation of human rights.

So I simply observed this change. Working on the judgments of the European Court of Human Rights made me think that there was a new movement underway. It made me think that there was a process of internationalization of law and that it was very important to understand the nature and evolution of law in the contemporary era. At the same time, I

[18] Mireille Delmas-Marty, *Pour un droit commun* (Paris: Seuil, 1994), *Towards a Truly Common Law: Europe as Laboratory for Legal Pluralism*, translated by Naomi Norberg (Cambridge: Cambridge University Press, 2002).

began to wonder whether or not similar movements were taking place worldwide.

V DESCRIPTIVE AND PRESCRIPTIVE DIMENSIONS OF LEGAL SCHOLARSHIP

JMC: As you are trying to understand how change takes place in law, as you are trying to describe and analyze processes of change, you are also trying to find out how these changes could lead to a better world. Does it mean that there is also a prescriptive dimension to your work?

MDM: Now you are asking a question that, in fact, is very difficult. For a scholar, the risk is always to slip from the descriptive to the prescriptive. When a scholar is a legal scholar, this is almost inevitable, and this is the case because law is a normative domain. Yet, as a scholar, and as a legal scholar, it is important to try separating the descriptive part from the prescriptive part.

In this context, a significant aspect of my studies has been trying to understand and describe as accurately as possible the movements that exist in the internationalization of human rights, which also exist in economic law, particularly in the area of trade. Similar developments have taken place with the creation of the World Trade Organization (WTO), which has a quasi-judicial system, which is binding for states. Then there is another area where internationalization is both regional and global, that is, the environmental field, in terms of climate change but also in terms of biodiversity. In all these areas, in my various books, especially in the past fifteen years, I have attempted to offer narratives, descriptive observations as a way to make the reader aware of the deep changes that are taking place.

JMC: Still, there is a prescriptive dimension, even a humanistic one in your work?

MDM: The prescriptive dimension exists, you are right. And it is my responsibility as a scholar to make it noticeable when my work, my reflection, passes from one level (descriptive) to another (prescriptive). It is true that I often ask myself not only what will the world order look like tomorrow, and what role will law play in this world order, but also what should the world order look like tomorrow, and what should be the role of law, including international law, in this world order. In this regard, there are several scenarios possible.

It could be a unified and uniform world order, which basically would be designed along the lines of what exists as the national order but then transposed on a global scale. This would also require a world state, or the equivalent of a world state. But do we really want this? This is where in my work I often move from the descriptive to the prescriptive. Indeed, I am not a supporter of a world order that would be unified and uniform. What I am afraid of when it comes to the scenario of a unified and uniform world order is that it could be, that it would be, a hegemonic world order, that is to say one world imposed by the most powerful country. Today the United States is probably in this position. Tomorrow it could be China, and after tomorrow another country, as it is difficult to say with precision what the future holds. But a unified and uniform world order would be imposed by the greatest power of the world, whoever this power is. And I am really afraid of this type of world order.

JMC: Are you afraid of this type of world order because it runs the risk of having law essentially reflecting a power situation and being put at the service of power, with very little attention given to the demands of justice?

MDM: And also because it could reduce human diversity, and then, human creativity. But legal scholars have to be modest when it comes to the relationship between law and political power, and law and philosophical or ethical justice. We have to recognize that law cannot do everything. Law operates to the extent that political, economic, and sometimes cultural contexts make certain choices possible. In this perspective, what law and legal scholars cannot do is to change the economy, the culture, let alone the world. What they can do is to provide instruments, tools, in order to allow giving shape to choices. In this perspective, if I had a recommendation to make for law to be able to play such a role, I would suggest that "plural law" could be a path for the future.

VI ORDERING PLURALISM

JMC: What do you mean by "plural law"?

MDM: I also use the term of "ordering pluralism." "Ordering pluralism" is more expressive because this expression contains two words that, in a way, are in contradiction. Traditionally, pluralism is the opposite of legal order. It means multiple orders. And you can play on words (for instance in French we have "orders" and "disorder" ("des ordres" and "désordre"). So, the notion and the ambition of ordering pluralism are quite paradoxical. Yet I think that, for the way forward, it would be politically a desirable path, especially in order to avoid the hegemony of one system over others and the disappearance of human diversity and human creativity.

JMC: When you refer to this notion of "ordering pluralism," do you also have in mind the need to coordinate pluralism?

MDM: Certainly. Ordering does not mean deleting all differences. It means harmonizing them, putting them in harmony, making them compatible. Moreover it can mean coordinating them in a purely horizontal way. We talk more and more of the dialogue of judges. For instance, in the United States, the dialogue between the judges of the Supreme Court and judges of other foreign courts is a kind of coordination that occurs spontaneously and without hierarchy.[19] At the international level, it could be something a little more hierarchical but without leading for this to complete unification. Hence the reference in my work to the process of harmonization, which is a type of convergence around common principles that we commit to respect, that each state commits to respect, but this while maintaining their autonomy, their difference.

What I am telling you here is a bit abstract. So let me give you a very concrete example taken from the jurisprudence of the European Court of Human Rights having to do with practices of wiretapping. Wiretapping, when considered broadly in terms of values, is contrary to the protection of privacy. At the same time, it is needed in some cases, for national security reasons. So between the demands of privacy and the demands of security, we must find a balance. As part of trying to find such balance, the European Court condemns a state that would wiretap a whole population under false pretenses. But at the same time, the European Court does not produce identical rulings vis-à-vis all states because the handling of wiretapping can vary from one European country to another. For instance, in France there is an independent system of administrative authority for wiretapping. In England a judge decides. In Germany there is a parliamentary committee. Also, the European Court recognizes and leaves to states a margin of appreciation, or of interpretation in terms of what is appropriate for deciding whether or not to go ahead with wiretapping. To be sure, this margin of appreciation can become larger as the differences in practice get stronger from one state to the other. But, still, this is a margin. This means that there is a limit not to be exceeded. There is a

[19] See Stephen Breyer, Julien Cantegreil, and Mireille Delmas-Marty, eds., *Regards croisés sur l'internationalisation du droit* (Paris: Société de Législation Comparée, 2009) and Stephen Breyer, *The Court and the World: American Law and the New Global Realities* (New York: Knopf Doubleday Publishing Group, 2016).

threshold of compatibility which should not be exceeded. And this is what I have in mind when I talk about "ordering pluralism." It is the idea that there is an order, but it is a flexible order. One could also talk of a "fuzzy" order, by reference to "fuzzy logics," and it is a form of order that can be scalable.

JMC: The notion of "ordering pluralism" also entails a certain amount of plasticity?

MDM: Plasticity, yes, and, more importantly, a possibility of some dynamism, as it refers to something like a process rather than a concept.

JMC: You argue that at the European level we have a form of "ordering pluralism" in the legal relationships that exist between the European Union and member states. Does such "ordering pluralism" exist at the international or global level?

MDM: At the international level, we have with the WTO, or the climate regime, the idea of common but differentiated responsibilities, which in a way is a form of ordering pluralism. The notion of "Common but differentiated" somehow incorporates the idea of a margin, that is to say there is a shared commitment to achieve common objectives but contextual differences are acknowledged as well.

JMC: Does this make it easier in the field of the environment to come up with a successful methodology to address climate change as a global risk?

MDM: When it comes to the environment, it is very difficult to reach an agreement on common objectives. At the same time, we would find even less of an agreement if we did not acknowledge this national margin. Climate change has to be addressed differently in each country according to needs and capabilities. We fight against climate change in the name of the concept of sustainable development, and the concept of sustainable development is geared toward the future. The same is true of the notion of "future generations." To which developing countries answer: "But we must also look at to the past."

JMC: And the present?

MDM: Indeed, the past and the present: Who is responsible for the current situation? Developing countries say "Not us." So if we want sustainable development to be accepted by all countries, sustainable development must be fair. It must therefore introduce an element which holds a sense of differentiation according to the history of each country. We cannot reach an agreement if we do not have this idea that sustainable development must also be fair, if we do not take into account the history of each country.

JMC: From this point of view, in your last book, Aux quatre vents du monde,[20] *you seem to think that the Paris Agreement on climate change*[21] *is a real step forward. Why do you think this agreement is a real step forward? More specifically, what are the extent and limits of this agreement?*

MDM: The Agreement is universal in the sense that it has been approved by all present member states (197 out of the 200 members of the United Nations, including the most polluting countries) and has managed to establish common goals (article 2, paragraphs a, b, c). These goals are, first, quantitative, such as "(H)olding the increase in the global average temperature to well below 2° C above pre-industrial levels and to pursue the efforts to limit the temperature increase to 1.5° C above pre-industrial levels ..." The objectives are, second, qualitative, such as "increasing the ability to adapt to the adverse impacts of climate change and foster climate resilience and low greenhouse gas emissions development ... ", and "making finance flows consistent with a pathway toward low greenhouse gas emissions." Despite all of the reluctance of industrialized countries, the Agreement recognizes that the adaptation "is a global challenge faced by all ... " and "that it is a key component of and makes a contribution to the long-term-global response to climate change to protect people, livelihoods and ecosystems" (article 7, paragraph 2).

To be sure each objective is addressed in the context of sustainable development and poverty eradication. Concerning the aim to reach global peaking of greenhouse gas emissions (article 4), developed country Parties should continue taking the lead by undertaking economy-wide absolute emission reduction targets while "developing country Parties should continue enhancing their mitigation efforts and are encouraged to move over time toward economy-wide emission reduction or limitation targets in light of different national circumstances" (article 4, paragraph 4). Additionally, "(T)he least developed countries and small islands may prepare and communicate strategies ... reflecting their special circumstances" (article 4, paragraph 6). But this process of contextualization allows to factor in the "ecological debt" of

[20] Delmas-Marty, *Aux quatre vents du monde. Petit guide de navigation sur l'océan de la mondialisation.*

[21] The Paris Agreement (French: L'accord de Paris) is an agreement within the United Nations Framework Convention on Climate Change (UNFCC) dealing with greenhouse gases emissions mitigation, adaptation, and finance. The language of the agreement was negotiated by representatives of the countries present at the 21st Conference of the Parties of the UNFCC in Paris and adopted by consensus in December 2015.

industrialized countries. And at the moment this process does not force present generations to give up their development and their economic welfare.

However, we still need a mechanism of control and, ultimately, of sanction in order to avoid that this universal agreement does not bring about a renationalized universal. Hence the importance of the debate on the constraining dimension of the agreement. It happens that the Paris Agreement envisions neither a committee of control nor any measure that could appear as a sanction. A number of commentators have concluded that, because of the lack of provision concerning sanctions, states will do whatever they want and nobody will be in the position to stop them. In reality, the situation illustrates the ambiguities of the distinction between *hard law* and *soft law*. In French, "hard" can be translated by "dur," but its contrary in English, "soft," sometimes is translated by fuzzy (flou), sometimes by optional (mou), sometimes by not envisioning sanctions (doux). The Paris Agreement plays on the three levels: it is fuzzy (flou), it is not optional (mou), but it partially does not envision sanctions (doux).

JMC: Can you please elaborate?

MDM: This agreement is fuzzy in the sense that the commitments are differentiated according to the national context, a fact that is probably necessary considering the disparities between national contexts. But at the same time, contrary to what has been said or written, the agreement is not soft but hard, in the second meaning of the word, because by its legal status it is obligatory. It has the value of an international treaty and must be executed in good faith by the parties. This although it contains a lot of clauses in the form of the present (*shall*) and the conditional (*should*) (article 4–4 mentioned above). As a result, each state will be under the obligation to establish its national contribution, implement it, and revise it every five years (articles 3 and 4).

Finally, the Paris Agreement is softer than the Kyoto Protocol because it does not entail a control mechanism and sanction mechanism. However, it contains a "transparency framework" ("cadre de transparence") called MRV (*monitoring, reporting, verification*), which will apply not only to developed countries, like with the Kyoto Protocol, but to all countries (article 13). This mechanism, very detailed, could bring about, even if this is not expressly mentioned, sanctions. At the international level, it can challenge reputations (through naming and shaming) and at the national level it could generate sanctions for the non-respect of commitments. Sanctions can be carried out by some of the national judges, if a case is referred to them by an NGO or scientists. It is in this perspective that a Dutch court of The Hague District has condemned in June 2015 The Netherlands to reduce its greenhouse gas emissions. Refusing to consider the cost of such a measure as a valid argument, as well as the argument of interference in the international policy of the country, judges have put forward a duty to protect the environment and humankind partially in the name of human rights. The condemnation is not final but similar cases have been deemed admissible in Europe (Belgium and Norway) but also in Pakistan and The Philippines, and even in the United States. Bridges can exist between soft law and hard law.

That said, the project of protecting climate in an effective way implies also engaging more broadly the responsibility of all non-state actors, and to begin with the multinational corporations because the rebalancing between competition and cooperation is facing first the obstacle of the economic and profit logic of business.

VII LAW AND THE EVOLUTION OF SOVEREIGNTY AND THE NATIONAL INTEREST

JMC: In others words, the differentiated approach can be an expression and instrument of equity?

MDM: It is an expression of equity and fairness, and it takes time to develop because each state defends its national interests first. To reach an agreement of shared responsibility, or "co-responsibility" we must give up some of our autonomy, and it is very difficult. It is very difficult, but I believe that it is the only way.

Earlier you mentioned my last book, *Aux quatre vents du monde*.[22] In this book, I talk about the need to move from a world of "solitary sovereignty" to a world of "solidarity sovereignty." In other words, we have to develop a culture of interdependence as central and iconic as the culture of independence developed for a long time and reinforced during the period of decolonization. The interdependencies between human beings and the nonhuman world, that is to say between the various components of the Earth's ecosystem, have been recognized in international politics since the Earth Summit at Rio, in 1992: "Recognizing the integral and interdependent nature of the earth, our Home." But at the same time, interdependencies are growing and reinforced by the influence of new technologies, between human collectivities, especially among states. This is why it is time to identify the change of representation that should result from it. Traditionally, people, united by their history and its

[22] *Ibid.*

particularisms, had adopted declarations of independence. Today, the inhabitants of Earth, if they want to unite in the desire to protect the future must recognize their interdependence in order to transform it into a common destiny. The goal is not to move toward an improbable fusional universal, and quite frightening if it were going to be imposed upon all by a dominating power, but rather toward the promotion of common goals.

By integrating common goals in their national system, states do not lose their sovereignty. This sovereignty does not diminish. On the contrary, it widens into a type of sovereignty that I suggest to present as shaped by *solidarity*. In contrast, short of having common goals, states go back to their traditional sovereignty, *solitary*, because it is limited to the national interests. We can see this with global terrorism, one of the domains in which the traditional national sovereignty approach continues to prevail. Failing at establishing a real agreement on common goals, which presupposes a definition of terrorism, states are going back to the old sovereignty model. While the agenda should be to fight against a global phenomenon, each state follows its own approach, runs *its* own war against terrorists.

In any case, we are in a transition period. As such, it is very difficult to think about law in a transition period because several models of the legal order coexist which apparently are not compatible. A number of states or political leaders continue to think according to the traditional sovereignty the model–of the state fully sovereign and independent of other states, and defending its national interests. But reality has changed. The reality that states now face is one of interdependence. In terms of climate, even the strongest state in the world cannot alone solve the problem of climate change. This is true as well for other global risks, such as terrorism. States cannot act alone; they need each other. So the classical or traditional model of sovereignty no longer works.

JMC: Are diplomats and political leaders, people who in general are responsible for the conceptualization and negotiation of the global, open to this type of idea of interdependent sovereignty?

MDM: Sometimes they are. For instance, for several years, one of my most loyal auditors at the Collège de France was a leading French diplomat, former ambassador of France to China. Another example is the fact that there is now a unit of globalization within the French Ministry of Foreign Affairs,[23] which

[23] See Direction générale de la mondialisation, de la culture, de l'enseignement et du développement international, Ministère des Affaires étrangères et du développement, diplomatie.gouv.fr.

focuses on these issues. So, yes, the diplomatic community is changing, is evolving and giving more and more attention to these issues.

On these issues I also had a lot of exchange through the ID Networks ("réseaux ID" – three networks, French-America, French-Brazilian, and French-Chinese, focusing on the internationalization of law and the imagination of law,[24] where the acronym ID refers to both "internationalization of law" and "imagination and law"). I helped establish these networks where academics meet diplomats and high-level practitioners because I do believe that we must invent new models and therefore be creative. At the same time, I am a member of the international Collegium (which was chaired for many years by Michel Rocard, a Former French Prime Minister[25]).[26]

So, awareness is growing on these issues. That said, as we know, we have witnessed in the past years the emergence of a very popular populist trend, in the United States and in Europe, that calls for going back to a form of independent and solitary sovereignty. There is therefore more work to be done in this area to find a balance between the two models of sovereignty, solitary versus solidarity, as we have not yet shifted toward a purely universalist model.

JMC: Nor have we shifted toward a post-national model.

MDM: Nor post-national, you are right. So we must come together to think about law as occurring at a variety of levels, inside of the state, outside of the state, and between states.

JMC: I guess this means we need to rethink law. But for diplomats and political leaders who are in charge of the negotiations at the international level, and for academics, is it not true that there is also the need to rethink the national interest?

MDM: Yes, we must also rethink the national interest. I think doing this is the hardest thing for a political leader or a diplomat. To include in their thinking and actions the idea that we must defend both the national interest as well as broader human and globally cooperative interests, is very challenging for them, intellectually and politically. For instance, when one is a European leader, one must consider the national and the regional interest and, more

24 See website of the Collège de France.

25 Michel Rocard served as French Prime Minister from 1988 to 1991.

26 See *dialoguesenhumanite.org: Enjeux juridiques droit mondial.*

broadly, the global interest. For a person in a position of political responsibility, this is not easy.

JMC: These are a lot of layers to consider.

MDM: Yes, there are a lot of elements to think about and to factor in. Moreover, one of the challenges associated with the idea of global or worldwide interest is that no one is directly responsible to defend it. Even international organizations are not positioned ideally to do so. Most of them are quite fragmented, and when they have a broader jurisdiction, like the United Nations, they have little power. Furthermore, those with the most power, like I think is the case of the World Trade Organization, have limited skills. That is why the defense of the common interest or of global public goods is so weak.

JMC: What are the implications of your understanding of international law and international institutions? If the new Secretary-General of the United Nations elected in the fall of 2016, António Guterres,[27] *reads your work, what should he conclude with regards to international institutions and the future of global governance?*

MDM: I would be delighted if he could read my work. Indeed, I think the Secretary-General of the United Nations is one of those leaders in the best position to protect the common interest in the world. The work that was done around the notion of the Responsibility to Protect (R2P)[28] is an illustration of this state of affairs. The then Secretary-General of the United Nations, Mr. Kofi Annan, played an important role in the fact that the United Nations took on board this notion. If the UN Secretary-General is probably the closest and the most aware of the demands associated with the idea of a common interest in the world, one of the difficulties to solve at the global level is to get the various international fields compatible and to get the organizations to interact constructively and efficiently. For instance, how to get the International Labour Organization (ILO) to be consulted on issues that concern at the same time this organization and the World Trade

[27] António Guterres, who was Prime Minister of Portugal from 1995 to 2002 and the United Nations High Commissioner for Refugees from 2005 to 2015, was designated the 9th UN Secretary-General in October 2016. He took his position on January 1, 2017.

[28] The Responsibility to Protect (R2P) is a new international human rights norm designed to improve the ability of the international community to prevent and stop genocides, war crimes, ethnic cleansing, and crimes against humanity. It was endorsed by all member states of the United Nations at the 2005 United Nations World Summit. On R2P, see for instance Ramesh Thakur and William Maley, eds., *Theorizing the Responsibility to Protect* (Cambridge: Cambridge University Press, 2015).

Organization. A real challenge is how to ensure that there is cooperation among international organizations, like the ILO and WTO, which deal with related issues.

JMC: Based on your latest research, what would your advice be for the UN Secretary-General?

MDM: Growing interdependence leads to identify common goals. A very telling example of this is offered by the agreement signed in New York in September 2015, concerning the seventeen Sustainable Development Goals (SDGs), conceived as a way to complete by 2030 the efforts initiated in the context of the eight Millennium Development Goals (MDGs), adopted in 2000. But we still have to identify and regulate the contradictions at work in the context of globalization. This is why I suggest the metaphor of "rose des vents," of a compass as a new framework in order to understand the processes characterizing the contemporary world. Indeed, law needs a minimum of stability. When a certain level of instability has been reached, law disappears. In this perspective, by suggesting a typology of the dominating trends, or winds, the "rose des vents" does not establish a static framework but on the contrary makes it possible to envision a provisional stabilization of global governance and as such allows not only to identify the contradictions at work in globalization but to regulate them as well.

In order to identify the contradictions, I propose, first, to refer to four dominating trends or winds, illustrated by the two examples of borderless terrorism and climate change. They are: The spirit of security and the spirit of liberty; and the spirit of cooperation and the spirit of competition. In a complementary fashion, these examples suggest that when it comes to the four dominating winds other trends or winds exist, such as the spirit of innovation (between liberty and competition) and the spirit of conservation (between security and cooperation), or the spirit of exclusion (between competition and security) and the spirit of integration (between cooperation and liberty).[29]

But how can we regulate these contradictions? I would propose to the United Nations Secretary-General a second image or metaphor, "dancing with the winds" ("ronde des vents"), suggesting how global governance could contribute to an equilibrium that would be created, like in a dance, by the dynamics created by the contradictions themselves. A little, also, like a system of alternative breathing for the world. If breathing stops, for instance if security becomes the primary right, or if competition suffocates the spirit of

[29] Delmas-Marty, *Aux quatre vents du monde. Petit guide de navigation sur l'océan de la mondialisation.*

cooperation, then globalization will quickly suffocate itself. In contrast, cooperation without competition amounts to no dynamism and liberty without security amounts to chaos.

Within each of the contrary winds, it would be therefore necessary to have a "regulatory" principle allowing the replacement of the "or" that opposes by an "and" that brings together. In order to balance liberty and security, the principle of equal dignity of all human beings; in order to balance competition and cooperation, the principle of planetary solidarity; concerning the pair of innovation and conservation, the principle of precaution (or rather of anticipation); finally, in order to balance exclusion and integration, the principle of ordering pluralism, because at the global level a legal order is necessary but it can only be pluralist.

VIII THE FUTURE OF LAW AND HUMANITY

JMC: *Would you say that one of the key questions posed by your work is how to ensure that normative orders, the various existing legal orders, enter into dialogue and amount to a meaningful system of global governance? If this is the case, what does this mean for current international institutions and even international law?*

MDM: It is effectively one of the most important questions. I think that the international legal order that would seem – and now I am being prescriptive – the most acceptable is an order that would be interactive. What this implies is interaction, instead of strict hierarchy, between national and international law and between different national laws, or different sectors of international law. As a consequence, this interactive legal order will be more complex and less predictable than a traditional legal order. It is what I call the "tragedy of the 3 Cs," that is: more Complexity means less Coherence and less Continuity or Completion in the hierarchical chain.[30] The result seems to be more effectiveness from the empirical point, but less predictability (because of the discontinuity in the chain) from the logical point of view, and less legitimacy (because of the lack of common values) from the axiological point.

JMC: *But how do we manage this interactivity, and how do me institutionalize it?*

MDM: I think that in practice this is already in the making. What strikes me is that, in the legal vocabulary, we more and more use a terminology that

30 *Ibid.*

introduces elements of what the future of law, of what future law, could look like. We can think about the notions of sustainable development, but also of sustainable peace. In this regard, it is not enough to want peace. What we want above all is a lasting peace.

JMC: A lasting peace, which is not simply an armed peace, or a war in waiting?

MDM: Yes, we want peace to be sustainable. The future of law, future law, can also already be seen at work in the introduction of this concept of "future generations." For a long time, law only dealt with present generations. But in the past twenty years, we have seen international law more and more concerned with the future, with how to secure the future, with the next generation and even further. In particular, for example, with the concept of common heritage of humanity, which was launched as early as in the 1960s, the idea is borne that we must also address the protection of future generations. All of this introduces a temporal dimension, which did not exist before in law.

JMC: But in a way law has always had a time dimension, for instance with the fact that it is oriented toward and cultivating predictability.

MDM: It is true that the time dimension is, here anyway, a part of law. But future generations were not considered. There has been a reluctance to project law into the future and use law to project into the future. For example, the French Declaration of 1793 (which never entered into force) said that we could not legislate for future generations. In the Papers of Thomas Jefferson, we find the same idea: "according to natural law, a generation is to another one what an independent nation is to another independent nation."[31] That said, if future generations had their own sovereignty because they were independents, it is now logical to see that the concept of future generations is entering the legal discourse while independent sovereignty moves toward an interdependent one.[32]

JMC: How do you explain the introduction of the notion of "future generations"?

MDM: Personally, I think it is not only related to growing interdependences but also related to awareness, a growing awareness of the fragility of the planet and, consequently, of the fragility of humanity. It is also related to scientific

[31] François Ost, *Le temps du droit* (Paris: Odile Jacob, 1999), p. 217.

[32] Mireille Delmas-Marty, *Résister, responsabiliser, anticiper, ou comment humaniser la mondialisation* (Paris: Seuil, 2013).

progress, to a better knowledge of our history and our future. We are now discovering not only that civilizations can disappear but also that humanity itself can disappear. Except by colonizing other planets, the risk of exhausting resources and the risk of climate change, all these phenomena remind us our finitude as human beings.

JMC: This is something new?

MDM: Yes it seems to be, particularly in the field of law. Incidentally, this awareness of fragility can feed the culture of fear of which we spoke about earlier. But, here too, there is an ambivalence that I find quite interesting.

On the one hand, fear, when it is fear of others, can be a bad advisor. It brings a wind of hatred, rejection, exclusion. In this situation, when we build walls instead of building bridges, which has been very much the case recently, especially in Europe, in reaction to refugees coming from Syria, Iraq, Afghanistan, or Eritrea, foreigners become the collateral victims of the "war against terror." Since the middle of the 1990s, European States, obsessed with the "migration risk," have spent a lot of energy to keep refugees out and forbid access to their territory. And the terrorist attacks of 2001, and even more so the ones of March 2004 (Madrid), July 2005 (London), and then January and November 2015 (Paris), and again of March 2016 (Brussels), taking place in an international globalized context, have further hardened European policy in the areas of immigration and asylum, two areas that had been transferred to the European Union in 1999 (Amsterdam Treaty [effective 1999] and Tampere Summit [1999]). In this regard, the terrorist attacks of November 13, 2015 have taken place at a critical time, when the European Commission was facing difficulties in terms of placing asylum seekers in European countries more and more opposed to the spirit of hospitality and integration.

On the other hand, when the fear of global risks is the awareness of a common destiny, it can create a sense of belonging to the same human family. In fact, the term of "family" is used in the preamble of the Universal Declaration. It suggests that all human beings are members of the same human family, that we are all aboard the same fragile ship. As such, awareness and fear of global risks may have positive effects if they contribute to building a community of values and encourage a commitment to our common destiny, associated with a quest for solidarity.

JMC: This is the theme of one of your recent books on the community of values?

MDM: Yes. The book's title is a question: *Vers une communauté de valeurs?*[33]

JMC: What would a community of values look like?

MDM: Actually, a global community of values is not a community that would ignore and get rid of history. This is not a community that would give up the cultural diversity that is now also qualified by the 2005 UNESCO Convention on the Protection and Promotion of the Diversity of Cultural Expressions[34] as part of the common heritage of humankind. A community of values does not consist in imposing the same behavior for everyone. It is not a uniform community. This is an interactive community. That is to say that it is a community in which we are enriched by each other, and by a better knowledge of each other. This is also a bit of a utopia. But I think it is an energizing utopia.

JMC: It is a combination of universality and particularism?

MDM: Yes, sort of. The idea is one of a process, to use a word that I like, a process where the humanization should be engaged on a reciprocal basis. There is no predestined population that will humanize the rest of the world. We must go through a process of mutual humanization. We have something to learn from each other, and therefore interactively. That is the condition for a world community of values.

JMC: So we should adopt a position of mutual learning, without ever having an actor who is in the position of "I know better" vis-à-vis other countries, other cultures?

MDM: Yes, it is a little bit like humanizing and civilizing each other. And that is why I am very interested in other societies, in other cultures, China for example.

IX CHINA AND LAW

JMC: You have been interested in China for a long time. What is the relationship between your interest in China and your research agenda on law?

MDM: As far as I remember I have always been interested in China. I started studying Chinese at the same time I was a law school student. Then my studies

[33] Mireille Delmas-Marty, *Les forces imaginantes du droit (IV). Vers une communauté de valeurs?* (Paris: Seuil, 2011).

[34] The UNESCO Convention on the Protection and Promotion of the Diversity of Cultural Expressions was adopted by the UNESCO General Conference in October 2005.

in Chinese were interrupted by the birth of my son. But at the time I thought that at one point I would return to Chinese and even do a Ph.D. on Chinese law. But when I reached the time, in my law studies, to start writing my Ph.D. dissertation, China was engulfed in the Cultural Revolution and law had almost disappeared in China. So I went to see my law professors in order to get their advice, and they told me: "Listen, if you want to prepare for the 'agrégation de droit' (aggregation of law),[35] this is really not the time to do a dissertation on Chinese law." It was already a bit odd to want to focus on Chinese law. But in the context of the Cultural Revolution, it did not seem to make sense. So I gave up. By, then, my connection with China came back in the late 1970s. During those years, in France we began to receive very good Ph.D. students from China. Then in the early 1990s, I was fortunate enough to be appointed as a member of the *Institut Universitaire de France*,[36] which gave me the resources to undertake research without having to enter into a preestablished framework. I decided to reconnect with my former students from China in order to set up a Franco-Chinese project. So off we went. It was in 1992/93. The research project was not officially supported by the university but simply tolerated. I remember the first preparatory meeting hosted in a quite popular neighborhood of Beijing, where these scholars were living.

JMC: What was the topic of this research project?

MDM: The internationalization of law and, since most of my former students had studied criminal law,[37] the research project focused on the internationalization of criminal law. In this field, we came to think about the internationalization of law in two ways: First the internationalization of economic crimes, and, second, the internationalization of violations of human rights. This research project lasted several years and led to the publication of a series of books, both in French and in Chinese. We also organized other initiatives in the context of the University of Paris 1, particularly a program for Chinese students on European Law (French and Comparative Law, also European Market Law and European Human Rights Law).

35 In France *agrégation de droit* (aggregation of law) is a selective civil service competitive examination leading to the position of university professor in the field of law. In law, aggregation exists in the fields of private law, public law, and legal history. Professor Delmas-Marty took the aggregation in private law and criminal law.

36 The Institut Universitaire de France(IUF), created in 1991, is a French service of the Minister of Higher Education that each year distinguishes a small number of university professors for their research excellence.

37 In the early part of her career Mireille Delmas-Marty developed expertise in criminal law.

JMC: Why your initial interest in China?

MDM: Well, this is a mystery. But when I started studying Chinese, I found this language absolutely fascinating. Later on, when I came to teach to the Collège de France, I had the opportunity to work with my colleague Pierre-Étienne Will, who is a leading scholar of Chinese history and who was interested in the history of Chinese law. So, together, for two years, we taught a seminar on Chinese Law that led to the publication of a big book titled *China, Democracy and Law*.[38]

JMC: I also saw that one of the non-Western legal scholars who influenced you is Professor ONUMA.

MDM: Yes, Professor ONUMA is Japanese, but he is also a great specialist of China.[39]

JMC: He focuses on the inter-civilizational dimension of law.

MDM: Of human rights, especially. I wrote a foreword to the recent publication of his work in French.[40]

X THE FUTURE OF THE INTERNATIONAL LAW

JMC: Did your interest in China lead you to reflect on the need to maybe integrate other traditions of international law in mainstream international law, which is essentially Western?

MDM: Absolutely. This is what attracted me to the work of ONUMA. That said, there are already inter-civilizational elements in the early work of the drafters of the Universal Declaration of Human Rights. There was a representative of China, Peng-Chun Chang, as well as other non-Western contributors, involved in the drafting of the Declaration. Chang, by the way, was a diplomat, not a jurist. Among other things, Chang challenged the reference to "reason" in the text of the Declaration (see Article 1, related to human beings with reason), as too Western-centric. He argued that a word other than "reason" was needed for the text of the Declaration to have universal value. He suggested the addition of the term "conscience," which he understood as an application of the Chinese notions of "ren" (by and large

38 Mireille Delmas-Marty and Pierre-Etienne Will, eds., *China, Democracy, and Law* (Leiden: Brill, 2011).

39 See ONUMA, Yasuaki in this volume, Chapter 10.

40 ONUMA, Yasuaki, *Le droit international et le Japon. Une vision transcivilisationnelle du monde* (Paris: Pedone, 2016).

referring to the notion of humanity, of being human) and of "liangxin," which was translated by "conscience" but does not fully express the underlying idea of "moral conscience" and "innate goodness" implied by the characters *liang* and *xin*.[41]

JMC: Yet, in the end, the final text of the Universal Declaration is very much a Western text?

MDM: Yes, and perhaps what is needed for the Universal Declaration is to be enriched by the interpretations that major non-Western humanist philosophies can give of it, by their interpretations of it.

Indeed, legal texts, especially legal texts that have a global normative value, do not have to be interpreted in a narrow fashion, exclusively making reference to Western considerations. For instance, interpreting international human rights by calling upon non-Western approaches could be a way to at the same time illustrate and enrich their universality. It is interesting for example to see how criminal judges of the courts of the former Yugoslavia and Rwanda, who have come from all around the world, and now the judges of the International Criminal Court, who also come from all around the world, have widened the interpretation of legal texts. Because every time a text is somewhat imprecise, a solution can be to search for answers in the national legal traditions. This is how a sort of hybridization, a blending of different legal traditions can happen.

JMC: Do you think that hybridization is likely to influence the future of international law, is likely to be one of the forms of the internationalization of international law in the years to come?

MDM: I do not know if the movement is truly irreversible. We cannot predict the future. But if the movement continues, there will inevitably be a work of hybridization that will have to be done. We already see it at work in some fields of international law. For instance, at times, international criminal law has made reference to commissions of truth and reconciliation, which were invented in South Africa and have been used widely in Latin America. They were not born of a Western tradition. Of course, I do not consider the commissions of truth and reconciliation as a panacea. It does not always work perfectly. But it is still an interesting alternative to traditional criminal justice as it developed from the West. The problem is that hybridization is perhaps happening too late. This may be one of the lessons of the South African decision, in the fall 2016, to withdraw from the ICC, while the then

41 See Delmas-Marty and Will, *China, Democracy, and Law*, p. 868.

president of the African Union, Robert Mugabe, was talking about the idea of an African International Criminal Court.

JMC: In terms of the future of law, do you think that the growing global importance of China will have an impact on the evolution of law?

MDM: Yes, I tried to address this question in an article I published a few years ago, "In the Age of Globalization, What Can we Learn from Chinese law?"[42] Here let me add that the importance of China will be growing if other juridical spaces such as the EU or institutions like the ICC disintegrate. This will change the overall balance. Nevertheless, I hope that we will continue moving toward what could be a multipolar order.

JMC: So is it still possible to imagine what we could call a "multipolar global law"?

MDM: Well, I hope so. In this regard, it is interesting to note that Europe is perhaps the only region in the world where law is constructed in a multipolar way. This is the case because in Europe there is not really a hegemonic country. And maybe, maybe, there is a chance that on a global scale, we are going to witness in the future the construction of an international legal order that will be not hegemonic.

JMC: But in the European context, multipolar law relies on both a desire for integration and a reality of integration.

MDM: Apparently, but at the same time European countries and their culture find themselves in a situation that are similar to the global one, where one finds many cultural differences. Presently, European integration is weakened as it appears that the process of disintegration is not excluded (see Brexit), even if cultural differences are less profound at the European level than on the global scale.

JMC: Is there globally a desire for integration and a reality of integration that would allow for the possibility of a multipolar law?

MDM: In order to answer your question let me go back to the notion of global risk I mentioned earlier. A desire for integration can still emerge through the risks which we run together. I think that what can unite the world in a community of values are, for example, the common ecosystem and, more specifically, the issue of its protection.

[42] In *Etudes chinoises*, Association française d'études chinoises, Vol. XXXIV-2 (2015), 37–51.

JMC: The idea of shared risk?

MDM: Yes, but not only the fear of common global risk. There is also the will to promote what economists call "global public goods."[43] This is where the idea of solidarity comes to play a central role. And it is true that among young people, maybe not all of them but a growing number of them are aware, more than previous generations, of these common risks associated with the degradation of the ecosystem.

JMC: You believe that the issue of the environment is more likely to generate the idea of a shared risk, and therefore the idea of an emergency that has to be addressed, than a sensibility to human rights?

MDM: I think that climate change is an opportunity to imagine what global governance may look like. But human rights remain also a central topic, and a more positive one. I will answer by sharing with you a personal story. At the end of a training session on human rights that I organized in the past for my Chinese law students, I asked them what they thought on human rights. They said: "When we arrived in France, we did not care much for issues of human rights." I asked them why. Their answer was that for them, initially, human rights were an ideological discourse invented by the West against other non-Western countries, including China. So I asked them: "What about now?" "Well, now we have changed." And they had changed because they had all been in training at the European Court of Human Rights, and they had seen that at the European Court there was no talk about China. It was all about issues of human rights in Europe. They could see that countries such as the United Kingdom, France, Germany, etc. were condemned in turns. So they discovered that human rights were not a pure ideological discourse imagined to criticize China. It may be a legal one, put to work in the defense of people. This shows, among other things, that human rights, instead of being viewed as an ideology in the non-West, could become an instrument of accountability and justice.

JMC: So, your idea is to pursue the idea of justice associated with human rights without being paternalistic?

MDM: Yes, I do think we must avoid pretending to hold a truth that others do not hold, and which we give generously to them. It does not work.

43 Delmas-Marty, *Vers une communauté de valeurs?*, pp. 281 sq.

XI TEACHING LAW

JMC: Let me ask you also a question on the organization of teaching and research in the field of law. Your practice of legal research is of course very different from what is taught in traditional law schools. So how can we transform the way law is taught in universities in such a way to make more room for the types of questions you are exploring in your work?

MDM: It is true that it would be a radical change if traditional law schools were making room for the kinds of questions I explore in my work. It would require an opening up of disciplines, an education that is both much more focused on comparative law and international law, but not as two different subjects but as two disciplines in interaction. It would also require working more on the processes, on the flows. I was asked a few years ago, when I was invited by Renmin University, in Beijing, along with other academics from around the world, to reflect on this exact question of how to teach law at the time of globalization. So the Chinese have begun discussing this question, which in my opinion is an indication that they are perhaps more advanced than we are presently in Europe and particularly in France on this issue.

JMC: How do you explain that?

MDM: Maybe because the Chinese are confronted more directly than we are with the fear of a legal system being imposed from outside. For them, Western laws appear behind global law. So the idea of an international law, becoming inter-civilizational law, in the words of Onuma, may be more urgent even if more difficult to imagine. They are still sensitive to American power, and thus to the importance of American law. The new challenge is teaching national and international law in such a way that it is possible to imagine, as a kind of reciprocal hybridization, a "truly common law,"[44] which requires an opening of the cultures to each other. During the conference in Beijing, I had the opportunity to see that the young Chinese legal scholars and professors in attendance were clearly more interested in a model opposed to globalizing law by expanding a single national model.

JMC: In the Western context, even in the European context or in the French context, what would be your recommendations to make it possible that the way in which law is taught in universities is more in tune with the current developments which you mention in your books?

[44] See Mirielle Delmas-Marty, *Toward a Truly Common Law* (Cambridge, UK: Cambridge University Press, 1994).

MDM: That is very difficult because we are old nations attached to our national law. In France we are very attached to our Civil Code, which is kind of a national symbol. And the more the law is rooted in culture, which is the case in France, in Germany, in Italy (and this also is the case in English law, which although not written law is still identified to national identity), the harder it is to agree to think in terms of ordering pluralism.

JMC: But, at the same time, there is a danger if we do not adapt.

MDM: Yes, but we do not see it. It is true that what can help us and force us in a certain way to think differently is Europe because, whether we like it or not, Europe exists and has a significant impact. For instance, France has begun to learn to change its case law and legislation according to European case law. Europe forces us to think differently about law. That said, changes in this domain come more from legal practitioners than from academics.

JMC: The university is a little behind the times then.

MDM: Yes, I think we can say that.

JMC: If the systems of knowledge we teach, including in terms of law, are a bit behind our time, what does this mean in terms of training, preparing the new generations?

MDM: It is a very difficult problem to solve in France because the educational structures, the structures of the recruitment of professors for example, are built on the premise that law is identified with the state, which means that even the little adventurous theories which would work toward the junction of French law, comparative law, European law, global law, are not always appreciated by the professionals of law, professors and scholars for whom the state framework is the main reference. So there is a phenomenon of self-reproduction. This entails the risk of undermining the relevance of mainstream academic knowledge.

This is why I think that the evolution may come from practitioners, who could gradually force universities to update themselves. In this regard, we can think about the series of lectures organized by the French Council of States (Conseil d'État) in 2015, on *Le droit comparé et la territorialité du droit*, or the book mentioned earlier by Justice Stephen Breyer on the United States Supreme Court, titled, *The Court and the World*.[45] In essence, what we need is a pluralist common law, and in order to realize this we must, first,

45 Breyer, *The Court and the World: American Law and the Global Realities*.

acquire a good knowledge of our national legal tradition but, then, make sure that it is open, eager, and able to learn from and dialogue with others.

JMC: We must both immerse ourselves in our national legal traditions and open them to others?

MDM: Yes, we have to go deeper in this direction. This is what the philosopher Paul Ricoeur said very well about religions: To deepen ourselves in our own identity, we have to be able to go to others: "A la surface la distance est immense, mais si je m'approfondis, je me rapproche de l'autre qui fait le même chemin."[46] The question is to know if we will be able, together and soon enough, to follow this path in order to improve the conception and teaching of law.

JMC: Finally, what would be your advice to a young scholar starting in the field of justice?

MDM: I should say "open the doors," or "build bridges." This means at least two things: Organize teams and promote cross-fertilization techniques to combine positive law and theory of law and knowledge in history of law, comparative law, and international law; and provide transnational, interdisciplinary, and transgenerational teams to avoid dogmatism spirit and legal fundamentalism.

46 J. P. Changeux and P. Ricoeur, *Ce qui nous fait penser. La nature et la règle* (Paris: Odile Jacob, 1998), p 19. See also *Vers une communauté de valeurs?*, p. 19.

10

International Law and the Question of Its Transcivilizational Possibility

Onuma Yasuaki*

I BEYOND EUROCENTRISM: THE HISTORY OF INTERNATIONAL LAW

JEAN-MARC COICAUD (JMC): *In your work[1] you clearly put forward the idea that international law, the way it currently exists, is too Eurocentric. You also add that this has not always been the case. For instance, in your work you refer to a time when there was a coexistence of regional civilizations, in the context of which international law was not as Eurocentric as it is today.*

ONUMA YASUAKI (OY): Well, during most of human history the globe was not unified either by economic, or military, or ideational terms. There were various types of regional civilizational spheres with their distinctive normative ideas. For example, in East Asia there was a Sino-centric civilizational regional system with Confucianism, Buddhism, Taoism, and some other religions, and ethical and normative ideas underlying these civilizations and cultures. In major parts of Eurasia there were Islamic civilizational spheres where people generally believed in Islam. There was of course great diversity according to region and according to time. There were various types of Muslim dynasties, Muslim political and religious entities. All were flourishing with their normative ideas, mainly focused on Sharia.[2] They had very active relationships. In addition, they had trade

* In this conversation, the names of the people are expressed with respect to their own culture. For example, Chinese, Japanese, and Korean names are expressed family name first followed by given name. To avoid misunderstanding, their family name is expressed in upper case when both family and given names are provided.

[1] See in particular ONUMA Yasuaki, *International Law in a Transcivilizational World* (Cambridge: Cambridge University Press, 2017) and A *Transcivilizational Perspective on International Law* (Brill: Pocket Books of The Hague Academy of International Law, 2010).

[2] Islamic law based on the religious texts of the Quran and Hadith.

and intellectual, and even military relationships with the European world, and with the East Asian world.

Similarly, in Europe, there was a regional civilizational system centered on Christianity with medieval decentralized political structures. People lived at the same time as Christians and as members of small communities. Generally speaking, in those days Europe was less developed than the Muslim world and the East Asian world.

These three areas constituted major civilizational areas actively engaged in exchanging material and spiritual goods. They were prosperous, arguably the most prosperous regions of the world. In other regions, for example in the Indian subcontinent, American continent, Oceania, and Africa, there were also various types of regional civilizational areas, although they were not so distinctive and active. Each regional civilization had a specific normative system, regulating both domestic and inter-societal relations.

It is only in very recent years that one normative system, Western-centric international law, came to prevail on a global scale. People tend to forget the existence of various regional systems before modern Western-centric international law came into existence. Mainstream history of international law has had the tendency of being self-congratulatory, focusing on how European international law has globalized. It tends to characterize the development of modern international law exclusively as a positive development, without paying much attention to the destruction that it has often meant for other normative systems. Once the sovereign states system and international law originating from Europe became prevalent, the Euro-centric perspective came to define the way of thinking about humanity.

Needless to say, what I have just said is a very simplified, sketchy picture of the world history from the viewpoint of international normative systems. But I think that this picture gives you an overall idea of how humanity came to be in the situation where we are now.

JMC: You are referring to a time when international law was essentially a regional exercise because it was attached to these regional civilizations, right?

OY: As I have just mentioned, the prototype of today's international law was born in modern Europe. Before it was globalized, people communicated with others based on their respective normative systems. Each normative system presented itself as more or less the "natural" or "superior" one. Therefore, there was almost always normative conflict when people belonging to different civilizations sought to communicate with each other. However, they had ways to deal with, or "tolerate," the existence of other normative systems.

For example, Christianity and Euro-centric ways of communicating among the various entities were taken for granted by Europeans. They served as the framework of interactions within this system. It is on this basis that Europeans sought to communicate with people outside of their world. However, when Europeans found it difficult to establish or maintain relations on their terms they accepted the norm and practice of the other side. When the Ottoman Empire was powerful, for example, the Europeans maintained relations with it generally on the terms that the Ottomans regarded as natural. It was only after the Ottoman Empire came to decline that the Europeans came to be able to redefine the relations based on European terms. In contrast, the Europeans "applied" their norms and practices from the very beginning when they "discovered" the "new world" at the end of the fifteenth century.

Even when a party had normative difficulties in maintaining friendly relations with the other party, they sought to justify maintaining economic and cultural relations to gain practical benefits through such relations. For example, the Muslims had a concept of coexistence of various religious communities which was used to bridge the Self and the Other. The Islamic world was in this respect more accommodating – or even generous to – different religions than was the Christian world. You may recall that after the Reconquista of the Iberian Peninsula by Catholics in 1492, many Jews and other non-Catholic peoples were expelled or escaped from the Iberian Peninsula to North Africa and other regions where Muslims reigned. Catholicism was much harsher than Islam to other religions at the time.

In the East Asian world, similar mechanisms for accommodation functioned so that communications and interactions with the Other could be maintained. During the premodern period, Sino-centrism prevailed in the region. As you know, Sino-centrism had a strong sense of superiority centered on China. According to this view, all non-Chinese peoples were regarded as barbarians: Japanese were "East barbarians," and Europeans were "Southern barbarians." Incidentally, Europeans were called Southern barbarians because they came from the South, not necessarily from the West.

This sense of hierarchy at the core of Sino-centrism was a source of difficulty, because non-Chinese peoples naturally detested being treated as inferior to Chinese. But both China and peoples wishing to have economic and cultural relations with China were pragmatic enough to maintain such relations. Peoples who wanted to participate in the Sino-centric tribute system paid due respect to the Chinese emperor, and were rewarded with economic, cultural, and ideological benefits. They also sought to explain internally as if they maintained the relations on an equal footing. China condoned such behaviors as long as they were not too apparent. The Sino-centric tribute system was flexible in allowing the coexistence of various types of diverse belief systems in different countries.

That said, we should admit that the world of premodern international law had problems. Tensions and conflicts were always in the cards. The terms and modalities of communication and interactions among peoples with different civilizations were to a large extent based on the power relations existing at a given time. For instance, as I alluded to before, when the Ottoman Empire[3] was powerful, the relationship between Muslims and Europeans was generally maintained based on the Islamic notions of norms and diplomacy. But as the Ottoman Empire declined and Europeans became more powerful, Euro-centric international law and diplomacy became more prevalent. The Ottoman Empire was brought to a more subjugated position. They were no longer in a position to impose their terms and *modus operandi* in interacting with the Europeans. Over time, the Ottoman Empire ended up being more and more pressured, to the point of being vanquished.

As exemplified by such a case, the downside of the normative plurality that characterized the premodern world was that it tended to reflect and depend directly on power relationships between societies, peoples, kingdoms, or empires. This is not to say that current international law is immune from such power influences. Even international law in the twenty-first century is shaped and influenced by power structures. Still, compared with the premodern period, current international law is more independent from power relations.

JMC: So, you are saying that prior to the emergence of modern international law and its projection globally, on the one hand normative and legal plurality existed among the main regions of the world but, on the other hand, as you just mentioned, this plurality and the types of relationships that could exist with it fluctuated with the evolution of power.

OY: Well yes, for a long period of time, prior to the time when Europeans took over and became a global, worldwide force and actor, you might talk about the existence of a sort of parity among major civilizational spheres, such as between the Sino-centric, Islamo-centric, and Euro-centric spheres. From the viewpoint of these three spheres of civilizations, a parity in the loose sense of the term might exist. However, in my view, it is difficult to characterize their relations as distinctly legal and expressing a form of strict

[3] The Ottoman Empire was created in 1299 and was dissolved in the aftermath of World War I, in 1922.

parity. One may be able to argue there were some kind of normative relations, but I doubt whether we could say there was strict parity between them.

II COEXISTENCE, STATE SOVEREIGNTY, AND GLOBALISM

JMC: Everything changes with the "unification" of the world. At the same time, you talk about the coexistence of regional civilizations in the pre-twentieth-century period. Does it mean that you think that from the fifteenth century all the way to the twentieth century some sense of coexistence existed among these regional civilizations?

OY: Yes. One of the characteristic features of Euro-centric international law is that, while undermining the existence of the plurality of regional civilizations with their own systems of norms, it did not eliminate the existence of pluralistic cultures. As a matter of fact, modern international law accepted coexistence on its terms. Modern international law has been a crucial part of the sovereign states system. And the coexistence of sovereign states has constituted the core of modern international law. States are free in determining their own political, cultural, economic, or religious systems within their own territories. Even though Western European powers and the United States have been extremely influential in this Western-centric global international legal system, to some extent civilizational and cultural diversities have survived within the territories of sovereign states. The existence of the principle of nonintervention among states is part of this story. Thanks to this principle of nonintervention, various kinds of political and economic systems, as well as social, and cultural, and religious practices survived, even during the modern period. Fundamentally, even the powerful Western states did not possess enough economic and military power to eradicate such diversity of states existing on a global scale.

It should also be noted that the sovereign states system has functioned hand in hand with the European colonial system. To a certain extent, European religions and cultures have penetrated the colonies, particularly in the American and African continents. Still, various premodern cultures, religions, languages, and other civilizational factors survived even in these regions. In the case of Asia, where far larger numbers of humanity live, the degree of the penetration of European civilization was far more limited. Many Asian leaders sought to modernize, or Westernize, their societies, but the adoption and penetration of European civilization in Asia was selective.

Toward the end of the twentieth century, because of the increasing influence of the universal idea of human rights, the normative power of the nonintervention principle deteriorated. We all remember how in the 1990s, in the immediate aftermath of the Cold War, issues of humanitarian interventions became a major topic of debates in the context of the conflicts in Somalia, Kosovo, and Rwanda. The fact that a genocide took place in Rwanda made the question even more urgent. With these crises and the growing awareness of the international community, the idea of the Responsibility to Protect emerged. More recently, with the collapse of Gaddafi's regime in 2011 and the ongoing civil war in Syria, discussions surrounding the Responsibility to Protect have made a comeback.

Even if the idea of the Responsibility to Protect has not been fully recognized by the entire international community, it is becoming more and more difficult to resort to the principle of nonintervention to ward off criticisms coming from the outside. This is a positive development because human rights must be protected anywhere in the world. But there is also a downside to this recent development. Civilizational, cultural, and religious diversity, which was preserved even during the period of a Western-centric world system, has been threatened by Western-centric globalization in economic, social, and cultural terms. Especially, more than a few Muslims believe that their sacred religious precepts and practices are being attacked by the predominant Western civilization. This is one of the dangers we must address in the twenty-first-century world.

In my view, even if human rights – in a move that makes national sovereignty more and more conditional, based on how human rights are respected – are often presented as the main justification for transgressing national sovereignty, this should not necessarily mean that there is an inherent contradiction between human rights and sovereignty. Sovereignty is a key norm and instrument for protecting human rights. This is why international law imposes on the state a major responsibility in the protection of human rights. If one sees a situation in a failed state where the state has collapsed and human rights cannot be secured by state mechanisms, one can understand that a well-functioning state and sovereignty is prerequisite for the protection of human rights. The most important human right, the right to live in safety, can be secured only when a sovereign state carries out its fundamental task to protect humans under its jurisdiction.

JMC: And this move toward making national sovereignty more conditional, more benchmarked on human rights, at least in principle, is a major development that has taken place in the last twenty years.

OY: Exactly. However, rather than simply accepting this development as something good, we should regard it as an important change calling for reconsideration of human rights in a more holistic manner. We need a more transcivilizational, including historical, approach to the question of human rights. It is understandable that people tend to criticize traditional discriminatory practices remaining in many parts of the world, especially in the non-Western world, from the viewpoint of human rights and humanitarian considerations. I myself have been a human rights activist since the late 1960s. As such, I have been engaged for many years in a variety of initiatives in order to enhance the value of human rights.

Yet, one should take into consideration how people react when they are criticized and attacked in that their religions, cultures, and social practices violate fundamental norms of human rights. These people have believed in their belief systems for hundreds of years, for thousands of years. And all of a sudden, within just a few decades, they are criticized for what they have believed in. They are now asked to give up their long-standing practices. Considering that it took centuries for Europeans and US people to give up their long-standing practices that were in conflict with human rights, you can understand how difficult it is to demand the same thing of Muslims and other non-Western people within just a few decades.

Finally, when it comes to the issue of human rights and their violations, it is important for us to make clear the following distinction. On the one hand, there are human rights violations in the context of violent conflicts. They are relatively easy to identify and explain, at least from an academic standpoint. On the other hand, when it comes to issues of so-called human rights violations associated with societal beliefs and practices which are at odds with "universal" – often in fact "Western" – beliefs and practices, they are more difficult to deal with. People in non-Western societies, like people in Western societies, have a right to their identity, be it individual or collective. To respect their identity and beliefs is a part of human rights.

JMC: Concerning the question of the relationship between law and power, don't you think that it is an element that is part and parcel of the nature of law? In a way, when it comes to international law, it has always been an expression and a projection of a power situation? For instance, during the nineteenth century, international law was used as a way to justify colonialism.

OY: Well, yes and no. International law up to the early twentieth century was overwhelmingly Euro-centric. It was basically a tool of Western colonial powers, of leading powers such as the United Kingdom, France, and other major European powers. As such international law functioned as an instrument to justify colonial rule, racial discrimination, gender discrimination, and economic exploitation. All these practices and policies were tacitly or explicitly endorsed by international law at the time.

But in the twentieth century, especially after the decolonization period, the content of international law began to change, although not fundamentally. Non-Western nations became a majority in international society in terms of the number of independent states. Following decolonization, the number of member states at the United Nations increased, with formerly colonized territories becoming independent and joining the UN. This greatly changed the make-up, the composition of the UN and its institutions.

In terms of membership, the UN General Assembly became much more representative of the world at large than it had been before. The decolonization and new states joining the UN had an impact on the global discursive space to a certain extent. The concerns of the non-West were given more attention, more publicity. As a result, today, although the global public space is still predominantly shaped by Western media and intellectuals, one could say that room has been gradually made for non-Western concerns, voices, intellectuals, and people.

I will give an historical example in the field of human rights to illustrate this development that has taken place with decolonization and continues to unfold to this day. Indeed, history does not stop. The development that started in the early years of the decolonization period continues even today. In a way, the importance that we give to diversity, both globally and nationally, is a part of this story.

If you compare three prominent instruments of human rights in the twentieth century, you can find an interesting development. First, the Universal Declaration of Human Rights (UDHR) was adopted in 1948, when decolonization had not yet begun at full scale. Second, the International Covenant on Economic, Social and Cultural Rights (ICESCR), and the International Covenant on Civil and Political Rights (ICCPR) were adopted in 1966 after decolonization started. Third, the Vienna Declaration on Human Rights (the Vienna Declaration), was adopted in 1993, when non-Western nations were the majority in terms of the number of independent states. Further, in 1993, the idea to respect cultural and civilizational diversity was accepted worldwide. And my point here is that the later the instrument was adopted, the more diverse views on human rights were reflected.

As such, if you compare the UDHR with the ICESCR and the ICCPR, the views of non-Western nations were much more reflected in the latter two instruments than in the UDHR. While the notion of self-determination of peoples was included in article I of the ICESCR and the ICCPR, the UDHR did not have a provision embodying it. The Vienna Declaration of 1993 expresses even more diverse, transcivilizational views on human rights. Immediately after the end of World War II, the Western nations had an overwhelming power to define the content of the UDHR, and the voices of non-Western nations influencing its spirit and content were extremely limited. Toward the end of the twentieth century, when the Vienna Declaration was adopted, this was no longer the case.

Although slowly and gradually, the content of international law has been changing. From the viewpoint of global legitimacy, however, it has not sufficiently changed. To this day, the views and the ways of thinking of Western nations, which occupy only slightly more than 10 percent of humankind in terms of the population, possess an enormous influence in drafting multilateral treaties and other international normative instruments, interpreting them, and implementing them on a global scale. We need more changes in international law-making and implementation. In this regard, the international redistribution of power now underway with the resurgence of Asian nations represented by China and India may have an impact on such changes. This is one of the most important questions that we will face in the twenty-first-century.

III THE PROBLEM OF POWER AND PRINCIPLE IN INTERNATIONAL LAW

JMC: So throughout the twentieth century, I guess you would say starting in the 1920s all the way to the 1990s, although international law has really been a Western paradigm, it gradually made space for non-Western actors through notions such as self-determination, sovereignty, and nonintervention. This has made it possible for what you call civilizational diversity to be preserved and in fact, at times, even enhanced. And now you are saying that in the past twenty-five years or so, a period which very often has been viewed as progressive and corresponding to a more active, if not a better United Nations, an evolution that is rather negative has taken place. Especially with the erosion of the principle of nonintervention, civilizational diversity is now more at risk than in the past.

OY: Well, the last twenty-five years have been an interesting period from the viewpoint of changing power relations in global history and the globalization of humanitarian values such as human rights. However, as I have already noted, the simultaneous development of these two factors may also be dangerous for a stable and peaceful international order. If China, India, and other resurging Asian nations acquire greater economic and military power, and the US and Western European nations continue to maintain an enormous ideational power capable of defining the way of thinking, of setting the agenda, and producing normative instruments on a global scale, humanity will face a serious discrepancy between the material power possessed by Asian nations and the ideational power possessed by Western nations.

If, for example, the US and Western power continue to think and behave on the presumption that they still are the dominant powers, people in the non-Western world, especially in Asia, will end up being very frustrated. We should recall that Chinese people held Sino-centric views for a long period of time. It has been rooted in their mind as the predominant way to see the world. It is natural, whether one likes it or not, that they will tend to behave according to this deeply rooted Sino-centrism when they become more confident in their material power. It will be extremely difficult, however, for the people in the US – and to a certain extent those in Western Europe – to liberate themselves from the Western-centric (for US people, US-centric) way of thinking, which they have regarded as natural for more than a century, and to appreciate Sino-centrism prevailing on a global scale.

JMC: In essence you are saying that in order to achieve, preserve, and enhance international stability and international order we have to make sure that power and ideas or principles are aligned. If we have disconnect between them we run the risk of having instability.

OY: As you know, law has generally two aspects. One is ideational. It is about pursuing normative values and ideals, such as equality, justice, fairness, well-being, etc. In the field of human rights, environment, or international humanitarian law, you can see this aspect most clearly. But law is also tightly connected with power. To a large extent it reflects power. Here, power means economic and military power. Law cannot be born without power, and law cannot be maintained without power. Usually, law is created and realized as a sort of equilibrium between the pursuit of normative values and the power of privileged people seeking to manipulate law. To some extent, there is always a discrepancy between the two. If, however, this discrepancy is too huge, the legal order may be destabilized.

JMC: And you feel that at the moment the danger is that there is a sense of disconnect between the distribution of power at the international level, particularly with the rise of China, and the fact that we are still basing our thinking on Western principles and ideas?

OY: Yes. Let me give you an example. You and I communicate in English. Though you are French and I am Japanese we take this for granted. This fact reflects the predominance of the English language on a global scale. This again reflects the power of the US, which succeeded the hegemonic status of the British Empire. Although English used to be a minor language, that of the English people, it has become the global language with the expansion of the economic and military power of the English-speaking people.

Yet, people who speak Chinese as a national language are the largest population in the world. From a Chinese perspective, they may feel that the present situation is unreasonable. Today, many people in China are eager to learn English. But when China becomes the largest economic power, superseding the US, they may think and argue: "Why do we have to learn English? Is it not more reasonable that the US and other peoples learn Chinese?"

In the twentieth century people over the world took for granted that humanity should communicate with each other in English. Today, the situation has not changed significantly. However, the present situation is not based on some moral or ethical ground. Nor is it based on some reasonableness of English as a language. From the perspective of linguistics, one cannot say that English is the most reasonable language of the world. The predominant situation of the English language is simply based on the fact that English is the mother language of the two most powerful nations in the world from the nineteenth century onwards, the UK and the US. If this is the case, we should not be surprised if at one point the Chinese people would argue that peoples over the world should communicate in Chinese rather than in English when China becomes even more powerful, superseding the US in the course of the twenty-first century.

And this is not limited to languages. There are many other areas in which the Western way prevails. There are many such institutions which people take for granted today, but in fact they are Western, at least in origin. The institution of the Christian calendar and meridian are some of the examples. Why is meridian 0 in Greenwich not in Delhi or in Beijing? The current institution of meridian reflects the power of the British Empire. We need to keep these kinds of things in mind as the world is changing.

JMC: You are saying that the requirements for global order, for global stability, call for having power and principles aligned. What about the requirements for global justice? I would imagine that in order to have global justice we also need to have an alignment between power and principles, and, perhaps more importantly, we need to have power being put at the service of principles of justice agreed upon?

OY: Even in the field of global justice there are always elements of power. For example, think of the following situation: Someone on the African continent living in a very poor village has a great idea, an idea that is far better for humanity than one put forward by a columnist of the *New York Times* in terms of justice. Yet, it is unlikely that this better idea on justice coming from a person in a poor African village would be universalized and realized. It would be unlikely to be universalized because there is no medium for this idea to be disseminated and shared on a global scale, whereas the view appearing in the *New York Times* may be accepted by the political and intellectual leaders of the world and globally shared. So even when it comes to the problem of global justice, we must take into consideration the element of power, which includes the ideational power structure of the world. For justice for humanity to prevail, we must change this excessively Western-centric discursive space, which is dominated by Western intellectuals and media.

Only when ideas coming from a variety of human traditions, such as Confucianism, Hinduism, or Islam, can be evaluated on an equal basis with those originating in Christianity, the Enlightenment, and many other Western ideas, will we be able to talk about global justice in the true sense of the term. In the field of justice, we may be able to find better ideas in the non-Western philosophy or religions. For example, we have today an extremely important idea of human rights, which was born in Western Europe in the modern period and in which I personally believe. Yet in the future we may be able to find out better ideas than human rights. But for this to happen, we need to have some space, more room, so that more diverse ideas, ways of thinking, traditional or new, can be shared and globally disseminated.

JMC: You are calling for a greater globalization of the public discourse, of public scholarship and so on, which is partly also a de-Westernization of public discourse, of scholarship? Ultimately, you wish for a widening of the market of ideas; you wish to make the public and global discourse richer and much more diverse?

OY: Exactly. You may call it "*de*-Westernization" because the present discursive space is excessively Western-centric. But this is not at all an *anti*-Western argument. Through this change, Western people will also be enriched. For anyone, to be able to encounter better ideas for humanity and become familiar with them is a great advantage. Non-Western people have learned tremendously from great European or Western culture and knowledge since the nineteenth century: Human rights, democracy, various discoveries of modern science, etc. Only very few intellectuals in the Western world have had such privilege to learn from non-Western great ideas. In the twenty-first century, however, Western people may be able to enjoy such privilege on a far larger scale. Advocating de-Westernization is not an aim or end. It is an intellectual device to invite people to enjoy wider, multicivilizational, and transcivilizational ideas and ways of thinking, thereby enriching them in ideational terms.

IV BROADENING THE SCOPE OF INTELLECTUAL TRADITIONS IN INTERNATIONAL LAW

JMC: In practical terms how could this multicivilizational and transcivilizational orientation happen? For instance, in the field of international law I agree with you that there is a need to de-Westernize and encourage what we could call the internationalization of international law. But, in practical terms, how do you go about this, both from the perspective of legal scholarship, and then from the perspective of practice? What would be your recommendations to make this happen?

OY: As to the first question, I have been arguing that Western international lawyers, international relations scholars, or any other intellectuals should learn the non-Western intellectual history of humanity, such as Confucianism, Buddhism, and other intellectual ideas and histories. I have also been arguing that non-Western intellectuals themselves must liberate themselves from Western-centric ways of thinking, which they have adopted unconsciously. The first task we should carry out is, for both Western and non-Western people, to liberate themselves from the predominant way of excessively Western-centric thinking, which is deeply rooted in today's people in an unconscious manner.

In 2011, I gave a lecture at the Fourth European Society of International Law Research Forum. In this lecture I explored various issues on the problem that you have just raised, arguing that non-Western intellectuals may be Africans, Asians, etc., yet their brain has been strongly influenced by Western ideas, and may be alienated from their own traditional cultures and civilizations. I must confess that I myself have been very Western-centric. For many years I focused on modern Western ideas and ways of thinking, studying Hugo Grotius, Thomas Hobbes, Hans Kelsen, Carl Schmitt, etc. It is only after I turned fifty years old that I seriously started studying Confucianism and other non-Western systems of thought.

JMC: You are saying that it is not only needed for Westerners to de-Westernize themselves. It is also imperative for non-Westerners to de-westernize themselves.

OY: Yes. I would say that it is even more important for non-Western intellectuals and academics to de-Westernize themselves. Frantz Fanon was correct in pointing out that non-Western intellectuals are generally so

Westernized and detached from the realities of their own people that they cannot represent deeply felt aspirations and desperations held by their own people. They tend to align themselves with Western intellectuals and communicate in Western-centric terms. We should be aware of this fact and rectify it through conscious efforts.

This is not an easy task. For instance, in non-Western universities, curricula and the research agenda are generally shaped by Western knowledge and intellectual production. Very often those identified as the best students in the developing world often continue their graduate studies in US and Western European universities. These constitute obstacles to intellectual de-Westernization. It tends to underscore and reinforce the claim of superiority of Western ways of thinking. To go back to my own experience and intellectual journey, I have found it very difficult to change my own way of thinking, which is Western-centric at an unconscious level.

Another problem is that intellectuals tend to overestimate or glorify their own cultural or civilizational traditions when they pursue a de-Westernized approach to academic undertakings. There have been numerous arguments that illustrate such egocentric ways of thinking. The argument that "our civilization, religion, culture or nation" – such as Confucianism, Hinduism, Islam, Eastern civilization, China, India, or Japan – had the notion of human rights, democracy, etc. since the very old days is one such example. Also, some Chinese scholars in international relations and other fields have begun to talk about the study of international relations "with Chinese characteristics." Unfortunately, many of these arguments tend to be egocentric and superficial, often justifying the policy of the national government of their nations. As a whole we must seek to overcome any kind of egocentric way of thinking, whether it is Euro-centric, US-centric, Western-centric, East-centric, Sino-centric, Hindu-centric, etc.

JMC: Going back to the issue of relations with the Other, in the West we are not learning much about or from the Other. As such, in a way, we are not seeing the Other. But, in the non-West, and this is probably equally problematic, as you alluded to above, often intellectual and political elites are ignorant of their own traditions because they have been so Westernized. In this regard, is it not true that if you do not see yourself, you cannot see the other?

OY: Exactly. I have already discussed this issue. But let me add a few thoughts on this. As to your first point, concerning the Western intellectuals not seeing the Other, I can cite an example from the field of human rights. Western liberal leaders often criticize discriminatory or violent policies and social practices in the non-Western world. They tend to characterize the resistance or rebuttal coming from the non-Western world to such criticism as a convenient tool or mere excuse to tolerate such policies and practices. When such rebuttal comes from a government or intellectual leaders always seeking to justify their governmental policies, this view is correct.

But what Western liberal leaders often fail to see is that such rebuttal also comes from a sense of national pride, from a rejection of interventionism. It is also caused by the feeling that there is hypocrisy in the West, as Western governments have hardly any problem supporting authoritarian regimes in the non-Western world when it suits them. Moreover, as I have referred to earlier, human rights activists in the non-Western world do not necessarily represent properly the feelings of their own people because they are often detached from them. This is a sad story, but the story that must be told when discussing complex relations between the "West" and the "East," or between the "developed" and "developing" countries.

JMC: The diagnosis that you are putting forward is not simply about the divide between the West and the non-West; it is also about the divide existing in the non-West between Westernized elites and the local people.

OY : Exactly. I have always been critical of the idea of simply dividing the East and the West because both East and West are not monolithic. They entail a diversity of views and feelings. Even I, who have been arguing for reappraising non-Western values, may be regarded as too Westernized by ordinary citizens in Japan. Being in the position of an international law scholar may connote something alien to many Japanese citizens. "Professor Onuma, who speaks English in such a fluent manner and deals with international law, is different from us." This may be a widespread feeling among ordinary Japanese citizens, and this may be true for most non-Western intellectuals dealing with international or global affairs.

JMC: If this is the case, how does one find the right balance and pursue what is right in general, and as applied to human rights, without being self-righteous? How does one go about finding the right balance in normative and intellectual terms, and in political terms? What would be your recommendation?

OY: That is exactly why in the past decades I have been arguing for the need of a transcivilizational perspective in addressing various issues in international law and other global affairs. I must admit that there is no single solution, no "correct" answer to your very difficult question. What I can say is that at least we have to be more serious about learning from non-Western wisdom, non-Western thinking, non-Western ideas. On a superficial level and in principle almost all intellectuals agree with me that we need to learn more from non-

Western philosophy, from Confucianism, Islam, etc. in the twenty-first century. Yet, what most people actually do is to continue learning only from Western sources, paying little attention to non-Western intellectual heritages and assets. The argument for the need to overcome Euro-centrism dates back to the 1970s. Still, the progress is very slow. In the twenty-first century, when the power constellation is actually changing in terms of material power, the need to change our way of thinking is all the more evident.

JMC: This is not a problem that we only encounter in the field of law. It is also a problem in philosophy. Western philosophy has an ambition of universality, and yet its ambition to be universal is built on rather narrow cultural foundations, the Western ones, by and large in ignorance of the world beyond the West.

OY: I agree. I have myself learned a bit of Western philosophy, but often found that universalistic arguments are in fact based on the limited assumption of European or Western civilization. For example, John Rawls's *Theory of Justice* is a leading work of philosophy in the twentieth century. It appears to be a general theory or universal theory of justice applicable to anyone regardless of cultures and civilizations. Yet, its basic assumption is in many respects Anglo-American. Rawls himself came to be aware of this, and made serious efforts to overcome his narrowness. Thus, he wrote *The Law of Peoples*. I highly appreciate his efforts. Yet, I find that the arguments of the book are not satisfactory. Another leading philosopher, Jürgen Habermas, did not even seek to make such efforts. In the case of Ronald Dworkin, a leading scholar in jurisprudence, the Anglo-American assumption is even more apparent.

In the twenty-first century, I really hope that philosophers will critically reflect on their own universalistic assumptions and seek to establish a philosophy that is transcivilizational. They should seek to construct a theory which is not just universalistic yet in fact Western-centric such as those theories of the twentieth and nineteenth centuries. As I have been arguing in my work,[4] we must distinguish universality, universalism, and universalization. It is indispensable for any universalistic argument to be aware of its limits and its narrowness in order to become more universal and transcivilizational.

[4] See ONUMA, *International Law in a Transcivilizational World* and *A Transcivilizational Perspective on International Law*, footnote 10, p. 15.

V RELATIVIZING THE SELF: INTELLECTUAL JOURNEY FROM WESTERN TRADITIONS TO GLOBAL PERSPECTIVES

JMC: You mentioned that it is only in the past twenty years or so that you have started to be very serious about the kind of issues we just discussed. What have been the findings of these twenty years of intellectual journey, trying to go beyond, to see beyond the West?

OY: I think that one of the most important lessons of my intellectual journey, seeking to overcome my own ignorance of non-Western intellectual traditions, is that almost all major philosophical or religious systems of thought are universalistic, yet egocentric. Buddhism, Confucianism, Christianity, Islam, Kant's philosophy, Hegel's philosophy – all these are universalistic and somewhat egocentric systems of thought. This egocentric universalism was inevitable, it seems to me, because all these were born before the twentieth century, and it was difficult for those who created these thoughts to appreciate the multicivilizational landscape of the world, even if they were all gifted geniuses.

Another lesson that I learned from diverse civilizational ways of thought is that, through such learning, we can see how narrowly defined we are. After such an intellectual journey, one can raise doubt about approaches and assumptions that one takes for granted. We can reconsider our own assumptions or presumptions before engaging in discussing something with people whose way of thought is different from ours. By carrying out such "meta-discussion" – which is a clumsy neologism, but I hope you understand what I mean – work before engaging in discussions with others, we may be able to exchange our views in a more self-composed manner.

Thirdly, it seems to me that almost all these great religions, social ethics, and philosophies share egocentric universalism, but they differ significantly if seen from the perspective of proselytism of their ideas. For example, Sino-centric Confucianism seems less proselytizing than Christianity and Islam. For Confucianism, which regards modesty as a great virtue, proselytism is something you should avoid. You may "suggest" to others to believe in Confucian values and virtues. However, to proselytize them even by force is unthinkable for Confucianism.

In contrast, Christianity and Islam share a proselitizing zeal. This may be associated with the idea of salvation. As nonbelievers are destined to go to hell after death, there seems to be a theological motivation and sense of duty to convert nonbelievers, inviting or even forcing them – as the last resort – to join the community of faith, and of salvation. While Christianity and Islam have the concept of sacred war, Confucianism does not. This may not necessarily mean that Confucians are more peace-oriented and Christians and Muslims are more aggressive and war-oriented. Yet, there seems to be a difference over the issue of proselytism between Confucianism on the one hand, and Christianity and Islam on the other.

JMC: We now all talk about the fact that China is rising. In this perspective, one of the issues for the future is whether or not China will be able to transform its economic power into political power, that is beyond the political power and leverage that it has already acquired. Arguably, part of the answer to this issue is based on whether or not Chinese values can be universalized and whether or not there is a desire in China to become a global political power.

OY: Here is an irony about China. On the one hand, Chinese leaders have begun to emphasize Confucianism as an ideology for demonstrating the "greatness" of China or the Chinese nation. On the other hand, their policy is far from faithful to Confucian values: humanness, modesty, compassion, politeness, etc. The policy of contemporary Chinese government is extremely aggressive and violent to its neighbors. The Chinese leadership and citizens are obsessed with their memory of modern history. According to their interpretation of modern history, they have gone through a series of humiliations since the nineteenth century. They have been humiliated because, they believe, China was weak in military and economic terms. This is the history of China since the Opium Wars.[5] This has been the national narrative of humiliation and victimhood.

From such a perspective, in order not to repeat this tragic history of humiliation, China must be powerful, as powerful as possible. This is a major reason why China has been so aggressive in increasing its economic and military power. Although Chinese leadership has begun to realize and emphasize the importance of ideational power or soft power, contemporary China values first and foremost material power, which is military and economic. The Chinese government has been trying to spread or project its soft power by, for example, establishing Confucius Institute on a global scale. However, if compared with paramount soft power China once had up to the early nineteenth century, the soft power of contemporary China is desperately small.

[5] The first Opium War (1839–1842) was fought between China (Qing Dynasty) and Britain, and the second Opium War (1856–1860) was fought between China on one side and Britain and France on the other. The wars resulted in territorial concessions (Hong Kong) and commercial (opening of ports) and diplomatic rights in China for European powers. The Opium Wars led to the Treaty of Nanking (1842), which marked the beginning of unequal treaties.

In recent years, I have been telling my Chinese friends and colleagues and arguing to the Chinese people: "Remember your great history of the pre-nineteenth-century world. You were so respected and admired by neighboring nations or even by many European intellectuals. This was thanks to your ideational and cultural power and not because of your military power. At the time, you valued more this ideational and cultural power than military power. And yet, now, you are obsessed with only one century history of humiliation, forgetting all of your important cultural assets associated with valuing this cultural and ideational power."

My point here is that we have to tell people that it is not for the sake of military power that one nation is respected. We respect French people not because they possess nuclear power but because they possess a very sophisticated, elegant culture. We respect British people not because they possess nuclear power but because they have a long tradition of parliamentary democracy, attractive theatrical art, etc. Contemporary China, Communist China, is very young as a nation. They are obsessed with their short-term memory, by the memory of humiliation in modern history. They have to liberate themselves from this obsession.

JMC: You just said that one of the key findings when it comes to your intellectual journey is that most philosophies are egocentric and yet universalistic. Another finding is that Islam and Christianity have strong proselytism tendencies, which is not the case for the Sino-centric world. Any other key findings?

OY: I am not an expert of comparative civilizations, so I should not be boastful. The observations I have shared with you may be wrong. They are based on my rather superficial readings of comparative civilizational studies in the last twenty years as an amateur scholar and not as a professional scholar.

JMC: Going back to the idea of civilizational diversity under attack since the end of the Cold War and its implications for defending human rights beyond borders, how do we balance the fact that we have to do something to help people in need and yet do so without being self-righteous and without undermining civilizational diversity? How do you draw the line?

OY: There is no absolute answer to this question. Answers must be found out for each specific case. It may be useful to share my experience with you. I have seen many human rights activists and human rights experts in my life as a scholar and human rights activist. Among those, especially among US human rights activists, there are many people who have good intentions but are ignorant of cultural diversities. These kinds of people tend to bring about problems when they preach or proselytize the value of human rights.

We also have to recognize that the very idea of human rights is an historical product. As such it has changed over time and it will most likely continue to change. When the idea of human rights was born first in modern Europe, it was basically about civil and political rights. Later it came to include economic, social, and cultural rights. And now we are talking about a third generation of rights. Some human rights activists and experts, especially those in the US, still stick to the first-generation rights, civil and political rights, regarding economic, social, and cultural rights as something associated with socialist ideology. They are obsessed with excessive political and civil rights-centrism.

However, about this issue I am now rather optimistic. Major human rights NGOs such as Amnesty International and Human Rights Watch have gradually changed their policy. They used to be almost exclusively centered on civil and political rights, but came to be more and more interested in economic, social, and cultural rights. This move is most welcome and should be encouraged.

VI DEVELOPING A GLOBAL INTELLECTUAL AGENDA

JMC: Looking forward, what are the issues you intend to focus on in the coming ten years? What is your next intellectual agenda?

OY: Well, considering my age and health condition, it is difficult to consider my interest in terms of ten years. Let me share with you the record of my interest and work in the past decade, and try to think of my future concerns just in a general manner. During the last twelve years, I have spent most of my time rewriting a treatise (textbook) of international law first published in Japanese in 2005 in the form of a book in English. It was published in 2017 by Cambridge University Press, under the title of *International Law in a Transcivilizational World*. I also published a collection of my articles originally published in Japanese or English in the form of a book in French. It was published in 2016 under the title of *Le droit international et le Japon: Une vision transcivilisationnelle du monde* (Editions Pedone, Paris, 2016). Furthermore, I published a pocketbook entitled A *Perspective on International Law* (Brill, 2010), based on my Lectures at The Hague Academy of International Law in 2007. As the titles of these three books suggest, I have sought to express what I call a "transcivilizational" perspective in the field of international law as clearly and coherently as possible.

Following the publication of these books I plan to deepen my study on the problem of cultural heritage. Like the field of human rights – or any other field

– the problem of cultural heritage has been dealt with in an excessively Western-centric manner. If you look at world heritage sites, many are centered in Italy, France, Spain, etc. It is only in recent years that people began to seek a proper balance among various civilizations in preserving world heritage. In my view, this question of cultural heritage should be treated as a part of the global environment. Humans are not just physical beings. They cannot live without culture. Various kinds of communities have protected their cultures and have passed them on to the next generations.

Modernity highly values the well-being of the present generation. It is concerned with intra-generational implementation of values. It has not paid sufficient attention to generational succession of values and virtues. It has tended to deny the importance of such succession, regarding the past as something to be overcome by ever-progressing modernity. However, toward the end of the twentieth century, humanity came to be aware of the significance of such generational succession of values and virtues after having been confronted with the deterioration of global, regional, national, and local environment, caused by human activities only pursuing intra-generational materialistic well-being during the modern period.

The importance of generational succession of values is not limited to the natural environment. Cultures and cultural environment must be passed on to the future generation together with nature and natural surroundings. From these perspectives the problem of cultural heritage is an extremely interesting, and important, subject of study. Yet, very few scholars have been interested in this subject in a serious and substantial manner. I would like to deepen my transcivilizational approach by addressing the problem of cultural heritage and to invite the attention of younger generation scholars to this question. I have been fortunate that I can work on this topic with prominent members of an interdisciplinary study group, which I organized some ten years ago. They include international lawyers, scholars of international relations, cultural properties, cultural policies of diverse countries, history of architecture, policy-makers, journalists, and some others, all of whom share such interest with me. It is to this question of cultural heritage that I am going to dedicate my limited time and energy in the coming years.

JMC: *In terms of scholarship, what do you think are the questions in the field of law and in the field of philosophy – because you are also a philosopher –, what are the issues on which you think the next generation should focus?*

OY: Well, I am not a philosopher, but I think that in terms of educational schemes we should put more emphasis on history in terms of global comparative civilizational history. This emphasis on history should be appreciated in law school curricula and in graduate school curricula. In order to understand the world of the twenty-first century we definitely need the knowledge of different civilizational histories. So many people today are ignorant of history, especially the history of different civilizations. This calls for improvements. University curricula must be changed accordingly. I firmly believe in this.

JMC: As a professor and a scholar, what kind of advice would you give to young scholars in the West and in Asia in terms of trying to do a better job than the previous generation of scholars and intellectuals? Also, what would your recommendation be in terms of research agenda and teaching agenda for the future?

OY: Well, talking about the next generation, I have always advised my daughters and students to learn Chinese and English in order to survive in the twenty-first century. The choice of specific languages could be somewhat different. You may choose French and Hindi, or you may choose Spanish and Arabic. But I firmly believe that, if possible, one should learn foreign languages. This is key for expanding one's horizon and communicating beyond one's own national community. This will help liberate yourself from many of your assumed beliefs and ideas.

Learning at least one European language and one non-European language is more desirable than learning two European or non-European languages. You could then transcend not only cultural boundaries but also civilizational boundaries. I have been fortunate in that I am a native speaker of Japanese and have learned English, and to a certain extent French and German. I have been able to enjoy learning about both East Asian civilization and European or Western civilization.

Another consideration relating to the first point is that we still live in a predominantly Western-centric world. Despite my criticism of this state of affairs, I recognize that the modern Western-centric world has produced a huge amount of valuable knowledge and understanding of the world. As such, we have still much to learn from this accumulated knowledge and perspective. And yet, as we have discussed, we are desperately, excessively Western-centric, and hence often utterly ignorant of non-Western civilizations.

So, our future generation's task is twofold. On the one hand, whether they are in Paris, New York, or in Nairobi, Cairo, or some village in any country, they should learn about the accumulated achievements of modern Western civilization. On the other hand, they should relativize it; they should liberate themselves from an excessively Western-centric way of thinking, by learning Islamic, Confucian, Buddhist philosophy or some other non-Western ways of seeing the world. One should be as comprehensive as possible in the attitude of learning, always paying attention to the diversity of cultures and civilizations.

This learning process should not just be a superficial undertaking. You should spend time seriously reading the Quran in addition to reading Kant. This is not only theoretical advice. It is also a matter of practical advice. If you are a US business person in China, and if you can cite some famous Chinese poems, your counterpart will greatly appreciate your understanding of Chinese culture. Even in the context of practical relations, curiosity for the Other and showing a desire to learn from the Other is a sign of respect, and this does matter tremendously.

JMC: Finally, what would your advice be to young scholars starting to work in the field of justice?

OY: I have four advices. First and foremost, doubt your own assumptions, presumptions, and preoccupations. As a way to illustrate this thought, I will refer to famous scholars who referred to this idea: "Everything can be doubted" (René Descartes, Karl Marx, and others); "To doubt is a virtue" (KAIHO Seiryo, a Japanese Confucian thinker in the eighteenth century). Second, learn with critical spirit classical works not only in your own culture and civilization, but also in different cultures and civilizations. And here I refer to the following: "Seek not what the sages taught. Seek what the sages sought" (BASHO, a Japanese poet in the seventeenth century, based on the words of KUKAI, a Japanese Buddhist in the thirteenth century). Third, seek to listen to the voices of those who have been ignored or neglected, and whose voice has been unheard of. Fourth, be sensitive to the sin of omission. If you can communicate fluently with others in your own language and on your terms, you are in a privileged position: "Even if lotus flowers open, and Heaven is revealed before our eyes with its supreme light shining, so long as there remains a single man or woman in this world, weeping from misfortune, or enslaved to his or her desires, we shall not ascend to Heaven" (TAKAHASHI Kazumi).

11

International Organizations and Global Justice

José E. Alvarez

I THE DEVELOPMENT OF INTERNATIONAL ORGANIZATIONS

Jean-Marc Coicaud (JMC): *To begin our conversation, tell us how international organizations came to be.*

José E. Alvarez (JA): Most histories of international organizations start with the nineteenth-century conferences where lawyers got together from different countries for various treaty-making efforts. Dissatisfactions with those ad hoc treaty-making efforts – the fact that such initiatives were left to the discretion of the host state who decided to convene them, whom to invite, and what specific issues were on the agenda – led to initiatives for greater institutionalization to permit more coherent and continuous efforts to address global issues. The deficiencies of those nineteenth-century conferences led to the creation of permanent (brick and mortar) institutions with international secretariats. Over time, some of these institutions aspired to achieve universal or quasi-universal membership. Among the first was the International Labor Organization (ILO) in 1919 and later the League of Nations. This historical account relies heavily on functionalism. The premise is that international organizations (IOs) were the product of rational state actors driven by the need to fulfill certain functions requiring international cooperation.

This functionalist explanation for IOs is clear, for example, in Duncan Snidal and Kenneth Abbott's important article which distills these functions to two: states' needs for centralized actions and their need to rely, at least for some things, on neutral or independent actors.[1] States need to combine their efforts to achieve the level of resources, financial as well as intellectual, to resolve certain issues. They also need institutions like the International Court of

[1] Kenneth W. Abbott and Duncan Snidal, "Why States Act through Formal International Organizations," *Journal of Conflict Resolution* (vol. 42, no. 3, 1998).

Justice (ICJ) and independent international civil servants led by the UN Secretary-General because these third-parties, at some remove from states, are perceived as more capable of settling interstate disputes neutrally, allocating resources impartially, or carrying out in disinterested fashion the work of IOs.

JMC: And why did this need emerge in the late nineteenth century?

JA: These needs did not emerge for the first time in the nineteenth century. Centuries before, Grotius, for example, sought to establish rules that should govern maritime trade.[2] But globalization – the modern world's generation of continuous transnational flows of goods, people, capital, and ideas – generated ever more pressing needs by more and more states to coordinate their efforts, including to address the negative externalities of such flows. The increased interdependence of states, not just on economic issues but on lots of others, their need to resolve problems of the global commons, for example, emerged more forcefully starting with this period. States had to address not only how to encourage trade in goods among them but also how to prevent the transmission of diseases that may come with port traffic, for example – and the need to resolve the tension between these two goals by agreeing on certain rules became all the more acute with the turn to civil aviation.

JMC: And these needs which developed throughout the 1920s and 1930s grew even stronger in the aftermath of World War II?

JA: The UN system was indeed the product of World War II and would not have developed, at least not in the same way, without that conflict, including the horrors of the Holocaust. The last inspired the rise of the human rights revolution. The United Nations is itself a product of the perceived flaws with prior institutional efforts. Many of the provisions in the UN Charter are conscious efforts to correct the flaws of the League of Nations Covenant.[3] Organizations like the UN are products of a learning process. From the UN to the WTO, IOs are efforts to correct the past. The UN Charter is at least in part a backward-looking document that seeks to build a viable collective security scheme that would, unlike the League of Nations, enable a central organ – its Security Council – to take enforcement action and impose legally binding obligations on states. The absence of such a central organ in the League, along

[2] Hugo Grotius (1583–1645), Dutch Jurist and author of seminal works in international law including *De Jure Belli ac Pacis* (*On the Law of War and Peace*) (1625).

[3] José E. Alvarez, *International Organizations as Law Makers* (Oxford: Oxford University Press, 2005).

with its failure to delineate clearly the respective powers of all the League's organs, were flaws that the UN Charter sought to correct. The lack of institutional separation of powers in the League led to establishing a Security Council charged with "primary" obligations over peace and security, a General Assembly that is principally a talk shop for almost everything else but is also in charge of finances, and an ICJ presiding over "legal disputes." The drafters also omitted a provision to permit withdrawal, which they feared would only encourage future aggressors to exit from the organization. They sought to avoid the resulting loss of leverage that the League of Nations suffered with respect to Japan, for instance. The WTO and its relatively legalized Dispute Settlement Mechanism was established to respond to the inadequacies of the less formal GATT.

Of course, institutional learning does not just occur when IOs are first established. Organizations – at least healthy ones – learn from their own mistakes over time and adapt. The UN adapted to de-colonialization – the product of its own efforts to recognize the principle of self-determination. This led to a radical shift in the composition of the General Assembly, which went from a body that was under the control effectively of the United States and other Western powers to one that exceeded 190 members with no one country, least of all the United States, in control of a predictable majority. The UN has also had to adapt to first the Cold War – which practically paralyzed its collective security system for decades – and, later, the fall of the Berlin Wall, which, at least for a time, reactivated the Council and emboldened that body to take innovative actions, such as establishing war crimes tribunals.

II HUMANITARIAN INTERVENTION: A NEW ERA FOR INTERNATIONAL ORGANIZATIONS?

JMC: Would you say that the post-Cold War era – the 1990s and the 2000s – introduced qualitative changes in the nature and work of international organizations, especially the United Nations?

JA: Absolutely. In the immediate wake of the Cold War there was what some people have called "UN-euphoria," an optimism that a new world order was being born, as was suggested by Secretary-General Boutros-Ghali in his *Agenda for Peace*.[4] Belief that things had completely changed was encouraged by the Council's coming together to get Iraq out of Kuwait. For

[4] Boutros Boutros-Ghali, *An Agenda for Peace: Preventive Diplomacy, Peacemaking, and Peace-Keeping: Report of the Secretary-General Pursuant to the Statement Adopted by the Summit Meeting of the Security Council on 31 January 1992* (New York: United Nations, 1992).

some, that successful resort to Chapter VII action indicated that the collective security scheme was finally working as intended. Many thought, naively, that this meant that in the future there would be no exercise of the veto – that peacekeeping would become robust and that states would finally begin to agree in advance to provide peacekeeping forces under the standing arrangements as anticipated by article 47 of the Charter.

That post-Cold War euphoria ended in the wake of a number of UN embarrassments, including its inability to prevent killings in Rwanda and Srebrenica, its Oil-for-Food scandal, and a debacle involving peacekeeping post-Somalia.[5] Today, no one really expects easy consensus among the Council's Permanent Members. The Council obviously remains unable to respond to many critical threats to the international peace, from those between Israel and Palestine to humanitarian crises too numerous to mention. After 9/11 we entered another period of uncertainty where the Charter's security apparatus seems ill-suited to intrastate conflicts and threats posed by non-state terrorist actors. Some argue more broadly that IOs, established by states to respond to interstate functionalist needs, now confront a paradigm shift where much of the action needing attention requires the participation of non-state actors, including multinational corporations and prominent members of international civil society. How interstate organizations adapt to a world where states are far from the only relevant actors may be the most significant challenge they currently face.

JMC: While the 1990s was an eventful period in terms of legal developments within the UN, haven't legal developments since been less significant?

JA: I don't think keen observers of the organization would agree. While perhaps there have been fewer innovations as dramatic as the Council's seizing the reins of transitional justice in places like the Former Yugoslavia and Rwanda, the current period has seen more subtle legal innovations.[6] The Council's invocations of the responsibility to protect (R2P) principle with

5 See, e.g., Summary of the Independent Inquiry into the Actions of the United Nations During the 1994 Genocide in Rwanda, UN Yearbook (1999); Summary of the Report of the Secretary-General Pursuant to General Assembly Resolution 53/35: The Fall of Srebrenica, UN Yearbook (1999). In October 1993 the United States authorized a special ops mission supported by the United Nations Operation in Somalia (UNOSOM) II in Mogadishu, Somalia, to arrest two top lieutenants of warlord Mohammad Aidid. The mission led to an unexpected battle and eighteen US soldiers were killed and seventy-three wounded in action.

6 See generally, Sebastian von Einsidel, David M. Malone, and Burno Stagno Ugaret (eds.), *The UN Security Council in the 21st Century* (New York: The International Peace Institute, 2016).

respect to Libya,[7] for example, or its creative adaptation of the "reverse veto" to implement the deal with respect to Iran's nuclear weapons program,[8] may, over time, prove to be even more significant than the Council's role in reanimating hopes for international criminal justice by establishing war crimes tribunals.

JMC: Do you believe that there is a viable responsibility to protect in the sense of a new duty on states to protect their own populations and perhaps a duty on the international community to engage in humanitarian intervention if they do not?

JA: I am very doubtful about the latter but more hopeful about the former. The human rights revolution – and the rise of states' acceptance of a multitude of human rights obligations – makes it increasingly difficult for states to deny that they owe human rights duties to those within their territory. But the fact that states have duties to prevent human rights atrocities does not mean that the Security Council will act consistently when states fail to do what they should. The Council's inability to date to engage in or authorize humanitarian action in Syria[9] may indicate that the Council's invocation of R2P was merely a politically expedient label – to be used when convenient – but not a new legal principle that would be consistently applied.

JMC: Libya is an exception rather than the triggering of a new rule?

JA: I suspect that it is. Nor should we assume that the Libyan operation was either wise or legal. While the Security Council has the power to authorize states to use force, whether it authorized the kind of force that led to the collapse of the Gaddafi regime and Gaddafi's death is debatable. Certainly, some members of the Council who voted in favor of the limited Libyan operation were surprised by the extent of the actual NATO operation that followed, as well as its consequences. Apart from legality, given the outcome of the operation – including the killing of civilians and what has emerged since the demise of Gaddafi – there is surely a question about whether bringing down the regime without having something (or someone) to replace it was wise. A resolution, ostensibly based on protecting civilians, that authorizes

7 See Security Council Resolution 1973 (Mar 17, 2011) (authorizing in para. 4 "necessary measures … to protect civilians" in Libya and citing in its preamble, Libya's "responsibility … to protect the Libyan population").

8 See Jean Galbraith, "Ending Security Council Resolution," 109 AJIL 806 (2015) (discussing the innovations of S.C. Res. 2231 of July 20, 2015).

9 Referring to the ongoing Syrian civil war, which erupted with pro-democracy protests against the Assad regime beginning in March 2011.

only aerial action but not military occupation, may not be the best tool to protect civilians over the long term.

JMC: Why does the text of Security Council Resolution 1973 authorizing the use of force in Libya make you nervous?

JA: Because I am not sure what it means to say when it seeks to protect civilians but only to this extent. The compromises made to adapt this resolution led to disputes among NATO countries and others with respect to what was permitted: What kind of force? To what end? Does it permit or anticipate Gaddafi to stay in power even if civilians continue to be threatened? Is the real aim to remove him from power?

JMC: Yet, if we had answered all these questions it is quite probable that the resolution would not have been approved.

JA: All the more reason to question the ambiguous resolution that was adopted. When you authorize force – the most significant power any IO has – you should be absolutely clear what force is being authorized and for what purpose. As Colin Powell noted long ago, this kind of clarity is needed not only for the soldiers ordered to use force but also to give clear notice to those against whom they are fighting. Peoples' lives are at stake on all sides. You should also be clear about what it is you are trying to achieve. Are you trying to eliminate a regime or just trying to protect civilians from a specific threat for a specific period of time? Do you have a plan in place if you wound or kill Gaddafi about how the territory will be governed so that more people won't be killed in the aftermath of the conflict than before it? We rightly expect a lot from people who authorize killing others, even for noble reasons.[10]

JMC: And you did not foresee the Council taking similar action in Syria?

JA: Not without a considerable shift in alignment of the underlying political interests, including of Russia and the Assad regime. There is nothing in the law – or in the UN Charter – that requires the Council to authorize force consistently in response to comparable threats to the peace. The UN Charter drafters intended the Security Council to act for political reasons, whenever they secured enough votes to authorize action.

[10] In the course of the Libyan civil war, deposed leader Muammar Gaddafi (in office 1969–2011) was captured and killed on October 20, 2011.

III ON GLOBAL GOVERNANCE

JMC: To go back to some of the themes which are at the core of your work on international organizations, it seems that global governance has become a central notion when talking about international affairs and the management of the international system. So, do you feel that such a notion – which is quite vague and ambiguous – is appropriate and do you think that it can be used appropriately as a way to describe the role of international institutions in terms of managing the international system?

JA: Global governance is a vague concept, but we need some term to describe what is going on that is not "government." What a nation-state exercising control over law in its territory does constitutes a government. The world does not have an executive branch, a legislature, and courts. We do not have and probably do not want a world government. But we need a term to describe the complex interrelationships among states, international organizations, other hybrid (public/private) institutions, and NGOs that, in effect, govern the world. State and non-state actors are now deploying legal tools – soft and hard – that affect how states behave both inside their own territories and outside them. Whether you call that global governance or something else matters less than recognizing that it exists and that it needs to be closely examined and evaluated – as we do in all forms of law-making.

Global governance is not limited to actions by classic IOs like those of the UN system. It includes actions taken by the World Bank and the International Monetary Fund (IMF) that might be compared to how domestic administrative agencies regulate.[11] But what some call Global Administrative Law (GAL) includes much more, such as the regulatory impact of private non-state business actors and hybrid public/private institutions. Classic IOs do not regulate the Internet, ICANN does. Of course, there are different ways to describe these realities. The impact of public and private forms of governance can be described in terms of network effects, systems analysis, transnational forms of ordering, or even forms of constitutionalism.[12] The last seems especially apt when these transnational norms are enforced, as they increasingly

[11] See, e.g., Benedict Kingsbury, Nico Krisch, and Richard B. Stewart, "The Emergence of Global Administrative Law," *Law and Contemporary Problems* (vol. 68, 2005), p. 15.

[12] For a survey of distinct frameworks for understanding international organizations, see Alvarez, n. 3. See also Terence C. Halliday and Gregory Shaffer, (eds.) *Transnational Legal Orders* (Cambridge: Cambridge University Press, 2015); Jan Klabbers, Anne Peters, and Geir Ulfstein, *The Constitutionalization of International Law* (Oxford: Oxford University Press, 2009).

are, by a proliferating number of international courts or tribunals.[13] Other scholars, more normatively inclined, argue that these adjudicative bodies are helping to reshape international law into a species of "humanity's law."[14] On this view, transnational judicial communication among the world's adjudicators – including regimes such as trade and investment and not only human rights venues – is increasingly human rights discourse.

JMC: So, you are telling us that global governance corresponds to something which is real; it corresponds to a need which has to be filled and you feel that international organizations are really playing a strategic role in this arena of global governance. They are not being marginalized?

JA: Make no mistake: States are still the primary law-makers in the world and sometimes they marginalize IOs that they feel are not acting in their interests. But states and IOs are no longer (if they ever were) the only relevant actors in governance. There are lots of other players. These include individuals – such as those who serve as international judges or arbitrators, those who are now entitled to bring disputes before regional human rights courts or UN human rights treaty bodies, or investors able to bring an investor state dispute to the World Bank's International Center for the Settlement of Investment Disputes (ICSID). All of these are now involved in developing a kind of "jurisprudence constante" that may have an impact not just on the interpretation of a particular treaty but on customary international law. If we did not have a term like global governance to describe these complex legal effects we would have to invent one.

JMC: Is global governance enough for the needs that we have at the global level? More and more we begin to hear about the notion of global policy, or of global public policy. In fact the European Union itself is an exercise of global policy at the regional level. Does it make sense to think that perhaps global governance is not thick enough, is not really fulfilling all the needs that we have? Beyond global governance should we think about global public policy? If so, how do you see the role of international institutions in this new landscape?

JA: The global governance that exists is indeed fragmentary and rudimentary. Many lawless gaps exist. But, as a lawyer, I am skeptical of any claim that the law can be distinguished from policy. It is a manifestation of public policy;

[13] See Karen J. Alter, *The New Terrain of International Law* (Oxford: Oxford University Press, 2014).

[14] Ruti G. Teitel, *Humanity's Law* (Oxford, UK: Oxford University Press, 2011); Ruti Teitel and Robert Howse, "Cross-Judging: Tribunalization in a Fragmented but Interconnected Global Order," *NYU Journal of International Law & Politics* (vol. 41, 2009), p. 41.

indeed, that is why it can be changed – as policies change. Many of the gaps in governance are reflections of public policy; that is, they exist because powerful stakeholders do not want them filled. But if the implication of your question is that interstate organizations, such as those of the UN system, have to be made more powerful in order to deal with existing challenges, I would not agree. The world that I see reaches for a variety of public and private forms of governance, that is, a mix of different and rather eclectic approaches for exercising policy judgments (whether or not in the form of international law). In a world that increasingly relies on forms of democratic governance at home, I think that a pragmatic approach – where some things are left to the local and are not internationalized – is not a bad thing. Democracies do not want and probably do not need all-powerful international organizations or international courts with hierarchical authority – and they certainly show no inclination to establish only one such institution over themselves or all other organizations. And if the implication of your question is that we increasingly need hard law enforced by courts that can authorize credible sanctions, the turn to forms of "informal law" despite the proliferation of international courts casts doubt on that.[15]

IV GLOBAL GOVERNANCE AND THE INTERNATIONAL CRIMINAL COURT

JMC: *Do you feel that there is a need to go one step further or one step higher in terms of institutionalizing the sense of what we could call shared vulnerability? We hear this all the time in terms of trying to tackle issues having to do with development and environment and clearly the way things are working at the moment is not very satisfactory. So, do you think this is a sensible idea?*

JA: No one disputes that some global commons issues require global – in the sense of universal – solutions. You need the cooperation of every state from the US to China to resolve something like climate change. But such issues do not require the establishment of a new multilateral organization or court. Institutionalization should not be the go-to solution for global challenges. Nor do I think – despite the great clamor for greater transparency and participation – that resolving such issues necessarily requires the voice or participation of every major player. Even global commons issues may begin to be resolved regionally, and there is room for bottom-up action (as by

[15] Joost Pauwelyn, Ramses A. Wessel, and Jan Wouters, (eds.), *Informal International Lawmaking* (Oxford, UK: Oxford University Press, 2012).

provinces within states or even municipalities) – especially when innovative solutions are sought. In my own scholarship, I have been skeptical that international crimes need to be dealt with at the international level, by a single International Criminal Court (ICC).[16] Even as an adviser to the first Prosecutor of the ICC, I urged resort to "positive complementarity" – where the shadow of the ICC inspires local efforts to prosecute international crimes and where the ICC succeeds by being only a court of truly last resort. Ideally, perpetrators of international crimes should be prosecuted where they commit their crimes, that is, in local court: Where their victims can see justice being done.[17]

JMC: It seems that most of the cases in the ICC are coming from developing countries, possibly because in these countries the resources to prosecute are weak. As such, in the public opinion, at times, especially in developing countries, there is a perception of lack of balance. How should we address this problem?

JA: As Mr. Ocampo, the former prosecutor of the ICC, said on more than one occasion, it should not surprise anyone if the ICC does what it is supposed to do – that is, prosecute the most serious international crimes. Nor should anyone be surprised if those atrocities occur most often in countries that have the most serious rule of law problems. But the fact that the ICC has singled out African countries for prosecution and has managed to indict only sitting African leaders has created a serious problem of backlash, within the African Union. Of course, to the extent African prosecutions have emerged because of the Security Council's referrals of the situations in Libya and Sudan, the ICC should not be blamed. Apart from pursuing truly unbiased preliminary investigations – and of warranted prosecutions – anywhere that these are warranted, the ICC needs to embrace, more than it has, Mr. Ocampo's notion of positive complementarity. The ICC is supposed to step in only when states are unable or unwilling to do so. Unfortunately, the ICC's statute did not anticipate technical or other assistance to states to convince or enable them to prosecute in lieu of the Court. The Court lacks mechanisms to make this happen. At present the ICC is just a court; it exercises some leverage over states by threatening to prosecute but does not house mechanisms for rule of law assistance to enable positive complementarity to take root.

16 José E. Alvarez, "Alternatives to International Criminal Justice," in A. Cassese (ed.), *The Oxford Companion to International Criminal Justice* 25 (Oxford: Oxford University Press, 2009), pp. 365–480.

17 See, e.g., José E. Alvarez, "Crimes of States/Crimes of Hate: Lessons from Rwanda," *Yale J. Int'l L.* (vol. 24, 1999), p. 365.

JMC: Following up on this issue of the ICC and based on its now rather significant experience, do we have ways through which we could somehow improve the situation or is it too late?

JA: Other institutions have adapted to changing needs. The World Health Organization's (WHO) adoption of its International Health Regulations signals a real change in an organization that once avoided regulating anything other than certain specific diseases, for example. In a world that is now subject to increasing transnational health threats, including those posed by the intentional transmission of pathogens, that organization has had to adapt and become, in part, a security organization. A court is harder to change but even there the Assembly of State Parties exists precisely to enable adaptation over time. Whether the political will exists to enable the ICC to change its procedures – including on when and where it initiates a preliminary investigation – is another question entirely.

JMC: Why is a court harder to change?

JA: An international criminal court is designed to do one thing well: prosecute someone when it has jurisdiction to do so and provide a fair trial leading to a conviction or an acquittal. The ICC, unusually, has a second mandate: to assist victims through some forms of reparation. It is not clear that the ICC can ever accomplish this second goal, given the thousands of victims that may demand compensation in some cases and the scarcity of available resources. In the absence of unprecedented reforms undertaken by the ICC's Assembly of States Parties and a willingness to find additional resources for this effort, it is hard to see how the ICC can take on a third mandate: to become an engine to institutionalize, in fragile states, the rule of law.

V ON HORIZONTAL, VERTICAL, AND IDEOLOGICAL CRITIQUES OF INTERNATIONAL ORGANIZATIONS

JMC: Since you have dedicated much of your scholarship to international organizations one would assume that you see international organizations essentially in positive terms, but in fact your book provides a more balanced picture. On one hand you of course highlight the positive dimensions of international organizations, but on the other hand you also caution us against the dark side, if you will, of international organizations. Tell us a bit about why this is so.

JA: Early in my book *International Organizations as Law Makers* I rely on Robert Keohane for the proposition the study of international organizations should never ever be confused with their celebration.[18] If you are an honest scholar you look at the phenomenon under study without blinders and try to appreciate its pros and cons. Only then can you provide credible prescriptions for change. My book describes the horizontal, vertical, and ideological critiques these organizations have faced.[19]

The horizontal critique rests on the accusation that even though organizations like the UN are premised on sovereign equality, they do not really put all their members on the same plane. States are not equal members in most IOs and not only in the obvious ways (as with respect to the UN Security Council or the weighted voting procedures within international financial institutions). Even our "impartial" international courts or tribunals tend to privilege richer and more powerful states – if only because these nations have access to more or better lawyers. While IOs – like the WTO – are often established to "level the playing field," that field remains horizontally challenged.

JMC: Do you think greater equality would be a plus?

JA: Yes, overall, if we believe that states should be treated at least under the law on an equal basis. Equality of arms should indeed be the rule within international courts and tribunals in practice and not just formally. Even the perception that a Court like the ICC is biased is a serious problem. Courts need to avoid even the appearance of partiality. IOs face a legitimacy deficit to the extent they continue to face critiques from the Global South that intentionally or not they are tools of hegemonic power.[20]

But a second legitimacy deficit is the complaint, heard most loudly, but not only, in democracies, that rule by IOs suffers from a vertical disconnect. The problem is that law or norms imposed from above at the international level are not subject to the legislative or other procedures that legitimize national rules or norms from below. Even IOs that engage in law-making only through the route of traditional treaties that require state ratification are not immune from this critique insofar as treaty-making itself is seen as an initiative that inordinately privileges executive branches within governments and rarely involves the full transparency and consideration accorded to the making of national laws. This "democratic deficit" is all the more true with respect to less formal forms of IO governance not involving treaties. There is a perception that what happens in IOs, like what happens in Las Vegas, stays in IOs and is rarely

18 See Alvarez, n. 3, at xix.
19 *Ibid.*, at 627–645.
20 *Ibid.*, at 199–217; 643–645.

exposed to full public view, much less the checks and balances associated with democratic governance.

The final critique is one of ideology: The complaint that these organizations are pursuing certain normative agendas that reflect cultural, economic, or other ideologies preferred by some states or national elites. A common example is the contention that, at least in the immediate wake of the Cold War, international financial institutions like the IMF were bent on promoting the Washington Consensus approach to governance and economic development. The perception that some IOs were (and possibly still are) elevating the need to deregulate, protect property rights, and promote free flow of goods and capital above other goals de-legitimizes these institutions and undermines them.[21]

JMC: What about the lack of normative or cultural universality from which international organizations suffer? Professionally, I spent quite a bit of time in Asia and I came to realize that, in addition to essentially being a Western creation, international organizations tend to put forward a Western agenda; they often reflect a dialogue between Americans and Europeans that does not reflect the whole world. Don't IOs evince a kind of truncated universality?

JA: That critique combines the horizontal and ideological critiques noted above. Chinese scholars in particular are becoming much more vocal about the fact that China and other Asian states have been, for too long, rule-takers and that it is time for them to take charge and lead IOs in new directions. We may be seeing that happening sooner rather than later, especially with respect to trade and investment issues. There is no question that much of international law, including international organizations, is a Western construct. It is impossible to deny that the US, Russia, Britain, and France were the principal drafters of the UN Charter and much of the post–World War II IOs that we have been addressing. It is an ongoing project to try to make all of these organizations more representative. It is a scandal that the IMF and the World Bank should be headed by Europeans and Americans. That is a colonialist holdover not required by any law.

JMC: Will the rise of China and others affect the nature and functions of international organizations and for that matter international law going forward? Do you think that in the future we are going to be practicing international law differently? Does a global law program like NYU's need to be internationalized?

[21] Alvarez, n. 3, at 640–645.

JA: International law needs to be internationalized. The functions of IOs will change as a result of the rise of the BRICs and new forms of organizations are already emerging that may eventually displace (or complement) the ones that we have. Whether replacing the United States with China as the world's "indispensable nation" for achieving global governance is a desirable change, however, I am not so sure.

With respect to your question about international legal education: Making a single international law program, even one located in a cosmopolitan city within the United States, truly international is a real challenge – and not only because of language and resource constraints. No single institution, even one as relatively well off as NYU, can possibly involve persons from all over the world, but the resources of the web including social media make it easier to try. But the difficulties NYU faces pale in significance as compared to a law school located in Kuala Lumpur. How the world will train the kind of cosmopolitan international lawyers that it needs is a daunting challenge. We increasingly need to devote resources to the comparative study of international law.[22] We need more attention to understanding how international law is being received and implemented around the world. This is harder than it once was insofar as international law has expanded to become a curriculum. Increasingly, international lawyers have become specialists in particular regimes – such as the WTO – and it is easier to focus on the parts over the trees. Fewer people pay attention to how trade law is being implemented around the world. I suspect that if we actually took a close look, we would find that there is no one trade regime but many. Just as we are likely to find that different countries take different approaches to what the World Bank calls corruption. In all these regimes, we pretend that there is a single treaty text and a single best interpretation of it, but the truth is more complicated – and culturally determined.

JMC: In a sense you are telling us that not only is the law that we teach not the law which in fact exists but also it is not the law that perhaps we should be teaching?

JA: It is actually even more complicated. While some scholars have indeed paid attention to how international law "trickles down" and penetrates into different national legal orders so that, as translated, it becomes something different in practice,[23] this assumes that we know what objective international law actually is – and can tell when national implementation efforts get it

[22] See, e.g., "Symposium: Exploring Comparative International Law," 109 *AJIL* 467 (2015).

[23] See, e.g., Karen Knop, "Here and There: International Law in Domestic Courts," *NYU Journal of International Law & Policy* (vol. 32, 2000), p. 501.

wrong. But in reality some countries' particular views of international law "trickle up." Some national adaptations of international law affect, sometimes dramatically, the meaning of international law, especially if the country is powerful enough to assert its views like the United States or China. The United States has managed to expand the powers of states to respond to acts of terrorism through the use of force and through some influential Security Council resolutions since 9/11.[24] Similarly, China's current actions relating to the South China Sea and islands therein seem directed at changing the rules of the game.

VI REFORM OF THE INTERNATIONAL SYSTEM: BALANCING POWER AND PRINCIPLES

JMC: The generic problem seems to be the relationship between power and principles. Ideally, you would want to have principles being put at the service of power. But very often it is the other way around. So how do we connect law and justice so that actors identify the right principles and put law at their service?

JA: The connection between law and justice is quite complicated. We are now conducting this conversation in an office once occupied by Thomas Franck, who devoted his life to legitimacy and questions of fairness and justice. And Tom first approached it, as you well know, as a problem of legal legitimacy and said that fairness had to be left for a second day.[25] And then he tackled fairness.[26] That proved to be a much more difficult proposition because when we try to achieve fairness or justice we need to bring people other than lawyers into the room.

JMC: So you need to bring in philosophers and practitioners?

JA: And anthropologists and economists and many other disciplines. We have learned, thanks in part to lawyers' efforts to promote sometimes overly narrow views of what the rule of law demands, that achieving the good life requires attention to the diverse needs of people – and not only to securing the civil and political rights associated with Western rule of law states. Achieving sustainable welfare is a broad political project requiring the efforts of many others apart from lawyers.

[24] José E. Alvarez, "Hegemonic International Law Revisited," *AJIL* (vol. 97, 2003), p. 873.
[25] Thomas M. Franck, *The Power of Legitimacy Among Nations* (Oxford: Oxford University Press, 1990).
[26] Thomas M. Franck, *Fairness in International Law and Institutions* (Oxford: Oxford University Press, 1998).

JMC: Would you say that bringing more nonlawyers to the table is one of the key agendas of the future?

JA: Well, all too often the error is that too few lawyers are consulted before action is taken, but you are correct insofar as some matters are erroneously seen as exclusively the domain of lawyers. Consider the topic of bringing IOs to account for their mistakes. An age that increasingly expects governments to be accountable is bound to expect the same with respect to any other entity that purports to exercise governance. UN peacekeepers, whether engaged in rape or spreading cholera in Haiti, need to be held accountable – despite the immunity accorded to the UN in national courts.[27] Making sure that organizations like the UN – which purport to be spreading the rule of law to others – are themselves subject to it is going to be high on the agenda for UN reformers. But achieving accountability is not just about making sure IOs are subject to sanctions and forced to pay damages for violating the law. Making IOs responsible also requires serious efforts to address their horizontal, vertical, and ideological deficits discussed earlier. We have only begun to address some of the more obvious horizontal/vertical defects such as the lack of transparency or the need to correct weighted voting schemes (as within the IMF). Much more needs to be done.

JMC: Up until now we could afford to be thinking and acting under the delusion that Western law was the whole of law and that somehow the Western view was the whole of law. It is less and less possible, so wouldn't you say that somehow we have to revisit what law is?

JA: Absolutely. I have suggested that one of the core challenges that IOs will need to address in the near future is the very nature of the "law" that they are propounding.[28] This is why your original question about governance is so important. Once we start talking about "governance" and once we start taking seriously the fact that IOs are indeed "law-makers" (albeit creative ones), we are already taking a step outside the European–American legal positivist mindset that says all international rules have to take the form of the legal sources enumerated in Article 38 of the Statute of the ICJ. I have argued that while one could try to fit all forms of governance into the traditional boxes of

[27] José E. Alvarez, "International Organizations and the Rule of Law," *New Zealand Journal of Public and International Law* (vol. 14, 2016), p. 3.

[28] José E. Alvarez, *The Impact of International Organizations on International Law*, at 398–420 (Leiden: Brill/Nijhoff, 2016).

treaty-custom-general principle, doing so misses much about how states, businesses, and individuals are indeed regulated by IOs.

JMC: So you want an opening up of the sources of law?

JA: That is already happening whether I want it or not. But some legal positivists argue against "de-formalizing" legal ascertainment.[29] For some people, IOs are merely the repositories of states; IOs are merely their agents and have no real agency of their own and it would be a mistake to elevate IO actions short of treaty-making to the status of "law-making." As noted, I agree that states remain the principal law-making actors. Indeed, some international legal regimes appear to be subject to a historical dialectic whereby once they appear to threaten some state prerogatives, state forms of backlash emerge to restore some of that lost clout.[30] States retain many tools – including defiance of what IOs do – to protect their sovereign rights. But, at the same time, IOs and actors associated within them – from UN special rapporteurs to international judges – still exercise some relative autonomy. Indeed, as we discussed in terms of functionalism, IOs and persons associated with them were meant not to be wholly subject to state control. Moreover, collectivities of state representatives – such as those within the UN General Assembly – have the power to take action that is denied to any one of them. The United States could not prevent the Assembly from recognizing Palestine as an observer-state – or from the obvious consequence of that initiative, namely the ICC's acceptance of Palestine as a state party.[31] Of course, the actions of the collective are not always progressive or good.

JMC: All these questions are really big questions and they have to do with the reform of the international system and the reform of international institutions. Are you comfortable with the nature of the debates taking place on the reform of the international system and international institutions?

JA: No. Reform agendas within IOs are still relatively narrow. Security Council reform generally has consisted of different proposals to tinker with the numbers of permanent members with or without the veto. Few people

[29] See, e.g., Jean d'Aspremont, *Formalism and the Sources of International Law* (Leiden: Brill/Nijhoff, 2011).

[30] "Is Investor-State Arbitration 'Public'?" (forthcoming *Journal of International Dispute Settlement*); also available as NYU IILJ Working Paper 2016/6, at www.iilj.org/documents/Alvarez_IILJ_2016_6_GAL_final.pdf. See also José E. Alvarez, "The Return of the State," *Minnesota Journal of International Law* (vol. 20, 2011), 223.

[31] See, e.g., Alvarez, n. 29, at 185–189 (discussing the consequences of G.A. Res. 67/19 determining that Palestine is an "observer state").

really have any hope of deep reform of that body. A genuine reform conversation would be more expansive. It would consider, for example, what kind of collective security arm do we really want in the age of non-state threats to the peace? What ought to be the relationship between the Security Council and the General Assembly or other regional or security organizations (such as NATO)? It would consider more seriously the overlapping jurisdictions of our existing IOs and the prospects for forum-shopping between them or other forms of collaboration. We should be discussing these questions within these organizations and not just in academe.

JMC: So things are not really moving ahead?

JA: Some of the most serious forms of governance reform are occurring outside traditional IOs, not within them. International lawyers are partly to blame. International legal advisers, in government or IOs, tend to have narrow views of what is relevant or safe to discuss. They are likely to treat some things as sacred. They would be the first to suggest, for example, that the ICJ should not be reexamined – even if it seems to have a relatively small docket, it has difficulty handling fact-intensive cases, and still gives the Permanent Members of the Security Council exalted status. Lawyers' caution about establishing a precedent concerning the UN's liability is surely part of the reason why the UN took an unconscionably long time to issue an apology – albeit an ambiguous one – with respect to its responsibility for spreading cholera in Haiti.[32] Despite their ostensible commitment to the rule of law, the lawyers inside IOs are not likely to be leading the charge in favor of recognizing that the victims of IO malfeasance are owed a legal remedy as much as any other human rights victim.

JMC: But in fact what you allude to here is the difficulty for international law, for international lawyers, to conceptualize and to bring about change. Why is that?

JA: As we discussed, the UN system is essentially a recent, post–World War II product. Some of those present at its creation are still with us today. It is not surprising that we are still living in the shadow of those who believe that these institutions were (and remain) great (but still fragile) institutions to secure the collective against abusive state power. There is still great sensitivity to undermining these "progressive" efforts. The perception persists that these

[32] See Report of the Special Rapporteur on Extreme Poverty and Human Rights, UN Doc. A/71/367 (August 26, 2016).

are our babies and we should not criticize them before they are fully grown and can take care of themselves.

JMC: It seems that more often than not, if it were not for diplomats acting as decision-makers, change in the field of international law would not happen. Would you agree that all the changes that have happened in the field of international law in the 1990s have mainly taken place out of diplomatic activism, decision-makers' activism, and were not necessarily initiatives started by international lawyers?

JA: Yes and no. International lawyers tend to enable initiatives started by others. They facilitate and enable the change the policy-makers want. At the same time, certain visionary lawyers, including those present at the creation, were change agents. This often happens, at least within academe, when lawyers are exposed to other disciplines. That is why I applaud interdisciplinary efforts between say political scientists and lawyers. I think that those collaborations may enrich both sides: The political scientists will realize that law exists and can be made to matter, but the lawyers realize that what they are doing is politics in another guise.

JMC: What about philosophy and law?

JA: The same potential for beneficial collaborations exists. One of the positive things about the US legal academy is its strong tradition of hiring onto faculties of law those with doctorates in philosophy, economics, or other fields. We tend to hire more interdisciplinarians than others do in our law schools.

VII ON THE INTERNATIONAL INVESTMENT REGIME

JMC: Changing a bit the topic, you have published two books dealing with the international investment regime and are about to publish a third.[33] *This is not a new interest for you since, more than twenty years ago, you started your career working on these issues both as a legal scholar but also as a practitioner. Why return to these issues and why is it that you feel that these issues are particularly important today?*

[33] José E. Alvarez, Karl Sauvant, Kamil Gerard Ahmed, and Gabriela del P. Vizcaino (eds.), *The Evolving International Investment Regime: Expectations, Realities, Options* (Oxford: Oxford University Press, 2011); José E. Alvarez, *The Public International Law Regime Governing International Investment* (Leiden: Brill/Martinus Nijhoff Publishers, 2011); José E. Alvarez (ed.), *American Classics in International Law: International Investment Law* (Leiden: Brill/Martinus Nijhoff Publishers, 2017).

JA: The international investment regime interests me because it is one of the most active in terms of producing law. It is not just that over 3,000 international investment agreements (IIAs) exist but hundreds of arbitral awards are now producing a kind of case law rarely evident in international law. There is considerable investment governance going on – and considerable sovereign backlash in its wake. The regime highlights the vertical, horizontal, and ideological critiques of governance. It also interests me insofar as it is a regime that has been deeply influenced by US ideas and power – which go back to the earliest days of the United States as a nation. The United States is not party to many international courts and rarely permits supranational supervision over its laws but thanks to the NAFTA's investment chapter, the United States has become one of the leading respondent states before ICSID. This exposure to investor-state claims has generated buyers' remorse. The United States is having second thoughts about a regime that it once foisted on the world. It is now backtracking on providing investor protections in its more recent IIAs, and the US, along with many other states, is trying to restore more of its sovereign policy space. The regime is a perfect example of a system that has encountered challenges, is undergoing change, and happens to involve a leading economic player.

JMC: The field as it is now is very different from what it was twenty years ago?

JA: Absolutely. There is much more law – customary and treaty – to discuss than in the early days when the only game in town were the decisions rendered by the Iran–US Claims Tribunal and a handful of other rulings. In addition, for a regime that lacks an overarching multilateral bricks and mortar institution comparable to the WTO in Geneva, the investment regime offers much to students of IOs. It consists of more than bilateral investment treaties (BITs). The IMF, for example, is an investment regulator, as is, to an extent, the WTO itself and the OECD. In addition, there are many participants in the market who rank countries based on their investment risk and are de facto enforcers of the regime. States that expropriate or otherwise mistreat foreign investors are likely to face market backlash.

JMC: So you are building on your established expertise but you are also expanding expertise out of all these changes that have taken place in the last twenty years?

JA: The investment regime is an example of governance without government that also happens to operate without an overarching international organization dominating it.

JMC: All this assumes that legal regimes are self-contained and that it is possible for them to continue to work in a self-contained fashion. But in a world which is more and more globalized, in one which is more interdependent, is this the right assumption?

JA: No. I agree with Bruno Simma, who says that most of these regimes are probably not self-contained and should not be so treated.[34] We have rules that enable an investor-state arbitrator to draw from general public international law in interpreting a BIT. The Vienna Convention on the Law of Treaties itself says that you can refer to relevant rules of international law among the parties. Simma has argued in favor of using that rule to bring human rights issues into investor-state arbitrations.[35] Such cross-referrals are in fact happening. But I am skeptical that this will produce the "progressive" results intended. In my view, unless you change the investor-state arbitral system itself by changing who the arbitrators are, who can bring cases, the standing of others affected to participate – unless you change all of those things I am not sure that we can expect "humanity's law" to emerge from rulings issued by commercially trained arbitrators.

JMC: Do you think that these kinds of changes are likely to happen? One would assume that it is necessary to really have these changes taking place so that global governance become more effective?

JA: Earlier I referred to Ruti Teitel's and Rob Howse's view[36] that there are commonalities among these international adjudicators – whether in trade, investment, or international criminal courts; they argue that all these adjudicators reach for human rights values and therefore increasingly contribute to a more coherent "humanity's law." I am not as optimistic as they are because I think that the background of arbitrators or judges matter. I do not think that the background of, say, a judge on the ICJ or a judge on the European Court of Human Rights is the same as the background or training of an arbitrator in one of these investor-state disputes. The broader point has been captured beautifully in the critical scholarship of David Kennedy, who argues that international law has come to be dominated by narrowly grounded experts

34 Bruno Simma and Dirk Pulkowski, "Of Planets and the Universe: Self-contained Regimes in International Law," in *European Journal of International Law* (vol. 17, 2006), p. 483.

35 Bruno Simma and T. Kill, "Harmonizing Investment Protection and International Human Rights: First Steps Towards a Methodology," in C. Binder et al. (eds.), *International Investment Law for the 21st Century: Essays in Honor of Christoph Schreuer* (Oxford, UK: Oxford University Press, 2009).

36 See Footnote 14.

handicapped by disciplinary tunnel vision.[37] This means that where Teitel and Howse see the prospect for "humanity's law," others see "fragmented" law among international regimes, including international courts, as the more likely outcome.

VIII ACCOUNTABILITY AND LEGITIMACY

JMC: You have served as a special advisor to the prosecutor of the International Criminal Court. What was your role in this function and why did you decide to take on this additional responsibility?

JA: Mr. Ocampo was very persuasive. I was also honored to join his other advisors at the time: Catherine MacKinnon on gender and Juan Mendez on humanitarian issues. I advised the prosecutor on public international law matters that he brought to my attention. He sought my advice, for example, with respect to an initiative being taken by the Assembly of State Parties directed at the accountability of the Prosecutor's Office. As I have suggested elsewhere, I found that the proposal posed some conflicts with the Rome Statute's goal of establishing a truly independent Office of the Prosecutor.[38] It was an important example of how difficult it may be to achieve accountability without undermining the goals of these organizations. That particular example made me humble about how little international lawyers have contributed to the accountability debate.

Nor do I think that the International Law Commission (ILC) has made sufficient progress on this issue, despite their release of its Articles on the Responsibility of International Organizations.[39] I do not think that you can wave a magic wand and resolve this by simply declaring that IOs are sufficiently like states that we can replicate what the ILC has done in its entirely more successful Articles of State Responsibility. As the ICJ has told us, each international organization is a creature of its own charter. It is a legal person only insofar as those characteristics are needed to fulfill its function.[40] The legal personhood of the IMF or the OECD or the OAS may be different than

[37] David Kennedy, "Challenging Expert Rule: The Politics of Global Governance," *Sydney Law Review* (vol. 27, 2005), p. 2.

[38] José E. Alvarez, "The Proposed Independent Oversight Mechanism for the International Criminal Court," in Richard H. Steinberg and Fatou B. Bensouda (eds.), *Contemporary Issues Facing the International Criminal Court* (Leiden: Brill/Nijhoff, 2016), p. 143.

[39] International Law Commission, Draft Articles on the Responsibility of International Organizations, with commentaries, 2011, in ILC Report on its 63rd Session, UN Doc. A/66/10.

[40] Reparation for Injuries Suffered in the Service of the United Nations, Advisory Opinion, 1949 ICJ 174 (Apr. 11).

the personhood or the responsibilities of the UN. The responsibility owed by each needs to be resolved organization by organization. In addition, accountability is not reducible to "legal responsibility." Sometimes IO accountability may require court-ordered legally binding remedies comparable to those applied to states, but sometimes accountability may be satisfied by turning to, for example, an ombudsperson approach (as the Security Council has done with respect to some of its sanctions programs in the wake of the critical Kadi ruling by the European Court of Justice).[41] Sometimes IO accountability may mean creating other bodies within an organization that can check, through political action, the organ in question. Sometimes we can expect an international or even national court to act or engage in forms of "judicial review" over IO organs (even if without the possibility of enforceable sanction).[42] And some parts of an IO, such as the prosecutor of the ICC, were intended to be largely insulated from the possibility of state "corrective" action.

JMC: And to the extent that we continue to ignore these demands for accountability, where warranted the legitimacy of these organizations will be all the more put in question?

JA: Yes. The backlash against the investment regime provides an example. Ignoring or diminishing the need to make investor-state arbitrators more accountable has not made the problem go away. It has led for calls for changes in how those arbitrators can be challenged for conflicts of interest and proposals for codes of conflict to encourage more ethical behavior. There are rules about avoiding conflicts of interest and the appearance of impropriety when it comes to national judges as well as with respect to lawyers in a national context. To date, we generally have no such rules for international judges or arbitrators generally and no single coherent set of ethical rules apply to international lawyers, apart from the disparate ones that may apply to them at the national level. These are accountability and legitimacy issues that are very likely to become prominent over the coming years. Even the way international judges are selected is likely to merit increased scrutiny. While we like to pretend that these judges are above politics, the ways that they are selected suggests that this is not the case.[43] We like to pretend that our judges,

[41] Joined Cases C-402 and C-415/05P, *Kadi & Al Barakaat Int'l Found.* v. *Commission* (Kadi I), 2008 ECR I-6352; Joined Cases C-584, C-593, & C-595/10P, *Commission* v. *Kadi* (Kadi II), July 18, 2013.

[42] José E. Alvarez, "Judging the Security Council," *American Journal of International Law* (vol. 90, 1996), p. 1.

[43] See, e.g., Ruth Mackenzie, Kate Malleson, and Penny Martin, *Selecting International Judges: Principle, Process, and Politics* (Oxford: Oxford University Press, 2010).

including on the ICJ, are selected on a purely meritorious basis, but candidates for the ICJ have to campaign – as do the governments that nominate them – within the UN's system of regional blocs. Whether the result are the best candidates for the job remains to be seen.

JMC: And the same applies to heads of international organizations?

JA: Of course; as is true of those selected to become part of the international civil service. Only some IO positions – such as the head of the World Bank or the UN Secretary-General – get public scrutiny. We rarely examine closely less transparent appointments processes, such as those involving the selection of adjudicators for our twenty-four international courts or tribunals.

IX THE FUTURE OF INTERNATIONAL ORGANIZATIONS

JMC: Turning to the future, how do you see international organizations twenty or thirty years from now? Will they be more important or less important?

JA: I suspect that the growth period of traditional IOs with universalist aspirations is at an end. For one thing, the proliferation of IOs and other groupings of actors (e.g., the G20) that make governance claims on states poses the issue of overload. We have created a world where we are demanding almost too much from states, even in the form of reports or information. The UN human rights system alone demands so many reports from so many different bodies of a single state that it creates a substantial bureaucratic and logistical burden even for a country with the resources of the US. One can only imagine the burdens imposed on a state that has fewer lawyers or fewer resources. As is well known, states are notoriously late in providing reports to either UN human rights treaty bodies or comparable entities in the ILO. This in turn produces considerable cynicism about the credibility of human rights/labor enforcement – and helps to explain NGO resentments toward the relatively more efficacious trade and investment regimes. The legitimacy of IOs and international law is not furthered when one can say, with some justice, that the single most effectively protected human right today is the right to hold property (thanks to investor-state arbitration). As noted, one solution to this dilemma is to fold labor, human rights, and environmental into more "enforceable" regimes, such as trade and investment. That said, resistance by states is more likely to lead to another solution to the overload problem: Consolidation. Thus, some have argued for consolidating all human rights treaty bodies. But that solution creates its own set of problems. We established a distinct committee under the Convention on the Elimination of All Forms of Discrimination Against Women (CEDAW) to handle gender-related complaints because, while gender discrimination was already part of the mandate of the UN Human Rights Committee under the International Covenant on Civil and Political Rights (ICCPR), that committee rarely addressed such issues and historically was dominated by men.

Nonetheless, we are likely to see efforts to consolidate the work of IOs in the future in response to the demands of states. On the other hand, we are also likely to see devolution of what some global IOs now do to more regional groupings, particularly if the global IO appears to be incapable of responding to regional needs. We are seeing such devolution occurring with respect to the trade regime, in the wake of the demise of the Doha round, and some see forms of devolution to regionalism occurring with respect to peacekeeping.

JMC: So consolidation, devolution, and also diversification perhaps?

JA: All three. And this includes international courts. I foresee more experimentation with different forms of international adjudication. I, for one, never expected the ICC to fully displace alternative forms of making perpetrators of international crimes accountable.[44] International criminal justice is likely to see more experimentation over time. Since the 1990s, we have gone from two ad hoc war crimes tribunals enjoying primacy with respect to jurisdiction to hybrid tribunals subject to differing jurisdictions and compositions. The Lebanon Tribunal's jurisdictional mandate is quite different from the one for Cambodia, for example. We have come to realize that truth commissions – which themselves come in different flavors – fulfill some functions that international and national criminal courts cannot and that these courts may need to work alongside such commissions to achieve the diverse goals sought for transitional justice. As noted, we are also coming to realize that the ICC cannot achieve the exalted goals of some of its advocates and that it too needs to be supplemented by other efforts, including national and possibly regional criminal courts, even with respect to states that are parties to the Rome Statute. International criminal justice will, I suspect, be an exception to any trend toward consolidation or merger of IO functions and there are likely to be others. Of course, this means that those who are threatened by the existing forms of fragmentation among IO regimes and courts will not be pleased.

JMC: So the future is relatively open.

JA: Yes and it may not be pretty.

[44] See Alvarez, n. 16.

JMC: Finally, what is your advice for emerging scholars in the field of justice?

JA: Question everything – including whether turning to law furthers justice. Try to see law and its institutions from the perspective of nonlawyers, including from the perspective of victims of the law and lawyers. Law does not displace politics, economics, anthropology, or sociology; it is all of those.

PART IV

WORLD ORDER AND GLOBAL POLICY

12

Global Justice and Global Peace

Charles A. Kupchan

I STABLE GLOBAL PEACE: HOW ENEMIES BECOME FRIENDS

JEAN-MARC COICAUD (JMC): *A few years ago you published an important book,* How Enemies Become Friends,[1] *in which you ask two fundamental questions. First, how do we preserve existing systems of peace? And, second, how do we deepen and enlarge zones of stable peace? You begin by telling us that, in fact, on these issues we do not know much. Why is it the case? And why is it so important to find answers to these two questions?*

CHARLES A. KUPCHAN (CK): I think that the field that you and I are part of is in some ways biased toward writing about war. It is not just scholars, it is journalists, it is novelists, it is moviemakers. If you pick up on any given day the *New York Times*, or the *Washington Post*, or *Le Monde*, or *Die Zeit*, or any newspaper from around the world, I bet that you will find at least one and probably several stories about war. Iraq, Syria, Yemen, Libya, Afghanistan – there is no shortage of conflicts for journalists to cover. And no question that if you turn on the evening news the same will be true – lots of coverage of wars. At the same time, it is safe to assume that we will not pick up the paper tomorrow morning and see a headline that says "All quiet on the US–Canadian border" or "All quiet on the Franco-German border" and that is because when peace breaks out nothing happens. There is no noise, there is no blood, there are no bombs – and therefore there are no journalists.

In some ways I think the same is true of scholarship: We tend to be drawn to big events, and we do not spend enough time writing about nonevents. So I set out in this book to try to fill that gap, to address a simple puzzle based on the mundane observation that if I get in my car in Washington and drive north to the Canadian border, a border that runs thousands of miles, I will find a few

[1] Charles A. Kupchan, *How Enemies Become Friends* (Princeton, NJ: Princeton University Press, 2010).

border guards who are checking passports, but I will not find any tanks on either side. That is a quiet miracle, right? That is historically a revolution that you have thousands of miles of border that is undefended by both countries. The same is true in your country, Jean-Marc; you can now drive from France to Germany without stopping. You do not see a tank, no border guards, you do not change money. And keep in mind that the Franco-German border was for much of history a demarcation that spawned untold violence and death.

It was to answer the puzzle of how peace breaks out that I amassed a range of historical cases to study how states demilitarize their relationships, how they become so comfortable with each other that war becomes unthinkable. I started looking around for literature on how to explain this phenomenon and I found very little. The main literature on this question is about what scholars call a security community – groupings of countries that form communities in which war becomes remote or war becomes unthinkable. But there are literally only a handful of books on that topic, so I set out to try to extend that literature. I have gathered as many cases in history as I could find and then I narrowed them down to twenty cases to study how peace breaks out.

The earliest case I look at is the initial confederation of three Swiss cantons in 1291. That federation was the basis for what is today a stable, federal Switzerland. I look at a case in the 1400s: the Iroquois Confederacy. After many, many decades of killing each other, five Iroquois tribes in what is today upstate New York sat around a fire in a town that still exists today called Onondaga and fashioned a great oral law. For the next 300 plus years, not one Iroquois tribesman killed another tribesman in battle. And then I look at eighteen other cases right up to the present day trying to answer the key question of when peace breaks out; when do countries succeed in escaping war?

II THE FOUR PHASES OF PEACE

JMC: You tell us that the ideal goal of our efforts is peace but that in fact we tend to focus on war; and this is the case because peace is a nonevent. Against this background the question you set to address and answer in the book is: How do we account for this nonevent? You argue that stable peace breaks out through what you call a four-phase process: you talk about accommodation, the practice of reciprocal restraint, the deepening of societal integration between the partner states, and finally the generation of the new narratives and identities. Why do you think that these four elements are key for stable peace to break out?

CK: Well, the story that I tell in the book, which you very nicely summarized, was a story that emerged through the cases. Peace does not have to necessarily come about through that sequence. You could generate other hypotheses, but that is what I found. The story does not occur exactly the same way in each case, but the sequence of steps that you just articulated is generally the story that encompasses all of the twenty very different cases that I examine in the book. These cases span different time periods, different cultures, and different locations and parts of the world. So let me just pick one case, the Anglo-American case, since it is one of the more detailed cases in the book, and very briefly describe how peace breaks out.

The initial movement toward peace always begins amid a condition of strategic necessity. That is to say the opening move is not one of altruism. The opening move is one of necessity. In the case of Britain and the United States it occurred in 1895 and 1896 when a dispute broke out between British Guyana and Venezuela over their border. The United States, which was feeling more and more powerful at the time, sent a message to London saying "this dispute between your colony and Venezuela is occurring in the Western hemisphere and thus it is our backyard; we should have a say in how this dispute is resolved." The British cabinet met in London to discuss the US demand, and they sent back a message to Washington basically saying "get lost."

Then there was talk of war in Washington, that this response was an affront to American pride, and that the British were violating the Monroe Doctrine, which said that the Western hemisphere should be a US zone of influence. The British ambassador in Washington sent messages back to London saying the situation was getting serious and that the Americans are talking of war. And it is at that point that Prime Minister Salisbury and the cabinet consulted with the head of the Navy and the head of the Army, and said "can we go to war with the United States?" And the answer from the Navy was a resounding "no." Britain faced a rising Germany, a rising Japan, an uprising in South Africa that was soon to become the Boer War. Simply put, the British did not have sufficient capability to go to war against the United States without grievously exposing themselves in other parts of the empire and imperiling the homeland itself due to the rising German threat in Europe.

And as a consequence of that recognition of strategic deficiency the British decided to back down, and they proceeded to send a message to Washington that effectively reversed course and indicated that "we have rethought our position. We think you are right. We will take this dispute to arbitration." Arthur Balfour, who was a leading voice in the House of Commons, gave a public speech in which he recognized the legitimacy of the Monroe Doctrine.

So this was a clear message sent across the Atlantic to the United States saying we want to change the nature of our relationship with you. It was the opening gesture of goodwill.

JMC: In essence, accommodation comes from strategic necessity?

CK: Yes, in order to describe the first phase in the process toward peace, "accommodation" is key. The initial act of accommodation by Britain – agreeing to take the territorial dispute to arbitration at the request of Washington – is what sent the signal of the benign intent. In the other cases that signal is sent through similar kinds of gestures. Giving up territory, ending a border dispute, moving your troops away from the border, settling a disagreement over trade – the key is sending a signal of benign intent through an act of strategic accommodation, an act of strategic restraint.

Then, if that signal is correctly received and the party that receives it is interested in exploring a move toward peace, it reciprocates. And that is stage two, reciprocal restraint. The party that was initially accommodated then becomes the party that accommodates and sends its own signal of benign intent to its adversary. So, in the case of the United States it accepted the finding of the arbitration panel that ruled in favor of Britain, and then the US went on to settle a host of other disputes with the British, including over fishing rights in the Bering Sea, over the border between Alaska and Canada, and over whether the US could build and fortify the Panama Canal. So from roughly 1896 to 1898 the two sides engaged in a ping-pong game of mutual accommodation and restraint; they were trying to resolve their disputes, give ground to each other, and open the door to reconciliation.

JMC: And so beyond the initial disputes there was a widening effort to find common ground?

CK: Yes, you might think of it as a widening of the circle. The first stage you put your toe in the water; you send up a smoke signal that says "I would like to give reconciliation a try," and then the second stage you are feeling out the other party. You are engaging in a tit-for-tat strategy of restraint.

In the third stage the story moves from the realm of high politics, of signaling and diplomacy, to the realm of societal engagement. Stages one and two are often done outside the eye of the public because they are dangerous politically. When a leader reaches out to the enemy he or she takes a risk, so it is often done behind the scene. What happens after the stage is set through diplomacy is that leaders start going public; they start affirming that "we are trying to make peace with our adversary." And you begin to see traders, investors, tourists, novelists, public action committees, and other societal actors start to get engaged in the game. In the case of Britain and the United States you see the founding and the growth of the Anglo-American Chamber of Commerce; it meets regularly in New York and in London. When the group begins dinner they sing the Star-Spangled Banner and God Save the Queen, and behind the front table they hang the American flag and the British flag. You begin to see that kind of symbolism trickle down into the arts, into the newspapers, and there is a kind of outpouring of social engagement that lays a societal foundation for rapprochement.

The final stage of the process, which locks in the breaking out of peace, entails a change in narrative and identity among the parties. In the case of Britain and the United States you begin to see Americans and British talk about one another as friends, as kin, as cousins, as members of the Anglo-Saxon family. And by 1902/1903 President Roosevelt is saying publicly that "war between the US and Britain would be a civil war, it would be fratricide." British officials and British opinion writers are saying exactly the same thing on the other side of the Atlantic. And it is that sense that the other becomes the self, that there is a shared identity between Britain and the United States that really closes the deal and enables the British people and the American people to see each other as friends. As a narrative of commonality and kinship deepens its hold on both societies, the prospect of war begins to become unthinkable. The British Admiralty stopped planning for war against America. Britain withdrew its last contingent of troops from the Canadian border. The United States stops worrying about war with the United Kingdom at roughly the same time. In 1895 the process starts. By 1906 Britain and America had become family and members of a zone of stable peace.

JMC: So it is really through this four-phase process of accommodation, reciprocal restraint, societal integration, and then change in narrative and identity that stable peace breaks out. You give us the example of the US and the UK and it is a story that is rather well known. Can you give us another example which perhaps is less well known and that perhaps was more complicated?

CK: Sure, I will give you another example. Before I do, let me note that the process can run in both directions. That is to say that the sequence is not always accommodation, restraint, integration, narrative change. It can also go backwards. In other words, peace can unravel. There is nothing unidirectional about this process. It is fragile, it is tentative, and it is contingent. It is important to stress that.

JMC: And therefore it has to be constantly nurtured?

Yes, and if the process of rapprochement is left unattended and not nurtured, it usually loses its forward momentum and can slip into reverse. So it has to be looked after on a constant basis until it reaches a definitive point of no return. Then the parties in question constitute a stable zone of peace. But that point of no return often takes quite a long time. In the case of the United States, the US embarked down the path of federation in 1789; that is when our Constitution was ratified. We then enjoyed seven prosperous decades as a zone of peace – only to fall apart amid bloodshed in the 1860s.

JMC: Are you saying that while your model applies to relations among states it can also be used to understand how a nation comes into being and flourishes as a zone of peace?

CK: Yes, because often times nations emerge as the consequence of a merger of previously separate units like the United States, like Germany, like the United Arab Emirates – these are all cases I look at in the book. But to give you an example of a case that took quite a long time, I will mention the Swiss.

The initial confederation of three Swiss cantons took place in 1291, but it really was not until 1847 that Switzerland cohered as a zone of peace. And that is because from 1291 to 1847 that effort to form a stable union was deeply divided along socioeconomic and religious lines. The urban cantons became primarily Protestant, the rural cantons were primarily Catholic, and the fault line between Catholicism and Protestantism, between farmers on the one hand and merchants and the middle class on the other, stood in the way of the onset of stable peace for many decades. In fact, there were five civil wars between 1291 and 1847; only after these lines of cleavage are overcome does the Swiss Confederation cohere.

III THE CAUSAL CONDITIONS FOR ENABLING ENEMIES TO BECOME FRIENDS

JMC: In the book you also argue that what you call the causal conditions that enable enemies to become friends have to do with three elements: First, institutionalized restraint, second, compatible social orders, and third, cultural commonalities. Can you tell us about each of these three elements and how they work?

CK: Well, as we were talking about just a few minutes ago the first and second stages of rapprochement depend heavily on restraint, on the readiness of the parties in question to step back, to put one hand behind their back and say "I do not mean you harm." And so the state has to be capable of practicing restraint, and some states are better at doing so than others – such as those that have constitutions and institutions that put constraints on their exercise of power. But I found, quite interestingly, that all different kinds of polities, not just those with inherent checks on the exercise of power, are able to practice restraint. This leads to one of the important conclusions of the book. And that is that regime type is not a good predictor of when and where peace breaks out. The ability to practice strategic restraint is an important predictor, but I found that autocracies, military regimes, absolute monarchies, are good under some circumstances at practicing restraint and therefore should be considered to be potential partners in peace. Therefore we should not look so heavily at regime type to predict a state's international behavior.

JMC: This is indeed an important finding. In particular it goes against what supporters of democratic peace theory have been arguing, that is to say that democracies are less war-prone than nondemocracies and therefore should be better at making and preserving peace than nondemocracies.

CK: Democratic peace theory holds that democracies do not go to war with each other. My book does not speak to that proposition – although I must admit that I am skeptical of democratic peace theory. Democracy and nationalism go hand in hand, and nationalism causes competition between nations. I am pretty confident that if democracies were not getting into fights with nondemocracies, they would be getting into fights with each other. But that is an aside. As for my findings about stable peace, I did discover outcomes that challenge the conventional wisdom. One corollary of stable peace theory is that democracies have attributes – such as public accountability, transparency, and institutionalized checks and balances – that make them uniquely suited to forming peaceful relationships with other states. But I found that all kinds of regimes are capable of practicing strategic restraint and thus heading down the road of rapprochement and stable peace. Scholars and policy-makers alike err when they overlook the opportunities to advance peace with nondemocratic regimes.

JMC: If a given type of regime is not necessarily a good predictor for restraint, so then what would be a better predictor?

CK: Well, one is simply the readiness of the parties in question to practice restraint. And I in my book do not generate or offer a theory about when that happens, except to say that it takes place under conditions of strategic necessity.

JMC: So when leaders feel pressure to look for ways to alleviate strategic deficiency?

CK: Right. The second condition is compatible social orders. And that is because as polities begin to integrate with each other, if they have very different social and political orders, these order clash with each other; elites in one country are undermined by the process of rapprochement and they therefore stop it from continuing. Take the case of Syria and Egypt, which moved to forge the United Arab Republic in 1958. It collapsed after a few short years because Nasser[2] tried to nationalize the Syrian economy and therefore undermined and provoked resistance from Syria's bazaar merchants and the landed gentry, who then pushed the military to secede from the union. In the case of the United States, the union fell apart in 1861 because of a fundamental social incompatibility between the North, which was industrialized and a wage economy, and the South, which was agrarian and a slave-based economy.

JMC: When you talk about compatibility of social orders, required compatibility of social orders, do you mean to say that we need it simply at the top, among elites, or is it something that has to be deeper, throughout the whole society?

CK: It is a deeper question. It is industrialized societies versus agrarian, aristocratic versus egalitarian. In other words you have to have structures of politics and structures of economics that do not undermine one another; otherwise you get interest groups emerging to block the process of reconciliation. This is exactly what happened, for example, in the union between Senegal and Gambia. Senegal wanted to create a customs union with Gambia that threatened the main source of income among Gambians, which was re-export trade. The Gambian elite accordingly resisted societal integration with Senegal, and eventually the union unraveled.

JMC: In your research you have not encountered examples telling you that it is possible to have two entities coming together despite the fact that there is quite a high level of incompatibility in terms of social order?

CK: Well, I want to stress that I am focusing only on a very high level of integration: stable peace, the demilitarization of the relationship. You can get very far down the road of good relations and rapprochement without having

[2] Gamal Abdel Nasser Hussein, second President of Egypt, serving from 1956 until his death in 1970.

this deeper social compatibility. But in terms of locking in that more durable kind of peace, I did find that compatibility of social orders is an important variable.

JMC: Since you insist on the specificity of your definition of stable peace, perhaps you could unpack exactly what you mean by stable peace compared to peace in general.

CK: There are many kinds of peace out there in the world in the sense that you could say that the Cold War really constituted a stable peace because the United States and the Soviet Union never went to war with each other. You could say that Brazil and Argentina enjoyed peace for a long time, many centuries, because the last time they fought a war was, if I recall correctly, in the 1820s. I am not looking at "not war"; I am not looking at just the absence of conflict. Rather, I am looking at a relationship that becomes so deep that war is removed as a legitimate tool of statecraft.

JMC: It becomes unthinkable?

CK: Unthinkable. The countries no longer militarize their borders or have war plans against each other. So it is important to stress that that is a very high bar. You can get types of peace in the world that even if they fall short of that very deep kind of peace are nonetheless very important and we should pursue them. In this particular book I look on one particular, highly evolved kind of peace and that is this deeper form of demilitarization and removal of armed conflict as a legitimate tool of statecraft.

JMC: Evolved and very advanced.

CK: Very advanced, and therefore rare – and precious.

JMC: And then the third causal condition for stable peace is what you call cultural commonality, which, once again, is really quite demanding.

CK: Yes, culture is a notoriously elusive variable or concept and it changes over time. What is today's cultural other is tomorrow's cultural self. So I just want to preface this discussion with a caveat about the malleable nature of the concept of culture; nonetheless, I did find that cultural linkages – and by culture I am referring to race, ethnicity, religion – do matter and these linkages do make it easier for countries to find their way to stable peace. So, for example, Britain attempted rapprochement with Japan at the same time that it did so with the United States. It succeeded with the United States and not with Japan in part because of the distrust, the racially motivated distrust, that existed between Britain and Japan that was not present between Britain and the United States. If we look at the Association of Southeast Asian Nations, ASEAN has helped secure peace in Southeast Asia since 1967. But Australia and New Zealand are not members. Why not? Because they are populated mainly by immigrants from Europe, not by Asians. In that sense, inclusion in ASEAN is defined in part by cultural commonality. I am not making an argument that is Huntingtonian[3] in nature – that is to say that groups of countries that are of different cultures are destined to clash. I do not believe that. What I am arguing is that countries that share some type of cultural commonality find it easier to get to stable peace than countries that do not.

JMC: Why is it that, fundamentally, you do not believe in Huntington's argument?

CK: Although I believe that stable peace is more likely to form among countries that share a common culture, I do not believe that conflict and rivalry are inevitable among countries of different cultural backgrounds. Huntington in *The Clash of Civilizations* claimed that cultural dividing lines are the world's main geopolitical dividing lines, with fault lines emerging among the world's main civilizations. I simply do not buy the argument. There is more conflict and violence within civilizations than there is between them. And that is because conflict often arises over borders, land, resources, and security – and therefore takes place among states that live near each other and are of the same culture. People often talk of the clash between Western Christendom and the Islamic world. But there is much more violence within the Middle East than there is between the countries of the region and the West. Iraqis are fighting each other, Syrians are fighting each other, Lebanese are fighting each other, and the tension between Saudi Arabia and Iran is emblematic of the broader struggle taking place between Shiites and Sunnis. In similar fashion, today there is much talk of the coming clash between China and the United States. But China's main conflicts have been with its geographic and cultural neighbors, not with powers that represent different civilizational groupings.

JMC: At the very core of your book How Enemies Become Friends *is the notion of trust. So here my question is: how to generate trust so that we can have stable peace pursued and engineered. Of course, trust seems to be more complicated to achieve when there is a gap between the self and the other because of lack of compatible social order, lack of cultural commonality, and so on. But, precisely,*

3 Samuel P. Huntington, *The Clash of Civilizations and the Remaking of World Order* (New York: Touchstone, 1997).

how do you go about bridging this gap between the self and the other when these causal conditions that you mentioned regarding compatible social orders, cultural commonality, and so on do not exist? How do you go about establishing peace when the gap between the self and the other is quite deep?

CK: Well, I think that the story that I tell, the sequence that we were just discussing, would apply across cases. In cases where you do not have social compatibility or cultural commonality, one would, I think, be wise to lower the expectations about how quickly and how far the rapprochement will go. So, let us say you take the example today of the United States and Iran where you do not have a cultural commonality and you have a strong sense of self and other. I still believe that in the case of Iran and the United States accommodation, reciprocal restraint, and societal integration are possible and can advance rapprochement between the two countries. You might not get to a stable peace in which war becomes unthinkable, but you might be able to move away from the hardened sense of conflict that you have today. So, I think the model applies across time and space, but it is harder to pull off this game when there is greater distance socially and culturally.

JMC: You describe the relationship between the United States and Iran as a "hardened sense of conflict." Yet the Obama administration worked hard at trying to ease the tensions and finding some common ground? And of course it seems that the Trump administration has been working equally hard at reintroducing tensions between the two countries?

CK: The Obama administration did succeed in concluding the Iran nuclear deal. Whereas the deal did somewhat ease tensions between the United States and Iran, it did so only at the margins. The purpose of the deal was to stop Iran's nuclear weapons program, not to facilitate rapprochement. That having been said, by strengthening reformist voices and helping to rebuild Iran's economy and its middle class, the deal does have the potential to lay a groundwork for rapprochement – but that outcome is at this point very distant and would take time to evolve. Despite the deal, Iran has continued its provocative and dangerous behavior, advancing its ballistic missile program and contributing to sectarian violence in the region. In the meantime, the Trump administration has taken a much more confrontational stance toward Iran. That stance has contributed to a hardening of attitudes on both sides and effectively closed off, at least for now, any realistic prospect of winding down mutual hostility

IV THREE FORMS OF STABLE PEACE

JMC: Now, perhaps digging deeper in your argument on stable peace, you also put forward the idea that zones of stable peace can take three different forms. As for rapprochement, you have already discussed that in the context of the US–UK relationship. But you also identify two other forms: security community and union. Please tell us a bit about each of these different forms.

CK: Well I went out and I found lots of different cases that qualified as stable peace – instances in which borders have been demilitarized, war plans have been torn up, and warfare de-legitimated as a tool of statecraft. I ended up discovering that stable peace came in three different forms. One was rapprochement, where the countries in question are no longer rivals and come to enjoy peaceful coexistence. Britain and the United States before World War I were not in a "special relationship" and not bound together in alliance as they are today. But they did stop engaging in geopolitical competition and came to see one another as having benign intent. This is an example of rapprochement.

A security community is a more evolved form of stable peace; it involves not just the winding down of rivalry, but the building up of community, of rules for how the states in question will interact with each other – even though they remain sovereign and they practice their own foreign policies with regard to third parties. And then the union is the most highly evolved form of stable peace and therefore the most difficult to attain. Unions form when a security community gets so integrated and mature that the borders among the separate states cease to be geopolitically consequential; the states merge into a new sovereign state in which they no longer possess an identity or rights of sovereignty and no longer have independent foreign policies and relations with third parties.

JMC: A new country?

CK: Yes, a new country.

JMC: So, the European Union: is it a security community or a union?

CK: I would say that the EU is stuck right now in between a security community and a union – and, of great concern, seems to be sliding backwards. That is to say that until about a decade ago I would have said there is continual forward momentum toward union – not necessarily toward a federal union like that of the United States – but forward momentum. That is no longer the case. Especially in the aftermath of the referendum in favor of Britain's exit from the EU, the union's future is now in question.

V THE QUESTION OF THE EUROPEAN UNION AS A FORM OF STABLE PEACE

JMC: When it comes to the European Union why are we going backward?

CK: I think that there are several different forces at play. One of them is globalization, which is making individuals increasingly uncomfortable. It is at once causing economic dislocation and stagnant wages, yet at the same time making it more difficult for governments to improve economic conditions. So there is a gap between the governed and the governments and increasing voter disaffection. Immigration is certainly part of the problem, with dominant populations in Europe uneasy with the influx of newcomers. The threat of terrorism intensifies opposition to immigration, and spawns controversial debate about the challenges of integrating Muslim immigrants into European societies. Borders are coming back to life and I think that there is a worrisome trend in Europe today of politics drifting back down from the supranational level to the national level in a way that, if left unaddressed, could threaten the integrity of the European project.

JMC: You are right; it seems that we are witnessing what we call the renationalization of European politics. What would be a solution for this problem?

CK: You know, I wish I had some magic bullet that I could offer because I do worry that Europe is in very precarious shape today. As is the United States. I see three types of problems at work. First, and this is happening on both sides of the Atlantic, populism is undermining the political center. To counter this, we need to boost economic growth and ensure all citizens reap the benefits; we need to ensure that our working classes are earning a living wage and are optimistic about the future; we need to bring down inequality and adjust globalization to make sure that its benefits are widely shared. Second, and not unrelated, there is a dearth of sound leadership today in Europe. No European leader is making it his or her business to breathe new life into Europe. Europe thrived over the last six decades in part by being an elite project. Now Europe has been politicized; people in Germany, France, and all over Europe are talking about the EU, but they are not talking about it in positive terms; they are talking about in negative terms and politicians are not fighting back but are ceding the narrative to the critics. Politicians are being guided by public opinion, not guiding public opinion. A third problem concerns the European narrative. I think Europe needs a new narrative. Remember we talked a little bit earlier about the importance of narratives and identities. The traditional European narrative is "we need Europe to escape the past." That resonates with older Europeans, but not with younger Europeans who have come of age after the fall of the Berlin Wall. They do not know World War II, the Cold War, and a divided Europe. For younger generations you need a new narrative about Europe's place in the world, about what Europe's responsibilities are in the twenty-first century. That kind of narrative is needed to try to build new momentum toward a collective Europe. And, of course, with the election of President Trump, we have our own challenges of populism on this side of the Atlantic. Perhaps concern about where Trump will take US foreign policy will help encourage Europeans to band together and work to defend the rules-based international order that the Trump administration views as more of a hindrance than an asset.

JMC: *You alluded to the issue of political leadership, which you said is weak in Europe. You said that there is a need for having political leaders in Europe being more supportive of the European project. Is Germany the key here?*

CK: I think that Germany is a key player and that it is hard to imagine a path out of the current crisis in Europe without Germany leading the way, leading with the help of others. And that is simply because Germany is too powerful, its economy is too big, others cannot fill Germany's shoes. That having been said, I think there is no question that with Britain leaving the EU, we need a new mechanism for decision-making within the EU that decentralizes power, checks the influence of Berlin, and ensures that the voices of smaller powers carry weight. I do think that there does need to be in an urgent way a push to get Europe's leaders away from being so beholden to and so mired in domestic politics and again focused on the European project.

JM: *France has now a new president, elected in the spring of 2017, Emmanuel Macron. He is young and seems committed to strengthening, to revitalizing, the European Union. Do you think that he could have a positive impact?*

CK: Macron's election was a watershed event. It arrested the rising tide of populism and turned back Marine Le Pen's bid for the presidency. A Le Pen victory would have likely meant the end of the European project. In my own mind, French voters were reacting to the dark consequences of the Brexit vote in the UK and Trump's election in the United States – and saying, "no thank you. Not for us." Macron is pro-European and willing to stick his neck out to defend the European project. It has been long overdue for a prominent

European leader to take on the EU's detractors and remind European citizens of the value of their project of integration. Macron now has to work closely with his German and other EU counterparts to deepen integration on defense and to reform Eurozone institutions. European leaders must take advantage of the swing of the political pendulum back toward the center to upgrade EU institutions and make them better able to deliver jobs, growth, and security. Macron has also introduced important reforms to France's labor market – raising the prospect of a rebound in the French economy. Overall, the Eurozone is growing again – an important step forward in terms of re-legitimating the political center and the EU. However, the EU is by no means out of the woods. With Brexit unfolding on its western flank and illiberalism taking hold among some of its eastern member states, Europeans will need to address unemployment, immigration, domestic security, and other issues that have the potential to further strengthen the populist right and left.

JMC: European institutions themselves have a role to play and in fact in the past they have played such a role. So why is it that today European institutions seem so weak or not really able to provide the kind of leadership that is required at the European level?

CK: Well, I think that we are seeing a greater and greater gap emerge between Europe's institutions and Europe's politics. Europe's institutions are getting stronger and more collective. The Lisbon Treaty[4] really put Europe up on the next rung, giving it the ability to function as a more capable union. But just at the time that Lisbon was coming into effect the EU began to be negatively politicized and the political trends have since been anti-EU, populist, antiestablishment, and anti-immigrant. So you now have these European institutions that are getting more and more divorced from the "European street" and somebody has to come along and put the politics and the institutions back together again. Otherwise I really do worry that you could have these European institutions come crashing down because they lack popular legitimacy and popular support.

JMC: The need then is to realign or better dovetail European institutions, which are getting stronger and yet are quite weak partly because they are disconnected from European politics, and politics. The key is to reconnect politics and

[4] The Treaty of Lisbon (December 13, 2007) is an international agreement which amends the structure and functions of the European Union (EU) in order to accommodate the growing number of members.

institutions at the European level, right? I guess this is partly why you feel that there is the need for a new narrative?

CK: Yes, and that new narrative has to be part of a kind of rebirth of democratic politics and democratic legitimacy; these are things that you have written about Jean-Marc. The reconnection of democracy, legitimacy, and the European project, this is crucial. That is not an impossible task, but nobody's doing it right now; as a consequence, Europe is more and more fragile and vulnerable by the day, by the hour.

JMC: So, you worry. But, ultimately, do you think that there are still reasons to be rather optimistic about the whole situation? Do you think that for the way forward the European Union is going to be able to find a solution?

CK: I remain guardedly optimistic. I think it is hard today to be a Euro-optimist. I am someone who has always been an ardent supporter of the European project – it is one of the most significant and consequential accomplishments of the modern era. But at this point in time I am worried. I express these worries verbally and in writing not to pronounce a death knell for the European Union but, on the contrary, as a wake-up call – as an effort to say to Europeans: "Wake up, look around you, this project that has been so successful and has turned Europe into a zone of peace. It is perhaps one of the greatest geopolitical experiments in history. But it is today very fragile, and you must do everything you can to protect it and help it thrive."

VI DEMOCRACY AND GLOBAL PEACE

JMC: To go back to your book How Enemies Become Friends, *in the midst of your analysis about stable peace you put forward a number of striking propositions on which I want you to elaborate a bit. One of these striking propositions is the fact that you say that spreading democracy does not amount to spreading peace. Of course, as you have alluded to earlier, this goes against standard wisdom.*

CK: As I mentioned earlier in the conversation, I went into the project thinking that I would find that democracies are particularly good at making peace and nondemocracies particularly bad – this is what we are taught at university, and it is what we hear from our leaders. Our leaders get up on a regular basis and give speeches where they say "democracies are wonderful and nondemocracies are horrible and we must change them." Well, I found no basis to support that stark distinction when it comes to making peace. I found that democracies make peace with democracies, democracies with autocracies, autocracies with other autocracies, and that regimes that are quite nasty at home can be quite reliable peacemakers abroad. Brazil and Argentina embarked down the path to peace when they were both ruled by military juntas. Suharto, General Suharto,[5] who was really one of the most brutal dictators of the twentieth century, was also a great peacemaker. He is the one who backed away from confrontation with Malaysia and put Malaysia and Indonesia on the path to anchoring ASEAN. And there are many other cases, including Mao and Khrushchev. It was admittedly short-lived, but those two leaders formed a zone of peace between a communist and autocratic Soviet Union and a communist and autocratic China in the 1950s. So the message here is: Do not overrate the importance of democracy when it comes to reconciliation and making peace. Do not believe that you need to stay away from nondemocracies because they are intrinsically aggressive and unable to make peace.

JMC: What is the policy implication of this message?

CK: Well, in the case of the United States, the policy implication is that we should be choosing enemies and friends on the basis of other countries' foreign policies not on the basis of their domestic institutions. Let's not write off nondemocracies. As I alluded to earlier, I think President Obama acted on this basis, engaging traditional adversaries like Iran, Cuba, and Myanmar. The idea is to engage even nondemocracies in the service of giving rapprochement a chance and making the world a safer place.

JMC: So spreading democracy and regime change should not be part of the foreign policy agenda?

CK: I think that the United States, its European allies, and other democratic partners should continue to try to support the spread of democracy, but it needs to be only one component of foreign policy. And it needs to be done very carefully – through encouragement and inducement, not through coercion or force. Furthermore, regime type should not be the ultimate determinant for choosing enemies and friends. Nondemocracies can make good partners in peace.

VII COMMERCIAL TIES AND PEACE

JMC: The second striking proposition that you put forward in your book has to do with the fact that you argue that commercial linkages do not necessarily promote peace. Once again this goes against what we are being taught and told.

[5] Suharto, President of Indonesia (1967–1998).

CK: Yes, and again I was surprised because of the conventional wisdom about the benign geopolitical effects of economic interdependence. But in the twenty cases that I looked at, in only one case did commercial integration help clear the way for political reconciliation. That case was in Germany between 1815 and 1871 when the customs union and commercial integration among the different German states helped move Germany toward unification. In all the other cases that I looked at, commercial integration mattered only after the diplomats and the politicians had done their work. Only after they had settled the key diplomatic and geopolitical issues on the table were the traders and the investors able to come in and help seal the deal. And so the policy finding that comes out of this insight is that we can give money to Palestinians and Israelis, Bosnian Serbs and Bosnian Muslims, get Japan to invest in China, but unless the core geopolitical issues that foster adversarial relations are first successfully addressed, those investments will not pay off geopolitically. The causal chain is politics, diplomacy, and geopolitics first, commercial integration thereafter.

JMC: Which leads me to ask you about the US–China relationship because clearly it is something that a lot of people are thinking about. What would be your analysis of this relationship and what would be your recommendations to have the relationship becoming stable and peaceful?

CK: Well, I think we are in act one of a play that has at least three or four acts. The relationship between the United States and a rising China is going to be one of the defining relationships of the twenty-first century.

JMC: For the world?

CK: Yes, for the world. The rise of China and its interaction with the United States will fall into the category of a hegemonic transition. The current global hegemon – the United States – is going to be challenged by the rise of China. China in the not too distant future will surpass the United States economically and, over time will have the military capability to challenge the United States for hegemony in its own neighborhood (the western Pacific) – not unlike the United States challenging Britain in its own neighborhood (the Western Atlantic) at the end of the nineteenth century. At this point in the hegemonic transition the key is to avoid mutual provocations, to find ways in which China and the United States can work together to build trust, to deepen the dialogue and the modalities of cooperation between the two countries so that when we get to the point at which China begins to pull even with the United States, China and the US are not implacable geopolitical rivals. If we do not build a foundation for that trust soon – say, by 2025 – then we could see dangerous tension over strategic primacy in the Western Pacific – over Taiwan, Korea, Japan, the Philippines, a host of disputed islands – that could fuel geopolitical uncertainty and rivalry moving forward.

JMC: Do you feel that in Washington people who are in positions of power are eager, willing, able to understand China in terms of its rise and how it could transform its economic power into political power down the road?

CK: I think that Washington is well aware of this. The United States is coming off of two decades in which it has been almost exclusively focused on the Middle East because of 9/11, the war in Iraq, the war in Afghanistan, the Arab Spring, the war in Syria, and the war against ISIL. The Obama administration tried to free itself of commitments in the Middle East so that it could focus more on East Asia. But the Middle East would not let go. The Trump administration also appears determined to focus more attention on the rise of China. There is no question that the rise of China is very much on the minds of officials and foreign-policy thinkers in the United States. But I would say that there is no consensus on the big question of how to manage China's rise peacefully.

JMC: China is on the mind of people in Washington but do they have the right mind to address China? You often say that people in Washington tend to be in a bubble and they do not really see the world in a very open and lucid manner.

CK: Well, I think that there are many different opinions on China and that anyone who makes a definitive judgment about the implications of the rise of China is misguided – any definitive judgment is premature. Anyone who says that China will inevitably emerge as an implacable aggressor is just guessing – that judgment is premature because we just do not know. Anyone who says that China will follow a peaceful path as it rises is also jumping the gun. We simply do not know. The one thing that I think I would say with confidence is that China and the United States need to avoid moves that will push them as an unintended consequence toward rivalry. Prior to World War I, neither Wilhelmine Germany nor Britain wanted to go to war. But they got locked in a naval race and in a broader geopolitical rivalry which led them down a dangerous path that ended in war. China and the United States need to be very careful not to find themselves in a similar tit-for-tat struggle in which neither wants conflict, but they end up in a cycle of escalation that ends in conflict.

JMC: Precisely how do we think and how do we shape and envision policy and foreign policy in a context that is so uncertain, keeping in mind that we want to avoid this kind of slippery slope that you just referred to?

CK: I think that the key, and this goes back to accommodation and reciprocal restraint, is for the United States to put its cards on the table and make clear to China what its red lines are, but at the same time make clear that it does not harbor aggressive intent toward China. Washington should indicate that it is not attempting to block China's rise and that it in fact believes that China's rise can be good for the world as long as China plays by a certain set of rules and upholds a rules-based international order. I think the key here is to fashion an updated rules-based order rather than just let a more anarchic order prevail. For its part, China needs to lay its cards on the table and make clear that it expects to have more influence commensurate with its greater power. But Beijing also needs to take steps to demonstrate to its neighbors and the rest of the world that it does not have predatory intent and that it does not intend to use its military forces in a predatory way. This kind of mutual transparency and accommodation is key to avoiding an unintended slide toward geopolitical competition.

VIII NO ONE'S WORLD

JMC: As we get ready to conclude our conversation, tell us a bit about your most recent book, No One's World: The West, the Rising Rest and the Coming Global Turn.[6]

CK: As the title indicates, I believe that the next world will belong to no one; it will not be the American Century, the Western Century, the Chinese Century, or the Asian Century. We are heading toward a world in which there will be multiple models of governance and multiple centers of power. These centers of power will have different views of how to organize life domestically and internationally – and these views will compete in the marketplace of ideas. This era will be the first time in history that we will live in a world that is integrated, that is globalized, but without a center of gravity. The world really became integrated and globalized over the course of the nineteenth century, but it was integrated under the guardianship first of Europe, and then the United States. Now we are moving to a world that is even more integrated, but without that center of gravity, without a global guardian.

6 Charles A. Kupchan, *No One's World: The West, the Rising Rest and the Coming Global Turn* (Oxford: Oxford University Press, 2012).

JMC: In essence, you do not think that we are going to have a world integrated under the guardianship of China. In November 2017 I attended a conference on how globalization is likely to evolve in the coming decades, organized in Shanghai by the Fudan Institute for Advanced Study in Social Sciences. At this conference Chinese scholars' mood was quite upbeat. The feeling was that we are on the verge of witnessing the emergence of a Chinese century. Why do you think it is not the case? What prevents China from putting in place a world order under its guardianship?

CK: As I explain in *No One's World*, the great geopolitical challenge of our time will be managing peacefully the transition from a world dominated by the United States and its Western partners to a world without a captain at the helm. To be sure, China, India, and other emerging powers will continue their relative rise, and we will witness the transition from unipolarity to multipolarity, which will produce instability. But I do not see a world dominated by China, which will have neither the capability nor the inclination to create Pax Sinica. I foresee China's geopolitical, economic, and cultural dominance in its own region. But China is not a universalizing power; it is primarily a mercantilist power. It will venture out in the world to do business, not to dominate it or remake it in China's image. This means a more fragmented and regionalized world, not a Chinese century.

That said, although China does not have universalizing ambition, I do believe that we will see a contest over the ordering norms that help preserve international order. Emerging powers like China will want to change those norms, not simply embrace the rules-based system that the United States and its partners built after World War II. That contest over norms will be particularly important in light of the surge of illiberalism that has come to the United States and Europe. Discontent and dysfunction among the Western democracies will have to make alternative models more attractive in the global marketplace of ideas.

JMC: So, your prognostic is that the world will belong to no one, but I guess the key question that you are trying to address and answer in your latest book is how do we make sure that No One's World does not devolve into chaos?

CK: Yes, I seek to address how we might arrive at a consensus on the foundational principles of a new order – our approach to legitimacy, sovereignty, commerce, human rights, international law, war, and peace. How can we propagate throughout No One's World consensual principles in a way that widens the circle, in a way that is inclusive, not exclusive, and enables a more equitable, diverse, and pluralist world to function in an orderly and in a peaceful way?

JMC: It is a bit tricky because clearly global standards so far have really been coming from the Western world. So do we have to redefine them or is there a way for these notions to be embraced by non-Western powers? What's your analysis of this question?

CK: Well, I think the common view in the United States, in Washington, people like John Ikenberry, my friend and colleague, is that the Western order is on the cusp of being universalized, and even if the West loses its primacy, its principles will nonetheless be the principles for the future. I do not believe that that is the way the world will work. I think that when rising powers rise they want to reshape the world and recast the world in ways that advantage their interests and that are consistent with their own political cultures and their own societies. So I think that the Western world will continue to be just that – the Western world. And there will be a Washington Consensus but there will be a Brussels Consensus, a Beijing Consensus, a Delhi Consensus, a Brasilia Consensus, a Jakarta Consensus, and there will be no dominant model in the way that there has been for the last 200 years.

JMC: Then the question is how do we reconcile these models? How do we manage to have these models coming together; otherwise we will have rivalry and the disorder that usually comes with it?

CK: You get lots of different players in the room and you begin a conversation on the rules of the next world. You get input from the Chinese, and the Indians, and the South Africans, and the Brazilians, and other key players, and you attempt to forge a consensus. The idea that the Chinese and other emerging powers are going to embrace the rules-based order devised by the Western democracies after World War II is an illusion. It is not going to happen. So the only alternative is to say okay, let us all put our cards on the table; let us have a discussion about the founding rules for the world that is going to come next.

JMC: It has to be a totally new world in a way?

CK: I think it has to be. That does not mean that important elements of the Western order will not survive, that they will not be included in the rules of the next order. I think they should and will. But the West will have to compromise and make room for alternative views as it seeks to fashion a new consensus.

JMC: You believe that it will have to happen?

CK: I believe that the effort must be made; whether it is successful remains to be seen.

JMC: And it is going to be taking a long time? I mean this process of reconfiguring the principles which are now ruling the world; it is going to take ten years, twenty years, thirty years, forty years, what's your timeline?

CK: Well I do not think we have an enormous amount of time and that is because by 2030 China is poised to be the largest economy in the world. By the year 2050 of the top leading powers in the world only one of them will be from the West: the United States. All the others in the top five will be from what is today the developing world. So we need to figure out the rules of No One's World sooner rather than later because the world is changing at a very quick pace.

JMC: If what you are saying is correct, the coming changes are going to be enormous. What does this mean for the evolution of international relations as a field of scholarship? To this day, international relations as an academic field is dominated by US scholarship and thinking. If the changes you are referring to take place, do you think that there will be intellectual implications? After all, there is a strong link between political legitimacy and intellectual legitimacy. How should US universities and academics, and Western universities and academics more broadly, prepare themselves in light of the coming changes?

CK: For starters, scholars outside the West should contribute more fully to the core literature on international relations. That process of intellectual diversification has already begun, but it needs to broaden. If scholars from China, India, Brazil, and elsewhere think about the world differently and better understand the norms that shape their countries' behavior, the field needs to benefit from their contributions. At the same time, international relations programs in the West should diversify intellectually and scholars should seek to broaden the historical scope of their studies. For example, much international relations scholarship draws primarily on European history. Placing more attention on East Asia and other non-European areas could challenge or leaven prevailing paradigms and, at a minimum, expose scholars to different geopolitical, economic, and cultural settings.

IX OBAMA, TRUMP, AND CONCLUDING THOUGHTS

JMC: Early in 2017 you just stepped down from serving for almost three years on the National Security Council under President Obama. Has that experience changed your view of the world? What can we expect from President Trump?

CK: I feel very fortunate to have had the opportunity to work in the White House for President Obama. I learned a great deal about making and implementing foreign policy and about the many challenges that the current political and geopolitical landscape poses to the effective conduct of statecraft. I do not think the experience fundamentally altered my basic views of international affairs. If anything, it confirmed my conviction that we are rapidly moving toward No One's World – a global setting in which power is increasingly decentralized and in which Western norms and approaches to governance are challenged by alternative models. This world is arriving more quickly than I had initially anticipated.

As for President Trump, his brand of populist governance is certainly breaking away from the model of US statecraft that has been practiced since World War II. The voters in his electoral base feel that they are on the losing end of the open, rules-based order that the United States has taken the lead in constructing and defending over the past eight decades. It therefore remains to be seen whether Trump proceeds to actively dismantle that order or veers back to a more traditional approach to statecraft. That a similar brand of populism has prompted the United Kingdom to exit the European Union and is taking hold elsewhere in Europe underscores the systematic nature of the phenomenon – and the urgent need for liberal democracies to address economic hardship, discomfort with immigration, and the other underlying sources of voter discontent.

I remain a "theological optimist" about the United States. By that I mean that I am confident that the country will reclaim its position as a leading liberal democracy and a country committed to international cooperation in the service of promoting stability, prosperity, and liberal values. Demographically, the country is becoming more diverse and outward looking. The United States has the best universities in the world, an entrepreneurial and business community second to none, and liberal institutions that are so far working as they should and serving to check the excesses of the Trump administration. In addition, import elements of Trump's agenda will backfire and be reversed. For example, unplugging from globalization and embracing protectionism will harm, not help, the American economy. Yes, globalization needs to be adjusted to ensure that its benefits are more equally shared. But a return to economic nationalism and protectionism is not the answer. Democracies are self-correcting, and these underlying political and economic realities will push the United States back toward a more traditional brand of internationalism.

On the other hand, the country is deeply polarized and many of its workers, especially in the American heartland, are still suffering from disappearing jobs and stagnant wages. Identity politics and the "culture wars" – fights over social issues like abortion and gay marriage – are front and center. Trump is the product of an angry populist revolt that will not die out any time soon. And even if Trump is a one-term president, which seems likely, he can do quite a bit of damage to the United States and the international system during his time in office. In this respect, it may well be up to Europe to hold down the Western fort while the United States is missing in action. Our moment, which hopefully will not last long, is not a world without the West, but a West without the United States. That is a sobering thought.

JMC: Finally, what would be your advice to young scholars starting in the field of justice?

CK: Ask big questions. Insert yourself into the battle of ideas. We are entering what appears to be an uncertain and unstable era in international politics. Good ideas and tireless activism may be needed more than ever.

13

International Economics and Development

A. Michael Spence

I ON SUSTAINABLE ECONOMIC GROWTH

JEAN-MARC COICAUD (JMC): *Our conversation focuses on international economics and global justice. This is one of the issues you address in* The Next Convergence: The Future of Economic Growth in a Multispeed World.[1] *This is a book you published a few years ago but, like any important book, it continues to be very topical and relevant in light of the recent evolution of the global sphere and what it means for issues of development and justice, within and among nations. As a way to begin our conversation, tell us a bit about the work and findings of the Independent Commission on Growth and Development,*[2] *which you chaired in the late 2000s, because it seems to me the book grew out of what you learned in the context of this commission.*

A. MICHAEL SPENCE (MS): I had the privilege of Chairing the Commission whose members were largely political and policy leaders from developing countries. They had spent a good part of their lives struggling with the challenge of achieving sustainable growth and poverty reduction in their countries. I learned a tremendous amount from them about that process and when I wrote the book, *The Next Convergence: The Future of Economic Growth in a Multispeed World*, I really wrote it for two reasons. One was to share some of

[1] A. Michael Spence, *The Next Convergence: The Future of Economic Growth in a Multispeed World* (New York: Farrar, Straus and Giroux, 2011).

[2] The Commission on Growth and Development was an independent initiative, chaired by A. Michael Spence. Launched in 2006 it brought together twenty-two leading policy-makers, academics, and business leaders to look, from the theoretical and empirical standpoints, into key aspects of economic growth and development. Its work culminated in two publications, *The Growth Report: Strategies for Sustained Growth and Inclusive Development* (2008) and *Special Report on Post Crisis in Developing Countries* (2009). If issues of growth and inclusiveness were already central in the late 2000s, they have only become more important in the 2010s with the slowing of growth in many developed and developing countries and the rise of inequalities.

that learning about the process of growth and development and another one was to take note of the fact that this is a really important change in the economic pattern globally.

JMC: In the book, you clearly give central importance to the notion and the process of growth, including in terms of being able to achieve economic justice at the national and international global levels. Why is growth so important? Why should we care about growth?

MS: For the past 200 years, before and up through World War II, basically what now we think of as the industrialized countries were growing and the rest were not. But in the postwar period we have a complete change in the pattern, which I characterize as a century-long pattern of convergence, in which the developing countries grow at relatively high rates and eventually catch up with us – at least a large fraction of them. Probably 15 percent of the world's population was well to do, on balance, in 1950, and by 2050 (at the end of the 100 years which go from 1950 to 2050), it will probably be closer to 85 percent or maybe more. So we are now in a very different world.

And, of course, the other thing I am concerned with in the book deals with the fact that after about sixty years of this kind of rapid growth, the developing countries, especially the big emerging economies, are becoming extremely important and impactful in the global economy. So against this background the book is about reflecting about some of the opportunities and challenges that this situation is creating.

JMC: Continuing on the issue of growth, why is it that economic growth, especially sustainable economic growth, is so important?

MS: Growth is important if it is sustained for a long time because it produces massive shifts of peoples' material well-being. But, much more importantly, because of the opportunities that growth gives them, people do not struggle with daily life and trying to keep themselves and their family alive. Instead, they can be productive and enjoy the likelihood that their children and grandchildren will be better off than they are; they can also be creative, and do all the things that I think really matter to human beings, to be at least in certain dimensions free. And so it really is not growth so much that is itself important and more the fact it is an enabler of those more fundamental things.

That said, sustaining high growth is a subject that we are still trying to understand. And it is difficult to accomplish. I think that the experience of the last fifteen or twenty years in developing countries plus in academic and policy research has made our understanding better, although we still do not understand everything about growth. Further, we can talk about it later, growth alone is not enough. Some kind of good governance is equally crucial.

JMC: Are you saying that growth is not only about economics, and good economic practices, but that it requires other social elements in order to be possible and to have a positive impact?

MS: Indeed, growth, and more specifically sustainable growth, is not really just about economics. It is also about governance, good governance. A country that is poorly governed not just in form but in intent will never really grow. There are lots of versions of those pathologies and they occur in autocratic systems as well as in democratic ones.

I would even say that at the top of the list of what is required to ensure growth, let alone sustainable growth, and I am tempted to also add "meaningful growth," is not necessarily that a government is reasonably trying to pursue what an economist would call a "right model," a "sophisticated open economy model." What is equally, if not more, important is that a government is intending to make the lives of the people in the country, virtually everyone, better off over time. Once this critical condition is in place, I think the rest of the story is largely economic.

JMC: In your work in general, and more specifically in the book The Next Convergence, *you clearly distinguish two types of conditions required for growth to take place: external conditions and internal conditions. Can you tell us more on external conditions and why they are so important for growth, and sustainable growth?*

MS: A very significant aspect of external conditions is economic openness and the accessibility of the external global economy. After the British industrial revolution, the average rate of growth in real terms, real per capita terms, was probably 1.5 percent. In continental Europe and eventually in the United States and Canada and the European offshoots it was probably around 2.5 percent too. In comparison, in the developing countries when they hit high speed growth, they are in the 10 percent range. So the situation is completely different.

I think the fundamental reason for this difference is that once the basic conditions were in place, once the removal of the constraints of colonialism and so on took place, including the fact that the gap between developing countries and advanced countries in terms of the knowledge and the technology base of the economy had become so large, so when the catch up process started, and as long as it has been working, it produced extremely rapid increases in potential output for a developing economy just by virtue of transfer of knowledge. In this regard, one of the things we have learned in the past fifty years is that, ultimately, growth is dependent on the knowledge and technology base of an economy.

JMC: You would say that knowledge and technology transfer is an important dimension of the impact of external conditions on the high growth of a number of developing countries?

MS: Yes, and here, what is really happening is that high-growth developing countries are increasing the knowledge and technology bases of their economies by essentially learning from the rest of the world, in particular the advanced countries, at a very high rate of speed. That said, the other crucial ingredient of this story is that a relatively poor developing country that is just starting its process of development has a demand side of its economy (meaning what people want and can afford to buy) that is relatively small and, without making it sound pejorative, relatively uninteresting. This would constrain growth because specialization is impossible. But with the global economy, potential demand is vast. This is to say that no matter how fast you grow, you really never influence global prices for things you export. Once you find something you can compete in you can expand in that area for quite a long time before something starts to produce diminishing returns. For a developing country, in the tradable sectors, demand curves are not really downward sloping. The only exception to that is China. China finally got big enough in the tradeable sector of its economy where it was exporting enough that its market share was large enough that it actually was able to put downward pressure on prices of manufactured goods.

JMC: Is this an element that you understand as part of the context of internal conditions for growth?

MS: Exactly. Or to put it differently, external demand is crucial in enabling high-speed growth. Interestingly, the United Kingdom, where the industrial revolution started, basically bootstrapped this by generating its own demand, largely thanks to its colonial empire. This allowed a flow of trade that helped accelerate increase in income and wealth in a very asymmetric fashion. As such it was not quite standalone but it was much closer. Similarly, continental Europe and the United States have had the United Kingdom to rely on. We were basically collectively generating the demand side of the economy that we needed to rely on. In contrast, in the postwar period, for much of this period, developing countries in the early stages of growth have been relying on what was relatively huge developed country demand. Now, of course, developing countries are heavily dependent on China because of the size and growth of its economy. But that is a relatively recent development. This illustrates the point that what matters is not just that a country is advanced. It is that it is big as well.

JMC: You just alluded to the position in which developing countries find themselves today. But how does the centrality of external conditions, in particular economic openness, impact developing countries?

MS: A developing country does not determine the external environment. So in the postwar period, starting very soon after World War II, the global economy was systematically opened up through successive rounds of negotiations in the GATT. People will debate what the intent of that was (many say the motivation was war recovery in Europe and Japan) but the effect was that through an increasingly wide range of products and services, the global economy was opened in such a way that countries that could find a way to compete were able to access the global markets' knowledge and demand. This is to say that the external conditions, including of course the removal of the colonial constraints when the colonial empires collapsed, have been terribly important, even though it created new nations with lots of challenges in terms of creating national identity.

JMC: Are you saying that, on balance, external conditions and the openness of the economy have benefited developing countries?

MS: Yes. To be sure, also, there are some serious challenges. Still, on balance, we can say that it went very well in the postwar period and much better than at any other point in history. In this perspective, the externally oriented strategies of a developing country are probably in order of importance, access external knowledge and technology and know-how, and access external markets, and those are linked. A developing country will access external markets by, for example, having multinational companies engaging in foreign direct investment and bringing with them not only knowledge of production technology but knowledge of the global supply chain. This is how technology information and communication technology on the one hand and transportation and logistics on the other can bring about a huge boost.

II DEVELOPING COUNTRIES, INFORMATION TECHNOLOGY, AND GLOBAL SUPPLY CHAINS

JMC: Explain a bit the link between the global economy and information technology.

MS: In fact, this is one the central points that I try to explore in my book *The Next Convergence*. Information technology and progress in transportation and logistics have clearly increased the extent of integration of the global economy. Technologically speaking, thirty years ago you did not deliver services at a distance using the internet and information and communications technology. Now you do. And this state of affairs is not a matter of a policy decision. This is a technological issue.

JMC: In the past fifteen years or so the notion of "global supply chains" has become a buzz word in the world of international business. What is it and what is the link of this notion with the development of information technology?

MS: Global supply chains were starting to develop before the powerful effect of the internet came on but they were relatively hard to manage. They were relatively simple. It amounted to: produce in country A and sell to country B. They were inefficient. They took a long time to get organized. It used to be said that in order to get a new product designed and to production in the context of a global supply chain in certain industries it would take eighteen months to two years, which is a long time when you are trying to meet the needs of a rapidly developing market. That number would probably be down to about six months now. And that is enabled by increasing expertise and integration through information and technology. The way I think of it, information technology increasingly made global supply chains fast and efficient. And it allowed them to be more complex without being inefficient. By complex I mean a network with inputs from multiple countries.

JMC: Would you say that when it comes to global supply chains and the development of information technology, developing countries are not in a strong position? Are they at a disadvantage? Most of the time, in developing countries, what is missing are good systems of governance, good institutions.

MS: One huge challenge we thought ten or fifteen years ago was key was the question of the telecommunications infrastructure. Now, this problem seems to be solved, or is being solved. For instance, there is a huge powerful high-bandwidth fiber optic cable going down the eastern side of Africa, which vastly increases the bandwidth of their external connection to the rest of the world through the internet and video and telephones and so on.

The second thing that turned out to be a near miracle was that the cell phone technology (which has been much less capital-intensive and therefore much more affordable than landline technology) has started to connect practically everybody in the world (including the developing world) through its data capabilities. Furthermore a marvelous array of information and financial services is starting to be delivered using these little tiny devices. So I would say a reasonable guess is that whatever gaps between rich and poor countries there have been in the past, and they were very large, in the first half century of high-speed growth, these gaps will diminish dramatically.

III DEVELOPING COUNTRIES AND GOVERNANCE

JMC: Another impediment that often developing countries have to face is a negative role of government.

MS: Here the first question to think about is what is the right amount of government? There are lots of examples of governments trying to do too much. In this regard to take the extreme case, centrally planned economies all failed; it is pretty clear now that we have had sixty years of experiments in this. The bottom line is that you cannot live without some version of the market system with prices, decentralization, incentives, and enough definition of private property so that people are willing to invest thinking that they actually own the things that they invest in. So, at some level, the basic market system is just right. It is a key requirement. In the past some governments were trying to do too much of what the private sector, the market aspect, does. This approach generally adds problems or just fails completely. Over time this has led to the abandonment of those centrally planned policies and the gradual withdrawal of the public sector in areas where it should not get involved. A friend of mine in India says reform entails trying to reconfigure things to achieve a kind of sustained high growth. The first one is trying to get the government to stop doing things it should not be doing. So this is one side of the issue.

On the other hand, the notion that government should do as little as possible and try to get the private sector to do virtually everything may be a kind of viable strategy for an advanced country, although, frankly, most advanced countries do not do that either. But it is definitely not a workable strategy for developing countries. I think part of the process of achieving sustained growth is finding the right complimentary role for government. As such, it is right to say that the government's role is to support in a variety of ways, through policies and investment, the private sector, in particular the investment dynamics that go with the private sector, which is where the growth in incremental employment comes from and, ultimately, the poverty reduction. That complimentary role turns out to be very important and one element of it is investment in what are sometimes called "public goods," or partly public goods. Investment in infrastructure of a variety of kinds, and in education and human capital, turned out to be probably the two central items. When governments fall short on that, the growth does not get to high levels on a sustainable basis.

JMC: *In this perspective, the question of governance at the national level is not simply one of good governance; it is also one of governance adapted to the needs and specific conditions of a given country?*

MS: In developing countries, and in developed countries, the role of government not only can be but probably should be different. This is to say that the slightly more intertemporal version of the role of government in a developing country over its multi-decade journey, from wherever it starts relatively poor and not growing to the end, which is a relatively high income country, is complex. The role of government changes more or less continuously, and the reason why this is, I think, fairly easy to understand.

In a developing country not only the governmental institutions are not fully formed but the market institutions and capabilities are not fully formed either; and so it is a very pragmatic sort of "get-the-job-done division of labor" that seems to occur in successful cases. One way I try to describe this to people is to think about China in 1978, when it abandoned the centrally planned system under Deng Xiaoping, and decided to at least allow elements of a market system to work. China at that point had an economy in which the government had been dominant and, while the market institutions and capabilities were probably nascent, they certainly did not exist in full-blown form.

In this perspective, the Chinese economy (and the Chinese society), and this on the own account of the Chinese government, has been in transition for more than thirty years. In the process, it is clear that the role of government has shifted. The government had to do things that it probably does not have to do now. For example, in the early days, the market system clearly worked in some ways. The market system in agriculture had a stunning effect on output. But if the government or the central bank with whatever capabilities it had had tried to slow economic activity down, if the economy got overheated, by raising the interest rates, frankly nobody cared much. Nobody cared what the interest rates were; that was not how the economy worked. So, something which we take completely for granted in developed countries, i.e. that the central bank will raise interest rates and that that will reduce inflation and slow the economy down and prevent overheating, was simply probably not true in China. As such, the Chinese government had to use other means for both stimulating and slowing the economy.

JMC: Is this issue of finding the right type of governance for developing countries going through a high-growth process the only challenge they have to face?

MS: No. Another major challenge comes later. High-growth economies go through a transition which is very important and very difficult, called a "middle income transition" – often also called the middle income trap. It is basically trying to sustain growth when you get to about 4 or 5 thousand dollars of per capita income, and this when you are not really competitive in the areas that you used to export before. What we understand about that transition is that there is a major change in the role of governments. Its interventions in the economy become less targeted and they become much more like the way an advanced country supports its market economy.

JMC: If this is a key problem, how does the government of a developing country cope with success, since high growth is a form of economic success, and make it part of a successful social agenda for the country, and this including in terms of increasing in a sustained fashion economic and social inclusion, this being the ultimate goal?

MS: This is in some way the most interesting challenge and the hardest part for all high-growth developing countries and their people. We all try to think about the way the world works in somewhat static terms, whereas this is something which is in constant motion. If static analysis does not do the job, we tend to shift to cyclical patterns of change. But developing country growth does not lend itself to static or cyclical models.

That applies to developing countries and now that their impact on us is fairly large, it applies to the advanced countries as well. This also means it applies to the management of the global economy. In this regard, we have to recognize that we have now lots of challenges because the way we used to manage this global economy, with the advanced countries making the rules and having similar sorts of interests (and we were pretty generous about it so we did not make rules just for us), it is just not going to work anymore. We have the developing countries within a decade or less of being over half of the global economy. In fact, they are now more than half the global economy and the share continues to increase.

One of the biggest mistakes that gets made over and over is to find a successful formula, assume that the world will allow you to do it forever, and then just do it for too long. But we are living in a world of constant change. We have to be pragmatic about it. We have to adapt. We have to protect people when the transitions come and they get sideswiped and so on. Basically, we have to solve problems on a constant basis.

When I think about it, having spent time around and in the business world, I realize this is very much a business attitude. Businesses and dynamic industries do not think in cyclical terms. They think there are constant challenges. There is the challenge of innovation and staying ahead. There is the challenge of adapting to change and so on. In some ways, I think that this kind of attitude is appropriate, and that it needs to be transplanted to a much larger universe, which includes policy-makers and the way we run economies.

IV DEVELOPED COUNTRIES AND THE GLOBAL ECONOMY

JMC: For a long time, this "business attitude," this ability to produce change and adapt to change has been one of the signatures of developed countries. It is why they have developed and become successful. As the balance of power is shifting, how do you assess the situation of Western developed countries?

MS: In a number of countries, including the one I am a citizen of, I think we are wrestling with this now. We are an economy that was dominant after World War II because of the destruction that the war caused in a number of other places. We are less dominant now because Europe is a powerful force (despite all the problems it is currently encountering) and Japan has risen. The economically dominant position that we have enjoyed in the past is now less of a possibility for the United States. We are going to become less dominant in the future as the world's future economic giants take their place on the global economy stage.

I think right now we are at a crossroads in the global economy in the United States and other advanced economies. The emerging economies, because of their size and their increasing incomes and capabilities, are presenting challenges to us. And, at least thus far, I think in terms of mindsets and frameworks, we are not adapting very well. We are not even thinking about it very carefully. It is probably important for us to understand these powerful global forces and how they are shifting the parameters within which we all operate.

If I go back in time, when Deng Xiaoping asked the World Bank to come in the early 1980s to China, he said "you are a bank but we do not want money. What we need is knowledge." So his request was that they set up a process by which knowledge of economic management that had been developed in the advanced countries over the past centuries was transplanted to China. I think it is interesting that the person most responsible for the major change in China and for the spectacular economic results over the last thirty years, the first and almost the only thing he asked for was knowledge transfer.

JMC: At the same time, there is much innovation taking place in (Western) developed countries? So there is still a significant amount of technology and business dynamism in these countries?

MS: The business world in all of our countries has very dynamic elements and adapts continuously. I do not think the problem is there. In the American economy there are very innovative sectors. They are highly competitive in the global tradable parts of the economy where we interact. The same is true in France. Germany is also doing very well. To be sure there are a number of other countries who have to lift their game on this front.

There are also distributional issues. In this regard, the contrast between Germany and the United States is interesting. Germany seems to have adapted with a combination of private sector initiatives and dynamics and pretty sensible policies worked out with government, business, and labor participants, so that the benefits of the economic growth and dynamism are fairly broadly shared in the economy. Whereas, in the United States the middle class is not doing very well. We have had until recently an unemployment challenge. But more importantly we have an income distribution challenge as well. Without pretending to know all of what that is about, I think our policy frameworks and the way we think of policies, for adapting to current and future needs, require some serious change.

V THE WASHINGTON CONSENSUS AND BEYOND

JMC: Since you are alluding to the problems of developed countries and the need to introduce some serious changes, what do you think of the fact that, especially since the 2008 financial and economic crisis, the Washington Consensus seems to have fallen out of fashion?

MS: John Williamson is rightly credited with the Washington Consensus produced at the end of the 1980s. It has come to have a bad name, I think more than somewhat unfairly. If you read the main elements of the Washington Consensus and ask whether these correspond reasonably well to what we now understand to be the very important ingredients on the economic and regulatory side of high-speed sustainable growth and development, the answer is "yes they do."

There were two ways in which I think John's insights were misused. One was to think of this as a kind of formula: If you do these things, everything will be fine; as opposed to: These are some known necessary conditions, but they are probably not sufficient. What got lost was the idea of the constant adapting and problem-solving process. The second way, and this is a more serious problem,

I think, is that it was misinterpreted in a very stripped down form, as: Small government is the best, the smallest you can make it, stripped down to only things that the government can do, privatize everything else, open up your economy, more or less overnight, ignoring all the subtleties of the transitions that need to occur and so on.

I think this is the version which people associate with the Washington Consensus, with at least some of the countries in Latin America at that period of time where it seemed to be much less successful. Of course, there are people who do not agree with that, who argue that the Washington Consensus is fine and that where it did not work is where it was not implemented completely. I am not sure that we will ever settle that issue. My view, for what it is worth, looking at the countries that had this pragmatic experimental evolving role of government view of the matter but with sensible guidelines that looked very much like John Williamson's original list, is that they were the ones that tended to succeed.

JMC: Following the criticisms of the Washington Consensus, some have come to talk about the notion of Beijing Consensus, although in the past few years this notion seems to have somewhat faded away. Do you think that this notion and the reality it is meant to refer to has a future? Particularly in the context of the gradual slowing down of the Chinese economy?

MS: On balance, I think that the Beijing Consensus will not be a concept that will persist. Every country is idiosyncratic but China's growth dynamics are essentially consistent with their predecessors, with Japan and Korea and Taiwan, even the little Botswana and so on in a number of other Asian countries and other parts of the world. So I do not think, at least yet, that we can say that there is a new model that was invented in China.

China has contributed mightily through its experience to learning about key issues of development and those lessons are important. They are worthy of study on a broader front as they are in other countries. That said, China is interesting because it is a scenario that has never been tried on this scale, with 1.3 billion people and an economy that is going to be someday 20 percent of the global economy. So China is just a different case.

Now, there is an issue coming up in China that is sometimes confused with this question, i.e. whether they have invented a new growth model, which is the role of the state. In economic terms, in the past sixty years China has demonstrated both the failures and the successes of doing things, with the wrong way up until 1978 or 1979, and then the right way, which fits the description of where it was successful in the last forty years or so. Whatever the ideology of the past forty years or so, the fact of the matter is that during this last period of time the management of the Chinese economy has been based on reasonable economic principles combined with a pragmatic problem-solving approach and a very, in the case of China, high level of saving and investment. In that last sense, China is extraordinary. It is a complete outlier on the investment front. The other high-growth countries saved and invested at a high rate but China is just up on the right end of that distribution.

Going forward there is the issue about whether or not China's government structure, with its dominant party in the midst of it, will be consistent with the future evolution of its economy. I think that that is a question that the Chinese ask, not too loudly, internally. But we know that the political and government structures of developing countries tend to evolve along with the economy. We know that Japan, Korea, Taiwan, and probably others were dominant single party versions of a democracy that evolved into full multiparty democracies. But none of us knows, including the Chinese, where this particular form of governance is going to end up.

VI EMERGING ECONOMIES

JMC: A few years ago it was fashionable to talk about emerging countries, such as China, of course, but also India, Russia, South Africa, and Brazil. Now it seems, with perhaps the exception of China, that most countries labeled a few years ago as emerging are, each in its own way, in trouble. Against this background, what do you make of the future of emerging countries?

MS: Most of these countries in one form or another (with probably the exception of South Africa) had a fairly powerful planning function. It is funny when I talk about the emerging economies in the industrialized economies, I frequently get questioned on how can a planned economy grow that fast? And I sort of tip my head and laugh a little, and then say that part of the problem is that after the central planning period was over in the sense of a complete economic plan, China and India and others kept the word "plan." But the "plan" now in China or India is more like the French indicative plan of a number of decades ago, where you basically create priorities and create a shared sense of where everything is going to go as a way of coordinating economic activity. And I think that is more like what the plan is now in China. There are still elements of direct central direction: But the decentralized market part is much larger.

The plans in this modified sense are useful. It is very important in countries like that there is a pretty good understanding of what is supposed to happen and why it all fits together. The internal logic is important and then it is shared very widely, so that businesses, for example, know what direction policy is going to go.

To be perfectly honest, it seems to me that in the advanced countries we could use a little bit more of that in areas that have long-time horizons, like energy and environmental policies and so on. Europe does better than we do in America on that. But those (energy and the environment) are two territories where I think that kind of plan makes a lot of sense. Then, once you adopt this approach, the important role of government is to draw in the labor side and the business side and the civil society organization side of the structure, and get it done.

I should add here that the other useful input for later arrivals to the high-growth club, including China, was the models and examples of their predecessors. This was terribly important. Japan was by these standards the first high-growth case ever. Korea and Taiwan were very influenced by Japan, and China was influenced by all of them, so they had a number of previous models to look at and learn from. I think this accelerated the learning process of high-growth countries of emerging countries.

JMC: Still, there are significant differences among these countries, including in the Asian context?

MS: Korea followed the Japan model relatively closely, including the reluctance to allow foreign direct investment which was quite limited and so they found other ways. Foreign direct investment is known to be a pretty powerful channel of knowledge transfer so if you do not have it, you have to find alternative methods and they did. China did not follow that approach at all. It privileged not all investment, because there are still capital controls, but foreign direct investment really almost from the get go. And, certainly by the 1990s, when China had fully opened up, it was relying heavily on the knowledge transfer associated with foreign direct investment.

JMC: Are these countries likely to face problems similar to the ones advanced developed countries are now facing? For instance, are they likely to suffer from delocalization and deindustrialization due to lower costs of production in other (developing) countries?

MS: In a way the answer is yes. Economies, when they reach the middle income transition, must let go of the labor-intensive process of manufacturing and assembly. These migrate to lower income developing countries. But the real threat now to the poorer developing countries, the late starter if you like, is that the digital manufacturing technologies will replace the labor-intensive ones. That will lead to a kind of de-industrialization and some amount or relocalization. But it leaves the early-stage developing countries with the issue of where their comparative advantage will lie. Or to put it simply, digital manufacturing technologies may make the early stages of the Asian growth model obsolete.

JMC: Among these countries some of them have been supporters of protectionist policies. This is the case of Japan, or at least this is the perception we have of Japan in the West. What is the reality of these protectionist policies and what is their future in Japan?

MS: They protected certain parts of the economy in Japan, so that structures did not evolve very much. That may have been politically necessary but they have ended up with an economy that is not unique. That said it is that kind of structure where you have fairly high structural inefficiencies in part of it and then hypercompetitiveness in other parts. More specifically, Japan has a hypercompetitive and innovative industrial sector in the tradable part of the economy. But many non-tradable sectors are over regulated and inefficient.

VII GROWTH, INEQUALITIES, AND PROTECTIONISM

JMC: An important aspect of your work over the years is to reflect on the ability of growth to generate better distribution. Can you speak about the distributional aspects of growth and the problems encountered in recent times in this domain?

MS: The reason I think many of us have been enthusiastic about the general trends of the global economy, at least up to recent years, is that they have positively affected the lives of hundreds of millions of people with whom we share the planet. So at that very large-scale level, this is something justice is all about. Globally, income and wealth inequality are declining because of developing country growth.

That said I think the distributional aspects of growth are complicated but very important. In a country where everybody is poor you really cannot achieve anything without some growth. You cannot do it just by redistribution because there is not enough to go around.

JMC: So growth is key for the possibility of redistribution. That said, growth can also generate inequalities?

MS: As growth starts to occur it produces some kind of rise in inequality measured in terms of income or some other ways, and part of that is inevitable and not necessarily a problem. But I think that it is important to understand that if you let it get out of hand – it is close to out of hand in China, and maybe close to out of hand in the United States – then it causes problems of social tensions and social unrest, and political instability as well. That is one dimension. So, as with growth you are going to get inequality, you have to manage it carefully and you have to pay attention to it. A second element is the fact that in high-speed growth environments there are transitions occurring all the time. In particular, people lose their jobs. Hence the idea, in particular dominant in Europe, that you have to protect people, that you cannot just let the market dynamics work themselves without the social security and other safety nets, the access to basic services and what not, when you happen to be a victim of this kind of high-speed machine running.

JMC: Today protectionism seems to be gaining some appeal, following the downsides of globalization, including in terms of the growing gap between rich and poor in developed countries, especially in Europe and the United States. How should we handle the question of protectionism?

MS: Yes, the protectionism pressures are rising in part in response to asymmetrical benefits and costs absorbed in economies. In the end, protectionism has turned out to have higher costs than benefits. But to realize them, the distributional aspects of openness have to be managed. There are good and bad ways to do that. And one of the lessons of Europe is that you do not protect people very effectively in the long run by protecting companies and industries. It is better to try to protect people and families directly so you do not interfere with the sort of global competitive dynamics and structural change. You can say that you should try to protect people rather than jobs, and developing countries wrestle with this all the time. If you think about this in Schumpeterian terms, jobs are being created all the time, and jobs are being destroyed all the time by competitive processes, both internally and with the global economy. In this context, if the job destruction process gets ahead of the job creation process, then you have a major problem of economic performance and unemployment, and dashed hopes and expectations.

Another part of the equation is that you have to pay attention to whether job creation and job destruction are a reasonable match. One of the reasons countries do not open up in a sudden fashion to the global economy is they are cautious and have to manage this rate of exposure to foreign competition of the domestic economy. That has become standard practice. That said, to be successful in this involves judgment. There is no formula that tells you how to do that. So there are lots of tensions of that type, and for some time now we have been starting to experience them in the advanced countries.

JMC: In recent years, inequality, rising inequalities, especially in developed countries, has become a major issue and concern, and many people see this as a cause behind the spread of populism, particularly in recent years in the United States and in Western Europe. What are your views on this issue of inequality?

MS: The most serious form of inequality is exclusion. And by this I mean the absence of access to equality of opportunity if there is a significant group of people in the economy (defined however you want by caste, by religion, by tribe, even gender) that is excluded from the process. When this is the case, which is already the expression of a major problem, something will go wrong. And it will usually be in the way that there will be a failure of support of the overall system. Polarization, political paralysis, even internal conflict can result. None are conducive to growth and prosperity.

In this perspective, what the Growth Commission felt extremely strongly about is that the inclusiveness in all these dimensions turns out to be a critical aspect in all these long-term growth strategies, both in developed and developing countries. If you ignore it, something bad will happen and it is usually something that amounts to a loss of support for policies and investments to support the growth.

VIII THE AFTERMATH OF THE 2008 FINANCIAL CRISIS AND POST-NATIONAL GOVERNANCE

JMC: In these days it is common to link problems of growth with the international economic order and the fact that it is not managed so well, particularly by international and regional institutions. Would you agree with this?

MS: The most important process or experiment that has been under way for many years in terms of creating a multinational economic and other social structure is the European Union. That is a process that has cost a huge amount and encountered difficulties along the way. Among other things, it requires rethinking, reinventing leadership, even going back to the drawing board and asking if the original goals are clearly right.

I think the honest answer is something similar is going to need to happen globally. Growing economic interdependence without regulatory oversight by legitimate and accountable institutions does not seem to be a stable outcome. But that is where we are now. It will be a very long-term journey, probably the rest of the second half of this century of convergence, where we can develop and deepen the institutions that are needed for global governance.

I think that right now it is fair to say that interdependence in the economic sense has outrun the governance capabilities by considerable margins and that is an environment which is risky and volatile, as there are lots of problems with it. Here we have the G20. It has inherited the mantle from the G7, G8, to be the kind of setter of priorities. One of its problems is that it is not inclusive. In terms of international entities, we have the United Nations, the World Bank, and the IMF that are more inclusive in terms of shareholders. So if the G20 can learn over time how to build multinational policy coordination and consensus on things that really matter, that will be a huge step forward. But nobody really knows how to do that. That is kind of what we are doing now.

JMC: How do you compare the handling of the 2008 financial and economic crisis in Europe and in the United States – a crisis that, by the way, is still with us in many ways?

MS: America has had a reasonable recovery, though by no means complete. Japan has continued to underperform but that dates back before the 2008 crisis. Europe has struggled more in this respect, in part because the decentralization of key decisions, or the need for broad-based agreements, has meant that aggressive policy responses have been harder to mount. In Europe or in America, in slightly different ways, we have not really recovered from the crisis. One of the effects of the crisis was to cause fairly rapid increases in the public sector debt and deficits and so on. In Europe that takes the form of differences between countries and destabilizing problems in some of the smaller countries. In America it takes the form of a big federal government deficit that needs to be reined in by a sort of bipartisan plan that needs to be put together, and both of those things are pretty uncertain. So it is not a pretty picture. But, that is perhaps too pessimistic. We have learned some lessons. The financial sector is better regulated and safer. Developing countries have become better at managing in the face of external shocks and distortions. In the next crisis, it is more likely we will make new mistakes rather than repeat the old ones.

That said, when it comes to the aftermath of the 2008 financial crisis, I and others are a little bit schizophrenic about whether the glass is half full or the glass is half empty. I get up some mornings and think we will solve our problems in the advanced countries. Japan will recover because it is a very resilient place. The emerging economies have demonstrated resilient and enhanced capacity for withstanding shocks and restoring growth. Other mornings I get up and think if China goes down that will take the rest of the emerging economies down with it. The United States is running risks with its sovereign debt and the reserve currency. As for Europe, it is stumbling around of how to try to share the burden of helping these struggling countries out and all these risks are sort of correlated with each other. So if the dominoes start falling, it could be a pretty ugly picture. I just go back and forth on that. I guess I would say I am cautiously optimistic, but there does seem to be an awful lot of systemic risk right now in the global economy.

Right now it looks as if the global economy is recovering. On a fairly broad front. But there are clear vulnerabilities. High and still rising levels of global debt, the threat of an outbreak of protectionism, populist, nationalist, and anti-globalization parties, especially problematic in Europe. It is a very confusing picture at the moment.

JMC: Regarding this question of risk, including of systemic risk, do you see it at work the same way around the world, in developing and developed countries?

MS: While everyone is vulnerable to large systemic shocks, the nature and level of vulnerabilities varies considerably. To answer this question, we have to keep in mind that there are similarities in the technological and economic forces that operate in all of our countries but then there are some fairly important differences. I will give you one example. The American household sector got leveraged up to a tremendous and dangerous extent in the course of the build up to the crisis, and that is part of the reason why it is so difficult to recover. Severe household balance sheet damage cuts off consumption and produces an immediate downturn in the economy. I mean, it is very difficult to get consumption back and domestic demand, whereas in Italy, where I live part of the year, housing leverage is extremely low and the savings rate in the economy is extremely high. So, in Italy, while there are lots of challenges at the level of government debt, the private sector is in a very different condition. In this regard, it is very useful to live or be exposed to multiple places. It gives a variety of perspectives on the problems at hand and it helps to think out of the box. In this regard, I spend quite a lot of time in developing countries continuing to learn, and I find the perspectives that come from that are quite interesting as well.

IX AFRICA AND ISSUES OF LEADERSHIP

JMC: Since you are just alluding to the situation of developing countries, what is your take on Africa? Although it has great potential, in part due to its natural resources, it is a continent that seems to continue to be left behind, with conflicts and poverty remaining significant features of daily life in many African countries.

MS: I am actually quite optimistic about Africa. I tried to think about African countries in the context of countries that had thus far had trouble. I think about them as countries that are new, trying to establish an identity. In the case of Africa, many of these countries do not make sense economically. They are just the leftovers of the dismantled colonial empires, and they have struggled mightily with both governing issues and economic performance. But in the last fifteen or twenty years, it is starting to look better. Fine leadership and time has help countries come together with a proud sense of identity. Many of these countries have young leaders who are very effective. They take responsibility as opposed to blaming someone else. They do not want to be dependent on aid. They understand at a very basic level what sort of open economy growth dynamics are and the components of what needs to be done. Of course, it does not make it less challenging but the performance in terms of accelerated growth both before the crisis and now after the crisis is coming back and makes one cautiously optimistic.

I think managing the natural resource wealth, which is extraordinary high in Africa, is effectively going to be a key part of this. I have played a small part in what is called the Natural Resource Charter (now via a merger with Revenue Watch the Natural Resource Governance Institute), which is in some sense building on the work of the Extractive Industries Transparency Initiative. The goal is basically to help countries deal with complicated questions of the natural resource wealth and turn it into a sustainable pattern of growth. So that is a kind of challenge that is more prevalent in Africa. But on the whole there is a reasonable chance that in the second half of this century Africa will be the star performer that people predicted that it would be in the first half.

JMC: You alluded to questions of leadership in Africa. Do you see leadership, and of course good leadership, playing a role in this context?

MS: In poor countries there is not much growth happening; the challenge is to change the economic and political dynamics so that growth becomes possible. This means making a fairly big jump. In order to achieve this, you really need to change the patterns, mindsets, and vision that have been the norm. This usually means changing behavior, changing people's minds, and changing the vision of how the whole thing is going to run. And, that seems to me, is a function of leadership.

When I use the term "leadership" and when we did in the Growth Commission we did not mean just a single individual. It is frequently a group. In most of these countries we end up identifying a single individual. And sometimes a single individual, as in the case of Mandela, is just enormously important, though even there you could say his colleagues in the African National Congress were important. Sometimes a single individual is just crucial by virtue of its humanity and stature. But quite frequently it is a group. Leadership does not refer only to the group in power. Important leadership sometimes comes from groups that are out of power but have the ability to persuade people there is a better path forward.

X EVOLUTION OF INTERNATIONAL ORDER AND OF INTERNATIONAL INSTITUTIONS IN THE TWENTY-FIRST CENTURY

JMC: How do you see the evolution of international institutions, including the need to reform them and to create room for new powers? After all, most international institutions were created to reflect the balance of power in the aftermath of World War II. They appear as less and less adapted to the needs of the twenty-first century.

MS: There are two ways this could go. The good way is that we are going to have to reinvent and rebuild the global governance institutions, and that China, India, Brazil, and other countries (it is quite a long list) are going to be an important part of doing that jointly along with the rest of us. We do not know exactly what we are going to build or how we are going to get there. I think it is a generation's work, at least, to do it, and nobody has a blueprint. Nobody knows exactly how to balance national interests, on the one hand, with global interests, on the other. And nobody knows either how to institutionalize that in a way that works. We know where the starting point is, that national interests are dominant, and it makes it very difficult to achieve global coordination, even when the benefits are fairly easy to identify. So it is a hard problem, but it is not impossible to solve. The best hope/scenario would be to have India and China on board, with very different governance systems but probably with a fundamental shared understanding that we all have a collective interest in this enterprise of the global economy and its sustainability and so on, and we will participate in governing it. And both India and China will have very important roles in ten years (in fact China is now a major player on the global stage), as these will be the two economic giants if everything goes well.

The second scenario is when key emerging countries will get to that point where they will either disagree with each other or have very different models, and something bad will happen. The global economy will start to split apart. It is imaginable in the downside scenario that you would have an economy that splits apart in the way that the world did in the Cold War, with one side doing one thing and another side doing another. That is not a very stable world because natural resources, which are crucial and have been the source of wars in the past, are not distributed around the world nicely in the global economy to sort of make that whole structure work.

So I think the best hope is that it is not this second scenario that we will follow. But, you know, there are no guarantees. We have had countries that became powerful and then were aggressive in the past. So I think the best hope is that there is a shared understanding that ultimately that does not work, that it is in no country's self-interest to approach the world like that. So far I think we are on the right path.

JMC: In this regard, how do you see the role of China and India in the evolution of the global economy and international institutions?

MS: My impression from being in China is that they are relatively assertive. They want to be part of the governance structures, but they are not particularly interested in being an externally aggressive economic and political power in the future. What they want is an ability to protect their own interests. So China's military is building up but it is building up because if the world turned against China it could get cut off from natural resources and it still has the memory of the long period in the nineteenth century in which it uniquely experienced declining GDP. It almost never happened before. So I think a lot of this is more defensive than aggressive.

That said, China has now acquired a very large interest and a very large potential impact on the stability and the sustainability of the global economy. So the thing that is interesting about China is that they have acquired systemic significance because of the size of the population. And this has happened at a much lower per capita level than has ever happened before. Because of this, there is not really a very good set of historical experiences that tells China how to discharge this responsibility or to carry out this balancing act. This has been added to the agenda of things China is going to have to experiment and invent as it goes along.

The interesting thing is that India is going to have to go through the same thing. India is not quite systemically significant, although close. The per capita income in India is a little bit more than 1,500 dollars and rising rapidly. They are about thirteen years behind China in high-speed growth rates but they are not far away from having exactly the same situation that is relatively modest per capita incomes in enormous size in the global economy. I am amazed at India. Here is a country that is the world's largest and most complex democracy that admittedly took some time to reach a stage of rapid development (which is normal since democracies tend to be like that) to find a way to sort of sustain high growth. Whoever is in power in India, Indians are convinced that it will not be allowed to derail in any fundamental sense the current path of development.

In many ways, what you find in China and India is the same situation. You find very talented people in the private sector and you find leaders who are admirable, smart, pragmatic, and effective and who face up to the challenges that they have.

XI THE WAY AHEAD

JMC: As a way to conclude this conversation, what are the things on which you are currently working?

MS: Now in the advanced countries we have a new challenge with respect to inclusiveness and making sure that the global economy as it evolves is benefiting everybody in an appropriate way and not hurting people. It is a journey and there are challenges all the way along the journey. I think a lot of these challenges were dominantly in the developing countries in the past fifty years, getting things started, connecting with the global economy, learning how to manage the macro side of the economy for stability. All of these things can be chalked up to areas where there has been either a big achievement or major progress.

I think in the advanced countries there are some issues and I am studying the German case because the Germans, the people and their government, around the year 2000 faced and recognized a serious productivity and competitiveness problem. Part of it came from the enormous economic problem absorbing East Germany back into the unified Germany. But what I think is interesting and what I am just in the process of understanding is: What was the nature of the problem? How did the economy evolve? More importantly, how did institutions in the areas of labor, business, policy-making, and other areas function to address this problem? Because it really does look like Germany has been fairly effective. Once I have finished that I think I will turn my attention to France, at least on the advanced country side of things.

So the way I think of it at this stage, sixty years into this process of sharing the global economy in some real way with the developing world, these are the new challenges. It does not make me pessimistic because I think our countries and our economies are pretty well put together in the sense of values and constitutional underpinnings and so on. We may be pessimistic in the short run because we do not seem to be solving problems as fast as we ought to be or even recognizing what it is but, ultimately, we are probably collectively pretty good at addressing them. We have reasons to have faith in the future.

JMC: Finally, what would be your advice to a young scholar starting his research work?

MS: My advice is always the same. It is to find something that you find deeply interesting, something that gets you up every morning eager to engage. It may take time to find that. There are many areas that fall under the broad heading of global justice that fit this. And there is certainly no shortage of issues and challenges.

14

Principles and Institutions of Global Justice

David Held

I OVERLAPPING COMMUNITIES OF FATE: FROM NATIONAL TO GLOBAL POLITICAL THEORY

JEAN-MARC COICAUD (JMC): *Why do you think it is important to consider political theory today in a global context? Why is it that the national context is not good enough anymore when it comes to thinking about political theory?*

DAVID HELD (DH): For most of the history of the modern state, that is, since about the late sixteenth century, it has been presupposed that kings and queens, or later democratic politicians, could more or less set the fate and fortunes of a country. The argument was that rulers, whether monarchical, democratic, or otherwise, could exclusively make fundamental decisions for their countries, with major implications for their citizens.

Today this idea that states are silos, as it were, relatively self-enclosed silos, is more than ever in question. We no longer live in a world of national communities of fate but in a world of what I call "overlapping communities of fate," where the fate and fortunes of countries are increasingly intertwined. Whether one thinks of the fallout from the US subprime markets and the development of the global financial crisis, whether one thinks of 9/11 and the decade of violence that followed the declaration of the "war on terror," whether one thinks about climate change, or whatever global public bad we choose, the fate of human beings and the fate of humankind is increasingly interconnected.

At the level of political theory what this means is as follows. For most of the history of political thinking it has been assumed that the political good adheres in the state. However the idea of the political good was articulated – whether it was defined by the monarchy, state bureaucracy, or popular mandate – the assumption was that the political good could be articulated within a political association delineated by clear borders. This is no longer true in an increasingly interconnected world, where the fate and fortunes of peoples are, as

I said, intertwined. So, to think politically we cannot just think locally. We cannot just think nationally. We cannot just think regionally. We must also think globally.

And I would like to make just one final point about this. Some of the most pressing challenges that we face now – and our children and children's children will face – are all by and large challenges that cannot be solved by states acting alone. These are challenges that come from dealing with collective public bads, and trying to produce collective public goods on a global scale. There is a pyramid or, if you want to put it less optimistically, an iceberg of issues approaching us. These issues have, for example, to do with our environment and habitat, from climate change to water deficits, to desertification, and so on. In each and every one of these areas the life chances of human beings are at stake. The agenda now is not just national; it is partially global, and here I am afraid human beings have yet to show that they are capable of responding adequately to these global collective action problems.

JMC: You mentioned the fact that we are now living in a world in which we have what you call overlapping communities of fate and for you it is really introducing a qualitative change to the political landscape. Is there a way to date when this qualitative change has happened and what are the factors which triggered it?

DH: We often call this era the era of globalization, but the truth is that globalization has been present across centuries while its nature and form has changed.[1] What is distinctive about the current period is a set of new technologies – satellite communications, computerization, digitalization, the internet, and so on – which do not just make global communication possible as never before in real time, but shape other areas of human activity such as global financial markets, global production chains, and so on. That is to say, these technologies not only make human communication possible on a global scale but they also reorganize the possibilities of economic, political, communicative, and legal life.

Accordingly, we can have a global financial market that operates effectively on the basis of twenty-four-hour trading, and multinational companies that can produce products which tie into global chains of production and supply. When you go into your local supermarket you will find goods from all over the world, and when you check out information about your purchase it is sent back to headquarters, where computers are processing all such information, and

[1] David Held, Andrew McGrew, D. Goldblatt, and J. Perraton, *Global Transformations: Politics, Economics and Culture* (Cambridge: Polity Press, 1999).

sending out orders for the resupply of goods from across the world. Whether it is flowers from West Africa, whether it is textile products from India, whether it is beef from Argentina, this is a global supply chain which is made possible by these changing technologies. What has happened increasingly throughout the twentieth century, and in particular the last few decades, is that there has been a growing confluence of change across different areas of human activity, driven by new information technologies that makes the world more interconnected than ever before, and ensures that something that happens in one time zone can easily ricochet across the world.[2] This is a new era driven by new possibilities.

JMC: Initially, this qualitative change took place in the areas of technology and in the field of economy and then it had consequences in the political sphere. Does this mean that the nation-state or the polity as we knew it in classical terms is definitely finished?

DH: No. Look at the European Union as a paradigm, just for a moment. Prior to Brexit (assuming the process is completed), you could be a citizen of, for example, the city of Glasgow, voting in city elections, and vote as well in Scottish elections, UK elections, and EU elections. So, a citizen of Glasgow could be engaged in four overlapping forms of political membership, all of which have relevance at different levels. City politics is preoccupied, of course, with the distinctive issues of cities; national politics focuses on a whole range of issues that affect all citizens and position countries in relation to each other, and the politics of the superregional and global deals with bigger questions and challenges that link us all together – such as climate change. Moreover, global challenges in the current period are not just addressed by cities, regions, and nation-states. They are also "addressed" by global markets with all their problems because they produce externalities which can run out of control, and by powerful states who make decisions inevitably in their own interests, even though these have considerable impacts beyond their borders.

JMC: You are suggesting that what is skewing all this transformation is the notion of overlapping communities of fate, which makes sense because you started with this notion. This notion of overlapping communities of fate has found a political and legal framework at the regional level in the

[2] David Held and Andrew McGrew, *Globalization/Anti-Globalization* (Cambridge: Polity Press, 2007).

European context. But at the global level we do not yet have a political and legal framework to act upon it?

DH: Let me reflect on Europe and then go to the global level. Europeans do not like to recognize this, but Europe was the most warmongering region of the world for a substantial period of time. From the late sixteenth century Europe exploded onto the world in a process of colonization and empire-building which proclaimed certain standards for citizens living within European boundaries, and negated those standards for people outside those boundaries. And then after empire reached its zenith in the late nineteenth century and came under increasing pressure, European powers began to turn their force and violence against each other in two calamitous world wars.

Who would have thought that this most warmongering region of the world could have transformed itself into something of a Kantian pacific union? What is now unthinkable in Europe? War among European states. The idea of war among European states has effectively been removed by the establishment of the EU in the second half of the twentieth century, with *sui generis* legal structures, legal bodies, a human rights regime, and so on. This was almost unthinkable seventy or eighty years ago, and yet it has transpired. Now at the global level, of course, we do not have such a union. We have in fact a world of increasing multipolarity, and where the balance of power is shifting very quickly, notably to the East. We live in the context of new emerging powers, for example, China, India, and others who rightly want more influence on the global stage. But on this stage the institutions are rooted in the 1945 settlement protecting the interests of the old established powers, particularly those of the West, who were among the victorious powers in 1945. This is, of course, especially true of the UN and the Bretton Woods institutions.

Nonetheless, it is the case that the present global order splices together two things: the interests of sovereign states, on the one hand, and the universal values of the UN Charter, the human rights regime, on the other. And these things push and pull in different directions.

But the positive thing I want to say is that we see signs, as it were, not only of the development of elements of an EU-wide constitution but also of some stepping stones toward similar developments at the global level. I think of the law of war and the human rights regimes in particular as two sides of the same coin that seek to circumscribe the nature of sovereignty and sovereign power. In the seventeenth, eighteenth, and nineteenth centuries sovereignty meant effective power. Might made right. Today that is not true – at least in principle – in international law. Legitimate authority is circumscribed by claims to maintain certain democratic standards and human rights values.

This is a fundamental shift in law at the international level. The law of war and the human rights regimes together are two sides of a legal coin which are the beginnings – only the beginnings – of a universal constitutional order.[3]

At the start of the twenty-first century I think we can see a number of possible trajectories. We can see the gradual weakening of the UN system in the face of emerging powers which are not adequately represented in the UN system. We can see the fragmentation of the global order into competing rival powers much like the nineteenth century. Or we can see the beginnings of the development of this universal constitutional order into a more democratic and just global system. Whichever trajectory prevails, a number of tough questions will be faced by all involved. Can we solve the disputes over trade rules with fundamental consequences for social justice? Can we manage financial markets? Can we check and reverse nuclear proliferation? Can we agree on genetic research rules? Can we deal with climate change? And at the moment, the answers seem at best unclear and at worst beyond us.

II ON THE DEVELOPMENT OF GLOBAL GOVERNANCE: NEED, FRAGMENTATION, AND EMERGING POWERS

JMC: These three tendencies that you identified, first the gradual weakening of the UN system; second, the fragmentation of world order; and third, the beginning of the world constitutional order, are these, in your view, tendencies which are effectively happening or are these possible scenarios for the future?

DH: The UN system always spliced together cosmopolitan, universal values, on the one hand, with sovereign interests, on the other, often producing contradictory effects. Second, the UN system embedded, most visibly in the Security Council, the dominant interests of the victors of 1945, and not surprisingly they built these institutions to suit their interests. But the world is becoming very dramatically transformed from the era of 1945; multilateralism and economic globalization, one might say, are the victims of their own success. New emerging powers have developed in these contexts with great speed. China and India, for example, have been able to take advantage of selective or managed entry into the global economy to enhance their economic development in a way that was completely unanticipated.

[3] David Held, *Democracy and the Global Order: From the Modern State to Cosmopolitan Governance* (Cambridge: Polity Press, 1995).

The world, and the distribution of the power especially, is changing faster, I think, than at any moment in human history.

If we look at this as a three-dimensional chess game, the top level, the world of coercive power, is still highly dominated by the United States and Russia, with China rapidly developing as well, but at the second, economic, level the world is increasingly multipolar. As a result, the West can no longer write the rules of the global game as it once could because the new powerful emerging voices have a capacity to block and veto what is put on the table. And at the third level, the level, let us say, of cultural power, communication, soft power, and the internet, we have a battle of voices. Now in the age of empire, empires could cut down from dominant coercive power, through economic power, through culture in one container. Today, this is no longer true. There is huge complexity between levels such that being the most powerful military country in the world – the United States – does not mean that it has the capacity to win the peace in Iraq, Afghanistan, Libya, Syria, and elsewhere. We live in a much more fragmented global order where there is a battle of voices and discourses, and the question is: Is there a way of binding these voices together so they all find legitimate expression and can compromise with each other sufficiently to deal with the big issues of our time?

JMC: You mentioned the gradual weakening of the UN system and the beginning of a constitutional world order but is it possible to move forward in terms of the constitutional world order with a UN system which is weakened and which is running the risk of becoming irrelevant? Can we have a constitutional world order without a stronger UN?

DH: There are two points to make here. One could easily be pessimistic about the complexity of global politics today. I think the failure of international negotiations over trade rules, financial market reform, and peace in many areas in the Middle East, among many other things, do not point in a very positive direction. Nonetheless, it is a great mistake to read the politics of the present into the past and the future. Circumstances change. As I said, there were remarkable twentieth-century developments in Europe and in international law, and politics can be built upon these – the cosmopolitan stepping stones, as I call them.

We are now faced with a number of choices. We know what does not work in many respects. Market fundamentalist philosophy that stresses that markets alone are the best way of resolving collective action problems does not work in practice. Markets produce massive externalities; they can and often do run out of control; they produce environmental degradation, which needs politics to address and resolve it. Two, "non-democracy," the politics of small clubs taking decisions in their own interests, is also in my judgment not the way to go because that created the global financial crisis, the energy problems of the current world order, and climate change. It was the small clubs of industrial nation-states, acting to protect their interests, that established the financial standards (or lack of them) which eventually engendered the global financial crisis, and the patterns of energy use which have led to climate change. It is the small clubs regulating, as it were, many key aspects of human activity in their own interests that generalize models of risk across the world. The decisions taken by the few become, in other words, the risks borne by the many.

There are two simple tests which point to core constitutive features of modern politics. You would not call a modern state a modern state if it did not have some system of impartial taxation and some system of impartial representation. A state that depends for its revenue on the voluntary donations of the rich could not be called a modern state; a state that is represented by autocrats or monarchs could not be called a representative state. To be a modern state you need, on the one hand, some system of impartial authority, a sphere of deliberation that is not intruded upon and wholly manipulated by particular interests, and, on the other hand, a system of impartial taxation. If we could begin to meet these tests at the global level then we can start developing a global order that can move away from archaic and unjust principles of organization and toward a fairer and representative system of global governance. What does this mean?

At one level, it means reinventing how states and peoples are represented at the UN level, and developing a robust form of global governance.[4] Deliberative decision-making centers beyond national territories are urgent when those significantly affected by public matter constitute a cross-border or transnational grouping, and when "lower" levels of decision-making cannot manage and discharge satisfactorily transnational international policy questions. In this context, the Security Council has to become more representative, along with the World Bank and the IMF, and so on. At another level, the revenues which these bodies utilize in order to pursue global public policy and address global public bads cannot just be from the voluntary contributions of the rich states because they can block policy that they do not like. We eventually do have to have a system of global taxation – whether it is a global financial tax like the Tobin tax or a global carbon tax, one can imagine any number of possible proposals. But unless we move to a system that is more representative and better financed we will not have a UN or global governance system robust enough to meet the challenges ahead.

4 David Held, *Cosmopolitanism: Ideals and Realities* (Cambridge: Polity Press, 2010), pp. 93–116.

Now, Max Weber wrote that the character of public life is determined by the sources of its revenue. This is a profound statement. In other words, if the sources of revenue are the rich and powerful states they will always have a stranglehold on what it is that can be done. Accordingly, global institutions need to be more representative and they need to be funded more impartially to meet the collective action problems we face.

Finally, let me ask, obviously, is this feasible? Well you and I do not know in the long run whether it is feasible. It was Hegel in the Philosophy of Right who wrote that "the owl of Minerva spreads its wings at the coming of dusk." Wisdom comes when you look back in time not forward. However, I think there are some optimistic signs. In the last few years we have seen the weakening of the importance and influence of the club model of the G1, as I call the United States, the G4, the G5, the G7, and the development of the G20. This recognizes already that the global basis of discussion can no longer be just based on the rich countries, but must be broadened. Second, as a result of the global financial crisis we have seen increasing political participation in virtually all of the institutions of international financial governance. This would not have, could not have, happened before. Third, and most importantly, we do not see that the emerging voices of the developing world, the BRICS countries in particular, want out of global fora. They do not want to undermine the UN system of global governance; they want to be included in it on fair and equal terms. The challenge is not to include them; rather, it is to stop the West from continuing to exclude them on unfair and unequal terms. I will come back to these issues later (see Section IV).

JMC: On this very issue of rising powers, China and India and others, do you feel that they are committed to the possibility of a constitutional world order and, if it is the case, are they committed to a foreign policy which would not be the captive of a narrow understanding of the national interest? If so, how do they fit in the new institutional order at the global level and how does this institutional order evolve and change?

DH: I am not sure I would go along with your first point in saying that they necessarily want entry into the global constitutional order, as I am discussing it. The stepping stones of the law of war and human rights law were ultimately stepping stones created by Western powers, above all, after they reflected on the catastrophe of the two World Wars, of the Holocaust, Stalinism, and so on. Whether these values can be embraced by all the emerging powers with their often different discourses and different priorities is an open question, one that we can return to later. What I want to say now is something actually a bit more modest, which is that on the current evidence these new emerging powers, particularly China and India, want to be represented in the global system on more fair and equitable terms. They do not want to create a complete set of alternative institutions; they do not want to run from these institutions; they want their voices to count in the global dialogue about the core challenges of our time. The old and narrow clubs of the G1, 4, 5, 6, and 7 are too small a set of decision communities based on old Western interests. The G20 is a stepping stone to a wider discourse among a series of countries and populations and, therefore, it is a step in the right direction.

III COSMOPOLITANISM AND WORLD ORDER

JMC: What kind of values and principles would give this emerging order its normative framework? What values and principles do you envision for this new world order?

DH: In my work, I set out a number of principles, cosmopolitan principles, that I believe can be universally shared, and can form the basis for the protection and nurturing of each person's equal significance in what we can call "the moral realm of humanity."[5] Eight principles are key. They are the principles of: (1) equal worth and dignity; (2) active agency; (3) personal responsibility and accountability; (4) consent; (5) collective decision-making about public matters through voting procedures; (6) inclusiveness and subsidiarity; (7) avoidance of serious harm (social justice); and (8) sustainability. Clearly, the meaning of these principles needs detailed unpacking in order to fully understand their nature and implications. This would take us beyond the terms of reference of our conversation. But I would like to say a few things about them.

The eight principles can best be thought of as falling into three clusters. The first cluster (principles 1–3) sets down the fundamental organizational features of a cosmopolitan moral universe. Its crux is that each person is the subject of equal moral concern, that each person is capable of acting autonomously with respect to the range of choices before them, and that, in deciding how to act or which institutions to create, the claims of each person affected should be taken equally into account. The second cluster (principles 4–6) forms the basis of translating individual action, or privately determined activities more broadly, into collectively agreed or collectively sanctioned frameworks of action. Public power at all levels can be conceived of as legitimate to the degree to which principles 4–6 are upheld. The final

5 Held, *Cosmopolitanism: Ideals and Realities*, chapter 2.

principles (7–8) lay down a framework for prioritizing urgent need and resource conservation; that is, a way of ensuring that public policy is consistent with a focus on those who are most vulnerable and with global ecological balances which can help prevent the destruction of irreplaceable and non-substitutable resources.

It is important to distinguish two things that often run together: Questions about the origins of principles, and questions about their validity or weight. Both kinds of questions are relevant. If the first illuminates the ethical circumstances or motivation for a preference for, or commitment to, a set of principles, the second is the basis for testing their intersubjective validity. In this regard, the justificatory rationale of cosmopolitan principles is dependent on two fundamental "metaprinciples" or organizing notions of ethical discourse – one cultural and historical, the other philosophical. These are, respectively, the metaprinciple of autonomy and the metaprinciple of impartialist reasoning, as I call them.

The metaprinciple of autonomy (the MPA for short) is at the core of the democratic project. Its rationale and standing are "political not metaphysical," to borrow a phrase from Rawls.[6] A basic concept or idea is political, in this sense, if it represents an articulation of notions found in public political life and, in particular, if it builds on the distinctive conception of the person as a citizen who is, in principle, "free and equal" in a manner which people can readily understand. In other words, the MPA can be understood as a notion embedded in the public political culture of democratic societies or emerging democracies.

The MPA is part of the "deep structure" of ideas that have shaped the constitution of modern political life. It has roots in the ancient world, although many elements of its deep structure were not part of classical thinking. It was not until modern times that the MPA became more firmly entrenched.[7] It became entrenched in the pursuit of, and struggle for, citizenship, which has always been marked by "an urge," as Marshall put it, to secure "a fuller measure of autonomy" for each and every person. Autonomy here means the "stuff" of which modern citizenship is made.[8] Or, to restate the point with reference to the principles listed earlier, it has been marked by an urge to realize the core elements of an egalitarian conception of the person (with its emphasis upon people as free and equal, capable of active agency and

[6] John Rawls, *Political Liberalism* (New York: Columbia University Press, 1993).
[7] David Held, *Models of Democracy* (Cambridge: Polity Press, third edition, 2006).
[8] T. Marshall, *Class, Citizenship and the Welfare State* (Westport, CT: Greenwood Press, 1973), p. 84.

accountable for their choices), of the democratic regulation of public life (including consent, deliberation, voting and inclusiveness), and of the necessity to ensure that, if people's equal interest in self-determination or self-governance is to be protected, attention must be focused on those who lack the capacity to participate in, and act within, key sites of power and political institutions (that is, that there must be a measure of social protection).

Another way to put these points is to say that the MPA is the guiding political thread of modern democratic societies and that the first seven cosmopolitan principles, suitably unfolded from a commitment to moral autonomy and self-determination, are the basis for specifying more fully the core values and ideas that underpin a liberal and democratic order.[9] In short, these cosmopolitan principles are the principles of democratic public life, but without one crucial assumption – never fully justified in any case in liberal democratic thought – that these principles can only be enacted effectively within a single, circumscribed, territorially-based political community. The cosmopolitan principles do not presume, as principle 6 indicates, that the link between self-determination, democracy, and sovereignty can be understood simply in territorial terms. Hence, it is possible to have a modern democratic rendition of the Stoic aspiration to multiple forms of affiliation – local, national, and global. The cosmopolitan principles are the core element of democratic public life, shed of the contingent link with the borders of nation-states.

To test the generalizability of claims and interests, however, involves something more; that is, it involves "reasoning from the point of view of others." Attempts to focus on this "social point of view" find their clearest elaboration in John Rawls's original position, Jürgen Habermas's ideal speech situation and Brian Barry's formulation of impartialist reasoning.[10] These formulations have in common a concern to conceptualize an "impartial" moral standpoint from which to assess particular forms of practical reasoning.

This concern should not be thought of as over-demanding, although it often is. All that the impartiality thesis claims, as Thomas Hill once eloquently

9 I say "first seven cosmopolitan principles" because the eighth, sustainability, has traditionally not been a common element of democratic thinking, although it ought to be. It is only in the last few decades that sustainability has moved center stage in democratic thinking and human rights.

10 See John Rawls, *A Theory of Justice* (Cambridge, MA: Harvard University Press, 1973); Jürgen Habermas, "Wahrheitstheorien", in H. Fahrenbach (ed.), *Wirchlichkeit und Reflexion* (Pfüllingen: Neske, 1973); Jürgen Habermas, *Between Facts and Norms: Contributions to a Discourse Theory of Law and Democracy* (Cambridge: Polity Press, 1996); Brian Barry, *Theories of Justice* (London: Harvester Wheatsheaf, 1989); and Brian Barry, *Justice as Impartiality* (Oxford: Clarendon Press, 1995).

explained, is that if one raises questions about fundamental moral standards, the "court of appeal" that one addresses is a court in which no particular agent – individual, group, or country – has special standing.[11] Before the court, suggesting "I like it," "It suits me," "It belongs to male prerogatives," "It is in the best interest of my country," does not settle the issue at hand, for principles must be defensible from a larger, human standpoint. This social, open-ended, moral perspective is a device for focusing our thoughts and testing the intersubjective validity of our conceptions of the good. It offers a way of exploring principles, norms, and rules that might reasonably command agreement. I refer to it as the metaprinciple of impartialist reasoning (MPIR).

Together the MPA and MPIR provide the grounds, I think, of cosmopolitan thought. The MPA lays down the conceptual space in which impartialist reasoning can take place. It generates a preoccupation with each person as a subject of equal moral concern; with each person's capacity to act autonomously with respect to the range of choices before them; and with each person's equal status with respect to the basic institutions of political communities, that is, with an entitlement to claim and be claimed upon. It provides motives, reasons, and constraining considerations to help establish agreement on reasonable terms. The MPIR is the basis for pursuing this agreement. It is a device of argument that is designed to abstract from power relations in order to disclose the fundamental enabling conditions of active agency, rightful authority, and social justice. Of course, as a device of argument, it can be resisted by those who reject the language of moral autonomy and self-determination; but then we must be clear that this is precisely what they are doing.

JMC: These principles, equal moral worth, self-determination, consent and deliberation, social justice, and finally sustainability, they are clearly at the core of the democratic message but historically it has been so far a Western message. How do we use them as a basis to build a bridge with the non-West? Do you feel that the new rising powers mainly coming from Asia are sympathetic toward these principles?

DH: There are many things to say about this. First of all, to paraphrase the American philosopher Bruce Ackerman, there is no country in the world without women who do not seek equal standing and equal rights with men.[12] There is no country in the world without men who do not seek to

[11] Thomas Hill, "The Importance of Autonomy," in E. Kittay and D. Meyers (eds.), *Women and Moral Theory* (Towata, NJ: Rowman and Allanheld, 1987), pp. 129–138.

[12] Bruce Ackerman, "Political Liberalisms," *Journal of Philosophy* (vol. 91, no. 7, 1994), pp. 364–386.

throw off the yokes and demands of deference. There is no country in the world without people who do not seek to free themselves from the burden of physical need. The principles of equal moral worth, self-determination, the avoidance of serious harm, and so on are the conditions of a just democratic life in which pluralism can flourish, shaped and enabled by the consideration that each and every one of us has an equal interest in self-determination. So my first argument would be that these values, or cosmopolitan principles as I call them, are the basis of the yearnings of all human beings whenever and wherever they are committed to a life of choice, of self-determination, and self-governance. That is the first thing.

The second thing is we should distinguish the origins of principles, say in the West, with their validity, as I noted earlier. The fact that certain principles have their intellectual origins in the West says nothing about their intellectual validity in general. And, third, we would be wrong to say that democratic ideas belong exclusively to the West. Think of India, the largest democracy in the world; it would be very odd to say to the citizens of India that democracy was just a Western idea. My view is that these principles are the underlying principles that are embedded in every struggle of every human being everywhere to bring power to accountability, to create a space for self-determination, and to recognize their ability to make their own choices free of domination. And the way you do this without violence is through dialogue and, ultimately, democratic dialogue.

Let me build on what I said for a moment by a specific thought experiment, consistent with the MPIR. Just imagine if we thought of the whole world order as one tower block. Today at the top level you would have the United States living in the penthouse and Europe somewhere below, with helipads and water supplies and abundant energy, rapid lift services, reasonable health services, and so on. As you go down the tower block you would get more and more people packed into the floors living increasingly compact, compressed lives with less space, fewer resources, slower lifts, less access, and so on. Now, if you ask all these people to do a thought experiment and consider how they would design the world order if they did not know which floor they were eventually going to end up on in this tower block, what would they say? At the moment we all know where we end up, some as American citizens, some as German citizens, and so on; we know the floor where we will be living, so to speak. But if you strip us of the knowledge of where we will ultimately end up, and suspend that one assumption, and ask people to redesign the layout of the tower block, what would they recommend? I have discussed this question regularly with my students. Basically, they design a system with greater equality of opportunity, enhanced standards of living guaranteed for each and all, a fairer distribution of resources, a more effective system of accountability to give voice to all living in the building, and a greater concern with public goods and resolving public bads. More or less the concerns we are speaking about.

IV INSTITUTIONS AND PARTICIPATORY MECHANISMS FOR WORLD ORDER

JMC: And so on the basis of these principles, which you are telling us have universal reach and universal validity, what kind of institutions do we build?

DH: There is no simple institutional blueprint to create a more democratic global order. We just need to know the right direction of travel. If you think of the great works of political philosophy in the sixteenth and seventeenth centuries, of Machiavelli, Hobbes, Locke, and others, they developed concepts for a new world order in terms of the idea of the modern state, which took centuries then to crystallize into its contemporary form. Today we need to redefine what we mean by the political good, and we have to set out the stepping stones to a universal constitutional order marked by greater justice and democracy. We can say a little more about what that means. In the short term, it means a democratizing process at the United Nations. It means changing the representative structure of the Bretton Woods institutions. It means building institutions which are able to handle issues of environmental injustice and to manage climate change. We can start with small steps just so long as we are on the road toward applying our principles consistently.

We can take this argument a step further. We cannot any longer run the world on a club model based on the patterns of historical power from the sixteenth century to the late twentieth century. This world order is changing and if we want collective institutions that can govern in the name of the wider interests of humanity, we have to include these diverse voices in a more democratic, equitable, and sustainable order. Now this is a very, very ambitious project. I have written about it for many years.[13] There are no guarantees that we will move in this direction. Where we are today is not where you would ideally start if you wanted to travel in this direction! But knowing the direction of travel is critical to knowing how we can solve the policy debates that affect us today from those concerning trade rules, financial market rules, genetic research rules, climate, and so on.

[13] David Held, *Democracy and the Global Order*; *Global Covenant: The Social Democratic Alternative to the Washington Consensus* (Cambridge: Polity Press, 2004), and *Cosmopolitanism*.

Elements of a more just democratic order, or a cosmopolitan model of democracy and politics, as I prefer to call it, can be found in some of the most important achievements of law and institution-building in the twentieth century. These developments set down a conception of rightful authority tied to human rights and democratic values which can be entrenched in wide-ranging settings. In this perspective, political power is legitimate if and only if it is democratic and upholds human rights. In addition, the link between territory, sovereignty and rightful authority is, in principle, broken, since rightful authority can be exercised in many spheres and at many levels, local, subnational, national, and supranational. Accordingly, citizenship can be envisaged, as it is already in the European Union, as equal membership in the diverse, overlapping political communities which uphold common civic and political values and standards. Citizenship, thus conceived, is not built on an exclusive membership of a single community but on a set of principles and legal arrangements which link people together in the diverse communities which significantly affect them. Accordingly, patriotism would be misunderstood if it meant, as it all too often has done, "my country right or wrong." Rather, it comes to mean loyalty to the standards and values of rightful authority – to common civic and political principles, appropriately embedded.

Suitably developed, this conception of global politics envisages, I believe, a multilayered and multilevel polity, from cities to global associations, bound by a common framework of law, a framework of law anchored in cosmopolitan principles, democracy, and human rights. The state does not wither away in this conception; rather, it becomes one element in the protection and maintenance of political authority, democracy, and human rights in the dense web of global forces and processes that already shape our lives. Perhaps more importantly still, it points to a political order no longer exclusively anchored in raison d'état and hegemonic state projects but in principles of global cooperation and cosmopolitan association.

The European Union today articulates some of these complex ideas and trends. At its core, the EU can be characterized as a Kantian project: An attempt to create, from the wreckage of the Second World War, a peaceful union of European states, cooperating on all transregional issues. This ideal remains fundamental to the European project even though the reality is fraught with the compromises of geopolitics. The EU has been through turbulent cycles of deepening and broadening – first the core states, then Spain, Portugal, Greece, then, after the fall of the Berlin Wall, membership was extended to central and eastern European states. But behind all the turbulent transitions, European leaders were eager to move forward the

European ideal through the policy and practice of extending and entrenching the Union as a multilevel polity, combining elements of supranational, national, regional, and local governance. Of course, this ideal has been compromised by a series of regional and global challenges in recent times.

JMC: *At the same time, there are very powerful counter-trends to these things today. Would you not agree that many of them are highly vulnerable to populist and nationalist trends?*

DH: We are indeed at a crossroads. One road points to the inexorable rise of populism and authoritarianism, while another opens up a more hopeful cosmopolitan future. The path to authoritarianism can be created by the dangerous drift in the world order that follows from the failure to address many key challenges, from the financial crisis to migration, and a search for decisive solutions from "strong man" leaders faced with a world that is seemingly out of control, and where a retreat to the familiar (and away from the Other) offers a tempting way forward. We see such trends across many different kinds of countries, from Brexit Britain to Trump's America, Duterte's Philippines, Putin's Russia, Modi's India, and Erdogan's Turkey. Of course, we have been here before. The 1930s saw the rise of xenophobia and nationalism in the context of prolonged and protracted economic strife, the lingering impact of World War I, weak international institutions, and a desperate search for scapegoats. The 2010s has some notable parallels: The protracted fallout of the global financial crisis, ineffective regional and international institutions, and a growing xenophobic discourse that places virtually all blame for every problem on some form of Other.

But there are alternative routes. To begin with, we have the option of recalling where the pursuit of authoritarianism leads. The routes chosen in the 1930s all led to calamity and destruction, and the rediscovery in the 1940s onward of the dangers of simply putting up the shutters, pursuing protectionism, and denying the equal dignity of each and all. The architects of the postwar era set down elements of a universal constitutional order, as we have noted, in which the principles of the equal moral standing of each and every person, and the equal rights and duties of each and all, became the bedrock of peace and prosperity in the postwar years.

But the years since the turn of the millennium have cast a dark shadow over global politics in many respects. The wars and crises that followed 9/11 have put at risk the wisdom and achievements of the architects of the post–World War II era: Of the founders of the UN and EU, of those who established and advanced the human rights regime, of the many actors and agencies that have tried to mitigate climate change and other environmental threats, and of those who have struggled to address poverty and inequality, among many other pressing issues. Having said this, the achievements of the post-1945 era have not yet been undermined or damaged to the point of no return. The future is still in our hands. Our forebears created stepping stones to a universal constitutional order, and we can still walk across them and build on them further. This remains a future worth struggling for.

JMC: What of civil society? Has the era of civil society peaked? You say little about this so far.

DH: Civil society was thriving in the 1990s, and I think we can say that period was the high point of global civil society to date. Why did it stall? It seems to me that the momentum of civil society was halted after 9/11 and with the War on Terror that followed. This changed the political atmosphere of the first decade of the twenty-first century quite decisively. I would even go [as] far as to say that the response to 9/11 was partly designed to depoliticize civil society, and to create a state of warfare, a mentality of warfare between "us" and "them," the United States and the threat of Islam and Islamic fundamentalism. President Bush and his supporters sought to depoliticize American politics and demand a new form of patriotism. But this period of politics, I think, is largely discredited now. The American century proved to be an American decade at best. The United States has learned (well, some elements within the United States have learned) that it cannot project its power and will across the world without compromise, without negotiation, without consent. It has learned that the "coalition of the willing" cannot produce peace and win the consent of people or their hearts and minds.

Having said that, I think civil society in many parts of the world is still very active. Wherever you go there are NGOs and different kinds of constructive engagement and participation. But the real problem is this: We cannot simply ennoble civil society. Civil society – especially in the age of the internet and global communications – is an actual and virtual space for a huge diversity of voices. For example, some NGOs in the US are pro-abortion, while others are anti-abortion. In sub-Saharan Africa, some NGOs support the free distribution of condoms in order to protect people, particularly women, from the spread of AIDS/HIV; yet, there are others who are highly critical of this and believe that such a move encourages sexual relations outside of traditional marriage and, thereby, enhances the risks of contracting AIDS/HIV. In the Arab Spring, there were powerful social movements and NGOs seeking to champion civil and political rights and to bring an end to autocratic regimes; at the same time, there were others who opposed such attempts in the name of Islam and political order. Civil society is, accordingly, a highly contested terrain.

The critical thing is the vitality of civil society, and the plurality of opinion and interests. Civil society will always articulate a diversity of interests and voices, and needs to be mediated by a system of deliberation and representation in order to win legitimacy in a democratic process. Global civil society, in other words, is a significant element of a vibrant public sphere, but is insufficient alone to produce consolidated, scaled-up, and legitimate outcomes.

JMC: Historically, at the national level, political participation and representation have been through a certain level of institutionalization, which has also meant a certain level of professionalization of politics. Clearly, more often than not, this has been a source of major problems. The crisis of political representation unfolding in a number of Western democracies is a case in point. As you seem to ask for more popular participation and better representation at the global level, how do we avoid at the global level the types of problems we have been encountering at the national level?

DH: Politics at the local, regional, and national level can usefully be described in reference to the Weberian concept of hierarchical bureaucratic organization.[14] This is the political counterpart to large private enterprises; the notion that the centralized political party alone can organize the political system, by articulating and aggregating voices and interests, and bringing a measure of coherence to them. But the rise of these notions predates the age of new communications and digital technologies – the mobile phone, the internet, and the possibility of direct communications within and between the electorate. It also predates the age of national (and transborder) polls which allow almost instantaneous knowledge of citizens' views and choices on various sorts of questions. This is not any longer the nineteenth-century world of hierarchical bureaucratic organizations – whether industrial or party-based – but increasingly a much more decentralized, confusing world of multiple voices in new network communication systems. This suggests the possibility of changing our political imaginary away from the idea that you can only represent people's interests through party arrangements and mechanisms, to the recognition that we have the capacity to represent people's views directly through these new forms of network communications, a diversity of deliberative fora, etc. It is a different world of politics.

There are other considerations as well. We know that we are capable, as human beings, of committing the most horrific atrocities against each other, and we have reinvented our institutions to try to mitigate this. We have built the European Union to create a Kantian pacific union that abolishes war on

14 Held, *Models of Democracy*, chapter 5.

the continent. At the global level, we have created constitutional stepping stones to a new universal order. For all the limitations of these structures – and they are very, very limited – they are nonetheless achievements that embody the wisdom of the past that we now need to build on. And what do these developments tell us? They tell us that politics and institution-building in communities still matters. That politics in constitutional states still matters. That the governing capacities of supraregional and global polities still matters. But, since gridlock frequently pervades the politics of many of these arenas (see Section V), we also need new digital structures to give voice to peoples to address public goods and bads, and global goods and bads. We know what does not work. I have dwelt on this. Market fundamentalism does not work. The small clubs of geopolitical decision-makers who govern in their interests does not work. The unilateralism of large states does not work. What are we left with?

We are left with something fantastic. We are left with something absolutely glorious! The reinvention of the idea of the public realm and democracy. These were once based in city-states. They were then rearticulated as essential to modern nation-states. Since then the public domain has expanded again and now has a supraregional and global component. But these developments have not been linear with one kind of polity simply replacing the next. In fact, the processes have been far more enriching, allowing us to live now in multiple overlapping political communities that mirror, at least in principle, the world of overlapping communities of fate. Today, we have a vision of being citizens of cities, nation-states, regions, and the global domain, a world of potentially interlocking democratic fora that embed cosmopolitan principles, social justice, and human rights. It is this cosmopolitan vision, embedded in our past and present, that we must project forward if we are to address the global challenges of our time, many of which, like climate change and the spread of nuclear weapons, pose existential threats. So, I argue, realism is dead, market first philosophy is dead. But it is cosmopolitan democracy and justice that can become the new realism, if we deploy its concepts, insights, and achievements to address and circumvent the obstacles ahead.

V FURTHER THOUGHTS ON THE WAY FORWARD

JMC: Despite all the challenges, you are clearly very hopeful for the way forward. Your philosophical and political message is a very optimistic one. In this regard, let me ask you a few additional questions.

A question concerns global policy. So far you have not mentioned this notion of "global policy." Yet it is now an issue which you focus on a lot. In recent years you've published two books in this area, Gridlock *and, very recently,* Beyond Gridlock. *How do these enhance our understanding in this area?*

DH: The importance of a focus on global policy, and of the two books you mention in particular, is that they help steer us away from a straightforwardly philosophical and political message. You are right that I am optimistic in my philosophical and political reflections. But these need to be tempered by the findings of empirical-analytical analysis. The focus on global politics does this.

Political theory has always involved a number of different approaches: The philosophical, conceptual, and normative, the empirical-analytical, and the work of advocacy. A great deal of modern political theory too often rolls these different types of approach together. I have tried to distinguish these tasks in the various books that I have written. The focus on global policy keeps one on the empirical-analytical domain. This helps illuminate the opportunities and obstacles ahead.

As we discussed earlier, the postwar institutions were put in place to create a peaceful and prosperous world order. At the same time, they established conditions under which a plethora of other social and economic processes, associated with globalization, could thrive. This allowed interdependence to deepen as new countries joined the global economy, companies expanded multinationally, and once-distant people and places found themselves increasingly – and, on average, beneficially – intertwined.

But the virtuous circle between deepening interdependence and expanding global governance could not last because it set in motion trends that ultimately undermined its effectiveness. Why? *Gridlock*[15] explores four reasons for this, or four pathways to gridlock: rising multipolarity, harder problems, institutional inertia, and institutional fragmentation. Each pathway can be thought of as a growing trend that embodies a specific mix of causal mechanisms. Understanding these takes us into new important analytic territory.

First, reaching agreement in international negotiations has been made more complicated by the rise of new powers like China, India, and Brazil, because a more diverse array of interests have to be hammered into agreement for any global deal to be made. On the one hand, multipolarity is a positive sign of development; on the other hand, it can bring both more voices and interests to the table that are hard to weave into coherent outcomes. Second, the problems we are facing on a global scale have grown more complex, penetrating deep into domestic policies and are often extremely difficult to

[15] Thomas Hale, David Held, and K. Young, *Gridlock: Why Global Cooperation Is Failing When We Need It Most* (Cambridge: Polity Press, 2013).

resolve. Multipolarity coincides with complexity, making negotiations tougher and harder. Third, the core multilateral institutions created seventy years ago have proven difficult to change as established interests cling to outmoded decision-making rules that fail to reflect current conditions. Fourth, in many areas transnational institutions have proliferated with overlapping and contradictory mandates, creating a confusing fragmentation of authority.

To manage the global economy, prevent runaway environmental destruction, reign in nuclear proliferation, or confront other global challenges, we must cooperate. But many of our tools for global policy-making are breaking down or inadequate – chiefly, state-to-state negotiations over treaties and international institutions – at a time when our fates are acutely interwoven.

While gridlock describes key trends in world politics today, it is also incomplete as an argument in two distinct ways. Intellectually, it does not account for a number of exceptions and anomalies, empirical facts that any good social scientific theory must engage with. And normatively, it paints a bleak picture of a world locked into a downward spiral. As citizens, we need not just to understand gridlock, but to find ways to break it. These twin motivations were the genesis of *Beyond Gridlock*,[16] which shows us that there are still sound reasons to engage in contemporary politics.

Beyond Gridlock contends, first, that gridlock is indeed persistent and, second, that despite gridlock, global governance is more resilient, adaptive, and amenable to agency than the stream of grim headlines today suggests. Gridlock may be widespread and structural, but it is not omnipresent or determinative. The key points of this analysis highlight well how a focus on global policy can yield an understanding of how and when change is possible in global politics.

Looking at how gridlock does, and does not, apply across issue areas reveals a number of systematic pathways through and even beyond gridlock. These pathways of change describe a constellation of conditions and causal mechanisms that apply across various domains. We can group them into three baskets: resilience, innovation, and agency.

First, a number of global institutions are more resilient and adaptive than the gridlock argument suggests. In some areas, international institutions have retained or gained a degree of autonomy from their member states that allow them to work even under conditions of gridlock. For example, some institutions have tools at their disposal that can adapt to change, like the World Trade Organization's Dispute Settlement Mechanism. This quasi-judicial body has

16 Thomas Hale and David Held, et al., *Beyond Gridlock* (Cambridge: Polity Press, 2017).

developed its own jurisprudence to deal with situations not foreseen in the negotiation of the treaties that created it. Other institutions like the Intergovernmental Panel on Climate Change operate at a technical level that allows them to focus on problem-solving with some degree of insulation from the gridlock mechanisms.

Second, and perhaps most strikingly, *Beyond Gridlock* documents numerous innovations in global governance, often in direct response to gridlock. Many of these innovations involve new kinds of actors – like cities, businesses, civil society groups, and others – and new modes of global governance, often reaching into domestic politics. For example, the 2016 Paris Agreement on climate change shifted the regime to a "catalytic" model of governance that sets out a global target and asks countries, and also other actors, to make a progressive series of pledges to meet it. This allows for a plurality of action and actors to work toward a common goal, generating not fragmentation but synergy.[17] New ways of institutionalizing global governance have, moreover, not stopped at the border, but reached inside nation-states to mobilize domestic constituencies. For example, in the realm of human rights, international courts and review processes give voice and standing to groups fighting on the ground, sometimes shifting the balance of power within countries toward more cooperative outcomes.[18]

Third, agency matters. *Gridlock* is ultimately a structural theory focused on historical trends, but *Beyond Gridlock* shows how and where countries, but also other actors, can work around or even against the broader constraints they face. Obviously, the actions of great powers can be decisive, and under some conditions gridlock can shift their preferences toward global problem-solving. For example, the 2014 Ebola outbreak in West Africa can be attributed in part to the weakness of the World Health Organization's monitoring and rapid response facilities. But once the crisis threatened to spill across borders, the United States acted swiftly to contain it, along with other major powers. Non-state actors can also show agency of this kind. During the 1990s, coalitions of civil society groups and reformist states were able to bring real changes to global governance, such as the global treaty banning landmines, or the creation of the International Criminal Court. More recent movements like Occupy Wall Street or the Arab Spring, fueled by the digital revolution,

17 Thomas Hale, "Climate Change: From Gridlock to Catalyst," in Hale and Held, et al., *Beyond Gridlock*.

18 T. Pegram, "Human Rights: Leveraging Compliance," in Hale and Held, et al., *Beyond Gridlock*.

have yet to make this "inside-outside" strategy work, but it remains a significant potential lever for change.

Finally, in several areas, gridlock has produced not just stasis but leadership. After twenty years of deadlock, political entrepreneurs in the climate realm were able to articulate a new vision for the regime, and make the world buy into it. Inspired philanthropy from the Gates Foundation and others has helped to reverse the tide for some of the world's most deadly diseases.[19] In sum, gridlock is a barrier to progress, but not an insurmountable one. It can sometimes spur the very actions and innovations needed to unlock it.

None of the pathways through and beyond gridlock should be seen as silver bullets. What *Beyond Gridlock* offers instead is an analytical and comparative account of the key levers and processes through which change can be built over time. This creates the qualified optimism that while we cannot break gridlock overnight, there is important work to be done to build a better world over time.

Of course, this is just one reading of global politics and of the obstacles and opportunities ahead. But it does show how a focus at this level, and in particular on the changing form and dynamics of global policy, yields significant insights – and hopes.

JMC: You have created a journal, Global Policy, *to explore and develop an intellectual and policy agenda in relation with this notion. Can you tell us about it? Why did you set up this journal?*

DH: *Global Policy* was set up nearly a decade ago. It was designed to fill a space that had been left by political science and international relations. Neither of these disciplines focus systematically on the range of agents, forces, and processes that cut through the borders of nation-states and shape their fate and fortunes. Moreover, neither have historically focused on the great global challenges of our time and the global collective action goods and bads that shape our world, and will shape the century ahead, as we have been discussing. This is precisely the domain of *Global Policy*.

Global Policy is an innovative and interdisciplinary journal bringing together world-class academics and leading practitioners to analyze both public and private solutions to global problems and issues. *Gridlock* and *Beyond Gridlock* are my responses to these issues; by contrast, *Global Policy* is a hub that brings many of the most innovative thinkers together to focus on these major challenges and debate them.

19 G. W. Brown and David Held, "Health: New Leadership for Devastating Challenges," in Hale and Held, et al., *Beyond Gridlock*.

The two General Editors of *Global Policy* are Dani Rodrik and myself. But the main powerhouse behind it has always been its Executive Editor, Eva-Maria Nag. What she has done is bring together conventional print publishing with social media to make *Global Policy* a multimedia presence in the leading debates of our time. Eva-Maria co-founded the journal with me but has shaped its contribution and has turned it into a great "bridge" between academia and policy-making at the international and global levels.

JMC: Incidentally, this is not the first time you venture in the world of intellectual entrepreneurship, if I can use this expression. Besides your teaching and research activities, you have been part of Polity Press for many years. As such, why this interest in getting involved in the practical aspects of intellectual life?

DH: I founded Polity Press with two of my life-long friends, Anthony Giddens and John Thompson. Polity was founded in the mid-1980s in a pub in Cambridge called The Panton Arms. It was 1984 and a long hot summer. We spent a great deal of time together in the beer garden wondering why so many publishers were ineffective, and asking why we could not do better! Of course, this question was somewhat motivated by the beer we were drinking …

But the aim behind Polity has always been more serious; that is, to mediate between the great Continental traditions of thinking and the Anglo-American world. Since 1945 the social and political sciences in the UK and the US have become ever more specialized and defined increasingly by their methodological approaches. By contrast, the French, German, and Italian intellectual traditions of thinking about the social sciences have had a much more theoretical orientation. It was a risk that these different ways of thinking and working would never speak to each other, and something important would be lost.

Thus Polity was founded as a bridge (another bridge like *Global Policy*!) between different continents and different ways of thinking and doing social science. Translation became a very major part of what we did, making available many of the most important academics in Europe to the English-speaking world. In our first year we published six books, including volumes by Habermas, Bourdieu, Bobbio, and Giddens himself. Not a bad start! To this day translation remains a very important part of our work. But translation is demanding and expensive and we have always published a range of types of books from cutting edge contributions to disciplines to innovative textbooks. This range is critical to the commercial viability of the enterprise.

Today Polity is one of the leading social science publishers in the world and, whenever I travel giving lectures, people always want to know more about how Polity was founded and how it developed. I think it is, as we hoped, a contribution to the cultural politics of our time. It is a source of great pleasure. I have learned an enormous amount from engaging with Polity and the many people who have worked there, above all John Thompson and Anthony Giddens.

There is one other thing I should point out. My father was an entrepreneur from his youngest days to his 90s. There is no doubt that his entrepreneurial energy was passed to his son, who has always tried to bring it to bear on intellectual, political, and cultural endeavor.

JMC: My next question concerns the future of research and teaching in the field of political theory, and political philosophy. As you alluded to earlier, we no longer can think and practice political theory and political philosophy the way we did before, when the national realm was the frame of reference. Also, the fact that at the global level the balance of power is now shifting toward the East is likely to have implications in how we organize teaching curricula and the research agenda. What are your thoughts on these issues?

DH: As I mentioned earlier, political theory has always involved a number of different approaches: The philosophical, conceptual, and normative; the empirical-analytical; and the work of advocacy. I expect all three to continue to have a significant role in the years ahead, as all three are important. Philosophical analysis of concepts helps clarify their meaning in important ways, but the impact of this work beyond philosophical circles will always be limited unless we work out their relevance and potential for social and political practices. The illumination philosophy offers is in many respects, of course, unrivalled, but its impact will be very modest unless it is articulated in relation to the changing nature and forms of social practices. Likewise, the latter invoke philosophical concepts, such as social justice and sustainability, on a regular basis. But unless these concepts are rigorously understood they also risk being no more than rhetoric or empty slogans.

In my book *Models of Democracy*,[20] I offered a detailed account of the changing meaning of democracy over time. But I also tried to show that the advocates of various models of democracy either explicitly or implicitly require certain conditions of entrenchment for the models of democracy to function and work. The social and institutional conditions of, for example, direct, liberal, or deliberative democracy have to be understood and

20 Held, *Models of Democracy*.

embedded if these forms of democracy are to flourish. Concepts without grasping the conditions of their entrenchment will not take us far. At the same time, merely having a fine political and analytical analysis of society will not help us understand which of the "warring gods," as Weber put it, we should choose; that is to say, it does not help us understand alone which directions we should take, and why.

But even if we are well equipped with sound concepts and empirical analyses we still need something more for political theory to work with, what I like to call, "practical intent." The missing ingredient is what one might call policy analysis and advocacy, which helps us understand how we might go from where we are to where we might like to be. Even though it is a big task, political theory must involve these three elements now and in the future – philosophical and theoretical reflection, empirical work, and political know-how. Of course, these cannot be done all at the same time and not necessarily by all of the same people! But these separate ingredients make up a compelling political theory.

None of this is to say which concepts, norms, or ideals are relevant or which concepts should be the main focus of our attention. I am a great admirer of the hermeneutic philosopher Hans-Georg Gadamer and his remarkable work *Truth and Method*.[21] Gadamer argues that the history of hermeneutics, from bible readings through to political theory, shows that our understanding, even when it is critical, is always partial, one sided, and embedded in the language and traditions in which we find ourselves, and that there is no escape from this. The hermeneutic circle defines the circle of life; we understand a text or an event in relation to an anticipation of a whole, which we infuse with the language and traditions we come from. We correct our understanding as we go deeper and deeper into a text or event, but it is always the complex interplay between the part and the whole which shapes our understanding.

There are a number of important principles which follow from Gadamer's work. First, understanding cannot escape the historicity of traditions. Knowledge is generated within the framework of traditions; the discernment of truth has a temporal structure. Second, since we are ourselves constituted by history and traditions, the process of understanding aspects of the world contributes simultaneously to our self-understanding and self-formation. Third, the process of self-understanding, like the process of understanding of other things, can never be complete.

Gadamer shows that it is only through immersion in other traditions, and by grasping the language of others, that we can illuminate both what it is we mean

21 Hans-Georg Gadamer, *Truth and Method* (New York: Continuum, 2004).

when we speak and what it is that others mean when they speak too. In short, the mediation of traditions provides the basis for intersubjective understanding, however complex and difficult the process is. We understand ourselves better if we seek to understand others.[22]

The implications of Gadamer's work are many. But there is one that is particularly relevant now. As we shift from a Western-centric world to a more fluid and complex multipolar order, it becomes all the more important to understand not just our languages and traditions but those of others too. There is no opportunity for intersubjective understanding unless there is immersion in the language and traditions of others. For political theory this can be an exciting moment as we explore the interface between Western and non-Western traditions of thinking and their many complex interactions over time. Political theory must now be constituted both by a multiplicity of approaches and levels, and at the interface of the dialogue of cultures.

JMC: Finally, as someone who has been teaching and writing for a long time, what would be your advice to the next generation of scholars and teachers in the field of political theory? What should they focus on and how should they proceed so that they can contribute to make the world a better place?

DH: It would be useful if they grasped that political theory requires a number of distinct intellectual approaches. It would help if they understood that the mediation of traditions and discourses gives us access to truths about ourselves and others, and that it is unlikely that all the concepts we need to make sense of our world will be found in one set of traditions. Understanding the multiple sources of concepts and how they have been embedded over time in different contexts and traditions can extend our horizons. And, yet, we also need to distinguish, as noted earlier, the origins and validity of concepts and ideas. The latter will always need rigorous examination and testing.

Political theory needs to help us understand the nature and form of the political good, and how these change over time. Today, political theory needs to equip us to address a world of overlapping communities of fate, which now faces profound existential challenges. We need both sound philosophical concepts and practical tools to face the future and to ensure we follow pathways forward which are just, equitable, and sustainable. The position I have set out here is one response to this hugely important challenge.

In the end, it is about immersing oneself in the work of others before you and understanding the debates that have shaped the modern period. Also,

22 David Held, *Introduction to Critical Theory: Horkheimer to Habermas* (London: Hutchinson, 1980).

while acknowledging what has come before, do not be afraid to innovate and pursue new avenues of thinking. In addition, it is key to accept that while the challenges ahead are formidable for any kind of critical theory or, more broadly, for humanity itself in the twenty-first century, there is important work to be done. There are many ways to make a difference. And, finally, most important, enjoy it! It is the passion for ideas that will carry you forward.

PART V

CONCLUDING THOUGHTS

15

Tomorrow and the Quest for Justice

Jean-Marc Coicaud and Lynette E. Sieger

In this short conclusion, we address two issues. First, we identify a few lessons from the book and its conversations. Second, we refer to some pending issues related to justice in national, international, and global perspectives, and allude to what could be the way forward for thinking further on them.

I A FEW LESSONS

The objective is not here to offer a comprehensive analysis of all the lessons that can be derived from the various topics touched upon by the contributors in the conversations that the book brings together. Rather, the goal is to simply highlight a few of them. In this regard, seven lessons stand out. In no specific order of importance they are: (1) the differences noted by the contributors between national, international, and global justice; (2) the tensions at work in the contemporary landscape between giving importance to human rights and overlooking them; (3) the imperative to address the shortcomings of justice; (4) the realization that power and self-centered interests can trump justice; (5) the need to reform international organizations and international law; (6) the search for a new sense of universalism and the interculturality that comes with it; and (7) the changes in the international distribution of power.

The first lesson is the acknowledgment, made in one way or another by all contributors, that the conditions, scope, and depth of justice are quite different at the national, international, and global levels. While it is mainly at the national level that historically justice has been taken more seriously, at least in well-functioning countries with public institutions and political leaders seen as legitimate, justice is far less developed at the international level (which, in some measure, gives prime of place to state-rights) and even more so at the global level (which is focused on the rights of individuals). Some of the contributors see the differences existing among these levels as quite normal – this is David Miller's point of view, who favors a form of "weak cosmopolitanism" – while others, like Thomas Pogge, are supporters of a cosmopolitan approach fully dedicated to the rights of individuals.

The second lesson that can be drawn from the conversations concerns how they reflect on the relations between the national, international, and global dimensions and their actors, like individuals and states. In this regard two contradictory trends are at play today. On the one hand, there is a tendency toward a better and more just integration, national, international, and global, among actors, individual and collective – a tendency that is in part inhabited by cosmopolitan considerations and is symbolized by human rights increasingly being taken seriously by the international community. Mireille Delmas-Marty alludes to this in her conversation. On the other hand, there is a tendency toward disintegration that threatens the sustainability of political, economic, and legal national and international orders, with the risks of conflicts this entails. The second scenario to which Michael Spence refers at the end of his conversation for the future of international order is part of this story. Incidentally, in the process Spence hints that justice is neither external nor secondary to the quest for security. In this perspective, it seems reasonable to say that one of the best ways to achieve security is to take into account the demands of justice that actors may have, nationally and internationally.

The third lesson, on which all contributors agree, is the need to improve the world in which we live. Their approach for this may vary. For instance, while most contributors tend to favor the development of a positive agenda in support of justice, Avishai Margalit, who is no less committed to justice than the other contributors, thinks that preventing injustice is more urgent than promoting justice. But they are all adamant that justice is a nonnegotiable imperative.

A fourth lesson is that power and self-centered interests often continue to trump justice. As such, the contributors are not blind to the challenges associated with taking the demands of justice seriously. For example, Abdullahi Ahmed An-Na'im, Neera Chandhoke, and ONUMA Yasuaki, each in their own way, remind us that colonialism has had a traumatizing effect on those at the receiving end of it, and that the trauma has still not entirely disappeared. Others, like Boaventura de Sousa Santos and Thomas W. Pogge, stress that power and the interests of rich power-holders remain an obstacle to the establishment of a more equal and democratic world.

This brings us to a fifth lesson, the need for reform, in particular the need of reform of the international system and its institutions. In this regard, none of the contributors consider the *status quo* an option. Their rejection of the *status quo* is both descriptive and prescriptive. It is descriptive in the sense that they acknowledge that, *nolens volens*, the current international order is changing. And it is prescriptive in the sense that the transformations underway have to be as much as possible geared toward positive change. For instance, José E. Alvarez and David Held highlight the importance of renovating the global governance system.

Part of how this could be done is related to a sixth lesson: the search for a new sense of universalism and the imperative of interculturality this entails. Universalism is seen as a crucial tool to bring countries together at the world level. At the same time, the contributors seem to agree that such universalism cannot simply be a replica of the one put forward by the West since it started to spread globally in the late sixteenth century. In its values, norms, laws, and institutions, a twenty-first-century universalism would have to move away from the trappings of self-centeredness in the context of which dominant actors are upgrading themselves and downgrading others (see how the West came to present itself as the epitome of civilization). This is to say that it would have to be more inclusive and representative, including in terms of diversity and pluralism. Mireille Delmas-Marty, among others, espouses this view.[1] Interestingly, a more balanced, diverse, and pluralist universalism would have to rely on and mobilize a strong commitment to dialogue and interculturality, if only to widen and deepen communications and understanding between one another. This is one of the messages that Abdullah Ahmed An-Na'im, ONUMA Yasuaki, and Wang Hui convey.

The seventh lesson is the need to reflect on the international distribution of power currently unfolding. In particular, the rise of China threatens the hegemony of the West and what has been for centuries the West's ability to align the rules of the games with its own interests, values, laws, and institutions. The threat is all the more real considering that within the Western camp itself economic and political difficulties have been mounting. The crisis of political representation and the spread of populism illustrate the extent to which in the West a number of democracies are under stress. In this environment, as Charles Kupchan puts it, "the great geopolitical challenge of our time

[1] A more open universalism is needed as a way to make communication among cultures possible and better, and as a type of content of communication. That said, in light of the intellectual hegemony and institutionalization of Western ways of thinking, it can only be a challenging enterprise. This is illustrated in international law. To what extent is it possible to make international law more open, more international? Is it possible to do so in more than cosmetic ways? After all, a great deal of the non-Western legal traditions, nationally and internationally, have lost their force. In these conditions, what could be a path for a way forward?

will be managing peacefully the transition from a world dominated by the United States and its Western partners to a world without a captain at the helm."

II A FEW PENDING ISSUES AND THE WAY FORWARD

By sharing with readers the knowledge and views of some of the best academics in the field, a purpose for the book and its conversations was to come up with a sort of cartography exercise. It was to draw a map of issues that have emerged in the current era and identify directions of thinking and action to tackle them for the way forward. From this perspective, the conversations try to accomplish three objectives on core and related matters of justice and their interactions at the national, international, and global levels. First, they offer a description of where we come from and where we stand on a variety of fundamental questions connected to justice. Second, they provide a critical analysis of important trends of the period as they relate to questions of justice. Third, they hint at possible future directions for a progressive agenda.

Of course, reading through the conversations will not provide the reader with a comprehensive analysis and full understanding of the questions tackled. Considering the scope, depth, and complexity of justice matters as well as the rather fluid character of the current era, *Conversations* provides a window akin to an entry point to the contemporary social reality, its evolution, and challenges in connection with issues of justice.

Against this background, it might be useful to conclude by mentioning a few of the pending issues that the dialogues touched upon in part but that likely require further development. That is in particular so with four overlapping types of issues, which could be explored further in order to possibly expand and strengthen the culture of justice in the years ahead. They are normative, economic, institutional, and political issues.

1. When it comes to normative issues of justice, contributors favor greater inclusiveness, be it social, economic, political, and cultural, both within and among nations. This greater inclusiveness entails creating more room for diversity, increasingly a significant aspect of the sense of justice in the contemporary period. In this regard, the international redistribution of power underway, including the push for emerging countries to be better heard and recognized as valuable actors, introduces a further sense of urgency. The emphasis on diversity leads to a call for a more pluralistic form of universalism – universalism as expressed and projected by the system of global governance, its values, norms, law, and institutions, like international law and

international organizations. Following up on this line of recommendation presupposes addressing and answering the following questions: How do we engineer a more pluralistic universalism? Where and how do we draw the line between an acceptable universality and an acceptable diversity? When comprehensive political or normative systems are in fundamental contradiction with one another how do we negotiate space for peaceful coexistence? Does the fact that democracy is to some extent, and in various ways from within and from afar, on the defensive make addressing these questions more challenging? For the way forward, three types of considerations could help provide clarity on these issues.

First, as formal and substantive rights, both central to justice within and among nations, are threatened by a weakening of democracy and a capitalism less and less under check (two phenomena that are somewhat related), it is not superfluous to reaffirm the fundamental and mutually constitutive nature of formal and substantive rights. Second, building on and developing further the reflexive character of justice – meaning a sense of critical awareness that is as mindful of others' rights as of one's own rights – could help, especially at the international level. In Phillip Allott's words, "Justice is the constructive critic who will never be silenced . . ."[2] As such, justice calls for actors to be self-critical and give credit and recognize others on their own terms, an attitude the powerful West has been reluctant to embrace. Third, equally important would be to stress the importance of public ethics in relation to justice, and inquire about the ways in which public ethics could be strengthened. This presupposes, at minimum, making sure that power-holders are bound by the rules of the game, nationally and internationally. The precept that no person who holds power is above the law is indeed largely viewed today as one of the defining features of justice. And yet power-holders all too often ignore this golden rule of justice. The frequent expressions of entitlement by those in power, along with their insistence on having many rights and few duties, while asking of others, less powerful, to have few rights and many duties, is a recipe for disaster.

2. Most of the contributors to the volume see the current international order, particularly in its economic dimension and the disparity it brings about between rich and poor, as unbalanced and consequently dangerously unstable. Hence the question: How to address the asocial, if not antisocial,

[2] Philip Allott, *Eunomia: New Order for a New World* (Oxford: Oxford University Press, 1990), p. 85. On justice, Allott also states the following: "As love, in all its forms, holds out to us the possibility that we might, for a while or for ever, become more ourselves in becoming more than ourselves, so justice holds out the permanent possibility to society that it might become more than itself, might continually surpass, its successive selves" (Ibid., p. 84).

tendencies, among other things, that undermine workers' rights[3] in the current stage of capitalism? The fact that contemporary (democratic) societies present the rights of individuals and the sense of equality and empowerment (freedom) as a key source of their legitimacy and at the same time are increasingly influenced by economic policies creating structurally embedded inequalities amounts to a fundamental contradiction that makes answering this question all the more pressing. As a number of the contributors indicate, this situation calls for a serious examination of the possibility of reforming capitalism (since it is not going to go away), so that rather than treating people as expendable it contributes to producing the conditions for a decent and relatively secure life. At the national and international levels this agenda requires intellectual, policy, economic, and political actors coming together and pushing in the same direction. This leads to perhaps an even more urgent question: How to achieve this goal?

3. Part of the reform agenda entails improving institutions. In this regard, considering that the growing interdependence among countries and the global nature of the problems at hand render international cooperation and multilateralism imperative, it makes sense to want to improve the effectiveness of international institutions. This project, however, is a difficult undertaking, for which much work would have to be done. More specifically, it is an intellectual or conceptual challenge in the sense that it would require identifying the scope, depth, and expected outcomes of the reform, and exploring the sort of renewed institutions and overall institutional architecture that would best fit the evolutions underway. And it also poses a policy challenge because new policies more in line with the times would have to be put to work.

4. The fourth challenge, a political one, is especially important. It is crucial because on politics rests the ability to orchestrate, or not, cooperation at the national, international/global levels. Take, for example, the reform of international institutions we reference in this volume. Institutional reform at that level certainly cannot happen without the participation and cooperation of nation-states. This includes their willingness to align their interests, and in particular their respective national interests, with global interests and to invest

[3] In one of his recent books, *China's Twentieth Century: Revolution, Retreat and the Road to Equality*, Wang Hui indicates that China is now a country where, despite having become the factory of the world and lifting millions out of poverty, many have no means of enjoying the protection of labor contract law (p. 197). Western countries also find themselves in a difficult situation. Poor conditions of employment and unemployment have become part of reality for many, feeding a discontent that has facilitated the development of populism.

in a long-term vision.[4] Reform that incorporates those changes is proving an arduous task. The political challenge is crucial as well because of the context in which political institutions and leaders operate today. Economic forces in a time of globalization are having a considerable impact on the destiny of countries and their people. In the process, these forces can limit the role of politics and its capacity to govern.[5] That said, this fact does not make politics less important. To the contrary, regardless of the role economic forces play, politics is the only sphere and activity supposed to govern people, societies, and their relations, at the national and international levels. Hence the question: How to preserve this role of politics and, more to the point, how to make politics meaningful in the current circumstances? What adds to the difficulty of the political challenge is that it does not exclusively concern public institutions and political and administrative elites. It concerns as well the place and role of regular people and the conditions under which they can participate, directly or indirectly, but always in a meaningful fashion in decision-making processes and governing matters. It includes the need to construct systems of rule of law that hold power-holders in their economic and political transactions to account to the people over whom those interactions have a direct and pervasive effects. As long as we lack answers to these questions that are both compelling and practical, the fate of justice will remain uncertain.

4 Jean-Marc Coicaud, "Ethique et intérêt national ne sont pas mutuellement exclusifs," *La Revue internationale et stratégique* (Paris: Institut de relations internationales et stratégiques (IRIS), Number 105, spring 2017).

5 For more on the hijacking of politics by money in the United States, Martin Gilens, *Affluence and Influence: Economic Inequality and Political Power in America* (Princeton, NJ: Princeton University Press, and New York: Russell Sage Foundation, 2012).

Intellectual Profiles of the Contributors

Lynette E. Sieger

Each of the thinkers who contributed to this volume was asked to provide answers to the following six questions. (1) What are the key achievements (educational, professional, social) of yours that you would most like to have highlighted? (2) How did you come to identify or become interested in the key intellectual questions of your work? (3) Who have been the most influential thinkers for your intellectual development? (4) What are the central issues and questions around which your intellectual/social project is organized? (5) What are the issues on which you intend to focus in the future and why? (6) What is your advice for emerging scholars in the field of global justice?

In this section I have crafted biographical sketches based on the answers of each contributor to these questions. The answer to question 6 is not included here. Rather, as a way to conclude each chapter and to unify the volume as a whole, as the editors of this volume, Dr. Coicaud and I decided to give the reader a sense of how the future of global justice studies might be tackled by rising scholars and practitioners in the field. As such the reader will find the answer to question 6 at the conclusion of each conversation/chapter.

As a whole these questions were meant to shed light on the intellectual trajectory of the contributors and to find the thread that led from their personal experiences to their early scholarship and developed their thinking to where it is today. Each of the contributors answered the way they saw fit. In order to preserve the integrity of how each contributor communicated their experiences through the answers, the reader may find some discrepancies of format among the biographical sketches. For instance, the reader will find that some contributors offered personal experiences as having grounded their intellectual and social projects, while others focused on encounters with scholars and scholarship as the central theme around which they organized their intellectual projects.

A selected bibliography of books of the contributors has been added to their biographical sketch in order to facilitate the reader who is interested in deeper research on the topics that are covered. The biographical sketches have been reviewed by the contributors and are presented in alphabetical order.

Abdullahi Ahmed An Na'im, Charles Howard Candler Professor of Law, Emory University School of Law.

Dr. An Na'im was born in a village on the Nile in Northern Sudan in 1946, the eldest of eight siblings. His early education was in Atbara and Omdurman, and he went on to study law at the University of Khartoum, Sudan. Upon graduation in 1970, Professor An Na'im was sent on a University of Khartoum scholarship for postgraduate studies in law to the University of Cambridge, England. He went on in his studies to earn a Ph.D. in law from the University of Edinburgh, Scotland.

He returned to Sudan to teach law at the University of Khartoum from 1976 to 1985, and was visiting Professor of Law at UCLA (USA), University of Saskatchewan (Canada), and Uppsala University (Sweden). He served as Executive Director of Human Rights Watch/Africa, before joining the faculty of Emory University School of Law in 1995. An Na'im has been a full professor of law with tenure at Emory Law School since 1997, and Charles Howard Candler Professor of Law since 1999.

He is a prolific author in the areas of human rights, constitutionalism, and Islamic law and politics. In addition to many books, he is the author of more than seventy articles and book chapters in these areas.[1]

An Na'im primary research and scholarship regarding Islam, state, and politics continues the thesis that he presented in his 2008 book *Islam and the Secular State: Negotiating the Future of Shari'a*. Currently, he is working on a book manuscript under the working title *Decolonizing Human Rights: From State-Centric Legality to People-Centered Practice*. Previous major research projects were on (1) women's access to, and control over, land in seven African countries; (2) a global study of the theory and practice of Islamic Family Law; and (3) a fellowship program in Islam and Human Rights.[2]

Ustadh Mahmoud Mohamed Taha has had the most formative and transformative influence on Professor An Na'im intellectual and professional

[1] All of Dr. An-Na'im's articles and book chapters can be downloaded and printed free of charge at: https://scholarblogs.emory.edu/aannaim/recent-publications/.

[2] Each of those projects had a dedicated website for the duration of each study. With the termination of all three projects, those websites are no longer updated, but they are accessible in archive form at: https://scholarblogs.emory.edu/aannaim/project-archive/.

development since the time that he was a student at the University of Khartoum in the late 1960s. As a student of comparative constitutional and international law, human rights, and related fields, he has learned from many scholars in those academic fields, but *Ustadh* Mahmoud remains the sole, truly influential thinker in An Na'im intellectual development.

It is due to that formative and transformative influence of *Ustadh* Mahmoud that An Na'im came to identify and focus on themes of Sharia, human rights, and constitutionalism, as matters of personal as well as professional concern. The key intellectual question of his life's work is how to render sound and rigorous scholarship in the service of positive social change. While trying his best to follow the model of *Ustadh* Mahmoud of total consistency of thought, speech, and action, An Na'im also strives to accept responsibility for all three dimensions of his being. He sees complete consistency of his thought, discourse, and lived experience as essential for the intersection of the personal and professional dimensions of his scholarship and advocacy for change as a Muslim from Sudan.

These are the central issues and questions around which he has sought to organize his intellectual/social project for fifty years of his life. These are also the same issues that he intends to continue to focus on for the rest of his life because that is what he believes himself to be accountable for before God as a Muslim. In terms of issues of social justice and individual freedom in this world, there is no value to intellectual and professional achievement that is not rendered into daily and consistent action in the service of human beings everywhere.

English publications (books) include: *What Is an American Muslim? Embracing Faith and Citizenship* (2014); *Muslims and Global Justice* (2010); *Islam and the Secular State: Negotiating the Future of Shari'a* (2008); *African Constitutionalism and the Contingent Role of Islam* (2006); *Toward an Islamic Reformation: Civil Liberties, Human Rights and International Law* (1990).

José E. Alvarez, Herbert and Rose Rubin Professor of International Law, New York University School of Law.

Professor José E. Alvarez's interest in issues of international law and justice stemmed, at least in part, from his early childhood experiences. Born in Cuba, Professor Alvarez's family faced persecution as the brief yet intense Bay of Pigs[3] conflict between the United States and Cuba unfolded. His father, also named

[3] The Bay of Pigs (April 17–19, 1961) was a US CIA-backed operation in which 1,400 Cuban fighters were trained to invade and overthrow Fidel Castro's communist regime. In less than twenty-four hours of fighting, decisive victory went to Cuba.

José, was a small-business owner, selling tamales at a farmstand on the main road to Havana. Lacking any great wealth or political ties he was, nevertheless, arrested by the Castro regime on the mere suspicion that he was not sympathetic to the cause. Upon his father's release the family went to visit friends in Spain. In their absence José (Senior)'s property was seized and became state owned. At six years of age Alvarez immigrated to the United States with his family.

Given these origins it is perhaps not a surprise that Professor Alvarez cultivated a career in international law with an emphasis on human rights, including the rights of free speech and the right to own property. Upon entering Harvard College in 1973 as an undergraduate student Alvarez devoted his studies to examining Latin American history, politics, and culture – and the United States' projects that influenced these. Upon graduation Alvarez continued his studies in the field of law first outside the United States, receiving a scholarship to attend Magdalen College, at Oxford University. Studying outside of the United States began what became a life-long commitment to examining the law as something that need not be associated with the law of any one nation-state.

Continuing on to Harvard Law School – where he served as the Topics Editor for the *Harvard International Law Journal* – Alvarez gravitated to studying international organizations, especially the United Nations. His first position as a lawyer was at the US State Department, where he gained an education about what was then the emerging international investment regime. Five years later, Alvarez embarked on a career in academia. Based on his early legal training and practice, both international organizations and investment law became core interests of his research and teaching agenda.

Professor Alvarez's professional positions and achievements include chaired professorships at Columbia University and New York University. His lectures at The Hague Academy of International Law served as the basis for his book *The Public International Law Regime Governing International Investment* (2011).[4] In 2013 Alvarez delivered a series of fifteen lectures at Xiamen Academy of International Law (China), which also led to the publication of his book *The Impact of International Organizations on International Law* (2016).[5]

[4] *The Public International Law Regime Governing International Investment* (Brill: Martinus Nijhoff Publishers, 2011).

[5] *The Impact of International Organizations on International Law* (Brill: Martinus Nijhoff Publishers, 2016).

Having started his career at the US State Department, Alvarez realized the importance of bridging his interests in theory to practice as a way to positively contribute to the world. In addition to pro-bono activities on behalf of NGOs such as the Center for Reproductive Rights, in 2010 Professor Alvarez was appointed by Luis Moreno-Ocampo – the first Prosecutor of the International Criminal Court (ICC) – as Special Advisor on international law. In this role Alvarez assisted the prosecutor with public international law questions, such as those involving the relationship between the United Nations Security Council, the Assembly of State Parties, and the ICC.

In the legal community Alvarez is known for taking on leadership and mentorship positions notably within the American Society of International Law (ASIL), including as the Society's former President and Co-Editor in Chief[6] of the *American Journal of International Law* (AJIL).

As an author Professor Alvarez focuses on how international law affects people's lives, both negatively and positively. In his works he explores the horizontal, vertical, ideological, and rule-of-law challenges facing international lawyers and the peoples of the world. He sees that at their core, these challenges usually involve the exercise of various forms of power, soft and hard, and economic, military, social, or market-based. Today, power is exercised not only by states but by non-state parties, including individuals and private enterprises.

Alvarez's thinking has been influenced by, among others, his former colleague at Michigan Law School, the late Eric Stein,[7] whom Alvarez credits for helping him to see institutions in a more holistic light. He credits his former colleague at Columbia University, Oscar Schachter,[8] with providing a cosmopolitan take on the law and giving him daily lessons in humility and the many ways one learns from one's students. Of Thomas Franck[9] – the NYU professor whose office Alvarez now occupies – Alvarez says simply, "He made me a better human being."

For the future of his research agenda in areas related to global justice, Alvarez expects to continue to explore the meaning of the national and international rule of law and the interconnections between them. He sees

6 Serving from 2013 to 2018.

7 Eric Stein (1913–2011) was a member of the University of Michigan Law School faculty and an eminent scholar in international and comparative law.

8 Oscar Schachter (1915–2003) was Hamilton Fish Professor of International Law and Diplomacy, Columbia University, and a well-known eminent scholar of international law and diplomacy.

9 Thomas Franck (1931–2009) was Murry and Ida Becker Professor of Law at New York University, and an expert on international law.

that furthering the rule of law at the national and international levels has become a leading goal of policy-makers around the world. This Alvarez sees as essential to achieving everything from interstate peace to particular sustainable development goals. While Alvarez respects those who see this project and the liberal internationalist ideas that lie beneath it as part of an inevitable progressive narrative, he firmly believes that it is the task of intellectuals to question the underlying assumptions – and particularly the West's framing of the question and of the goals.

English publications (books) include: *American Classics in International Law: International Investment Law* (ed.) (2017); *The Impact of International Organizations on International Law* (2016); *The Evolving International Investment Regime: Expectations, Realities, Options* (ed. with Karl Sauvant, Kamil Gerard Ahmed, and Gabriela del P. Vizcaino) (2011); *The Public International Law Regime Governing International Investment* (2011); *International Organizations as Law-Makers* (2005).

Neera Chandhoke, Professor Emeritus of Political Science, University of Delhi, National Fellow, Indian Council of Social Science Research.

Dr. Chandhoke studied political science Honours at the undergraduate level, and then pursued a Masters in the same subject in the 1960s. Her studies focused on Karl Marx and Rosa Luxembourg. As a young teacher in the 1970s, Chandhoke was particularly interested in the formulations of Dependency theory.

Chandhoke credits a great deal of the inspiration for her thinking to English literature and Greek mythology – literature because it explores the ambiguities of the human condition, and Greek mythology for illuminating that there are no easy solutions to human predicaments.

Professor Chandhoke develops her work in the belief that political theorists ought to identify political predicaments, and offer how best to resolve them, situating intellectual projects in the interstices of political life and theory. She works at the crossroads of Indian politics and Western, but increasingly also Indian, political theory.

Civil society[10] is a core interest in the work of Dr. Chandhoke, an interest that was stimulated by the political events that followed the fall of the Berlin Wall, coupled with the hopes invested in civil society by political theorists of the 1990s. In this area Chandhoke's work is inspired by Hegel's understanding

[10] See *State and Civil Society* (1995).

of civil society as the theatre of history and Gramsci's exploration of civil society as the site of hegemony.

Chandhoke's interest in the concept of secularism[11] was sparked by the rise of the religious right in India in the 1990s, the targeting of minorities, and unthinking adoption of Western models of secularism by its supporters and friends. In India secularism emerged on the political scene during the freedom struggle, as equality between various religious groups, and as minority rights. The Supreme Court of India has interpreted secularism to mean equality of all religions. Chandhoke penned *Contested Secessions* (2012) because she felt that liberal theories of secession did not take into account troubled and complicated cases of secession. In 2014 Chandhoke published a book[12] on the Maoist uprising in Central India, and evaluated the achievement and the failure of the Maoists from the perspective of Mao's own theories of Guerrilla War, and theories formulated by Frantz Fanon, Che Guevara, and Amilcar Cabral.

Dr. Chandhoke is retired from Delhi University, where she taught the fundamentals of Western Political Theory to generations of students. She held a professorship in the postgraduate Department of Political Science. Many of her students came from disadvantaged families, and were doubly or even triply oppressed by reasons of caste, class, and gender. A number of her students thought that the subject of political theory was too abstract, too removed from daily life, alien, and even boring. Chandhoke not only acquainted students with theories that had been authored for and in foreign settings, but also inspired them to take cognizance of the way political theorists have tried to establish normative frameworks for the multiple transactions of societies. She showed them how stimulating, how contemporary, and how relevant for daily life the study of political theory can be. Dr. Chandhoke considers drawing in and engaging students in this way as one of her greatest achievement.

Her current work reexamines the concept of secularism. Dr. Chandhoke focuses on what she calls the central question that confronts scholars across the world. Namely, how can people who subscribe to different conceptions of the good live together in a degree of civility and peace? Chandhoke finds the question troublesome because the proposition that a society is plural because its members speak different languages is an empirical one. The proposition that pluralism is a value is a normative one. There is nothing to connect the first and the second propositions, unless we build a conceptual argument that

[11] See *Beyond Secularism: The Rights of Religious Minorities* (1999).

[12] See *Contested Secessions: Rights, Self-determination, Democracy, and Kashmir* (2012).

links the two. She asks, what other concept can bridge the gap except secularism? Chandhoke intends to argue that secularism is a property of democratic states, and that many of the tasks we have invested secularism with properly fall within the domain of democracy.

English publications (books) include: *Contested Secessions: Rights, Self-determination, Democracy and Kashmir* (2012); *The Conceits of Civil Society* (2003); *Beyond Secularism: The Rights of Religious Minorities* (2002); *State and Civil Society: Explorations in Political Theory* (1995).

Mireille Delmas-Marty, Professor Emeritus of Comparative Legal Studies and Internationalization of Law, Collège de France.

Professor Delmas-Marty began her legal studies in the 1960s. At the time, her publications centered on French positive law and criminal law. In the 1970s the ratification of the European Convention on Human Rights and its impact on national law in the European context, including France, played a key role in showing the importance of analyzing the internationalization of national law. Indeed, such internationalization transformed the legal order's hierarchical, static representation of law into an interactive, evolutionary one. International human rights instruments paved the way for an internationalization that also manifested itself in economic areas, for example with the European Common Market, Community, and Union. It was these processes that encouraged Dr. Delmas-Marty to develop her research in three areas: the legal techniques and logics affecting *legal formalism* (foreseeability); the ethical values concerning *legal humanism* (legitimacy); and the actors and powers involved in *global governance* (effectiveness).

Mireille Delmas-Marty's works focus on how the internationalization of law entails changes in certain legal categories and, more broadly, in what she refers to as a metamorphosis of the legal order. Whether they concern formalism, humanism, or governance, Professor Delmas-Marty sees legal changes as a way to transform the world's great legal disorder into a pluralist global order.[13]

Mireille Delmas-Marty regards her greatest achievements to include being a teacher, serving as an expert on law geared toward the public interest, at the national and international levels, and being a citizen of the world learning from and engaging with others throughout the span of her career.

[13] See *Towards a Truly Common Law*, Cambridge University Press (2002); *Ordering Pluralism* (2009); and *De la grande accélération à la grande metamorphose: Vers un ordre juridique planétaire?* (2017).

Professor Delmas-Marty's thinking on renewing legal formalism, particularly as it relates to comparative law and the harmonization of criminal justice, has been influenced by the French comparatist Raymond Saleilles (1855–1912) and the Chinese politician Sun Yat-sen (1866–1925), who derived a theory of "five powers" by crossing ancient China's "constitution" with the Western model. Another major theme in Delmas-Marty's work has been questioning the sense and nonsense of legal humanism. In this area she has been influenced by Hannah Arendt's work on the distinction between labor, work, and action, and her contributions to the debate on "human" rights showing that human life, limited by a beginning and an end, follows a linear movement distinct from nature's perpetual, cyclical movement. In the area of global governance Delmas-Marty finds Habermas particularly inspiring to her thinking as he was the first to highlight the specificity of the post-national constellation, leading the way in rethinking the role of civil society and the public political space and elaborating plans for cosmopolitan democracy.

The Caribbean-born French writer and poet Edouard Glissant's (1928–2011) message, urging one to seek a counterpoint to savage globalization not by retreating into oneself but promoting *mondialité*, as a world of solidarity and diversity (*diversité mondiale solidaire*), has also especially influenced Delmas-Marty's work. Solidarity in diversity is precisely what she seeks through "ordering pluralism."

Delmas-Marty's future research agenda focuses on the following theme, "Towards a universalizable 'common' law." As such she is now working on outlining the conditions of validity for a future worldwide "common" law, in light of collective memories of the past and the present. In order to do so she calls upon a dynamic method that considers the practices of "common" law as transformational processes destabilizing national orders,[14] bringing the various legal systems closer together while respecting their specificities. These processes, Delmas-Marty argues, have developed at various times and in various parts of the world. Their reappearance in fragments in the wake of globalization suggests the possibility of a worldwide "common" law that if not universal is at least "universalizable."

The goal of the research agenda in which Professor Delmas-Marty is now engaged is threefold: to illuminate the notion of "common" law by a historical approach; to describe the emergence of fragments of "common" law in the era of globalization; and to outline the conditions for a "universalizable common world of laws."

14 See *Aux quatre vents du monde. Petit guide de navigation sur l'océan de la mondialisation* (2016).

English publications (books) include: *Ordering Pluralism: A Conceptual Framework for Understanding the Transnational Legal World* (2009); *Global Law: A Triple Challenge* (2003); *Towards a Truly Common Law: Europe as a Laboratory for Legal Pluralism* (2002); *European Criminal Procedures* (2002).

David Held, Professor of Politics and International Relations and Master of University College, Durham University, and Visiting Professor of Political Science, Libera Università Internazionale degli Studi Sociali Guido Carli.

Dr. David Held received his Ph.D. from Massachusetts Institute of Technology and conducted his postdoctoral research at Cambridge University. It was during the late 1980s and early 1990s, while working at the Open University, that Held began to focus his intellectual interests on global questions. A defining moment in shaping Held's work came when his colleague Anthony McGrew read Held's book *Models of Democracy*. McGrew wondered whether democratic theory had anything to say about relations between states and countries given that the book focused on what happens within the boundaries of political communities. Held discovered through this intellectual exchange that the basic assumptions linked to the field of political science and international relations break down in an era of globalization when states are connected both externally and internally. Held attributes the exchange with McGrew for shifting the focus of his work from what he calls national communities of fate to a world of overlapping communities of fate, where the fortunes of countries are increasingly intermeshed.

The primary focus of Held's work has centered on the changing nature and form of political communities. He has undertaken this field of inquiry through (i) extensive empirical inquiry into the dynamic character, structural elements, and governance failures of contemporary society;[15]; (ii) investigating the changing nature and form of the modern state and the locus of the political good, examining the question of whether the nation-state alone – as typically assumed by conventional political theory – can be the sole home of democracy, accountability, and the rule of law;[16] and (iii) exploring how and in what ways one can move beyond the crises and dilemmas of politics and governance in the contemporary world.[17]

[15] See Held, *Global Transformations* (1999), *Globalization/Anti-globalization* (2007); *Global Inequality* (2007); and *Gridlock: Why Global Cooperation is Failing When We Need it Most* (2013).

[16] See Held, *Democracy in the Global Order* (1999); *Models of Democracy* (2006); *Cosmopolitanism: Ideals and Realities* (2010).

[17] See *Global Covenant* (2004); *Debating Globalization* (2005); and *Beyond Gridlock* (2017).

Professor Held's thinking has been influenced by Judith Shklar. While a Ph.D. student at MIT, Held cross-registered to take Shklar's postgraduate seminar on Rousseau at Harvard University. It was Shklar who taught Held that to engage seriously in theoretical debates one had to know what came before in the history of ideas, otherwise one risks repeating the mistakes of all those that have come before. In addition to Shklar, Jürgen Habermas' work has had an enormous impact on Held's intellectual development and his attempt to develop a contemporary version of critical theory with practical intent. Lastly, Held credits a great deal of his intellectual development to Antony Giddens, with whom he worked at Cambridge on his postdoctoral research.

Among his achievements, Held takes special pleasure in having developed a contemporary version of critical theory that departs from its old Marxist roots while maintaining the pursuit of knowledge with practical intent, aiming to make the world a better place. Unlike the Marxist project, which is essentially monologic and seeks to capture the truth for its agents to pursue, Held is interested in the way political theory can help illuminate the changing context of power in ways which help to better understand the constraints and possibilities ahead.

In 1984 Professor Held co-founded Polity Press, which publishes global scholarship in the social sciences and humanities, and he is General Editor of the journal *Global Policy*, which brings together the work of scholars and practitioners in the field.

In Dr. Held's future research agenda he intends to continue to explore the interplay between the changing structural contexts of the postwar order – gridlock – and the continuing scope agents have to pursue effective pathways of change. He sees the new multipolar order as raising complex questions about the changing nature of the global system and the role of cosmopolitan values in the decades ahead. As such, Held will continue to focus on and develop work on these issues.

English publications (books) include: with Thomas Hale and others, *Beyond Gridlock* (2017); with Pietro Maffettone, *Global Political Theory* (2016); with Thomas Hale and Kevin Young, *Gridlock: Why Global Cooperation Is Failing When We Need it Most* (2013); *Cosmopolitanism: Ideals and Realities* (2010); *Models of Democracy* (third edition, 2006); with Anthony G. McGrew and others, *Global Transformations: Politics, Economics and Culture* (1999).

Charles A. Kupchan, Professor of international affairs, Walsh School of Foreign Service and Department of Government, Georgetown University, and Senior Fellow, Council on Foreign Relations (CFR).

Charles A. Kupchan holds a B.A. in East Asian Studies from Harvard University and M.Phil. and D.Phil. degrees in Politics from Oxford University. Through his scholarship as well as public service, Kupchan has sought to serve as an intellectual bridge-builder between the worlds of academia and public policy. In his research and writing, he has produced a significant body of literature aimed primarily at the scholarly community, while also deliberately publishing work addressed to the policy community as well as a wider lay audience. Dr. Kupchan has spent the balance of his career in research and teaching positions – at Princeton University, Georgetown University, and the Council on Foreign Relations. He has also served in the US government. From 2014 to 2017, he worked in the Obama administration as Special Assistant to the President and Senior Director for European Affairs on the National Security Council. During the first Clinton administration, he served as Director for European Affairs on the National Security Council. As a scholar and public servant, Kupchan has sought to deepen understanding of the causes of war and peace, and to advance the prospects for a stable global order based on liberal values.

Professor Kupchan's research agenda has been guided by the lessons of history as well as by contemporary and emerging challenges to peace and liberal practices. His work is broadly focused on the thematic areas of war and peace, the sources of order and disorder, and the formulation and implementation of grand strategy. In keeping with his interest in public policy and his government service, much of his work is driven by and speaks to real-world problems and puzzles. His scholarship relies heavily on comparative historical case studies.

Kupchan's research agenda often emerges from his prior scholarship; as he concludes a book or article, he confronts a set of follow-on questions that shape his next intellectual project. In *How Enemies Become Friends* (2010), for example, he studied how long-standing adversaries can tame competition, pursue rapprochement, and find their way to lasting peace. The answers and new questions that emerged from that study led him to the core puzzle of his latest book: *No One's World* (2013). *No One's World* examines how the international system might peacefully move from a world materially and ideologically dominated by the West to one of multiple centers of power and political models, a transition that has the potential to produce instability and war.

Charles Kupchan's scholarly approach is theoretically eclectic. He tends to draw on whatever theoretical paradigm or paradigms are most useful in explaining the question under study. Kupchan locates his work in the tradition of "liberal realism." For Kupchan, liberal realists hold that geopolitical competition constitutes the default position in international politics, but that it is possible – although quite difficult – to tame such competition through reciprocity, institutionalized and rule-based cooperation, the generation of shared or common identities, and other peace-inducing practices. Kupchan's thinking has been more influenced by his reading of history and examination of contemporary challenges than by the works of individual scholars. He finds that reading history – across time and regions – is the best way to broaden intellectual horizons and to formulate questions for future research. He also believes that as a scholar and teacher of international relations it is important to have an informed and nuanced understanding of the key historical events that have shaped the world in which we live. Some of the scholars who have most influenced his work include Robert Gilpin, Paul Kennedy, and John Gaddis.

In his future research, Kupchan plans to continue pursuing these general lines of interest, although he intends to put increased focus on domestic politics and ideologies and their impact on foreign policy. Especially in light of the recent rise in nationalism and populism, Kupchan believes that scholars may need to pay more attention to domestic influences on the conduct of statecraft. He is currently writing a book about the political and ideological sources of American isolationism.

English publications (books) include: *No One's World: The West, the Rising Rest, and the Coming Global Turn* (2013); *How Enemies Become Friends: The Sources of Stable Peace* (2012); *The End of the American Era: U.S. Foreign Policy and the Geopolitics of the Twenty-first Century* (2002); with others, *Power in Transition: The Peaceful Change of International Order* (2001); *The Vulnerability of Empire* (1994).

Avishai Margalit, Schulman Professor Emeritus of Philosophy, Hebrew University of Jerusalem and former George F. Kennan Professor, Institute for Advanced Study, Princeton.

Dr. Avishai Margalit holds undergraduate and graduate (M.A. and Ph.D.) degrees in philosophy from The Hebrew University of Jerusalem. Margalit's writing is distinctive for its quality and style of documentary philosophy. Much of his thinking and subsequent publications come from engaging thought related to current events and the dynamics of how issues of today relate to literature in science, art history, poetry and fiction, history and economics, and of course, his primary area of expertise, philosophy.

The main questions that concern Dr. Margalit's work center around ethics and morality, and the politics in between. Margalit views ethics as dealing with the ways in which we regulate the morality of both our thick human relations and our thin human relations. As an Israeli caught in one of the world's longest ongoing tragic conflicts – Israel/Palestine – Margalit became an engaged activist and observer of the ethical and moral dimensions of the conflict as they emerged.

Professor Margalit's achievements include a number of prestigious awards, including the Israel Prize in Philosophy (2010), the EMET Prize in the Humanities (2007), and the Spinozalens Award (2001). Among his distinguished list of appointments, Margalit was the first Bertelsman Professor at Oxford University (2001). He counts among his greatest professional achievements the public reception and influence of his books *The Decent Society*[18] and *The Ethics of Memory*.[19] In 2005 Dr. Margalit delivered the Tanner Lecture, titled "Decent Peace," at Stanford University.

Being an avid reader in many fields, Margalit's thinking has been influenced by many scholars. He credits the work of Plato as having an immense presence in his life in addition to the work of Ludwig Wittgenstein. Rudolf Carnap influenced the early stages of Margalit's philosophical writing.

Currently, Margalit's work focuses on the relation between manipulation and human autonomy. He finds that current reality, at least in democratic countries, suggests that manipulation has more political bearing than naked force. Seeing a need for the issue of manipulation to be further explored given its significance to everyday lives, this is an area that Margalit will continue developing.

English publications (books) include: *On Betrayal* (2017); *On Compromise And Rotten Compromises* (2010); *The Ethics of Memory* (2002); *Views in Review: Politics and Culture in the State of the Jews* (1998); *The Decent Society* (1996); and *Idolatry* (jointly with Moshe Halbertal, 1992).

David Miller, Official Fellow and Professor in Social and Political Theory, Nuffield College, Oxford University.

David Miller's interest in social justice began as a graduate student and continued to be a preoccupation throughout his academic life. At the time of his graduate work Dr. Miller was dissatisfied with utilitarianism and wanted to develop an alternative. Over time he came to recognize that it was fruitless to discuss social justice without considering the conditions under which it could realistically be pursued, which sparked his interest in questions of national

18 (1996).
19 (2002).

identity and citizenship. This in turn led him to think about global justice, and the respects in which it was different from social justice.

At the most general level, Professor Miller's work centers on working out a political philosophy for social democracy as it developed in Europe in the second half of the twentieth century. This remains an incomplete political project, but Miller sees its achievements as now under threat from a variety of directions, including global capitalism, identity politics, and so forth. As such, it remains important to spell out the values that inform this project, and to investigate what conditions are necessary for it to be sustained. This also informs his approach to global justice, where Miller's main question is what the citizens of a democratic state owe to outsiders, consistent with sustaining their own democratic institutions and social justice policies.

Initially, Professor Miller was influenced by Alasdair MacIntyre's approach to the history of ethics, and his claim that ideas like justice had to be understood as internally connected to social practices. Brian Barry's work has always been important to Miller's thinking, for its robust style and also for bringing political philosophy and social science into contact with each other. Michael Walzer's pluralistic approach to justice has also served as an important influence on Miller's own thinking, as well as his understanding of the aims of political theory. Initially a sharp critic of Rawls's theory of justice, Miller now sees virtues in his work that as an early scholar he had overlooked.

Miller's future research agenda includes continuing his work on social justice, including recent experimental work on that topic. Recently, Miller has undertaken research on immigration and refugees, which he will continue. He is also planning a short book on self-determination, which will link to his interest in territorial rights.

English publications (books) include: *Strangers in Our Midst: The Political Philosophy of Immigration* (2016); *Justice for Earthlings: Essays in Political Philosophy* (2013); *National Responsibility and Global Justice* (2007); and *Principles of Social Justice* (2001).

Thomas W. Pogge, Leitner Professor of Philosophy and Professor of Political Science, Yale University. Research Director, Centre for the Study of the Mind in Nature, University of Oslo.

Thomas Pogge received his Ph.D. in philosophy from Harvard University, where his adviser was John Rawls. Subsequently, he taught in the Department of Philosophy at Columbia University, before moving to Yale University, where he is founding Director of the Global Justice Program. It is both Kant and Rawls, in this order, who have been the most influential thinkers on his intellectual development.

Thomas Pogge's interest in philosophy and the issues he has ended up spending his life working on came in stages, but very early in his life. In this regard, he had three formative experiences that led him to develop a passion for philosophy and issues of moral and political philosophy.

First, as a child, when he was about eight years old, he made what he calls a remarkable discovery. He found out that the country into which he had been born had, a few years earlier, unleashed a horrendous war on its neighbors and, during this war, had interned, enslaved, and murdered unimaginably many Jewish and other civilians in camps. Every adult he knew had played a part in these events, in one way or another. This discovery turned his world on its head. It was not a mere updating of information or a learning of new facts. It shattered what rudimentary order of the world he had begun to map out. In the world of his emergent understanding, it was inconceivable that the people around him could do such things to other human beings. This discovery of the Nazi crimes was the experience that he had misunderstood the world – completely. Rebuilding involved much questioning: What then is the world like? How is it possible to form reliable judgments about it when adult guidance is not trustworthy? Are flowers experiencing great sadness and pain when we cut them and sell them in shops? How would he be thinking about the war, the Jews, and the Slavic peoples, if Germany had won?

A second formative experience was his active involvement in protesting the US war in Vietnam, between 1969 and 1974. Prior to that period, Pogge had been rather well disposed to the United States thanks to their fight against Nazi Germany and their exciting space exploration. But he was deeply shocked to find the United States involved in the mass killing, with enormously superior technology, of a poor peasant population. He became a walking encyclopedia on the war and tried to convince everyone within reach to actively oppose any kind of support for the US war effort.

Third, a three-month trek in the summer of 1980 through Asia (including Turkey, Pakistan, India, Bangladesh, Thailand, Taiwan, Korea, and Japan), where Pogge encountered poverty of previously unimaginable depth and severity, had a deep impact on him. In India, people were starving in the streets, some not far from glittering shopping arcades for the superrich. In particular, the slums of Calcutta overwhelmed him and motivated him to try to do whatever he could to end this suffering. He understood then that the poverty problem was vastly larger in human terms and also vastly smaller in economic terms than was understood in the West.

All this led Dr. Pogge to dedicate his professional and intellectual life to thinking, writing, and teaching on issues of poverty. In this regard, the central issues and questions around which his intellectual trajectory has been organized amount to the following question: How can global and national institutional structures be reformed, so that they generate less poverty and inequality, and so that they allow all people to participate fully in the social, economic, and political life of their societies?

For the way forward, he is focusing on such research themes as climate change, access to medicines, offshore finance, and demilitarization/democratization of supranational decision-making. The first three are both hugely important and ripe for reform. The fourth is more remote (reform is less realistic) but absolutely essential for the long-term future of humanity.

English publications (books) include *Politics as Usual: What Lies behind the Pro-Poor Rhetoric* (2010); *World Poverty and Human Rights: Cosmopolitan Responsibilities and Reforms* (2008); and *Realizing Rawls* (1989).

Boaventura de Sousa Santos, Professor at the School of Economics, University of Coimbra, Distinguished Legal Scholar, University of Wisconsin–Madison Law School, Global Legal Scholar, University of Warwick, and Director, Centre for Social Studies (CES), University of Coimbra.

Boaventura de Sousa Santos received his LL.M and J.S. from Yale University and a Doctor of Laws, Honoris Causa from McGill University. The primary issue of Professor de Sousa Santos's scholarship centers on the question raised by Jean Jacques Rousseau: *Does science contribute to the well-being and happiness of society?* Contrary to Rousseau, de Sousa Santos's response has not been a resounding "no." In developing his ideas in relation to this question de Sousa Santos has exerted his thinking in defining what kind of science can contribute to building a better society and under which conditions it can be produced. His method has been twofold: first to know in depth the kind of science that is potentially harmful (what he refers to as the dominant kind) and to contribute to providing the epistemological and theoretical foundations for the type of science that can contribute to the liberation of humankind (a subaltern kind). This latter kind of science de Sousa Santos sees as being founded on the epistemologies of the Global South.

What drives Professor de Sousa Santos's work in the field of global justice is a constant soul-searching process of self-reflectivity. This he keeps always in close articulation with the social movements that he has been both working-with and knowing-with. This articulation has been crucial to de Sousa Santos in keeping his research and intellectual agenda open and ready to receive the surprises of emergent realities that do not fit models of received knowledge. The thinkers that de Sousa Santos identifies as having most influenced his work include Karl Marx, Mahatma Gandhi, Frantz Fanon,[20] Paulo Freire,[21] and Orlando Fals Borda.[22]

Among his achievements, de Sousa Santos has contributed to building a solid body of epistemological and social scientific work based on the experiences and expectations of the most excluded special groups, those that resist and struggle against what he identifies as the three main modes of domination of modern times: capitalism, colonialism, and patriarchy. Rather than knowing about them, de Sousa Santos strives to know with them, through what he has called in more recent times the epistemologies of the South.

Dr. de Sousa Santos's current and future research agenda focuses on working on the problem of political consequences of his proposal of the epistemologies of the South: Socialism as democracy without end, nonauthoritarian state, and rights of nature.

English publications (books) include: *The End of the Cognitive Empire: The Coming of Age of Epistemologies of the South* (2018); *If God Were a Human Rights Activist* (2015); *The Rise of the Global Left: The World Social Forum and Beyond* (2006); *Toward a New Legal Common Sense* (2002).

A. Michael Spence, Nobel Laureate, Professor of Economics, New York University Leonard N. Stern School of Business Senior Fellow, Hoover Institution, and the Philip H. Knight Professor Emeritus of Management, Graduate School of Business, Stanford University.

Dr. Spence received his B.A. in philosophy from Princeton University and studied mathematics at Oxford on a Canadian Rhodes Scholarship. From there he went on to receive his Ph.D. in Economics at Harvard University. Spence's work in informational asymmetries was spurred by his membership in a group discussing issues of market performance in

[20] Twentieth-century psychiatrist and philosopher known for his contributions to Marxism, critical theory, and postcolonial studies.

[21] Twentieth-century Brazilian philosopher and educator known for contributions to critical pedagogy.

[22] Twentieth-century Colombian sociologist known as a founder of participatory action research.

the late 1960s. During this time he became interested in the details of market structure and performance, especially with respect to incompleteness of information.

His work on development followed his time as an academic administrator – holding positions as Dean in the Faculty of Arts and Sciences at Harvard University and Dean at the Business School at Stanford University – and came from giving a lecture on investment at the World Bank[23] that turned into the Growth Commission.[24]

Dr. Spence's work is influenced by his doctoral thesis – which was titled *Market Signaling* and was awarded the David A. Wells prize for doctoral thesis – advisers Kenneth Arrow,[25] Tom Schelling,[26] and Richard Zeckhauser.[27] Spence's key achievements include developing early work on informational gaps and asymmetries in markets and resultant market performance and how they create risks for exploiting people and hence are relevant to issues of regulation, values, and justice. In 2001 Dr. Spence was awarded – with George Akerlof[28] and Joseph Stiglitz[29] – the Nobel Prize in Economic Sciences for his contributions to the field of the informational structure of markets.

Currently, Spence's principal intellectual interests are in transitions to growth patterns that are more inclusive and sustainable as the global economy evolves and becomes very large.

English publications (books) include: *The Next Convergence: The Future of Economic Growth in a Multispeed World* (2011).

ONUMA Yasuaki, Professor Emeritus, University of Tokyo.

As a junior high school student in Yamagata, a northern city in Japan, Professor ONUMA saw the movie *Watashi wa kai ni naritai* (*I Want to Be a Shellfish*), which addressed the problem of individual responsibility for war crimes. While

[23] "The Next Convergence: Structural Change, Growth and Employment in a Multi Speed World," December 5, 2011.

[24] Commission on Growth and Development (2006–2010) chaired by Dr. Spence.

[25] Kenneth Arrow (1921–2017), was winner of the Nobel Memorial Prize in Economic Sciences with John Hicks in 1972.

[26] Thomas Schelling (1921–2016). Economist and professor of foreign policy, national security, nuclear strategy, and arms control at the School of Public Policy at University of Maryland, College Park.

[27] Richard Zeckhauser, economist and Frank P. Ramsey Professor of Political Economy at the Kennedy School of Government at Harvard University.

[28] University Professor, McCourt School of Public Policy, Georgetown University, and Koshland Professor of Economics emeritus, University of California, Berkeley.

[29] University Professor, Columbia University.

a senior high school student, he read an article by OKUMA Shgenobu entitled "Senso, kokka, ningen" (War, State, Humans). Through these early experiences, he came to be interested in the problem of war and peace, and humans' involvement in war. ONUMA was greatly influenced by the "Student Revolt" in 1968–1969 and the anti-Vietnam War movement in Japan, and came to consider the problem of sins of omission. He also came to be interested in the problem of the West-centric structure of the contemporary world by studying the human situation in developing countries, and the history of ideas in the non-Western world.

ONUMA went on to study law and politics at the University of Tokyo, where he received his Bachelor of Laws (LL.B.) in public law in 1969 and a second LL.B. in political science the following year. In 1999 ONUMA received his LL.D. in law from the Graduate School of Law and Politics at the University of Tokyo. For many years ONUMA was a professor of international law with the University of Tokyo and later on with Meiji University. In addition, he has been a visiting professor in a variety of universities around the world, such as Harvard Law School, Princeton University, Yale Law School, Georgetown Law Center, University of Cambridge, University of Paris I Sorbonne, Ma-Planck Institute in Freiburg, the Graduate Institute in Geneva, Peking University, Tsinghua University, Jawaharlal Nehru University, and University of Sydney.

ONUMA's intellectual agenda focuses on how to pursue and realize ethical or normative values and virtues based on normative consciousness of ordinary citizens. In particular, he has been interested in exploring how people can liberate themselves from their assumptions and preoccupations that they take for granted and how to recognize and account for one's sin for omissions. His works focus on how to envisage a society where the suppression of disadvantaged minorities is minimized. His thinking is notably influenced by ENDO Shusaku,[30] KAZUMI, Takahashi,[31] Hans Kelsen,[32] and KOJI, Iizuka.[33]

Throughout his professional career Professor ONUMA has published many works in the context of which he challenges mainstream international law, international relations, history, and history of ideas.

Since 2004, together with OWADA Hisashi,[34] and other prominent Asian international lawyers, ONUMA has been engaged in the establishment and

[30] (1926–1993), Japanese novelist.
[31] (1931–1971), Japanese novelist.
[32] (1881–1973), Austrian jurist and legal and political philosopher.
[33] (1906–1970), Japanese geographer.
[34] Judge on the International Court of Justice since 2002.

management of the Asian Society of International Law. The Society was established in 2007, and has been an important center for Asian international lawyers to pursue academic and professional goals by working together.

In addition to his work as a scholar and professor, Dr. ONUMA has been engaged in human rights activities since the 1970s, specifically in the areas of (i) the legal and social status of the Korean minority in Japan, (ii) the repatriation of Koreans left in Sakhalin at the end of World War II to Korea, and (iii) the Japanese atonement for the former "comfort women." In these areas ONUMA has made significant contributions.[35]

For the future of his research agenda in the domains related to global justice ONUMA plans to focus on world cultural heritage issues beyond Western-centrism by taking a transcivilizational approach. In understanding cultural heritage, ONUMA plans to explore the intergenerational succession of values in relationship to attitudes and policies related to the environment and interpersonal engagement.

English publications (books) include: *International Law in a Transcivilizational World* (Cambridge University Press, 2017); *A Transcivilizational Perspective on International Law* (2010); *A Normative Approach to War: Peace, War, and Justice in Hugo Grotius* (1993).

Wang Hui, Professor of Literature and History, Tsinghua University.

Wang Hui was born and grew up in Yangzhou, on the north bank of the Jangtze river, in Jiangsu province, not far away from the provincial capital, Nangjing. Historically, Yangzhou was one of the wealthiest cities in China, known at various periods for its great merchant families, poets, artists, and scholars. Wang Hui's father worked for the local government and his mother taught foreign literature, mainly European literature from the Greek period to eighteenth century Enlightenment, and also had an interest in Japanese and Indian literature. Wang Hui's mother's academic specialization in literature had a strong influence on him, if only because in time he used her library to introduce himself to literature and the humanities. This certainly played a key role in the fact that Wang Hui was introduced at an early age not only to Chinese thought (Chinese classics but also modern Chinese thinkers, such as

35 See: *Saharin kimin* (*Koreans Left in Sakhalin*, (1992); 1993); *"Ianfu" mondai towa nandattanoka* (*What Was the "Comfort Women" Problem?*, (2007); Korean edition, translated by Jeong Hyun-Suk, 2008); and (ed.) *Sengo sekinin* (*Postwar Responsibility of Japan*, 2014).

Lu Xun[36]) but also to Western scholarship and thought. Hence what is one of his intellectual trademarks and strengths: mobilizing both Western and Chinese scholarship.

After spending some time, during the Cultural Revolution, in the countryside, he started college and then did his Ph.D. at the Graduate School of the Chinese Academy of Social Sciences, where he studied under a student of Lu Xun, himself a famous literature historian, Professor Tang Tao.[37] After completing his Ph.D., Wang continued at the Chinese Academy of Social Sciences as a researcher. In 2002 Wang Hui moved to Tsinghua University, where he continues to be a professor of literature and history. From 1996 to 2007 he worked as one of the executive editors of *Dushu*, an influential Chinese literary magazine, publication of which started in 1979.[38] In addition, over the years, Wang Hui has been Visiting Professor at Harvard University, Stanford University, and the University of Washington, among others.

Lu Xun has been an early and constant influence on Professor Wang. In fact, it is through Lu Xun that Wang Hui has come to be interested in the question of modernity – modernity in general and modernity in the Chinese context. In this regard, for Wang Hui, Lu Xun has been an entry point for both analyzing and trying to understand the relationships between Western modernity (European modernity and its intellectual figures, such as nineteenth-century German thinkers like Hegel, Stirner, Marx, and Nietzsche) and Chinese modernity. In addition to Lu Xun, other important Chinese intellectual influences come from the classics, Zhang Taiyan,[39] one of the most prominent scholars, thinkers, and revolutionaries of early twentieth-century China, and a professor of Lu Xun, as well as from Mao Zedong. On the Western side, critical modern theory, from the Frankfurt School[40] to French

[36] Lu Xun was the pen name of Zhou Shuren (1881–1936), a leading figure of modern Chinese literature. Writing in Vernacular Chinese as well as in Classical Chinese, Lu Xun was a short-story writer, editor, translator, literary critic, essayist, poet, and designer.

[37] Tang Tao (1913–1992) was a well-known essayist, poet, literary critic, and historian as well as an expert in Lu Xun studies. The various academic positions he held include being a research fellow with the Institute of Literature in the Chinese Academy of Sciences.

[38] For more on *Dushu*, see, for example, the conversation with Wang Hui in this volume.

[39] Zhang Taiyan (1868–1936) was a Chinese philologist, literary critic, philosopher, and revolutionary. His philological works include *Wen Shi* (文始 "The Origin of Writing"), the first systematic work of Chinese etymology. An activist as well as a scholar, he produced many political works.

[40] The Frankfurt School is a movement of social theory and philosophy founded in 1923, consisting at the time of neo-Marxist critique of existing capitalist, fascist, or communist systems. Early members of the school included Max Orkheimer and Theodor W. Adorno, and

theory,[41] especially Foucault, and the thinking trends represented by Edward Said, especially his book *Orientalism*,[42] also had a significant influence on his thinking.

As a whole, Wang Hui's scholarship is at the crossroads of history of ideas, literature, and social theory. His work also mobilizes sociology, history, and philosophy. The main thread of his work is to provide an analysis of the specificities of Chinese modernity as well as of its relations with the West. As such, over the years, the focus of his research has given much attention to three types of issues. First, making sense of Chinese modernity, from an intellectual and sociopolitical standpoint, has been a major aspect of Wang Hui's scholarship. This has led him to explore, in his four-volume book *Rise of Modern Chinese Thought*,[43] the historical currents that have influenced Chinese modernity from the Song Dynasty to present day. In the process, he challenges the West to revisit some of its basic assumptions about what it means to be modern. Second, and this is also a major concern in the *Rise of Modern Chinese Thought*, there is the question of the nature of China as a political entity. In this context, part of the thinking of Wang Hui is to reflect on the culture and status of China as an empire, as different from the nation-state as it has been built in the West. Third, Wang Hui has been spending much time exploring what it is to be Chinese and how the notion of "Chineseness" has been built over the years, internally and in relation with the "other(s)" of China. Incidentally, Wang Hui's thinking on these two latter issues, especially the relationship between universalism and particularism, is all the more important in the context of China becoming a global power. China's experience and views on these matters could in part impact how it relates to its global role in the future.

In terms of his current and future research, Wang Hui is now putting his energy into analyzing China in the twentieth century and what could be the ways forward in the various aspects of the development of Chinese society, including in its relations with the rest of the world. He is also going back to Lu Xun bringing together literature, and historical and archeological studies to at

later theorists with roots in Frankfurt School critical theory include Jürgen Habermas, Clauss Offe, and Axel Honneth.

41 French Theory is a corpus of philosophical, literary, and sociological work that emerged in France in the 1960s and became influential in American Universities in the 1970s. It adopts a critical approach. Some of the main authors of French Theory are Louis Althusser, Jean Baudrillard, Gilles Deleuze, Jacques Derrida, Michel Foucault, and Pierre Bourdieu.

42 Edward W. Said was a professor of literature at Columbia University. His most well-known book is *Orientalism* (1979).

43 Not available in English. For the Chinese edition, *Xiandai Zhongguo Sixiang De Xingqi* (2008).

the same time deconstruct and understand the meaning of "history" in the Chinese context.

English publications (books) include: *China's Twentieth Century: Revolution, Retreat and the Road to Equality* (2016); *China from Empire to Nation State* (2014); *The Politics of Imagining Asia* (2011); *The End of Revolution: China and the Limits of Modernity* (2010); and *China's New Order: Society, Politics and Economy in Transition* (2006).

Index